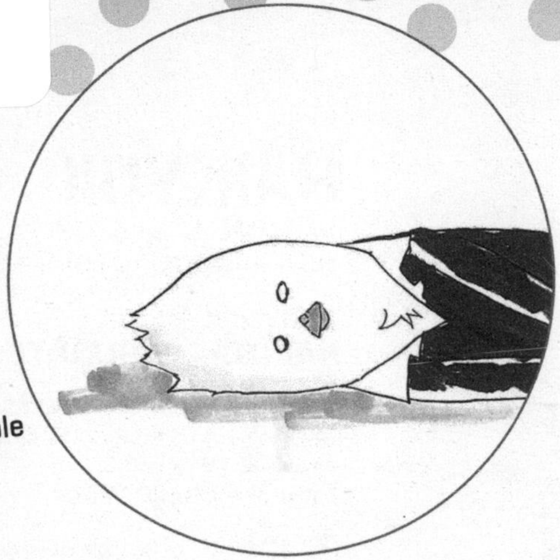

Thank you for picking up *Haikyu!!* volume 5. I'm drawing a series where everyone is getting lots of exercise, but I myself am woefully sedentary. I wonder if drawing people working out counts as working out.

HARUICHI FURUDATE began his manga career when he was 25 years old with the one-shot *Ousama Kid* (King Kid), which won an honorable mention for the 14th Jump Treasure Newcomer Manga Prize. His first series, *Kiben Gakuha, Yotsuya Sensei no Kaidan* (Philosophy School, Yotsuya Sensei's Ghost Stories), was serialized in *Weekly Shonen Jump* in 2010. In 2012, he began serializing *Haikyu!!* in *Weekly Shonen Jump*, where it became his most popular work to date.

HAIKYU!!

VOLUME 5
SHONEN JUMP Manga Edition

Story and Art by
HARUICHI FURUDATE

Translation **ADRIENNE BECK**
Touch-Up Art & Lettering **ERIKA TERRIQUEZ**
Design ❸ **FAWN LAU**
Editor ❹ **MARLENE FIRST**

HAIKYU!! © 2012 by Haruichi Furudate
All rights reserved.
First published in Japan in 2012 by SHUEISHA Inc., Tokyo.
English translation rights arranged by SHUEISHA Inc.

The stories, characters and incidents mentioned
in this publication are entirely fictional.

Printed in the U.S.A.

Published by VIZ Media, LLC
P.O. Box 77010
San Francisco, CA 94107

10 9 8 7 6 5 4 3 2 1
First printing, November 2016

www.shonenjump.com   www.viz.com

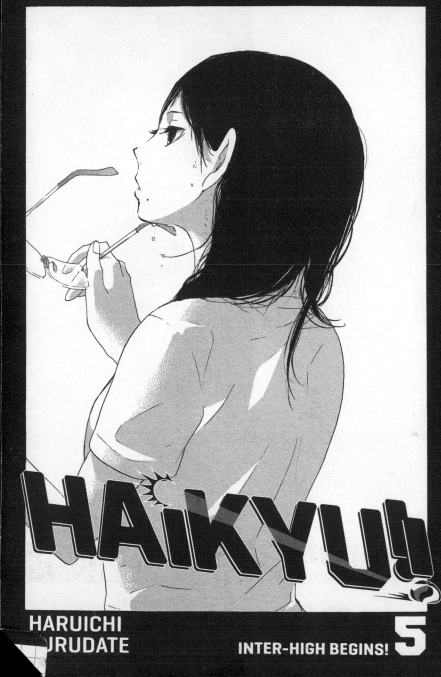

HAIKYU!!

HARUICHI
URUDATE

INTER-HIGH BEGINS!

5

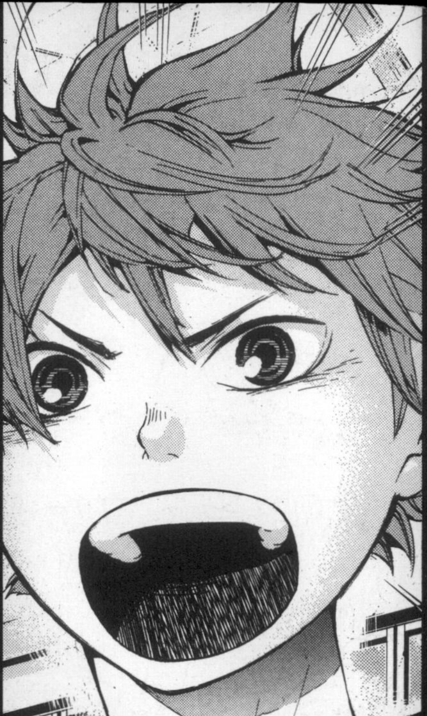
KARASUNO

SHOYO HINATA

1ST YEAR / MIDDLE BLOCKER

Even though he doesn't have the best body type for volleyball, he is super athletic. Gets nervous easily.

TOBIO KAGEYAMA

1ST YEAR / SETTER

His instincts and athletic talent are so good that he's like a "king" who rules the court. Demanding and egocentric.

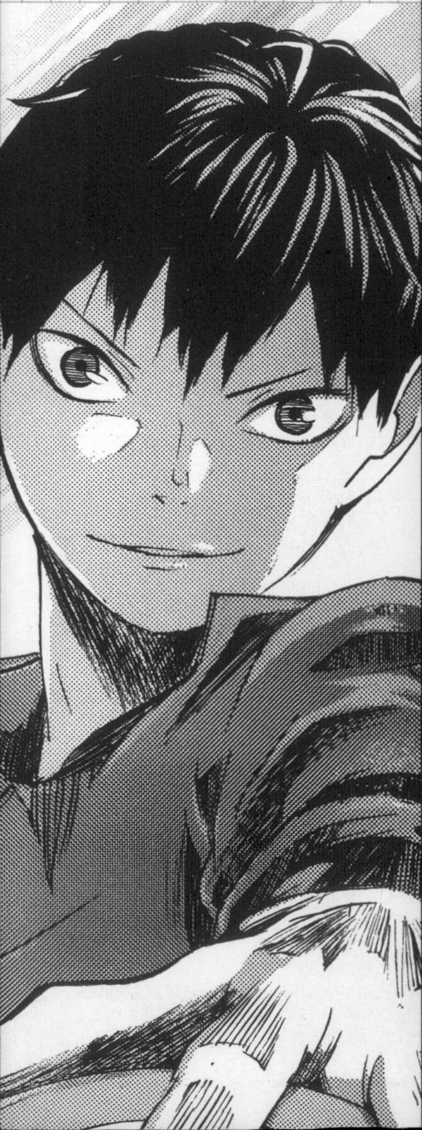

CHARACTERS

Karasuno High School Volleyball Club

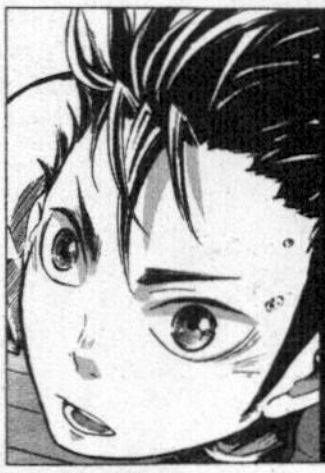
YU NISHINOYA

2ND YEAR
LIBERO

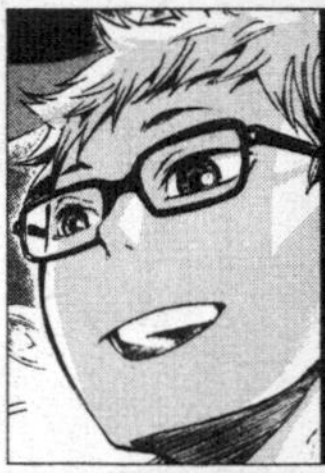
KEI TSUKISHIMA

1ST YEAR
MIDDLE BLOCKER

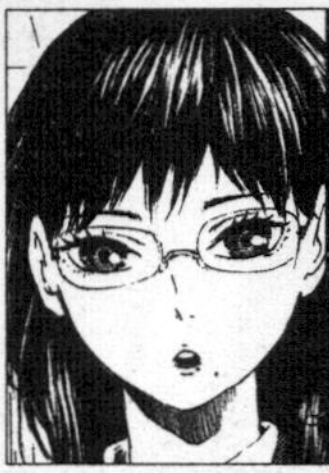
KIYOKO SHIMIZU

3RD YEAR
MANAGER

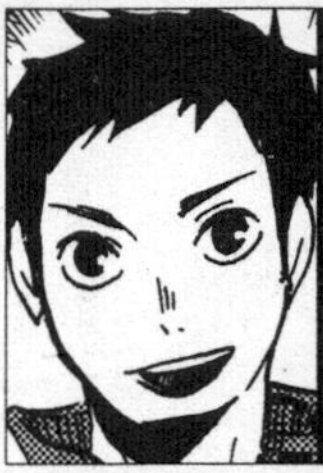
DAICHI SAWAMURA

3RD YEAR (CAPTAIN)
WING SPIKER

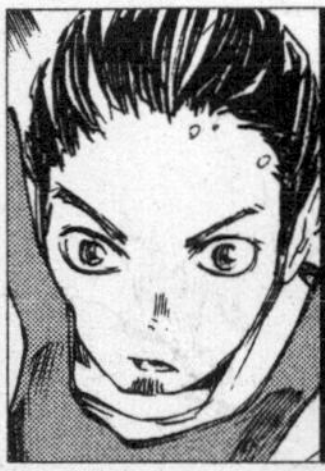
ASAHI AZUMANE

3RD YEAR
WING SPIKER

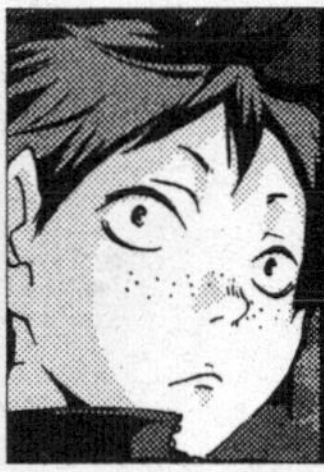
TADASHI YAMAGUCHI

1ST YEAR
MIDDLE BLOCKER

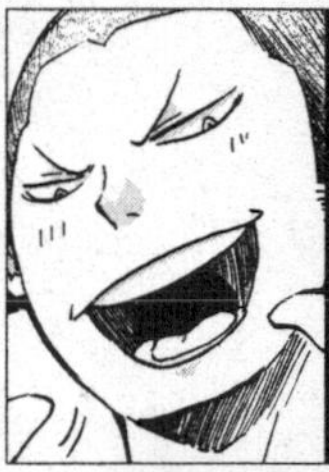
RYUNOSUKE TANAKA

2ND YEAR
WING SPIKER

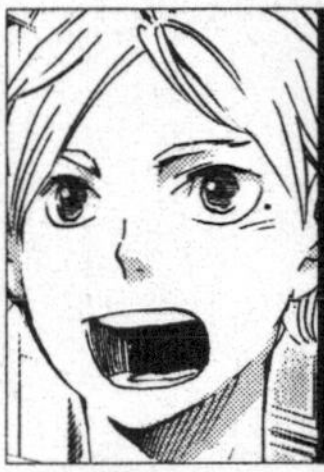
KOUSHI SUGAWARA

3RD YEAR (VICE CAPTAIN)
SETTER

Aoba Johsai High School

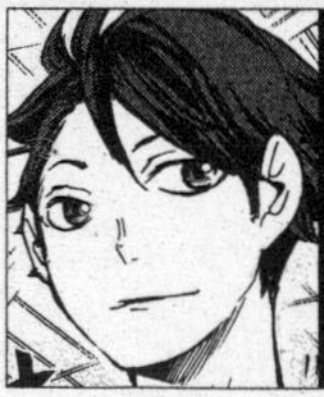
TOHRU OIKAWA

3RD YEAR (CAPTAIN)
SETTER

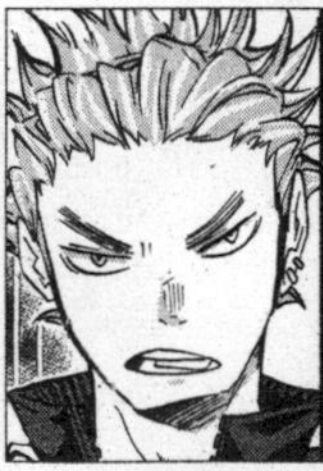
KEISHIN UKAI

COACH

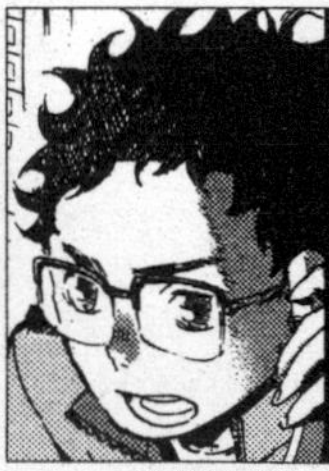
ITTETSU TAKEDA

ADVISER

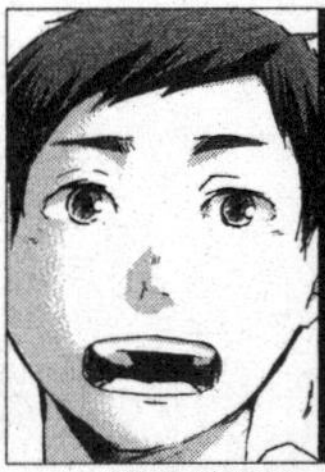
CHIKARA ENNOSHITA

2ND YEAR
WING SPIKER

Ever since he saw the legendary player known as "the Little Giant" compete at the high school national volleyball finals, Shoyo Hinata has been aiming to be the best volleyball player ever! He decides to join the volleyball club at his middle school and gets to play in an official tournament during his third year. His team is crushed by a team led by volleyball prodigy Tobio Kageyama, also known as "the King of the Court." Swearing revenge on Kageyama, Hinata graduates middle school and enters Karasuno High School, the school where the Little Giant played. However, upon joining the club, he finds out that Kageyama is there too! The two of them bicker constantly, but they bring out the best in each other's talents and become a powerful combo! In Karasuno's practice game against their old rival Nekoma, Kageyama and Hinata figure out new ways to improve their skills but ultimately lose to their opponent's consistent teamwork. Promising to get payback on the national stage, Karasuno gets ready for the summer Inter-High Tournament!

HAIKYU!!

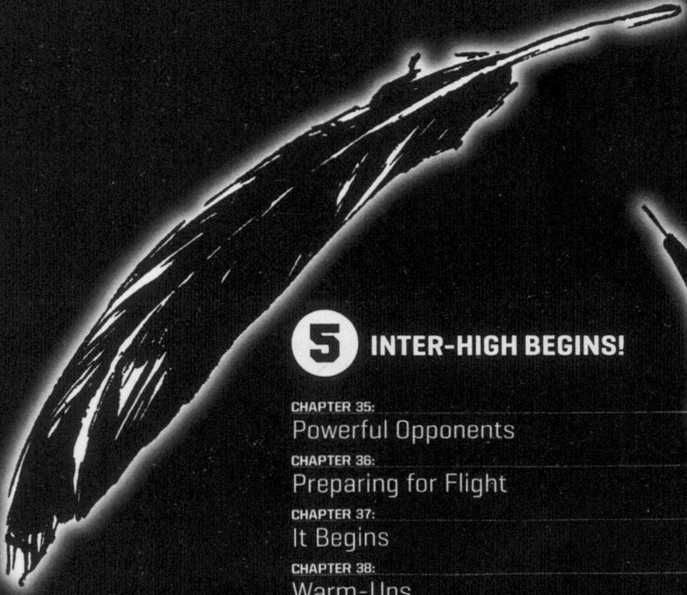

5 INTER-HIGH BEGINS!

CHAPTER 35:
Powerful Opponents · 007

CHAPTER 36:
Preparing for Flight · 027

CHAPTER 37:
It Begins · 047

CHAPTER 38:
Warm-Ups · 067

CHAPTER 39:
The Return · 087

CHAPTER 40:
Winners and Losers · 107

CHAPTER 41:
Round 2 · 129

CHAPTER 42:
The Iron Wall · 149

CHAPTER 43:
Freak Quick Unleashed · 169

CHAPTER 44:
The Greatest Decoy · 189

CHAPTER 35

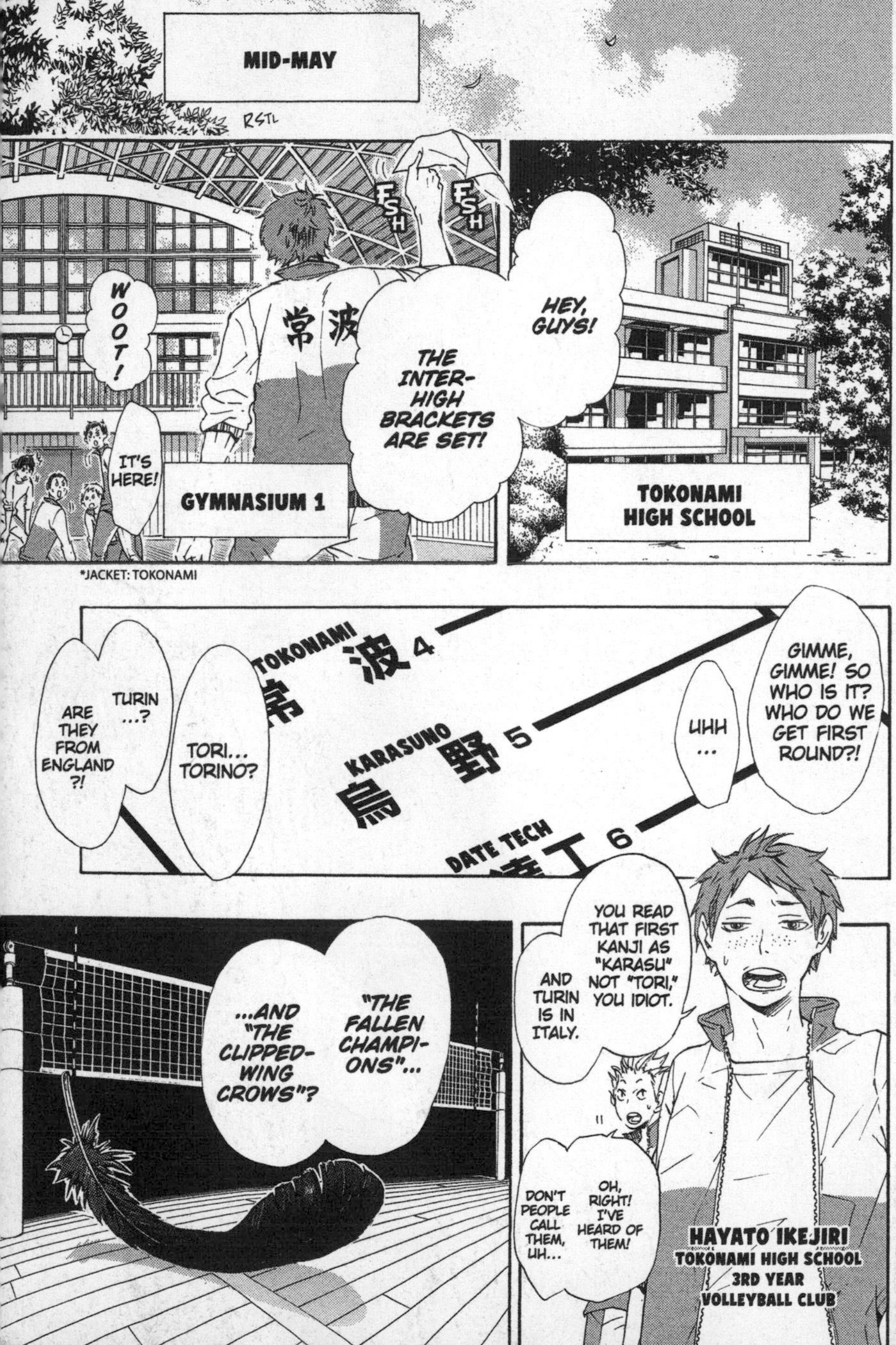

RSTL
MID-MAY
RSTL
TOKONAMI HIGH SCHOOL
FSH FSH
HEY, GUYS!
THE INTER-HIGH BRACKETS ARE SET!
常波
GYMNASIUM 1
WOOT!
IT'S HERE!
*JACKET: TOKONAMI
GIMME, GIMME! SO WHO IS IT? WHO DO WE GET FIRST ROUND?!
UHH ...
TOKONAMI 常波 4
KARASUNO 烏野 5
DATE TECH 6
TORI... TORINO?
TURIN ...?
ARE THEY FROM ENGLAND ?!
YOU READ THAT FIRST KANJI AS "KARASU" NOT "TORI," YOU IDIOT.
AND TURIN IS IN ITALY.
HAYATO IKEJIRI
TOKONAMI HIGH SCHOOL
3RD YEAR
VOLLEYBALL CLUB
OH, RIGHT! I'VE HEARD OF THEM!
DON'T PEOPLE CALL THEM, UH...
"THE FALLEN CHAMPIONS"...
...AND "THE CLIPPED-WING CROWS"?

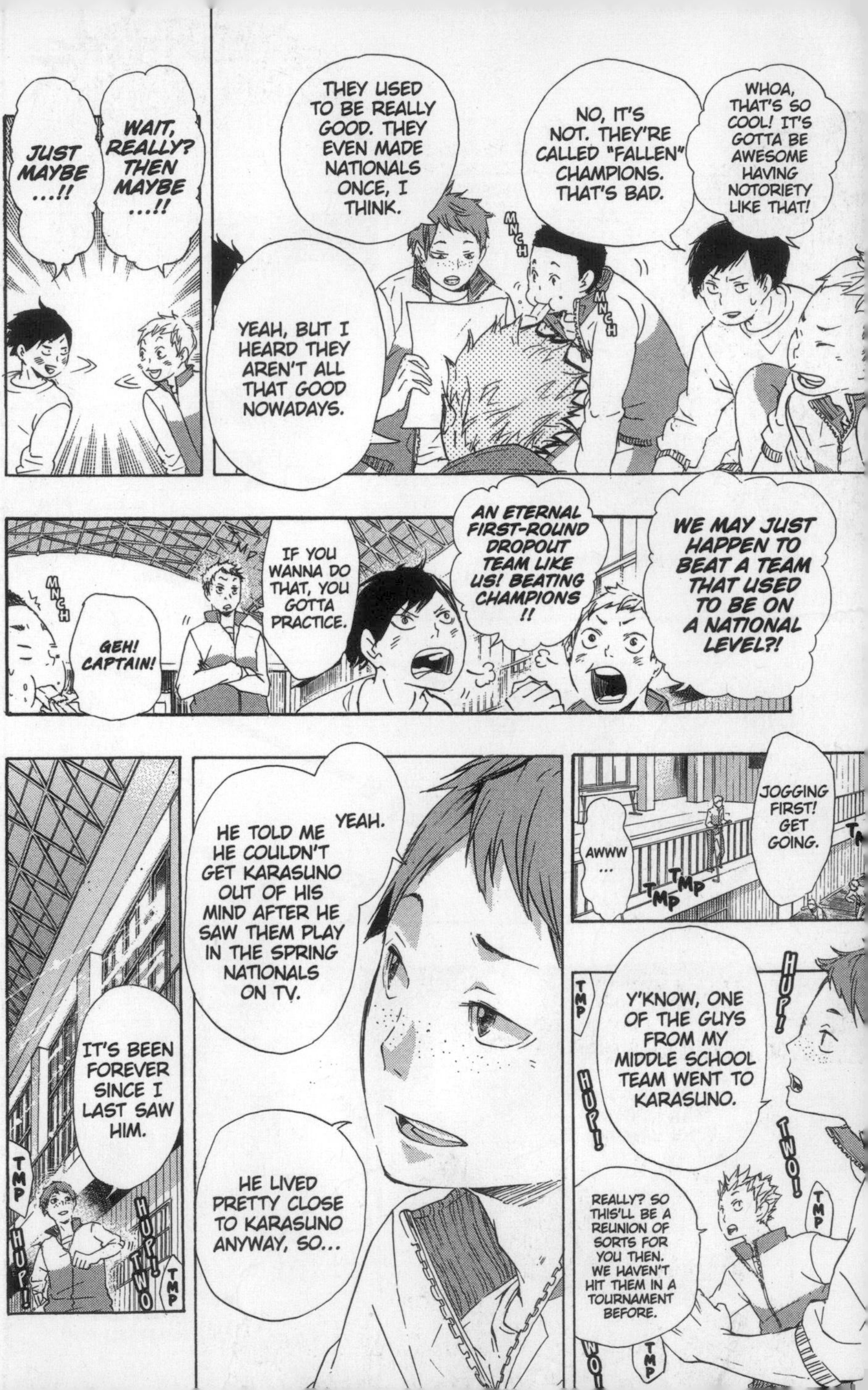
WHOA, THAT'S SO COOL! IT'S GOTTA BE AWESOME HAVING NOTORIETY LIKE THAT!
NO, IT'S NOT. THEY'RE CALLED "FALLEN" CHAMPIONS. THAT'S BAD.
MNCH
THEY USED TO BE REALLY GOOD. THEY EVEN MADE NATIONALS ONCE, I THINK.
MNCH
YEAH, BUT I HEARD THEY AREN'T ALL THAT GOOD NOWADAYS.
WAIT, REALLY? THEN MAYBE ...!!
JUST MAYBE ...!!
WE MAY JUST HAPPEN TO BEAT A TEAM THAT USED TO BE ON A NATIONAL LEVEL?!
AN ETERNAL FIRST-ROUND DROPOUT TEAM LIKE US! BEATING CHAMPIONS !!
TMP
IF YOU WANNA DO THAT, YOU GOTTA PRACTICE.
MNCH
GEH! CAPTAIN!
JOGGING FIRST! GET GOING.
AWWW ...
TMP TMP TMP
Y'KNOW, ONE OF THE GUYS FROM MY MIDDLE SCHOOL TEAM WENT TO KARASUNO.
HUP!
TWO!
TMP
HUP!
TMP
REALLY? SO THIS'LL BE A REUNION OF SORTS FOR YOU THEN. WE HAVEN'T HIT THEM IN A TOURNAMENT BEFORE.
TMP
YEAH.
HE TOLD ME HE COULDN'T GET KARASUNO OUT OF HIS MIND AFTER HE SAW THEM PLAY IN THE SPRING NATIONALS ON TV.
HE LIVED PRETTY CLOSE TO KARASUNO ANYWAY, SO...
IT'S BEEN FOREVER SINCE I LAST SAW HIM.
TMP
HUP!
HUP!
TWO
TMP

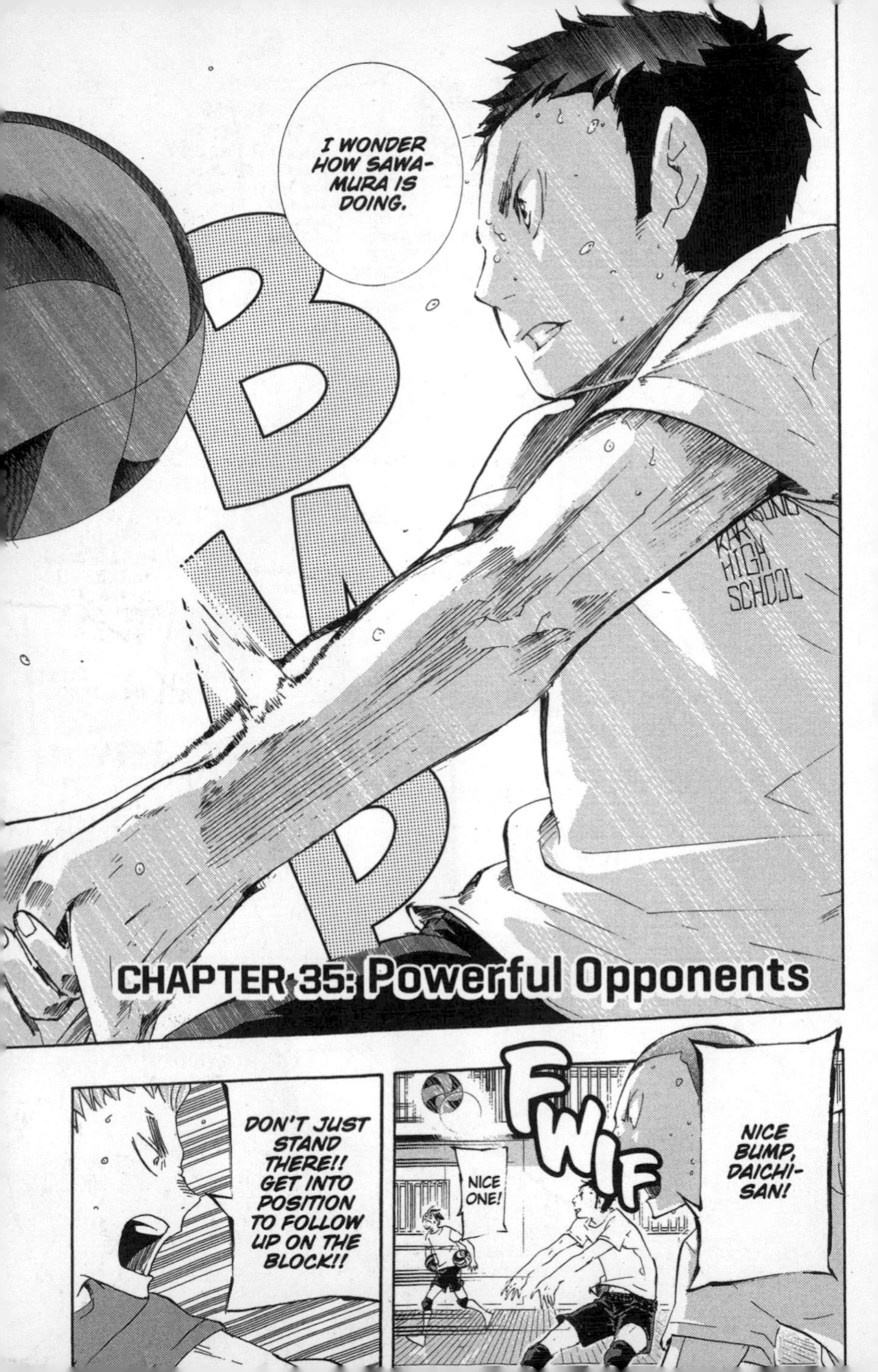
I WONDER HOW SAWA-MURA IS DOING.
CHAPTER 35: Powerful Opponents
NICE BUMP, DAICHI-SAN!
FWIF
NICE ONE!
DON'T JUST STAND THERE!! GET INTO POSITION TO FOLLOW UP ON THE BLOCK!!

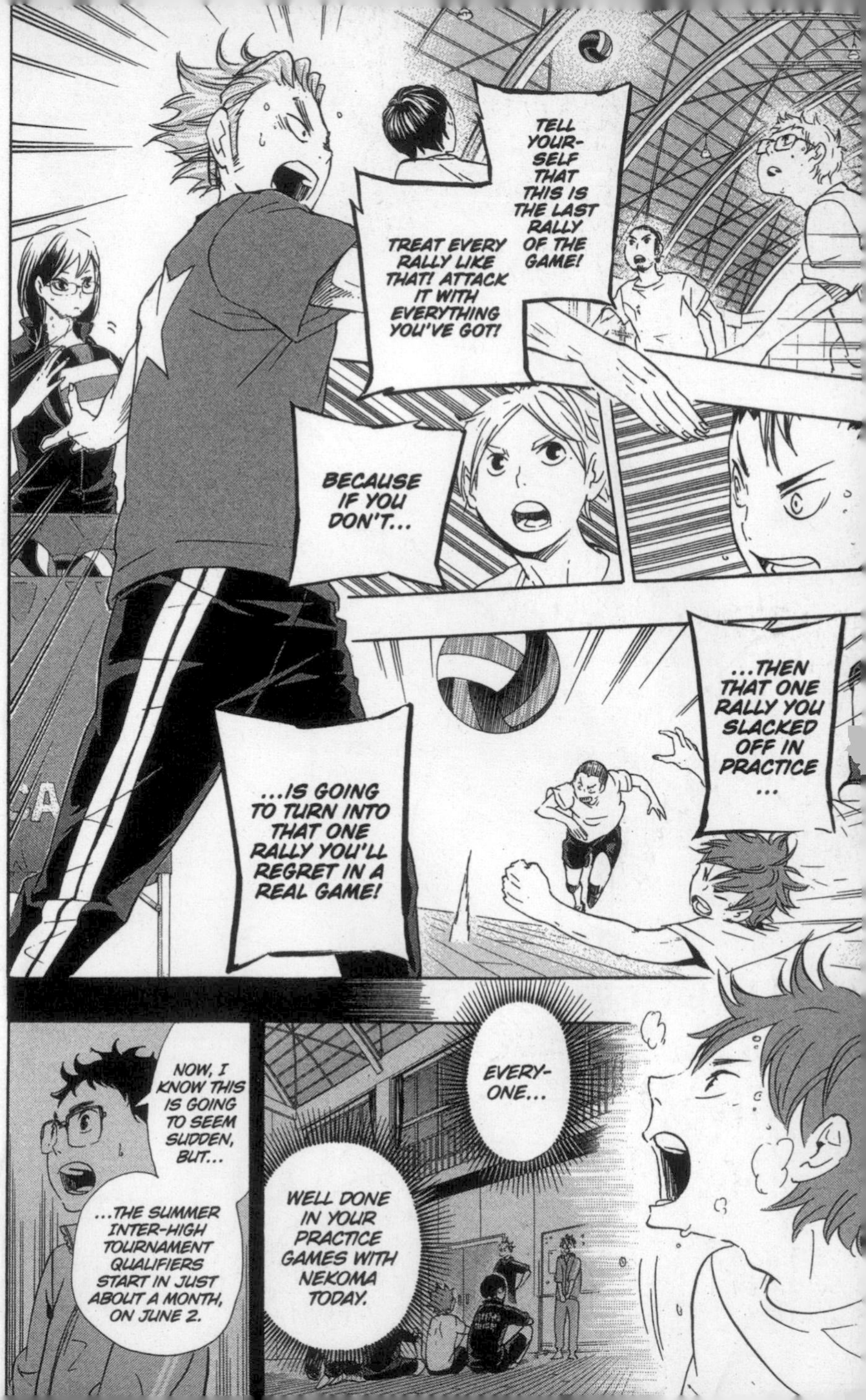
TELL YOURSELF THAT THIS IS THE LAST RALLY OF THE GAME!
TREAT EVERY RALLY LIKE THAT! ATTACK IT WITH EVERYTHING YOU'VE GOT!
BECAUSE IF YOU DON'T...
...THEN THAT ONE RALLY YOU SLACKED OFF IN PRACTICE...
...IS GOING TO TURN INTO THAT ONE RALLY YOU'LL REGRET IN A REAL GAME!
EVERY-ONE...
WELL DONE IN YOUR PRACTICE GAMES WITH NEKOMA TODAY.
NOW, I KNOW THIS IS GOING TO SEEM SUDDEN, BUT...
...THE SUMMER INTER-HIGH TOURNAMENT QUALIFIERS START IN JUST ABOUT A MONTH, ON JUNE 2.

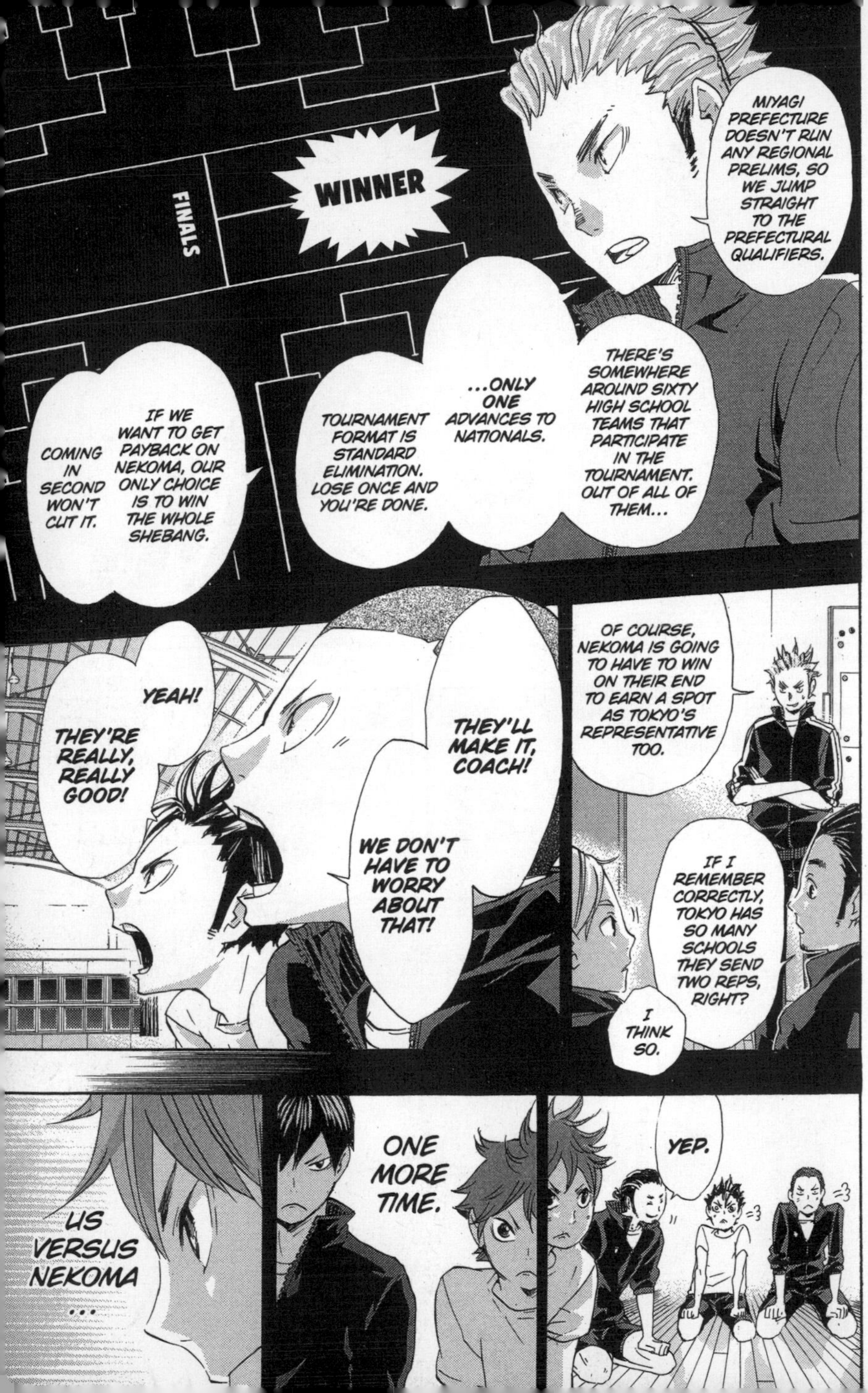
MIYAGI PREFECTURE DOESN'T RUN ANY REGIONAL PRELIMS, SO WE JUMP STRAIGHT TO THE PREFECTURAL QUALIFIERS.
WINNER
FINALS
THERE'S SOMEWHERE AROUND SIXTY HIGH SCHOOL TEAMS THAT PARTICIPATE IN THE TOURNAMENT. OUT OF ALL OF THEM...
...ONLY ONE ADVANCES TO NATIONALS.
TOURNAMENT FORMAT IS STANDARD ELIMINATION. LOSE ONCE AND YOU'RE DONE.
IF WE WANT TO GET PAYBACK ON NEKOMA, OUR ONLY CHOICE IS TO WIN THE WHOLE SHEBANG.
COMING IN SECOND WON'T CUT IT.
OF COURSE, NEKOMA IS GOING TO HAVE TO WIN ON THEIR END TO EARN A SPOT AS TOKYO'S REPRESENTATIVE TOO.
IF I REMEMBER CORRECTLY, TOKYO HAS SO MANY SCHOOLS THEY SEND TWO REPS, RIGHT?
I THINK SO.
THEY'LL MAKE IT, COACH!
WE DON'T HAVE TO WORRY ABOUT THAT!
YEAH!
THEY'RE REALLY, REALLY GOOD!
YEP.
ONE MORE TIME.
US VERSUS NEKOMA ...

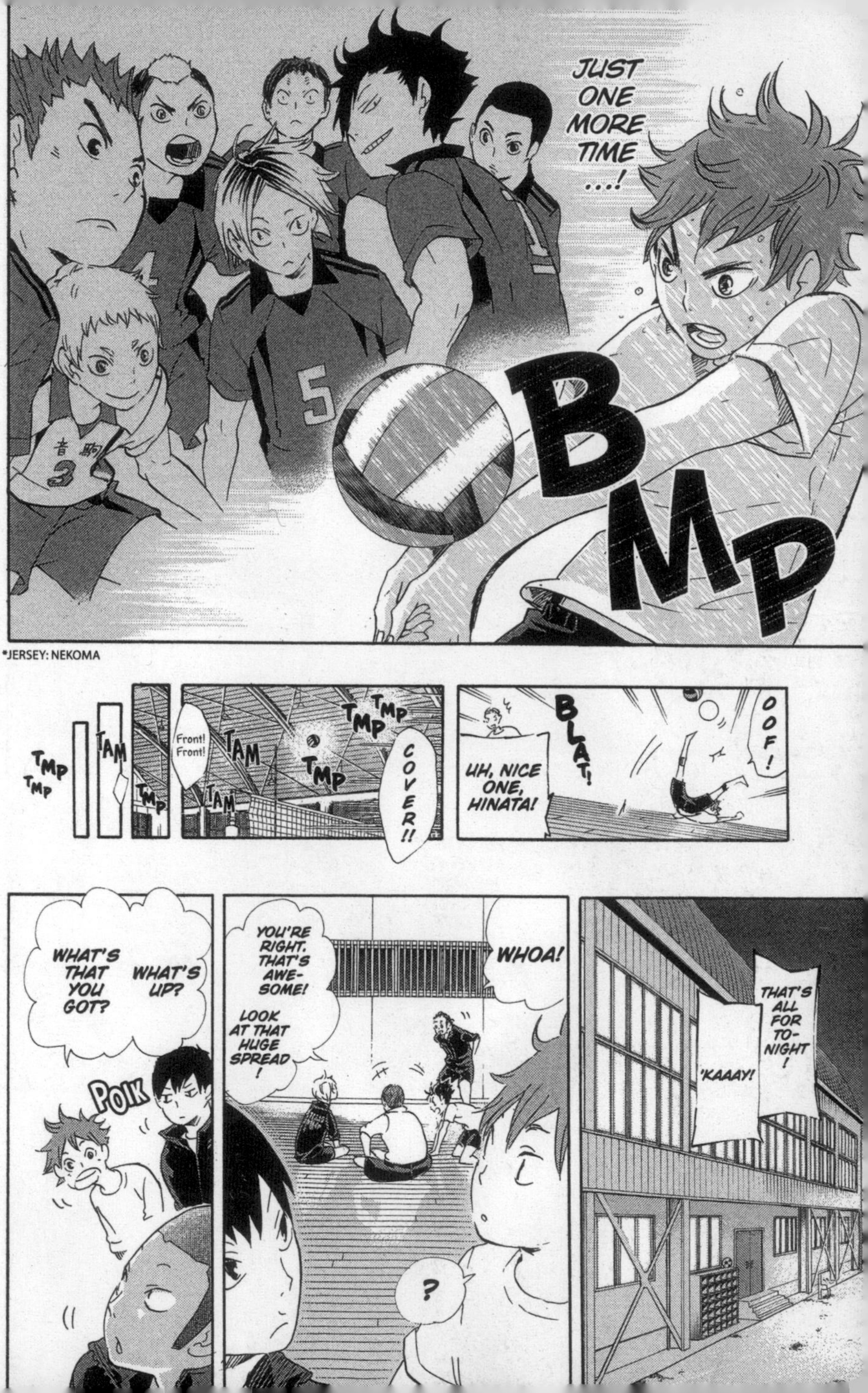
JUST ONE MORE TIME ...!
BMP
OOF!
BLAT!
UH, NICE ONE, HINATA!
COVER!!
TMP TMP
TMP
TAM
TAM
Front! Front!
TMP
TAM
TMP TMP
THAT'S ALL FOR TO-NIGHT!
'KAAAY!
WHOA!
YOU'RE RIGHT. THAT'S AWE-SOME!
LOOK AT THAT HUGE SPREAD!
?
WHAT'S UP?
WHAT'S THAT YOU GOT?
POIK
*JERSEY: NEKOMA

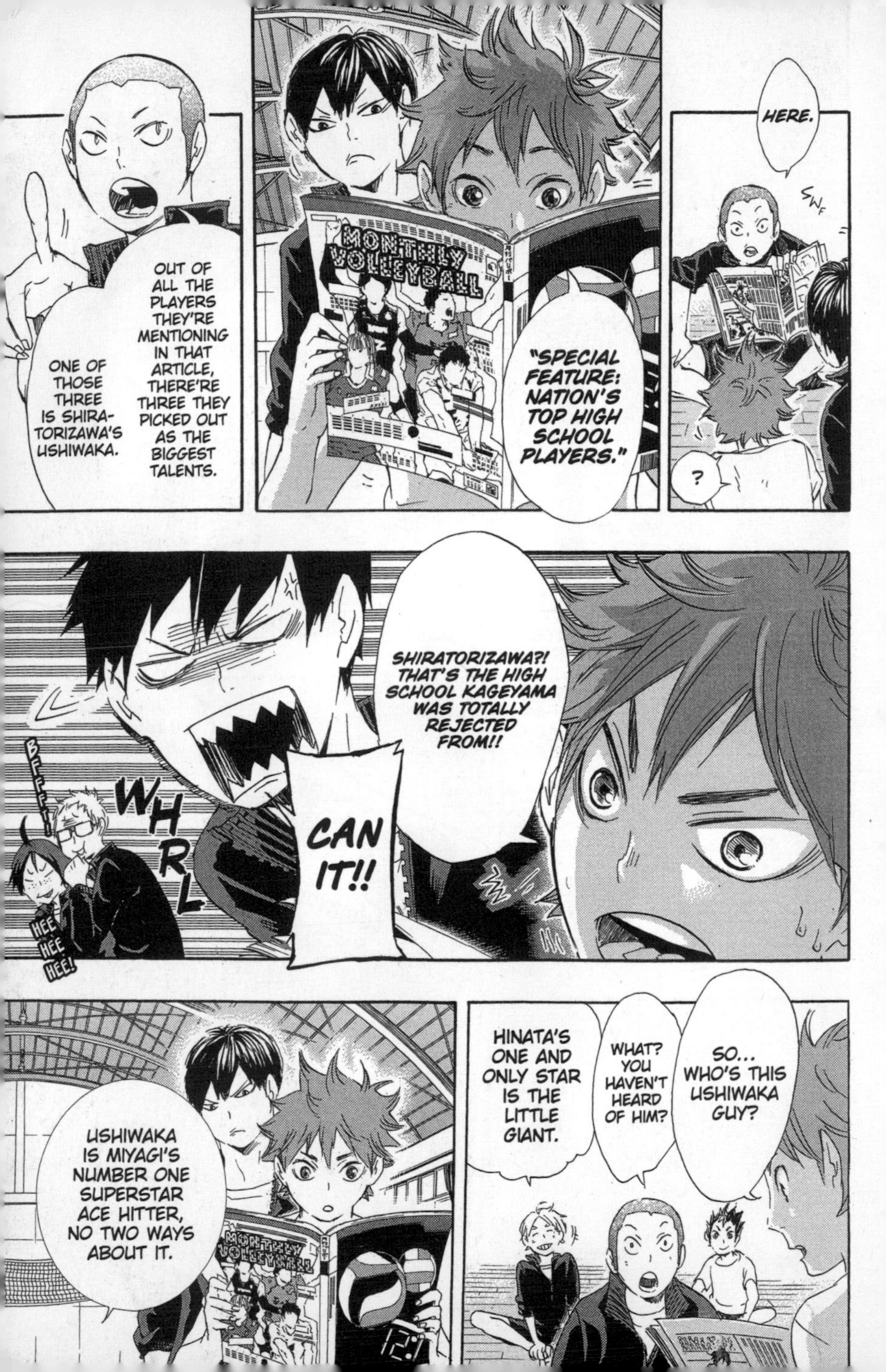
HERE.
SWF
?
"SPECIAL FEATURE: NATION'S TOP HIGH SCHOOL PLAYERS."
MONTHLY VOLLEYBALL
OUT OF ALL THE PLAYERS THEY'RE MENTIONING IN THAT ARTICLE, THERE'RE THREE THEY PICKED OUT AS THE BIGGEST TALENTS.
ONE OF THOSE THREE IS SHIRATORIZAWA'S USHIWAKA.
SHIRATORIZAWA?! THAT'S THE HIGH SCHOOL KAGEYAMA WAS TOTALLY REJECTED FROM!!
CAN IT!!
WHRL
BFFT!
HEE HEE HEE!
SO... WHO'S THIS USHIWAKA GUY?
WHAT? YOU HAVEN'T HEARD OF HIM?
HINATA'S ONE AND ONLY STAR IS THE LITTLE GIANT.
USHIWAKA IS MIYAGI'S NUMBER ONE SUPERSTAR ACE HITTER, NO TWO WAYS ABOUT IT.
MONTHLY VOLLEYBALL

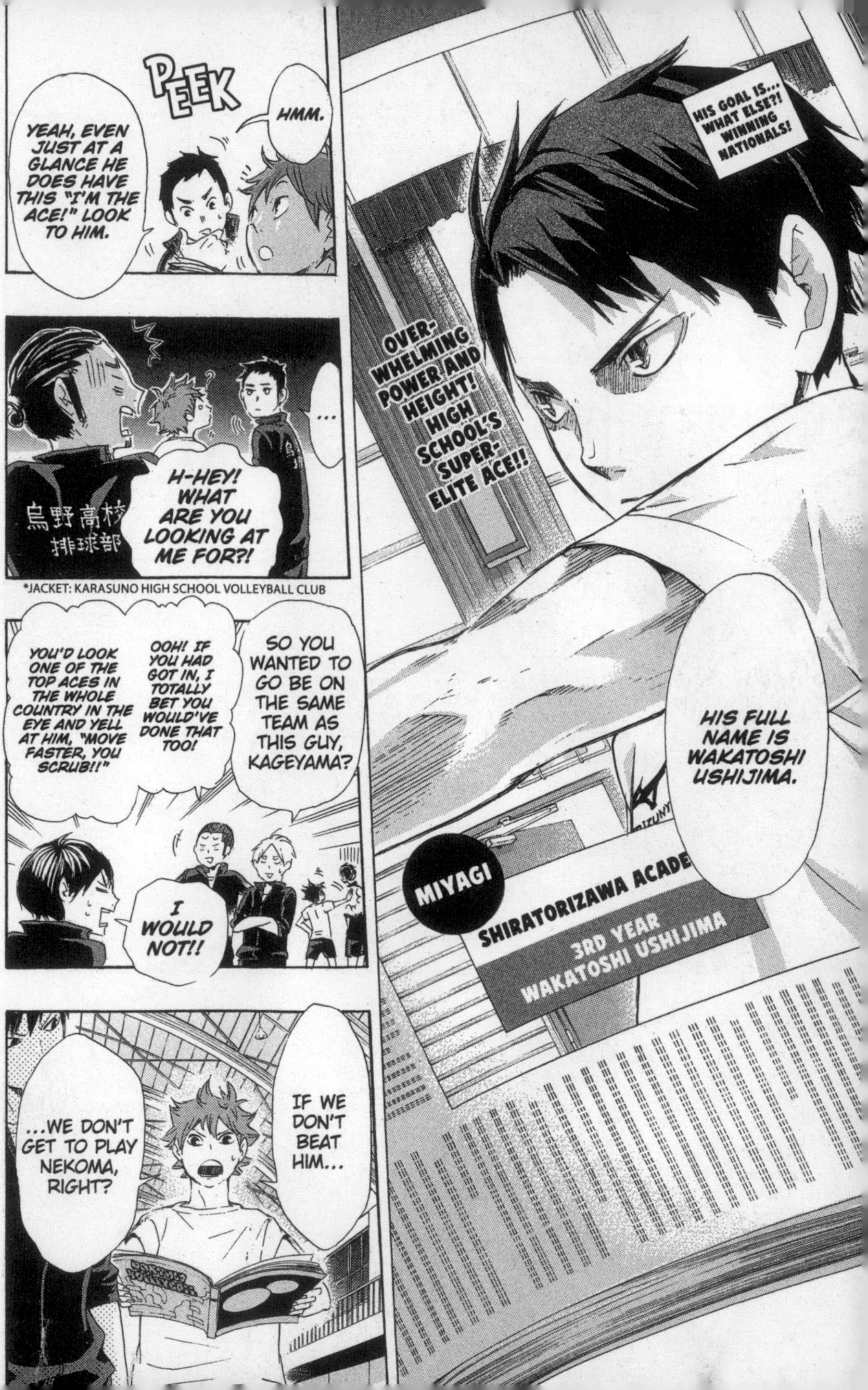
HIS GOAL IS... WHAT ELSE?! WINNING NATIONALS!
OVER-WHELMING POWER AND HEIGHT! HIGH SCHOOL'S SUPER-ELITE ACE!!
HIS FULL NAME IS WAKATOSHI USHIJIMA.
MIYAGI
SHIRATORIZAWA ACADE
3RD YEAR
WAKATOSHI USHIJIMA
PEEK
HMM.
YEAH, EVEN JUST AT A GLANCE HE DOES HAVE THIS "I'M THE ACE!" LOOK TO HIM.
...
H-HEY! WHAT ARE YOU LOOKING AT ME FOR?!
烏野高校排球部
*JACKET: KARASUNO HIGH SCHOOL VOLLEYBALL CLUB
SO YOU WANTED TO GO BE ON THE SAME TEAM AS THIS GUY, KAGEYAMA?
OOH! IF YOU HAD GOT IN, I TOTALLY BET YOU WOULD'VE DONE THAT TOO!
YOU'D LOOK ONE OF THE TOP ACES IN THE WHOLE COUNTRY IN THE EYE AND YELL AT HIM, "MOVE FASTER, YOU SCRUB!!"
I WOULD NOT!!
IF WE DON'T BEAT HIM...
...WE DON'T GET TO PLAY NEKOMA, RIGHT?

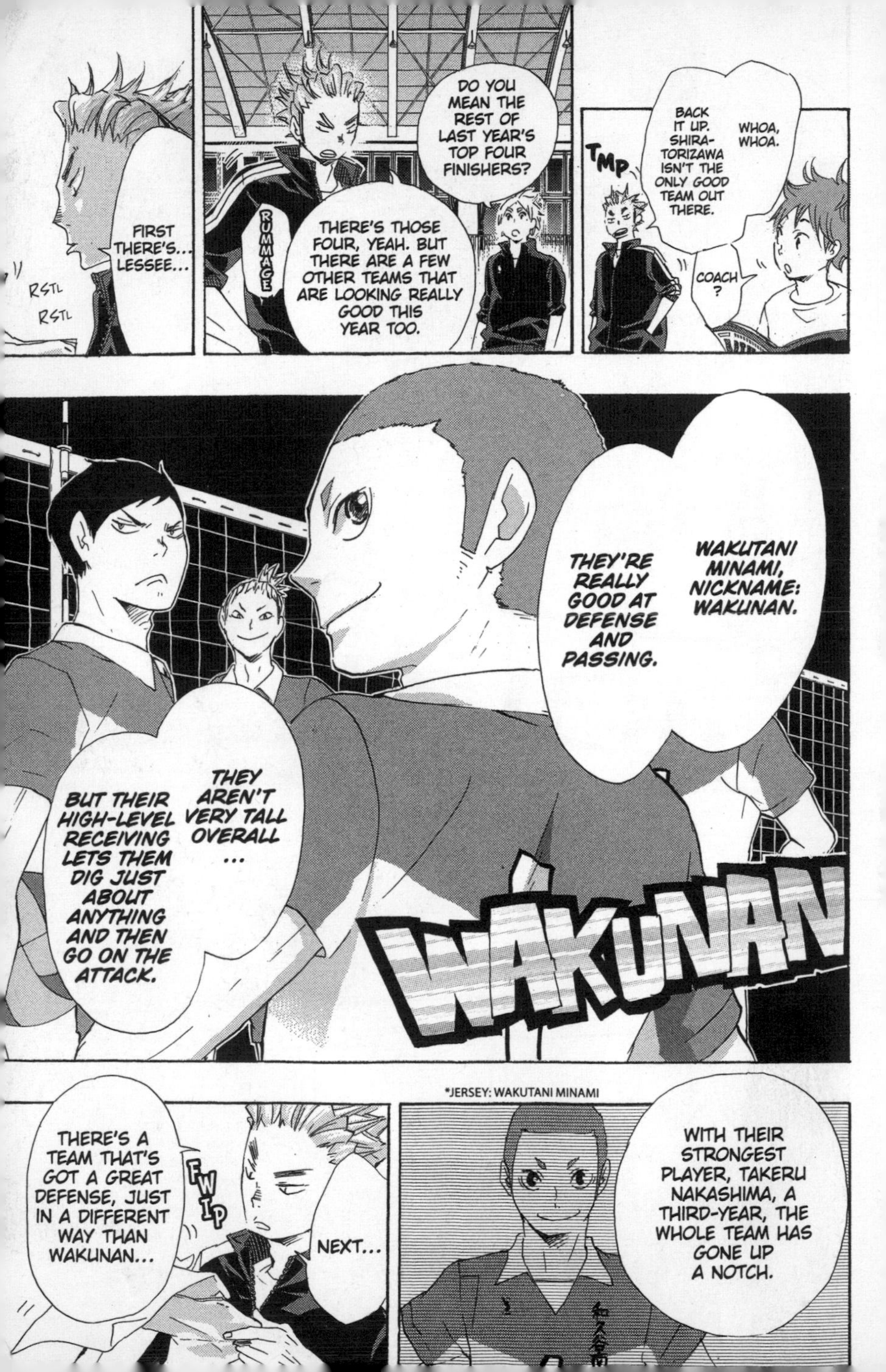
WHOA, WHOA.
BACK IT UP. SHIRATORIZAWA ISN'T THE ONLY GOOD TEAM OUT THERE.
TMP
COACH?
DO YOU MEAN THE REST OF LAST YEAR'S TOP FOUR FINISHERS?
RUMMAGE
THERE'S THOSE FOUR, YEAH. BUT THERE ARE A FEW OTHER TEAMS THAT ARE LOOKING REALLY GOOD THIS YEAR TOO.
FIRST THERE'S... LESSEE...
RSTL
RSTL
WAKUTANI MINAMI, NICKNAME: WAKUNAN.
THEY'RE REALLY GOOD AT DEFENSE AND PASSING.
THEY AREN'T VERY TALL OVERALL...
BUT THEIR HIGH-LEVEL RECEIVING LETS THEM DIG JUST ABOUT ANYTHING AND THEN GO ON THE ATTACK.
WAKUNAN
*JERSEY: WAKUTANI MINAMI
WITH THEIR STRONGEST PLAYER, TAKERU NAKASHIMA, A THIRD-YEAR, THE WHOLE TEAM HAS GONE UP A NOTCH.
NEXT...
FWIP
THERE'S A TEAM THAT'S GOT A GREAT DEFENSE, JUST IN A DIFFERENT WAY THAN WAKUNAN...

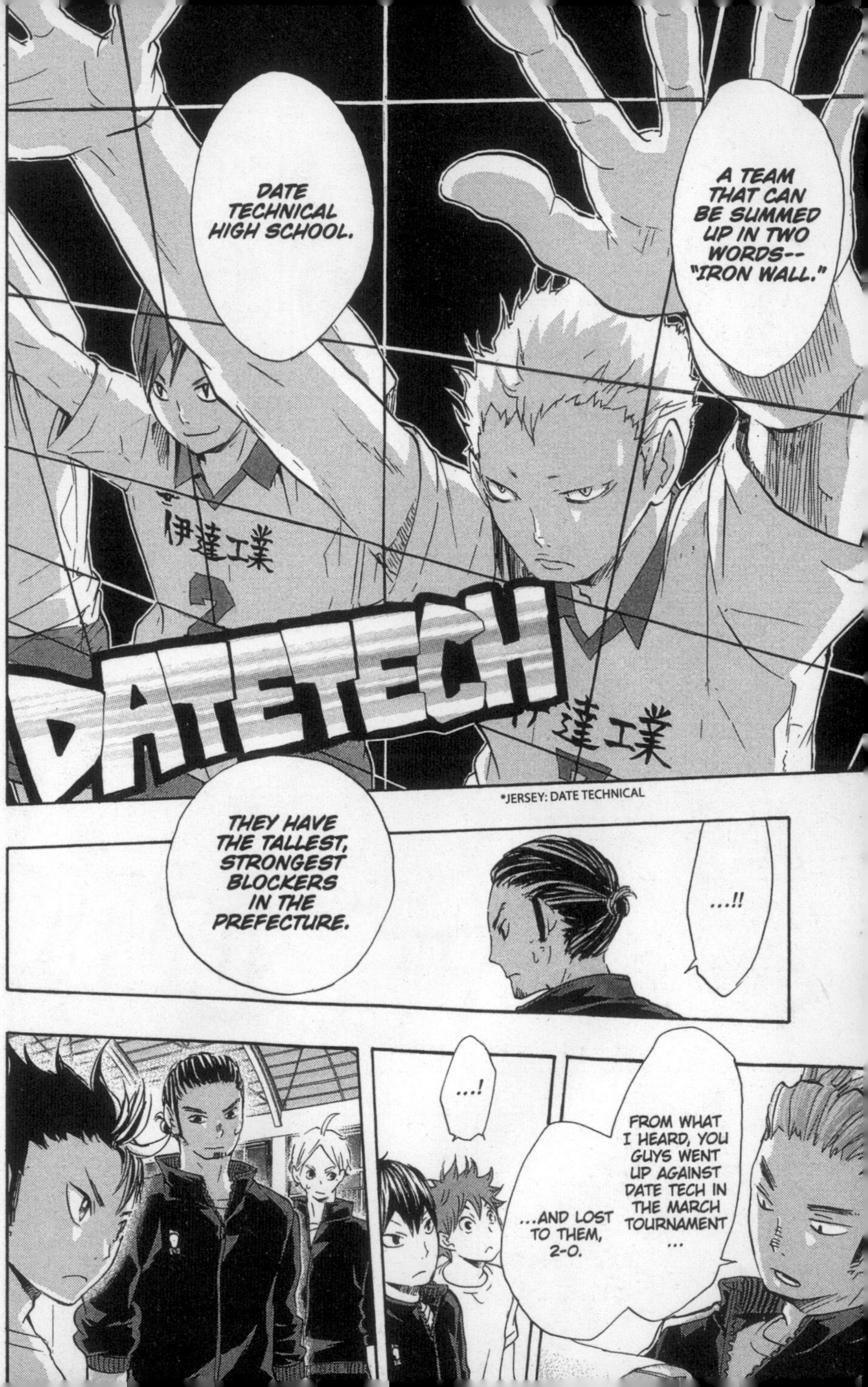
A TEAM THAT CAN BE SUMMED UP IN TWO WORDS-- "IRON WALL."
DATE TECHNICAL HIGH SCHOOL.
DATETECH
*JERSEY: DATE TECHNICAL
...!!
THEY HAVE THE TALLEST, STRONGEST BLOCKERS IN THE PREFECTURE.
FROM WHAT I HEARD, YOU GUYS WENT UP AGAINST DATE TECH IN THE MARCH TOURNAMENT ...
...AND LOST TO THEM, 2-0.
...!

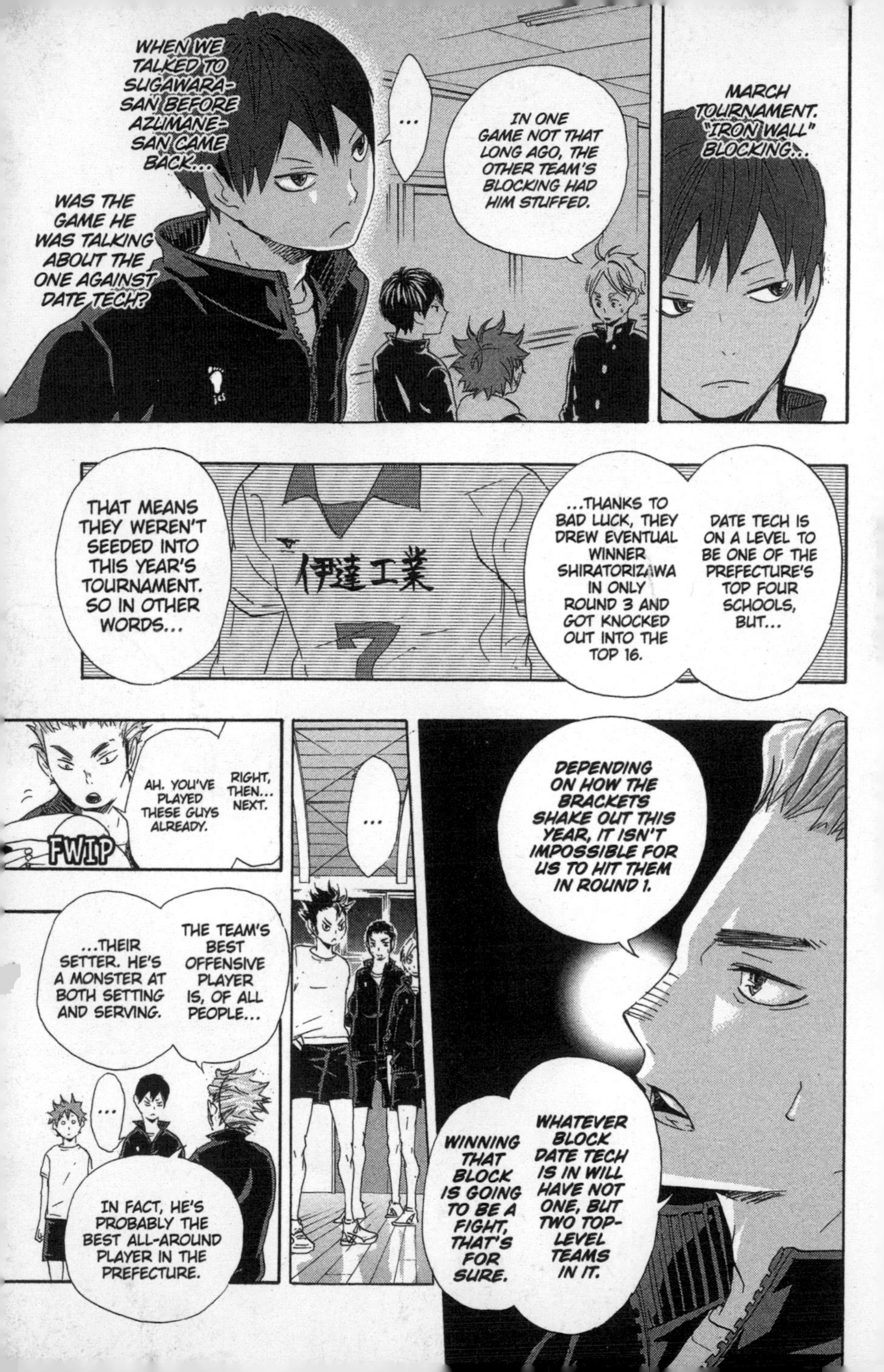
MARCH TOURNAMENT. "IRON WALL" BLOCKING...
IN ONE GAME NOT THAT LONG AGO, THE OTHER TEAM'S BLOCKING HAD HIM STUFFED.
...
WHEN WE TALKED TO SUGAWARA-SAN BEFORE AZUMANE-SAN CAME BACK...
WAS THE GAME HE WAS TALKING ABOUT THE ONE AGAINST DATE TECH?
DATE TECH IS ON A LEVEL TO BE ONE OF THE PREFECTURE'S TOP FOUR SCHOOLS, BUT...
...THANKS TO BAD LUCK, THEY DREW EVENTUAL WINNER SHIRATORIZAWA IN ONLY ROUND 3 AND GOT KNOCKED OUT INTO THE TOP 16.
伊達工業
7
THAT MEANS THEY WEREN'T SEEDED INTO THIS YEAR'S TOURNAMENT. SO IN OTHER WORDS...
DEPENDING ON HOW THE BRACKETS SHAKE OUT THIS YEAR, IT ISN'T IMPOSSIBLE FOR US TO HIT THEM IN ROUND 1.
WHATEVER BLOCK DATE TECH IS IN WILL HAVE NOT ONE, BUT TWO TOP-LEVEL TEAMS IN IT.
WINNING THAT BLOCK IS GOING TO BE A FIGHT, THAT'S FOR SURE.
...
RIGHT, THEN... NEXT.
AH. YOU'VE PLAYED THESE GUYS ALREADY.
FWIP
THE TEAM'S BEST OFFENSIVE PLAYER IS, OF ALL PEOPLE...
...THEIR SETTER. HE'S A MONSTER AT BOTH SETTING AND SERVING.
...
IN FACT, HE'S PROBABLY THE BEST ALL-AROUND PLAYER IN THE PREFECTURE.

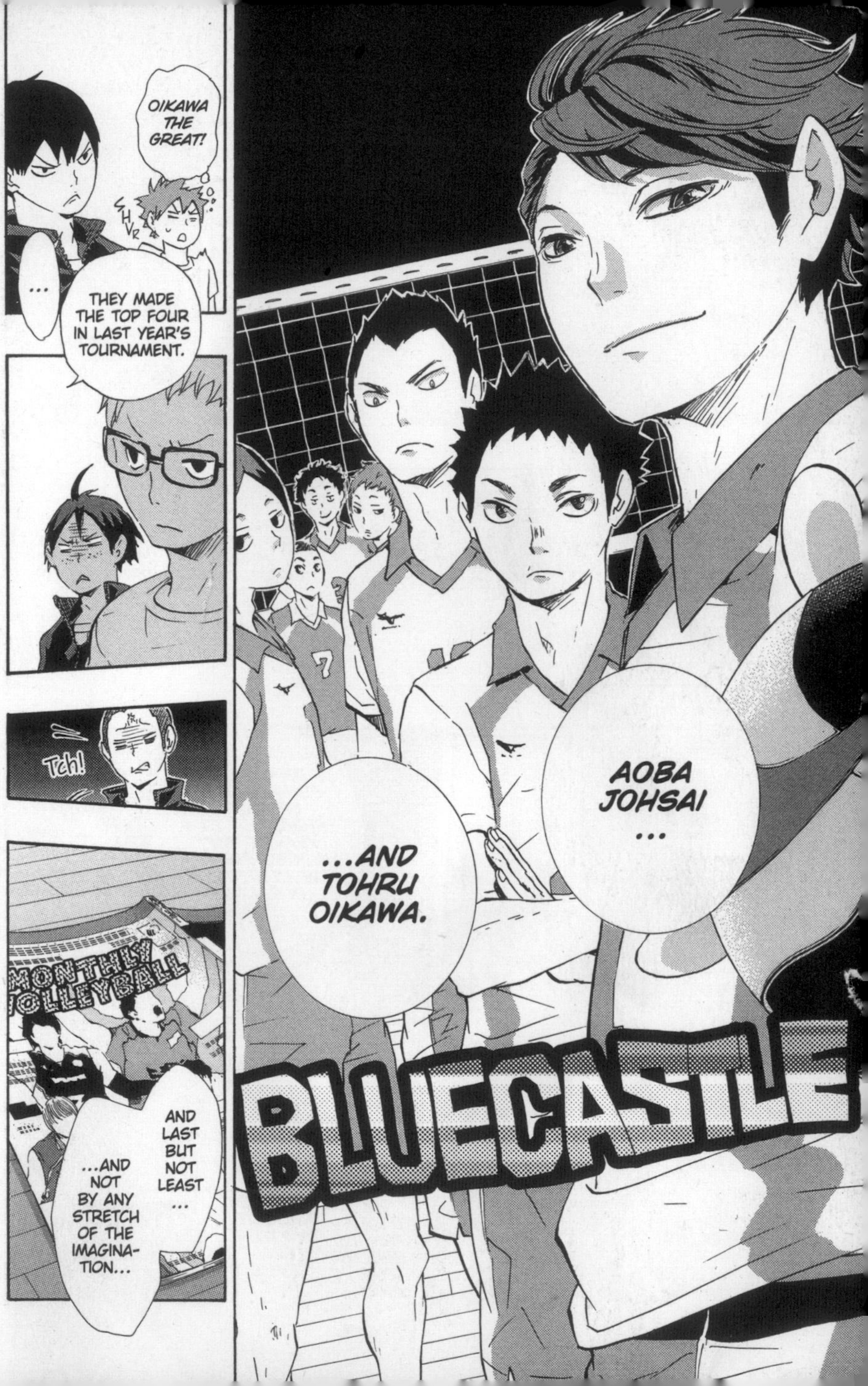
OIKAWA THE GREAT!
SHVR
THEY MADE THE TOP FOUR IN LAST YEAR'S TOURNAMENT.
...
Tch!
MONTHLY VOLLEYBALL
AND LAST BUT NOT LEAST ...
...AND NOT BY ANY STRETCH OF THE IMAGINATION...
AOBA JOHSAI ...
...AND TOHRU OIKAWA.
BLUECASTLE

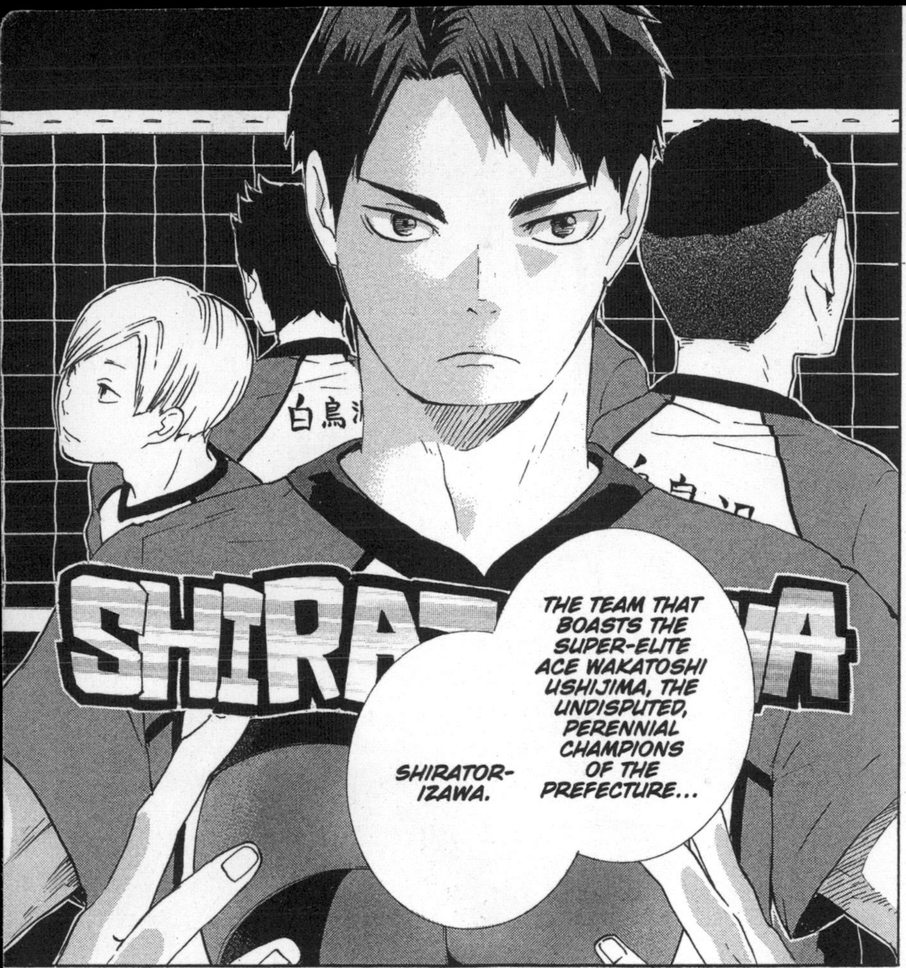
THE TEAM THAT BOASTS THE SUPER-ELITE ACE WAKATOSHI USHIJIMA, THE UNDISPUTED, PERENNIAL CHAMPIONS OF THE PREFECTURE...
SHIRATOR-IZAWA.
白鳥沢

*JERSEY: SHIRATORIZAWA

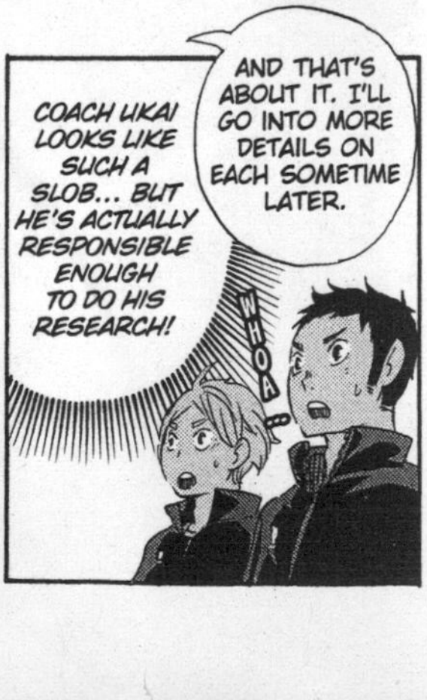
AND THAT'S ABOUT IT. I'LL GO INTO MORE DETAILS ON EACH SOMETIME LATER.
COACH UKAI LOOKS LIKE SUCH A SLOB... BUT HE'S ACTUALLY RESPONSIBLE ENOUGH TO DO HIS RESEARCH!
WHOA

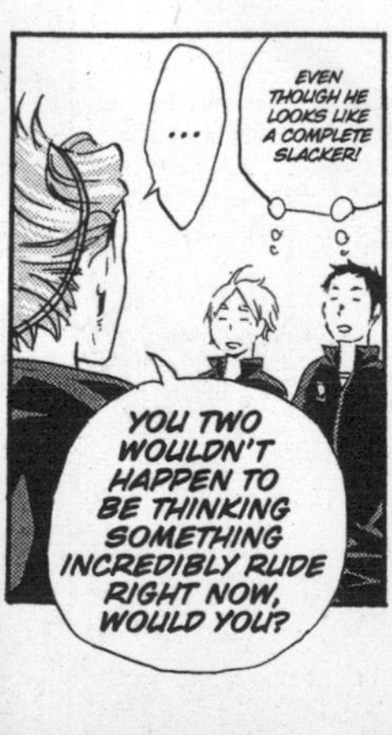
EVEN THOUGH HE LOOKS LIKE A COMPLETE SLACKER!
...
YOU TWO WOULDN'T HAPPEN TO BE THINKING SOMETHING INCREDIBLY RUDE RIGHT NOW, WOULD YOU?

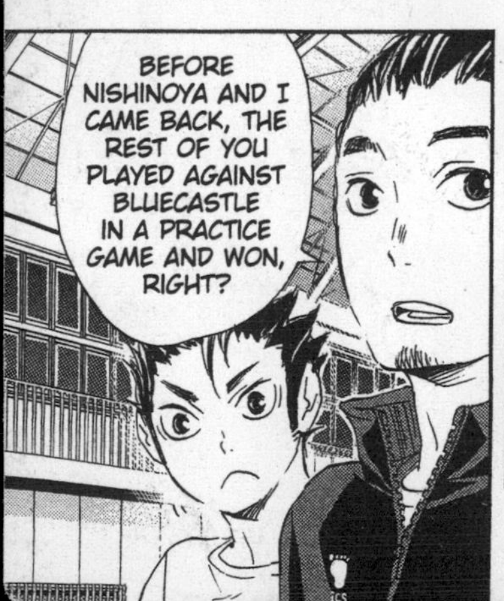
BEFORE NISHINOYA AND I CAME BACK, THE REST OF YOU PLAYED AGAINST BLUECASTLE IN A PRACTICE GAME AND WON, RIGHT?

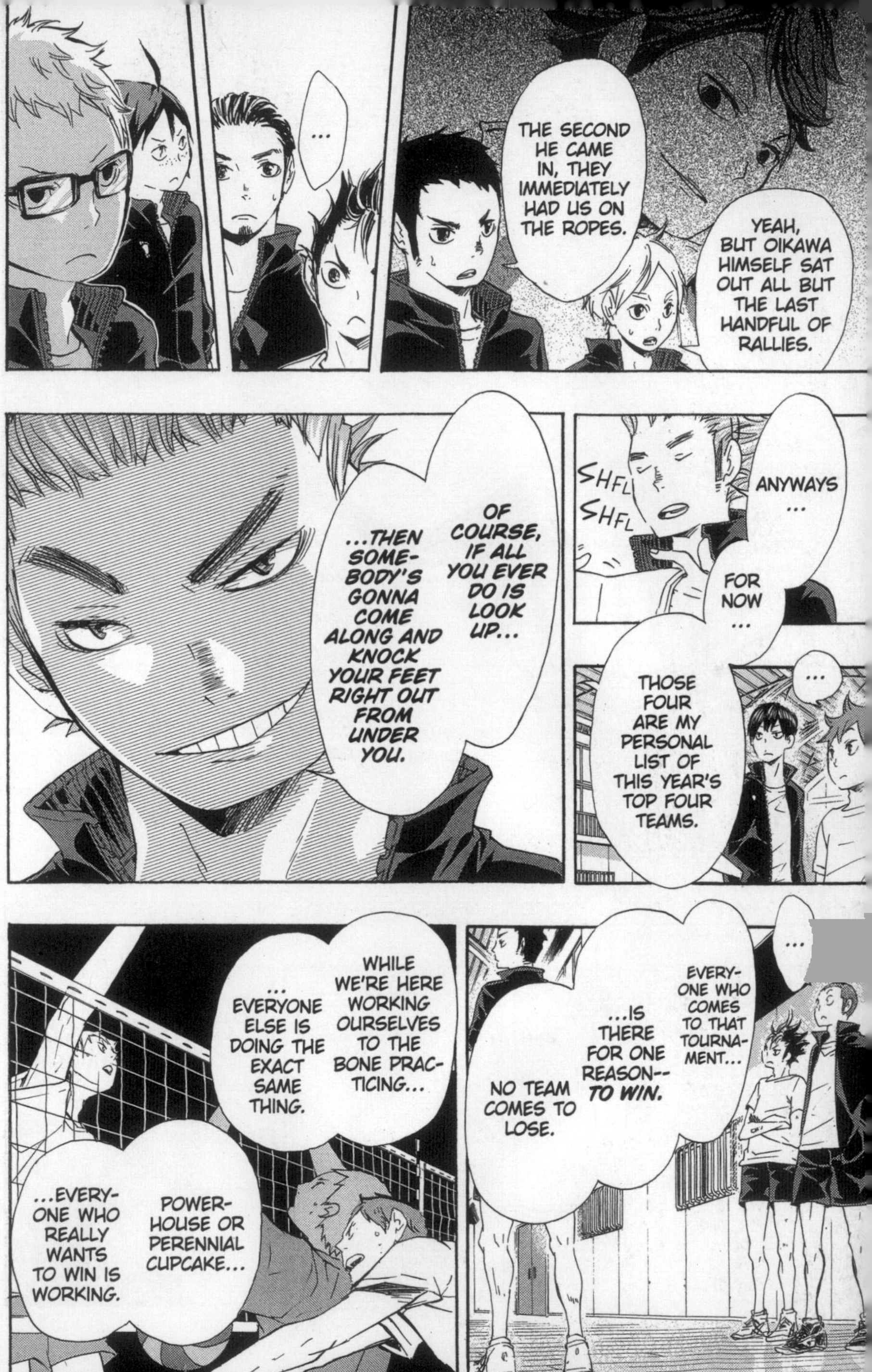
THE SECOND HE CAME IN, THEY IMMEDIATELY HAD US ON THE ROPES.
YEAH, BUT OIKAWA HIMSELF SAT OUT ALL BUT THE LAST HANDFUL OF RALLIES.
...
SHFL SHFL
ANYWAYS...
FOR NOW...
...
THOSE FOUR ARE MY PERSONAL LIST OF THIS YEAR'S TOP FOUR TEAMS.
OF COURSE, IF ALL YOU EVER DO IS LOOK UP...
...THEN SOMEBODY'S GONNA COME ALONG AND KNOCK YOUR FEET RIGHT OUT FROM UNDER YOU.
...
EVERYONE WHO COMES TO THAT TOURNAMENT...
...IS THERE FOR ONE REASON-- TO WIN.
NO TEAM COMES TO LOSE.
WHILE WE'RE HERE WORKING OURSELVES TO THE BONE PRACTICING...
... EVERYONE ELSE IS DOING THE EXACT SAME THING.
POWERHOUSE OR PERENNIAL CUPCAKE...
...EVERYONE WHO REALLY WANTS TO WIN IS WORKING.

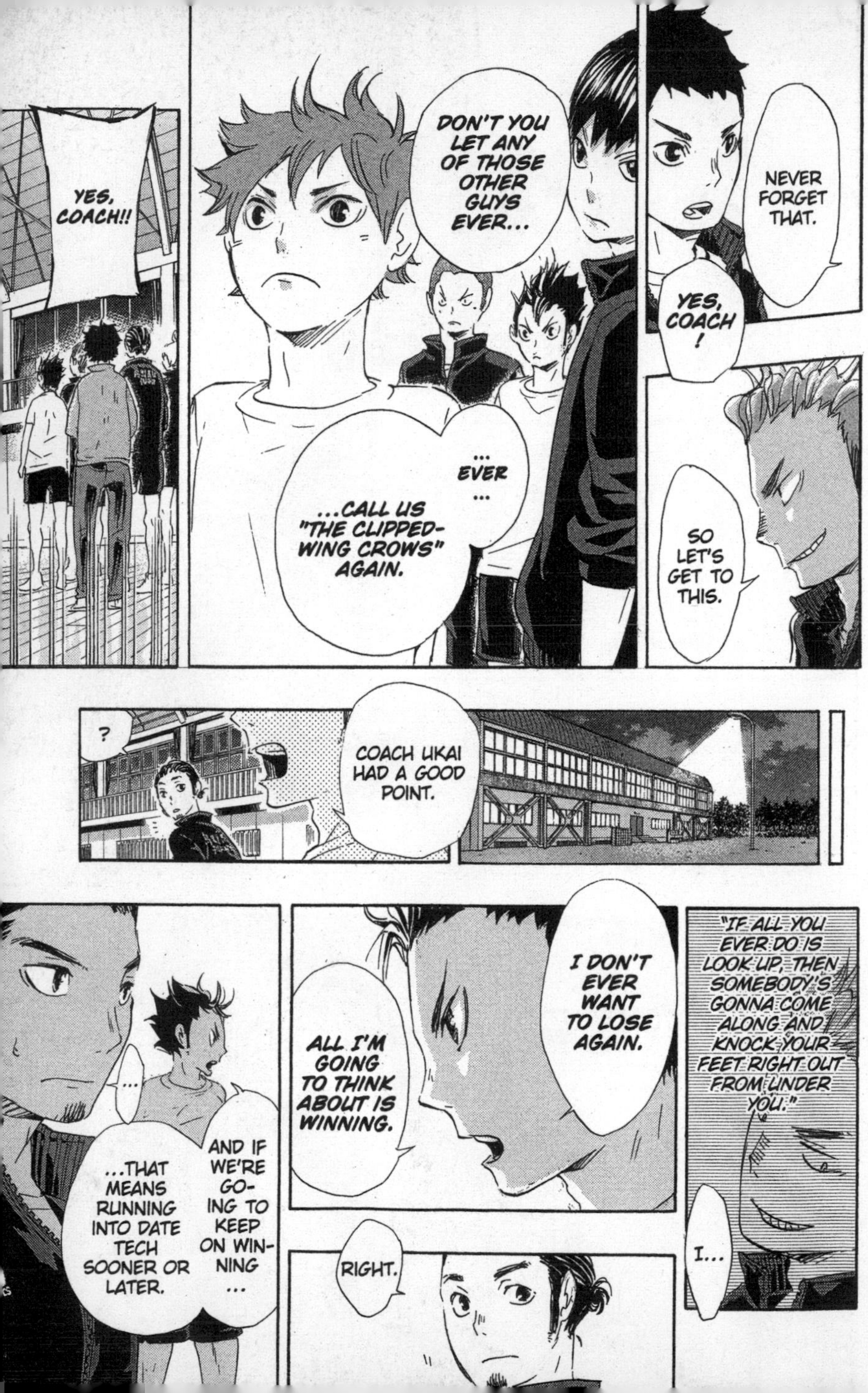
NEVER FORGET THAT.
YES, COACH!
SO LET'S GET TO THIS.
DON'T YOU LET ANY OF THOSE OTHER GUYS EVER...
...EVER...
...CALL US "THE CLIPPED-WING CROWS" AGAIN.
YES, COACH!!
COACH UKAI HAD A GOOD POINT.
?
"IF ALL YOU EVER DO IS LOOK UP, THEN SOMEBODY'S GONNA COME ALONG AND KNOCK YOUR FEET RIGHT OUT FROM UNDER YOU."
I...
I DON'T EVER WANT TO LOSE AGAIN.
ALL I'M GOING TO THINK ABOUT IS WINNING.
RIGHT.
...
AND IF WE'RE GO-ING TO KEEP ON WIN-NING...
...THAT MEANS RUNNING INTO DATE TECH SOONER OR LATER.

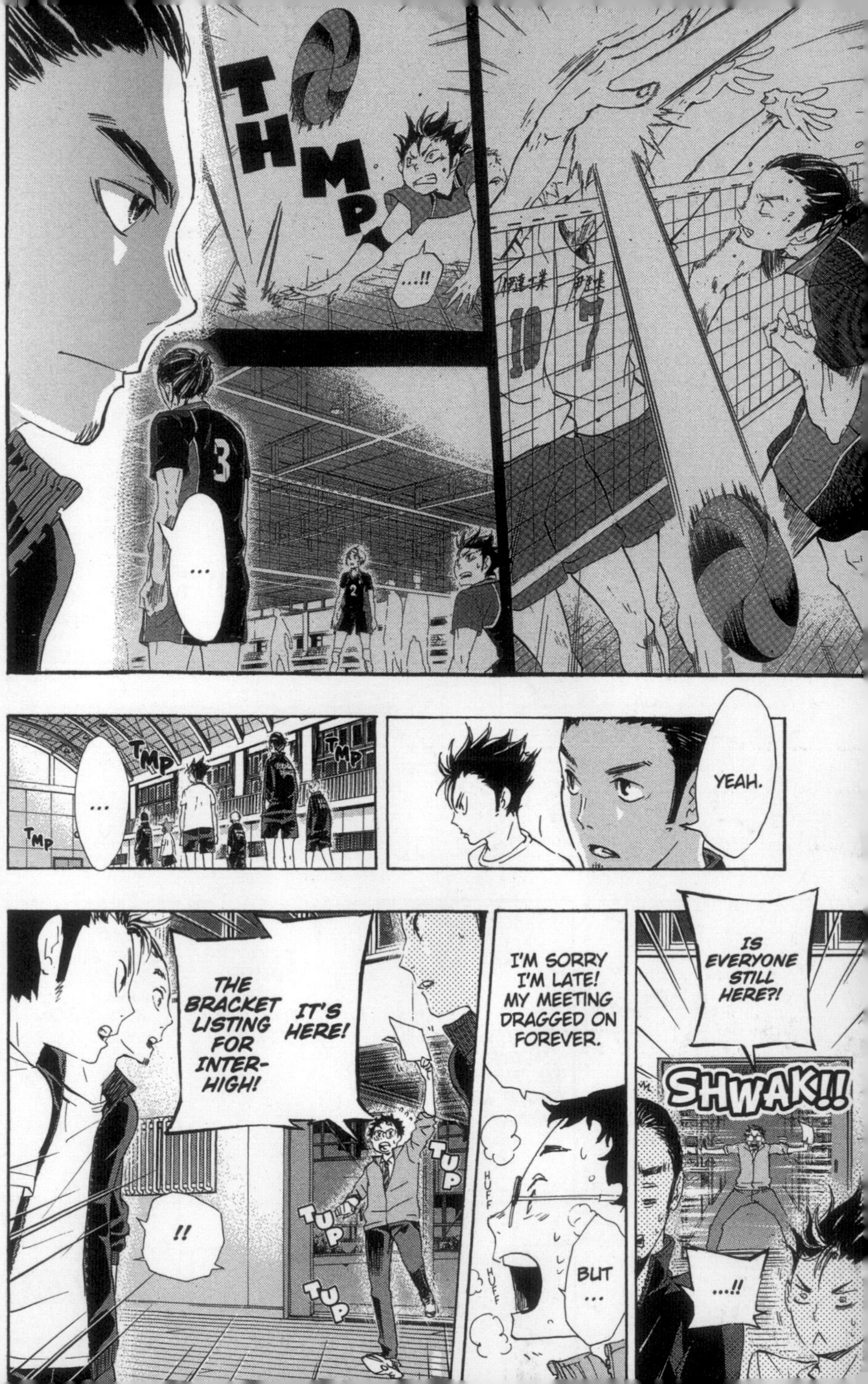
THMP
...!!
...
YEAH.
TMP
TMP
...
TMP
IS EVERYONE STILL HERE?!
SHWAK!!!
...!!
I'M SORRY I'M LATE! MY MEETING DRAGGED ON FOREVER.
HUFF
HUFF
BUT ...
IT'S HERE!
THE BRACKET LISTING FOR INTER-HIGH!
TUP
TUP
TUP
TUP
!!

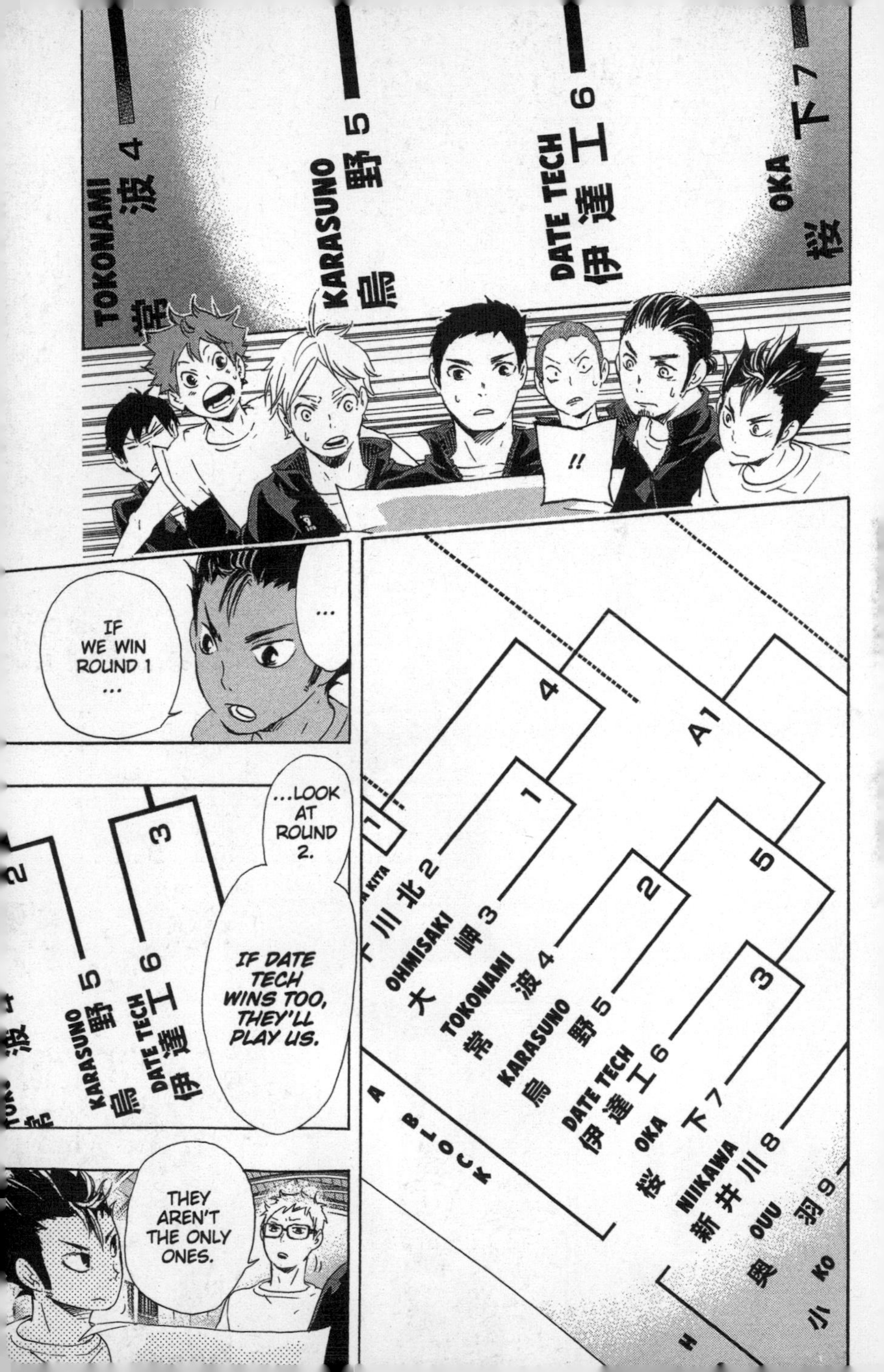

TOKONAMI 常波 4
KARASUNO 烏野 5
DATE TECH 伊達工 6
OKA 桜下 7
!!
A BLOCK
A1
OHMISAKI 大岬 3
TOKONAMI 常波 4
KARASUNO 烏野 5
DATE TECH 伊達工 6
OKA 桜下 7
NIIKAWA 新井川 8
OUU 奥羽 9
...
IF WE WIN ROUND 1 ...
...LOOK AT ROUND 2.
IF DATE TECH WINS TOO, THEY'LL PLAY US.
KARASUNO 烏野 5
DATE TECH 伊達工 6
THEY AREN'T THE ONLY ONES.

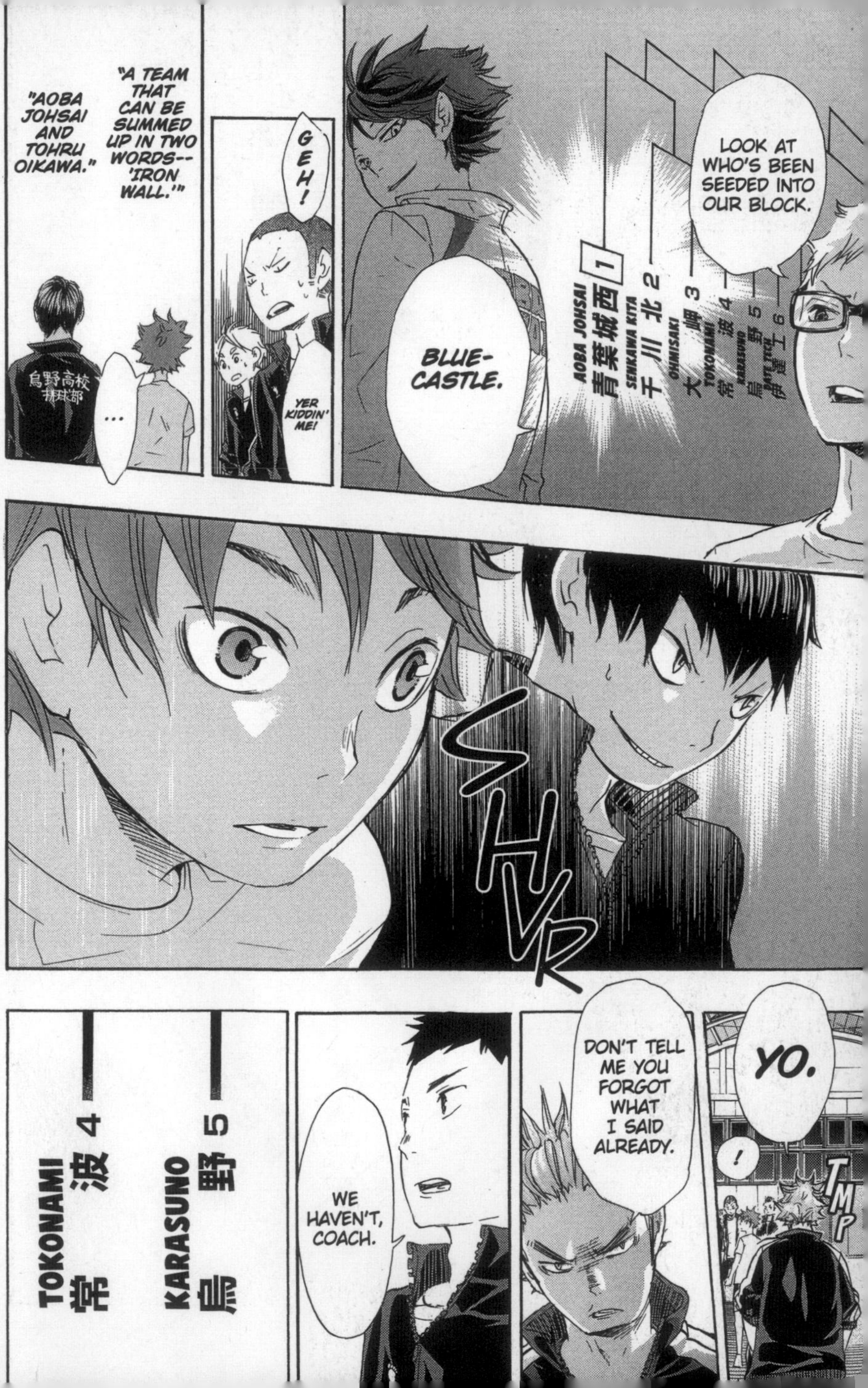
LOOK AT WHO'S BEEN SEEDED INTO OUR BLOCK.
AOBA JOHSAI 青葉城西 1
SENKAWA KITA 千川北 2
OHMISAKI 大岬 3
TOKONAMI 常波 4
KARASUNO 烏野 5
DATE TECH 伊達工 6
BLUE-CASTLE.
GEH!
YER KIDDIN' ME!
"A TEAM THAT CAN BE SUMMED UP IN TWO WORDS--'IRON WALL.'"
"AOBA JOHSAI AND TOHRU OIKAWA."
...
烏野高校 排球部
SHVR
YO.
!
TMP
DON'T TELL ME YOU FORGOT WHAT I SAID ALREADY.
WE HAVEN'T, COACH.
TOKONAMI 常波 4
KARASUNO 烏野 5

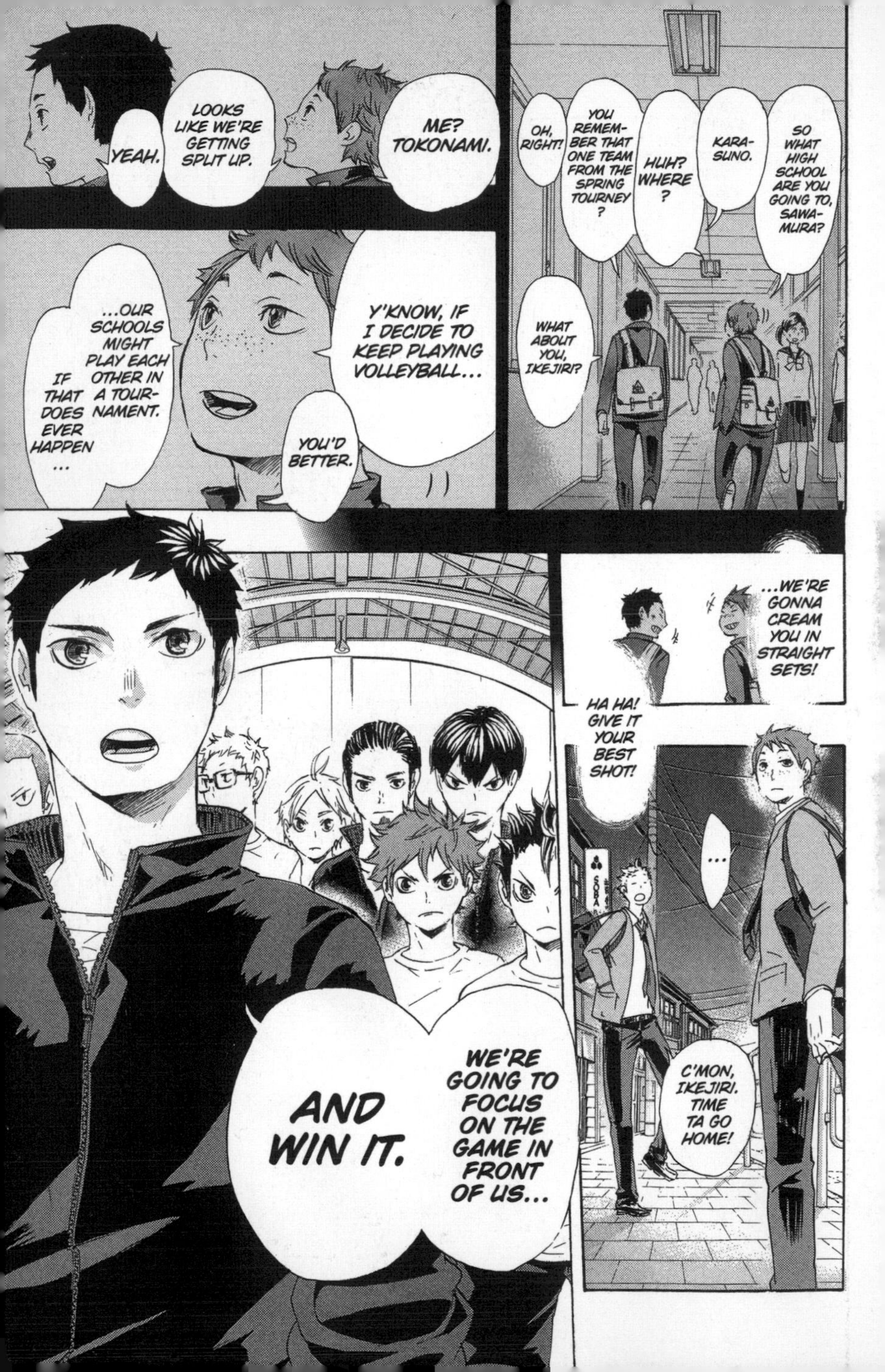
SO WHAT HIGH SCHOOL ARE YOU GOING TO, SAWAMURA?
KARA-SUNO.
HUH? WHERE?
YOU REMEMBER THAT ONE TEAM FROM THE SPRING TOURNEY?
OH, RIGHT!
WHAT ABOUT YOU, IKEJIRI?
ME? TOKONAMI.
LOOKS LIKE WE'RE GETTING SPLIT UP.
YEAH.
Y'KNOW, IF I DECIDE TO KEEP PLAYING VOLLEYBALL...
...OUR SCHOOLS MIGHT PLAY EACH OTHER IN A TOUR-NAMENT.
IF THAT DOES EVER HAPPEN...
YOU'D BETTER.
...WE'RE GONNA CREAM YOU IN STRAIGHT SETS!
HA HA! GIVE IT YOUR BEST SHOT!
...
SOBA
C'MON, IKEJIRI. TIME TA GO HOME!
WE'RE GOING TO FOCUS ON THE GAME IN FRONT OF US...
AND WIN IT.

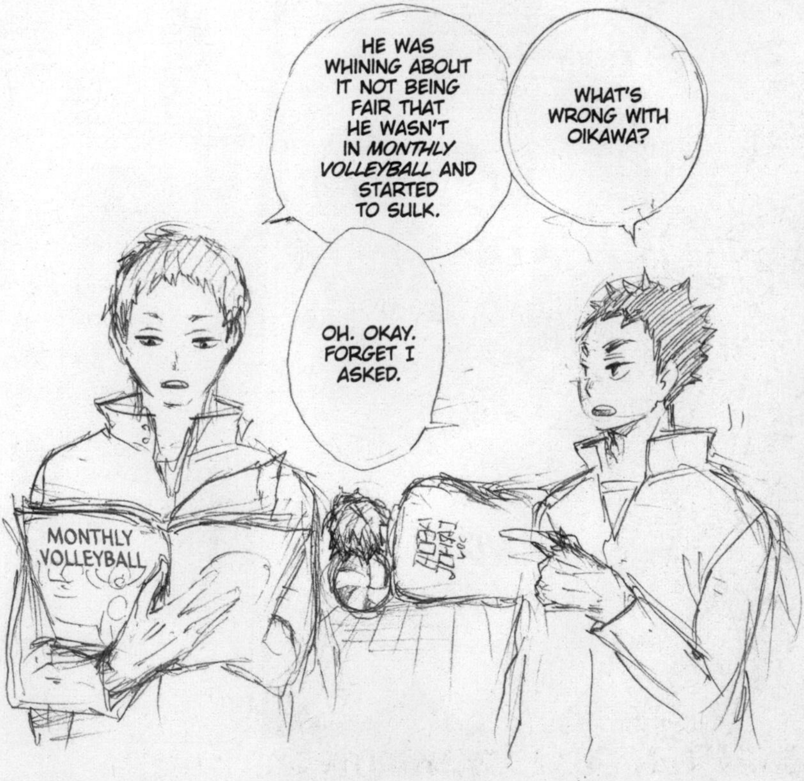
WHAT'S WRONG WITH OIKAWA?
HE WAS WHINING ABOUT IT NOT BEING FAIR THAT HE WASN'T IN *MONTHLY VOLLEYBALL* AND STARTED TO SULK.
OH. OKAY. FORGET I ASKED.
MONTHLY VOLLEYBALL

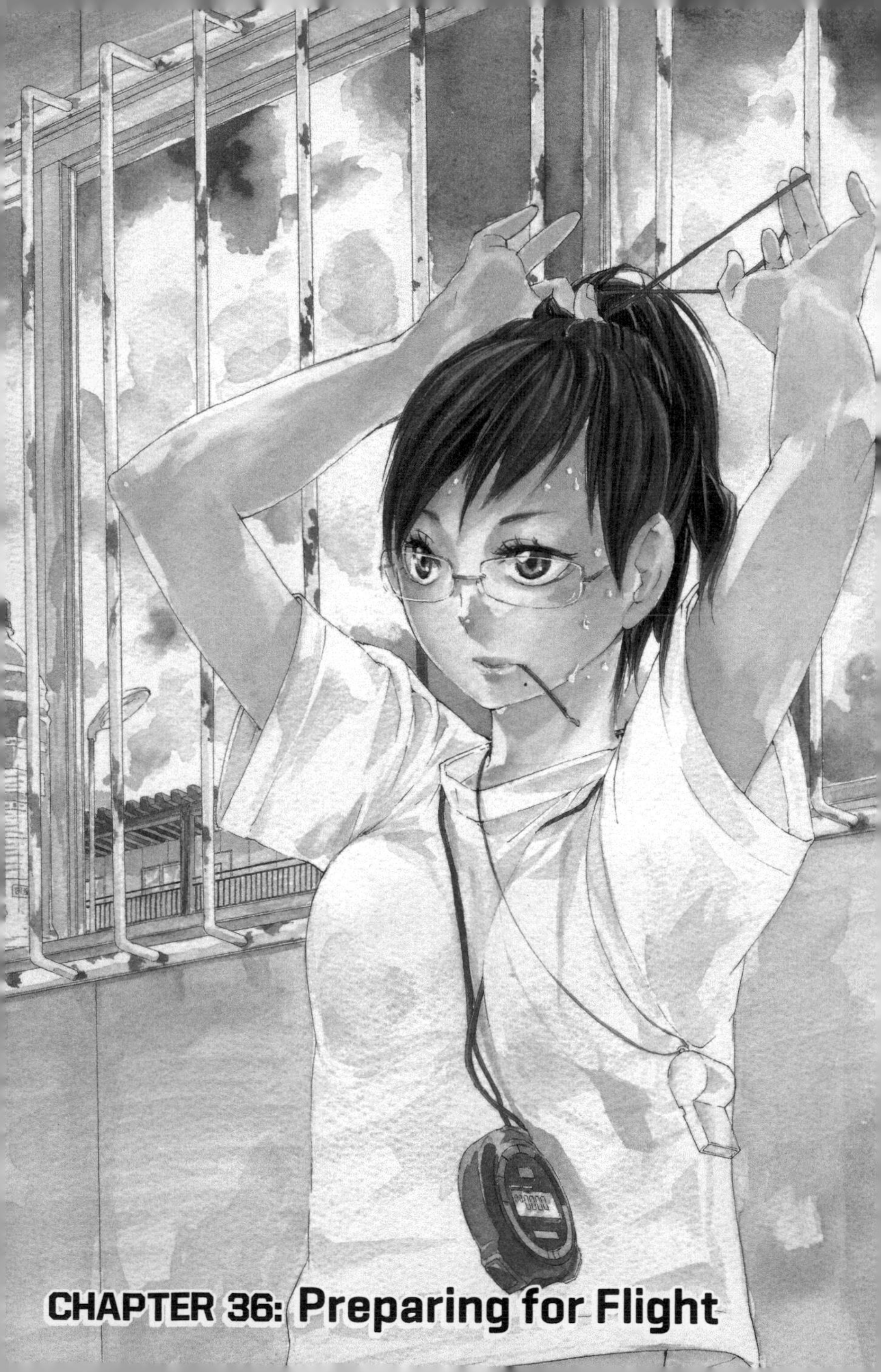

CHAPTER 36: Preparing for Flight

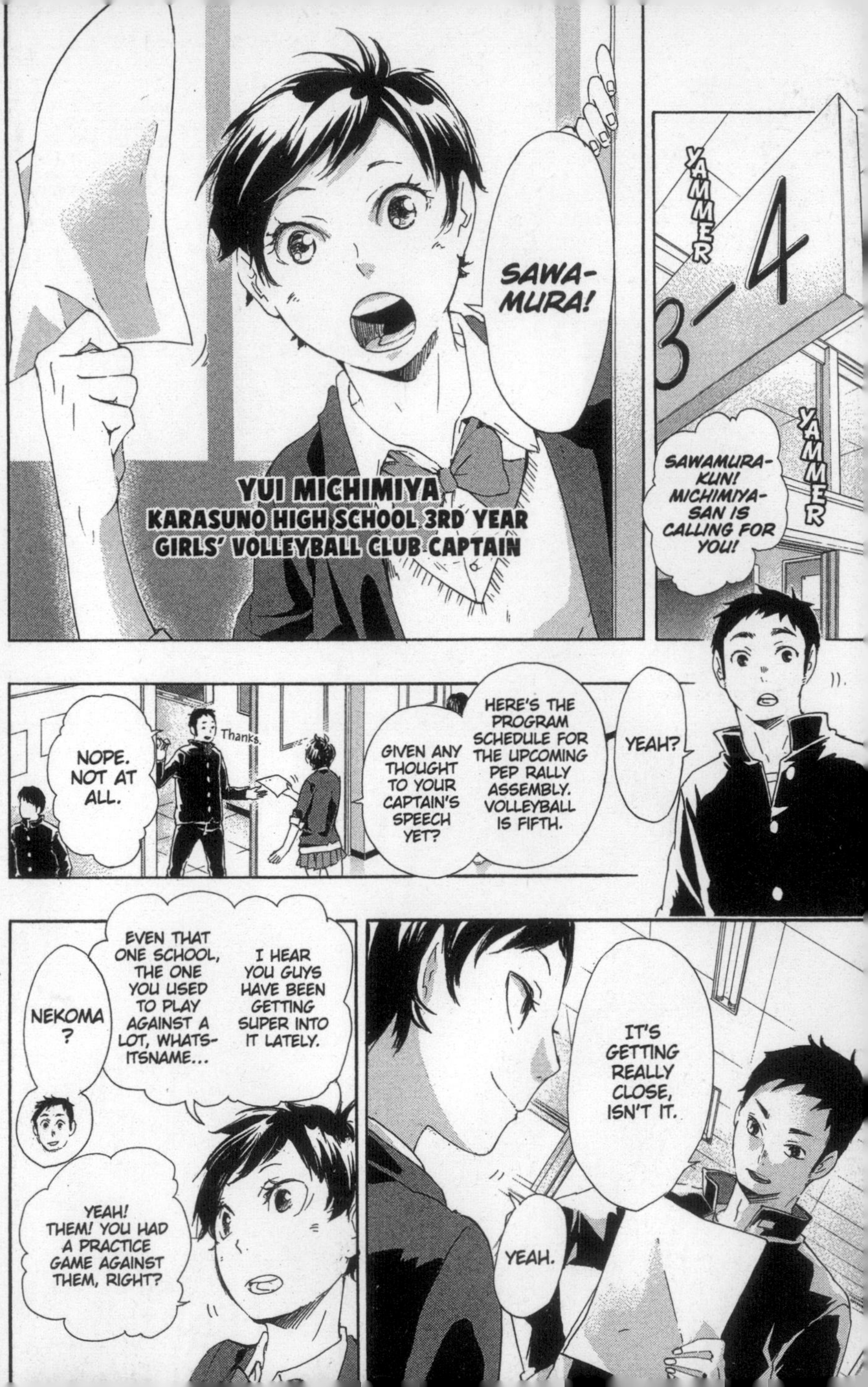
YAMMER
YAMMER
SAWAMURA-KUN! MICHIMIYA-SAN IS CALLING FOR YOU!
SAWA-MURA!
YUI MICHIMIYA
KARASUNO HIGH SCHOOL 3RD YEAR
GIRLS' VOLLEYBALL CLUB CAPTAIN
YEAH?
HERE'S THE PROGRAM SCHEDULE FOR THE UPCOMING PEP RALLY ASSEMBLY. VOLLEYBALL IS FIFTH.
GIVEN ANY THOUGHT TO YOUR CAPTAIN'S SPEECH YET?
Thanks.
NOPE. NOT AT ALL.
IT'S GETTING REALLY CLOSE, ISN'T IT.
YEAH.
I HEAR YOU GUYS HAVE BEEN GETTING SUPER INTO IT LATELY.
EVEN THAT ONE SCHOOL, THE ONE YOU USED TO PLAY AGAINST A LOT, WHATS-ITSNAME...
NEKOMA?
YEAH! THEM! YOU HAD A PRACTICE GAME AGAINST THEM, RIGHT?

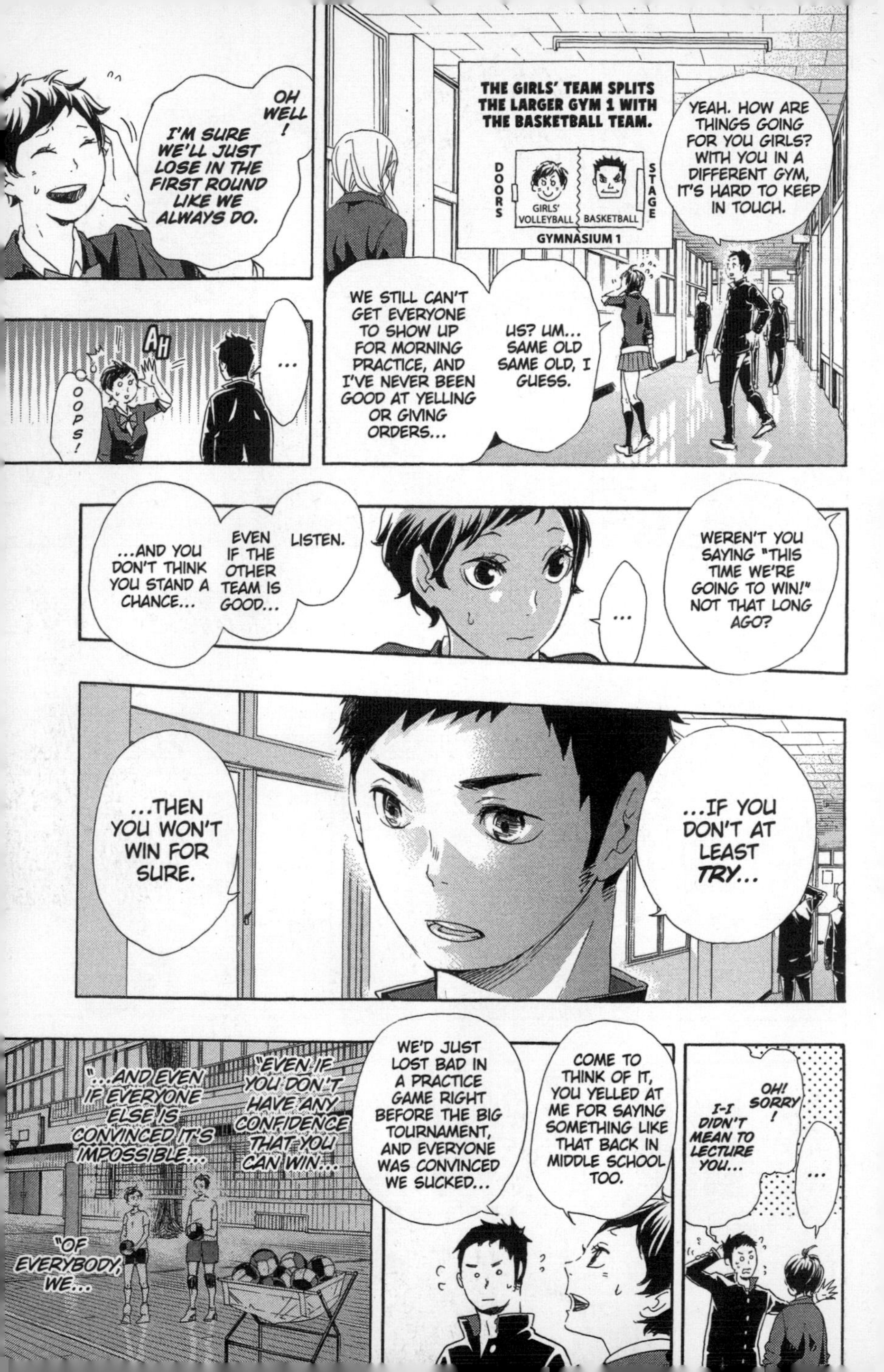
THE GIRLS' TEAM SPLITS THE LARGER GYM 1 WITH THE BASKETBALL TEAM.
DOORS
GIRLS' VOLLEYBALL
BASKETBALL
STAGE
GYMNASIUM 1
YEAH. HOW ARE THINGS GOING FOR YOU GIRLS? WITH YOU IN A DIFFERENT GYM, IT'S HARD TO KEEP IN TOUCH.
US? UM... SAME OLD SAME OLD, I GUESS.
WE STILL CAN'T GET EVERYONE TO SHOW UP FOR MORNING PRACTICE, AND I'VE NEVER BEEN GOOD AT YELLING OR GIVING ORDERS...
OH WELL!
I'M SURE WE'LL JUST LOSE IN THE FIRST ROUND LIKE WE ALWAYS DO.
...
AH
OOPS!
WEREN'T YOU SAYING "THIS TIME WE'RE GOING TO WIN!" NOT THAT LONG AGO?
...
LISTEN.
EVEN IF THE OTHER TEAM IS GOOD...
...AND YOU DON'T THINK YOU STAND A CHANCE...
...IF YOU DON'T AT LEAST *TRY*...
...THEN YOU WON'T WIN FOR SURE.
OH! SORRY!
I-I DIDN'T MEAN TO LECTURE YOU...
...
COME TO THINK OF IT, YOU YELLED AT ME FOR SAYING SOMETHING LIKE THAT BACK IN MIDDLE SCHOOL TOO.
WE'D JUST LOST BAD IN A PRACTICE GAME RIGHT BEFORE THE BIG TOURNAMENT, AND EVERYONE WAS CONVINCED WE SUCKED...
"EVEN IF YOU DON'T HAVE ANY CONFIDENCE THAT YOU CAN WIN...
"...AND EVEN IF EVERYONE ELSE IS CONVINCED IT'S IMPOSSIBLE...
"OF EVERYBODY, WE...

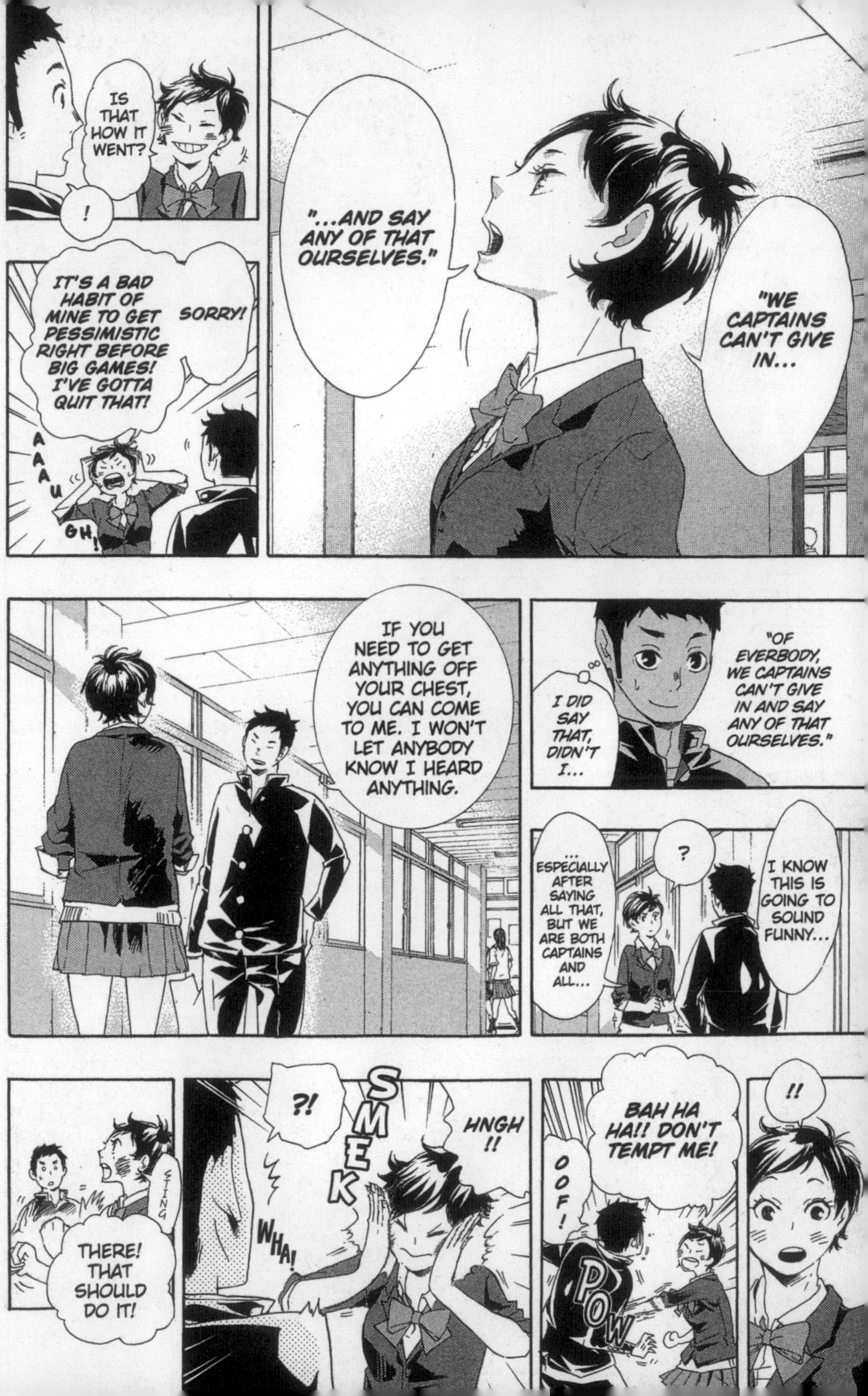
"WE CAPTAINS CAN'T GIVE IN...
"...AND SAY ANY OF THAT OURSELVES."
IS THAT HOW IT WENT?
!
SORRY!
IT'S A BAD HABIT OF MINE TO GET PESSIMISTIC RIGHT BEFORE BIG GAMES! I'VE GOTTA QUIT THAT!
AAAUGH!
"OF EVERBODY, WE CAPTAINS CAN'T GIVE IN AND SAY ANY OF THAT OURSELVES."
I DID SAY THAT, DIDN'T I...
I KNOW THIS IS GOING TO SOUND FUNNY...
?
...ESPECIALLY AFTER SAYING ALL THAT, BUT WE ARE BOTH CAPTAINS AND ALL...
IF YOU NEED TO GET ANYTHING OFF YOUR CHEST, YOU CAN COME TO ME. I WON'T LET ANYBODY KNOW I HEARD ANYTHING.
!!
BAH HA HA!! DON'T TEMPT ME!
OOF!
POW
?!
SMEK
HNGH !!
WHA!
STING
THERE! THAT SHOULD DO IT!

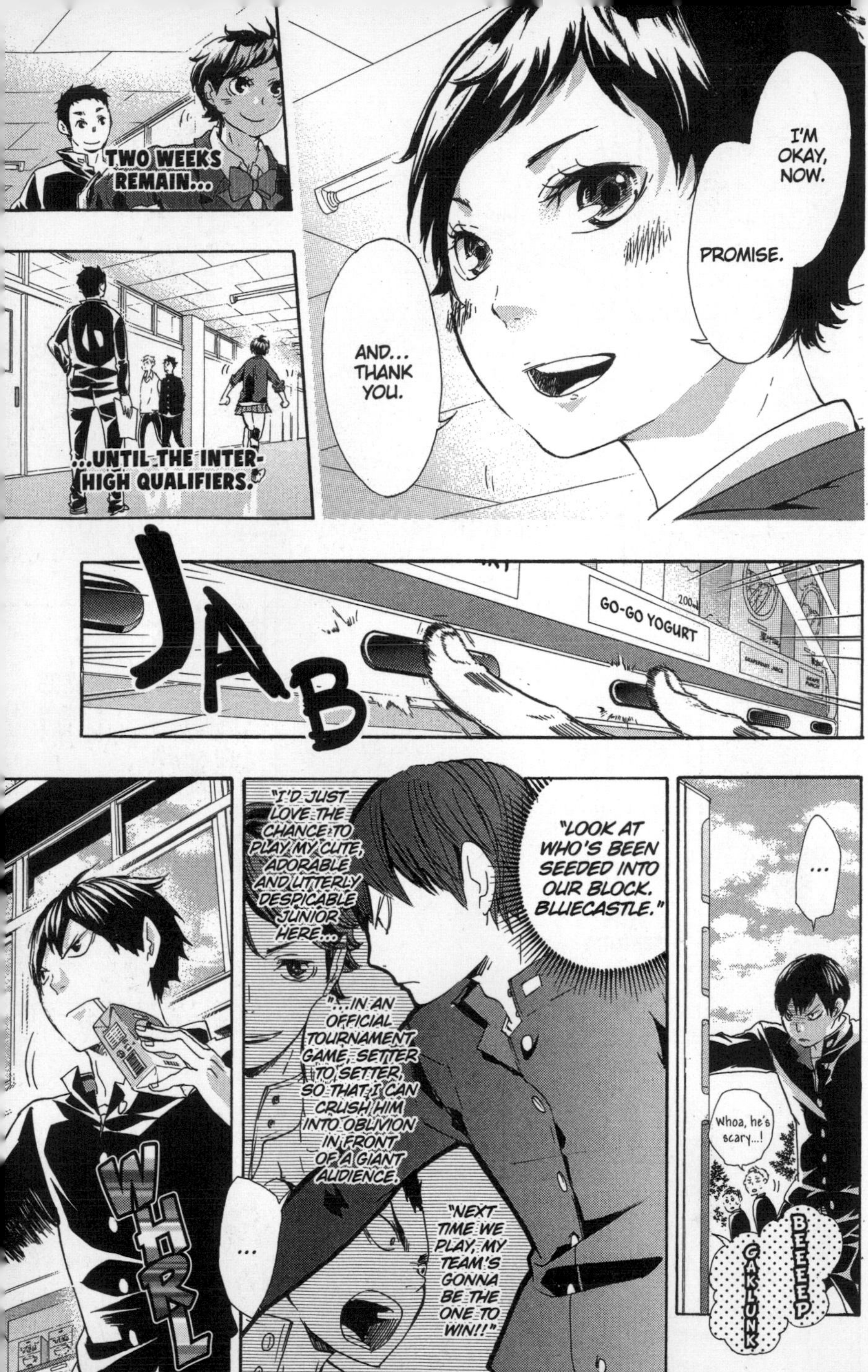
I'M OKAY, NOW.
PROMISE.
AND... THANK YOU.
TWO WEEKS REMAIN...
...UNTIL THE INTER-HIGH QUALIFIERS.
JAB
GO-GO YOGURT
...
Whoa, he's scary...!
BEEEEP
GAKLUNK
"LOOK AT WHO'S BEEN SEEDED INTO OUR BLOCK. BLUECASTLE."
"I'D JUST LOVE THE CHANCE TO PLAY MY CUTE, ADORABLE AND UTTERLY DESPICABLE JUNIOR HERE..."
"...IN AN OFFICIAL TOURNAMENT GAME, SETTER TO SETTER, SO THAT I CAN CRUSH HIM INTO OBLIVION IN FRONT OF A GIANT AUDIENCE."
"NEXT TIME WE PLAY, MY TEAM'S GONNA BE THE ONE TO WIN!!"
...
WHIRL

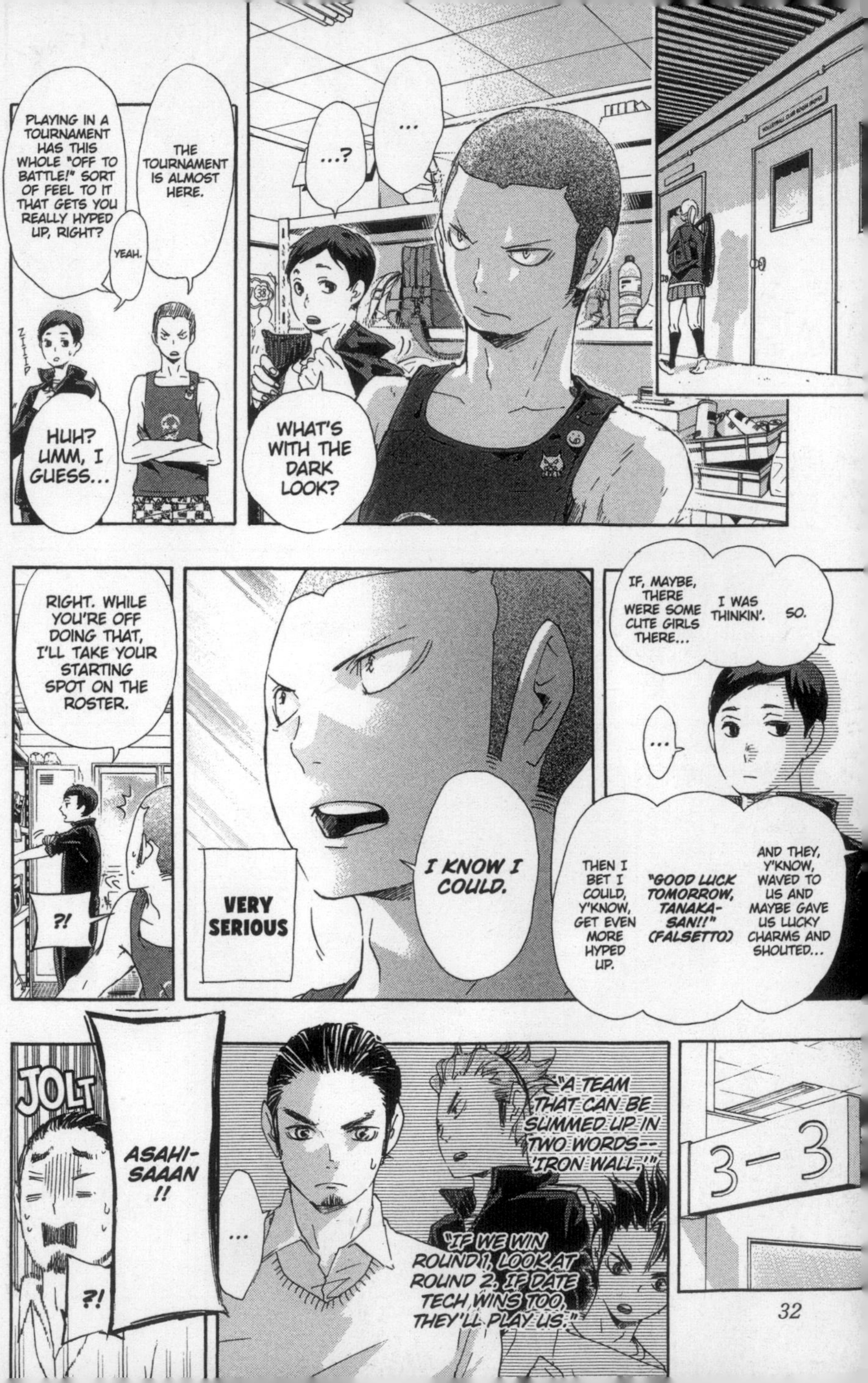
...
...?
WHAT'S WITH THE DARK LOOK?
THE TOURNAMENT IS ALMOST HERE.
PLAYING IN A TOURNAMENT HAS THIS WHOLE "OFF TO BATTLE!" SORT OF FEEL TO IT THAT GETS YOU REALLY HYPED UP, RIGHT?
YEAH.
ZIIIP
HUH? UMM, I GUESS...
SO.
I WAS THINKIN'.
IF, MAYBE, THERE WERE SOME CUTE GIRLS THERE...
...
AND THEY, Y'KNOW, WAVED TO US AND MAYBE GAVE US LUCKY CHARMS AND SHOUTED...
"GOOD LUCK TOMORROW, TANAKA-SAN!!" (FALSETTO)
THEN I BET I COULD, Y'KNOW, GET EVEN MORE HYPED UP.
I KNOW I COULD.
VERY SERIOUS
RIGHT. WHILE YOU'RE OFF DOING THAT, I'LL TAKE YOUR STARTING SPOT ON THE ROSTER.
?!
3-3
"A TEAM THAT CAN BE SUMMED UP IN TWO WORDS-- 'IRON WALL.'"
...
"IF WE WIN ROUND 1, LOOK AT ROUND 2. IF DATE TECH WINS TOO, THEY'LL PLAY US."
ASAHI-SAAAN!!
JOLT
?!

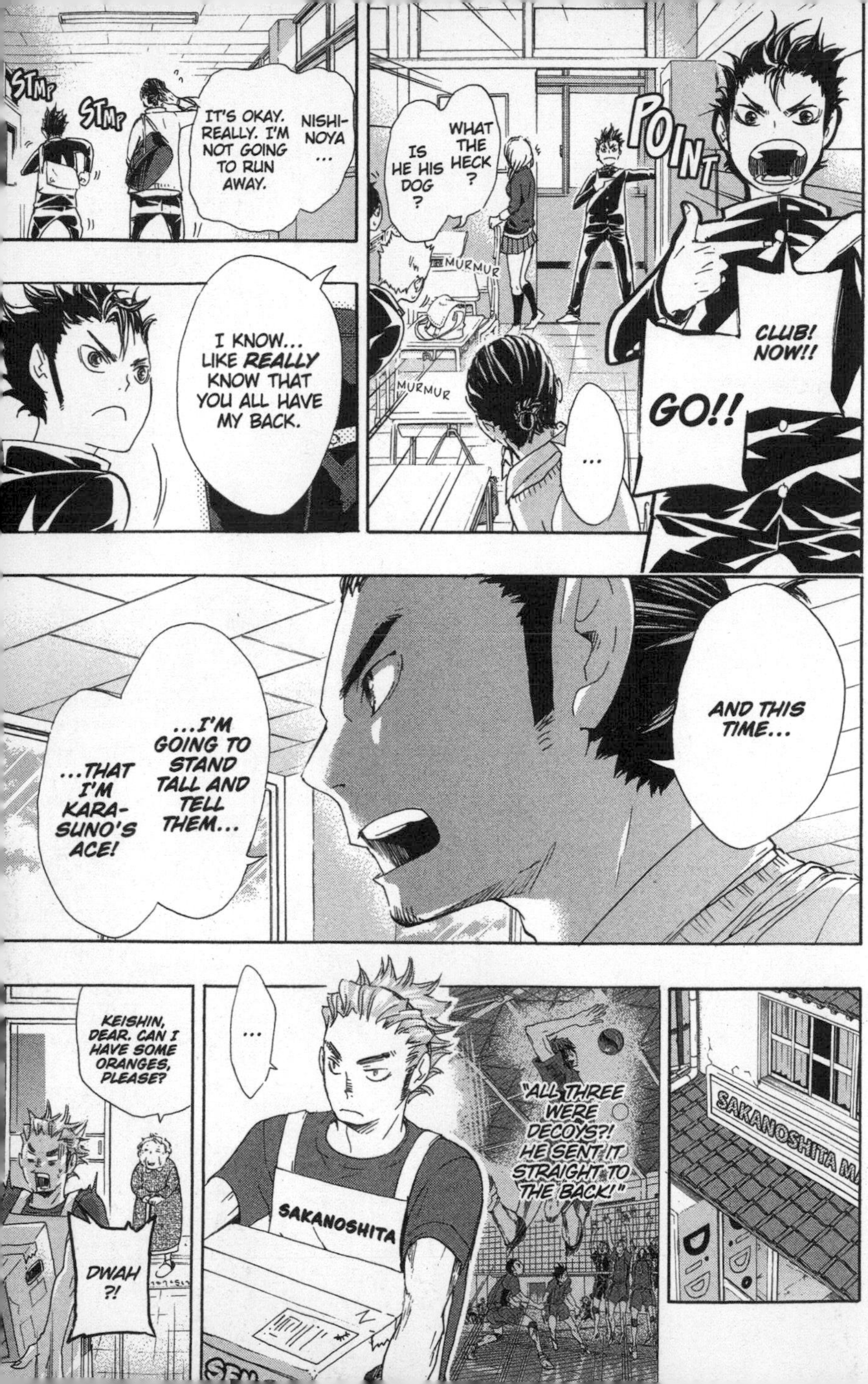
POINT
CLUB! NOW!!
GO!!
WHAT THE HECK?
IS HE HIS DOG?
MURMUR
MURMUR
...
STMP
STMP
NISHINOYA...
IT'S OKAY. REALLY. I'M NOT GOING TO RUN AWAY.
I KNOW... LIKE REALLY KNOW THAT YOU ALL HAVE MY BACK.
AND THIS TIME...
...I'M GOING TO STAND TALL AND TELL THEM...
...THAT I'M KARA-SUNO'S ACE!
SAKANOSHITA MA
"ALL THREE WERE DECOYS?! HE SENT IT STRAIGHT TO THE BACK!"
...
SAKANOSHITA
KEISHIN, DEAR. CAN I HAVE SOME ORANGES, PLEASE?
DWAH?!

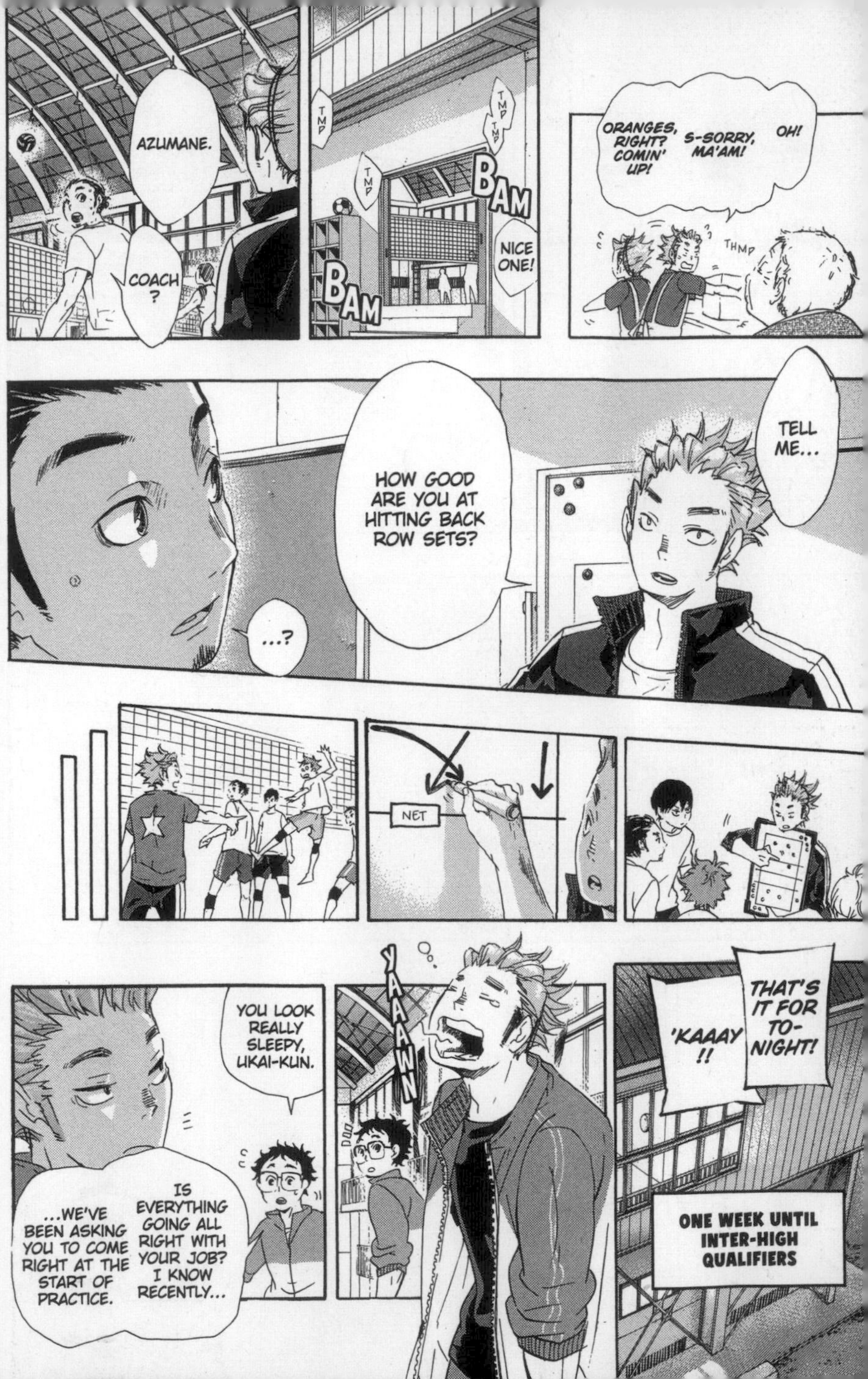
OH!
S-SORRY, MA'AM!
ORANGES, RIGHT? COMIN' UP!
THMP
TMP TMP
TMP
TMP
BAM
NICE ONE!
BAM
AZUMANE.
COACH?
TELL ME...
HOW GOOD ARE YOU AT HITTING BACK ROW SETS?
...?
NET
THAT'S IT FOR TO-NIGHT!
'KAAAY!!
ONE WEEK UNTIL INTER-HIGH QUALIFIERS
YAAAAWN
YOU LOOK REALLY SLEEPY, UKAI-KUN.
IS EVERYTHING GOING ALL RIGHT WITH YOUR JOB? I KNOW RECENTLY...
...WE'VE BEEN ASKING YOU TO COME RIGHT AT THE START OF PRACTICE.

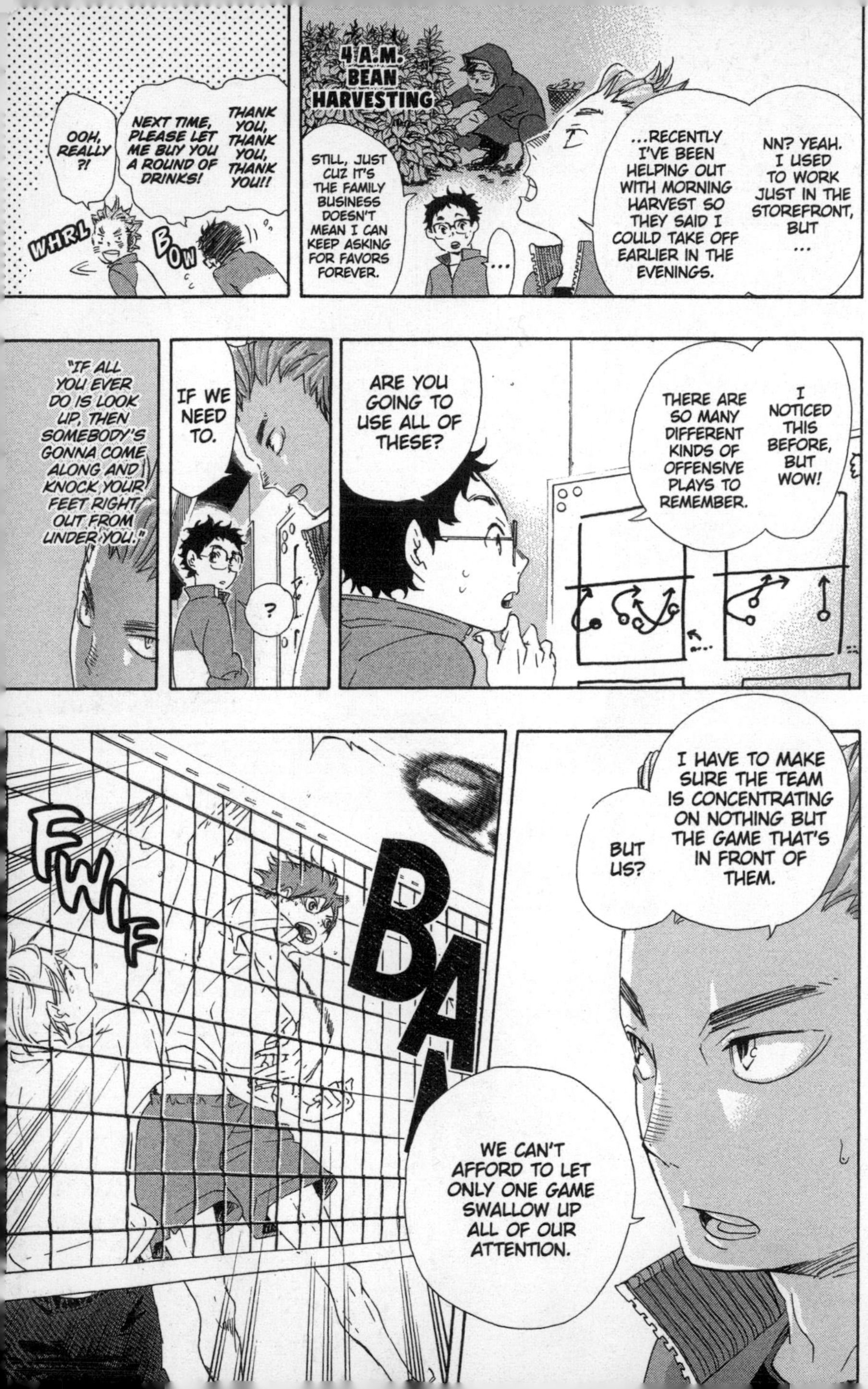

NN? YEAH. I USED TO WORK JUST IN THE STOREFRONT, BUT ...
...RECENTLY I'VE BEEN HELPING OUT WITH MORNING HARVEST SO THEY SAID I COULD TAKE OFF EARLIER IN THE EVENINGS.
4 A.M. BEAN HARVESTING
STILL, JUST CUZ IT'S THE FAMILY BUSINESS DOESN'T MEAN I CAN KEEP ASKING FOR FAVORS FOREVER.
...
THANK YOU, THANK YOU, THANK YOU!!
NEXT TIME, PLEASE LET ME BUY YOU A ROUND OF DRINKS!
BOW
OOH, REALLY ?!
WHRL
I NOTICED THIS BEFORE, BUT WOW!
THERE ARE SO MANY DIFFERENT KINDS OF OFFENSIVE PLAYS TO REMEMBER.
ARE YOU GOING TO USE ALL OF THESE?
IF WE NEED TO.
?
"IF ALL YOU EVER DO IS LOOK UP, THEN SOMEBODY'S GONNA COME ALONG AND KNOCK YOUR FEET RIGHT OUT FROM UNDER YOU."
I HAVE TO MAKE SURE THE TEAM IS CONCENTRATING ON NOTHING BUT THE GAME THAT'S IN FRONT OF THEM.
BUT US?
WE CAN'T AFFORD TO LET ONLY ONE GAME SWALLOW UP ALL OF OUR ATTENTION.
BA
FWIF

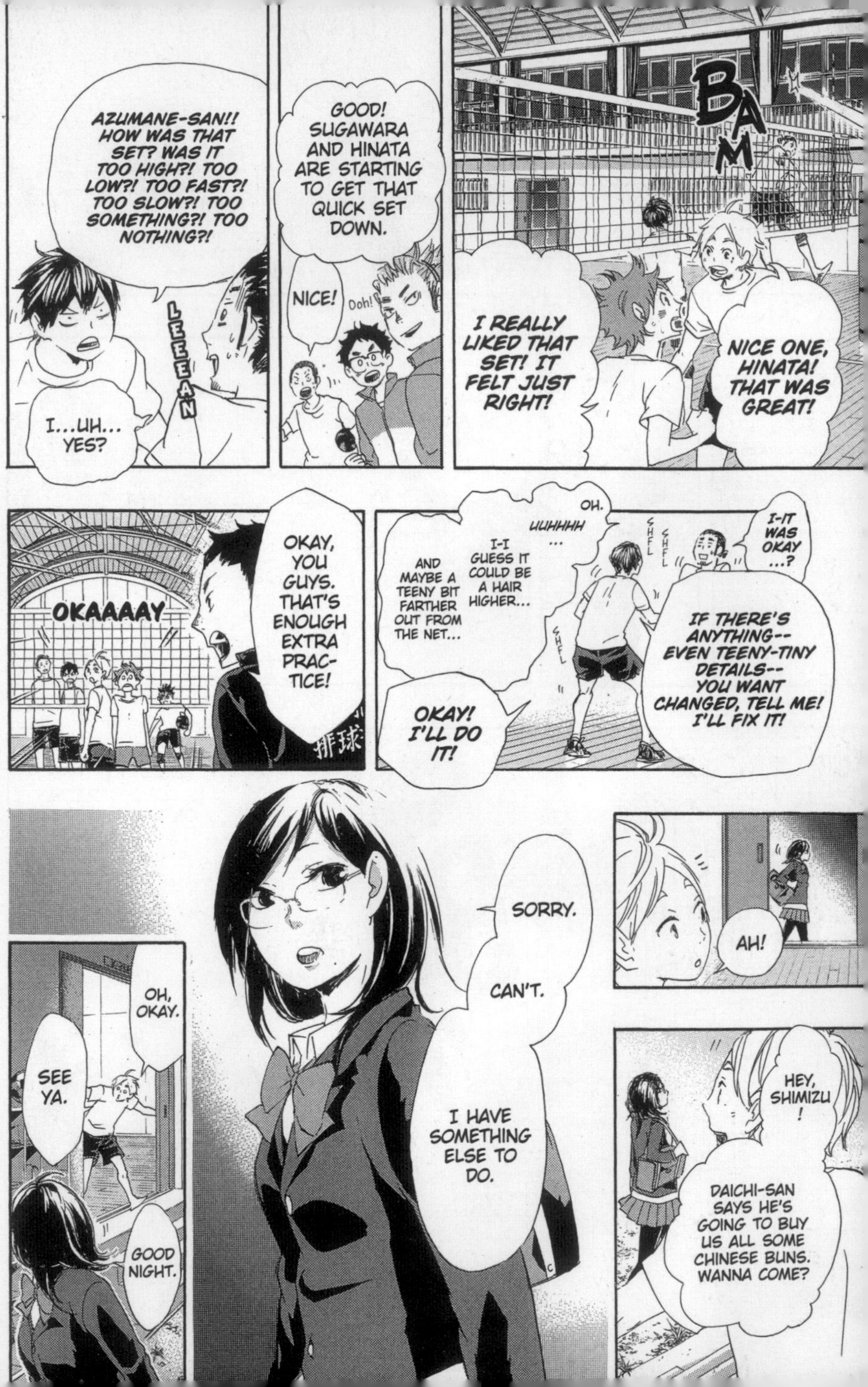
BAM
NICE ONE, HINATA! THAT WAS GREAT!
I REALLY LIKED THAT SET! IT FELT JUST RIGHT!
GOOD! SUGAWARA AND HINATA ARE STARTING TO GET THAT QUICK SET DOWN.
Ooh!
NICE!
AZUMANE-SAN!! HOW WAS THAT SET? WAS IT TOO HIGH?! TOO LOW?! TOO FAST?! TOO SLOW?! TOO SOMETHING?! TOO NOTHING?!
LEEEEAN
I...UH... YES?
I-IT WAS OKAY...?
SHFL SHFL
OH.
UUHHHH...
I-I GUESS IT COULD BE A HAIR HIGHER...
AND MAYBE A TEENY BIT FARTHER OUT FROM THE NET...
SHFL
IF THERE'S ANYTHING-- EVEN TEENY-TINY DETAILS-- YOU WANT CHANGED, TELL ME! I'LL FIX IT!
OKAY! I'LL DO IT!
OKAY, YOU GUYS. THAT'S ENOUGH EXTRA PRAC-TICE!
OKAAAAY
排球
AH!
HEY, SHIMIZU!
DAICHI-SAN SAYS HE'S GOING TO BUY US ALL SOME CHINESE BUNS. WANNA COME?
SORRY.
CAN'T.
I HAVE SOMETHING ELSE TO DO.
OH, OKAY.
SEE YA.
GOOD NIGHT.

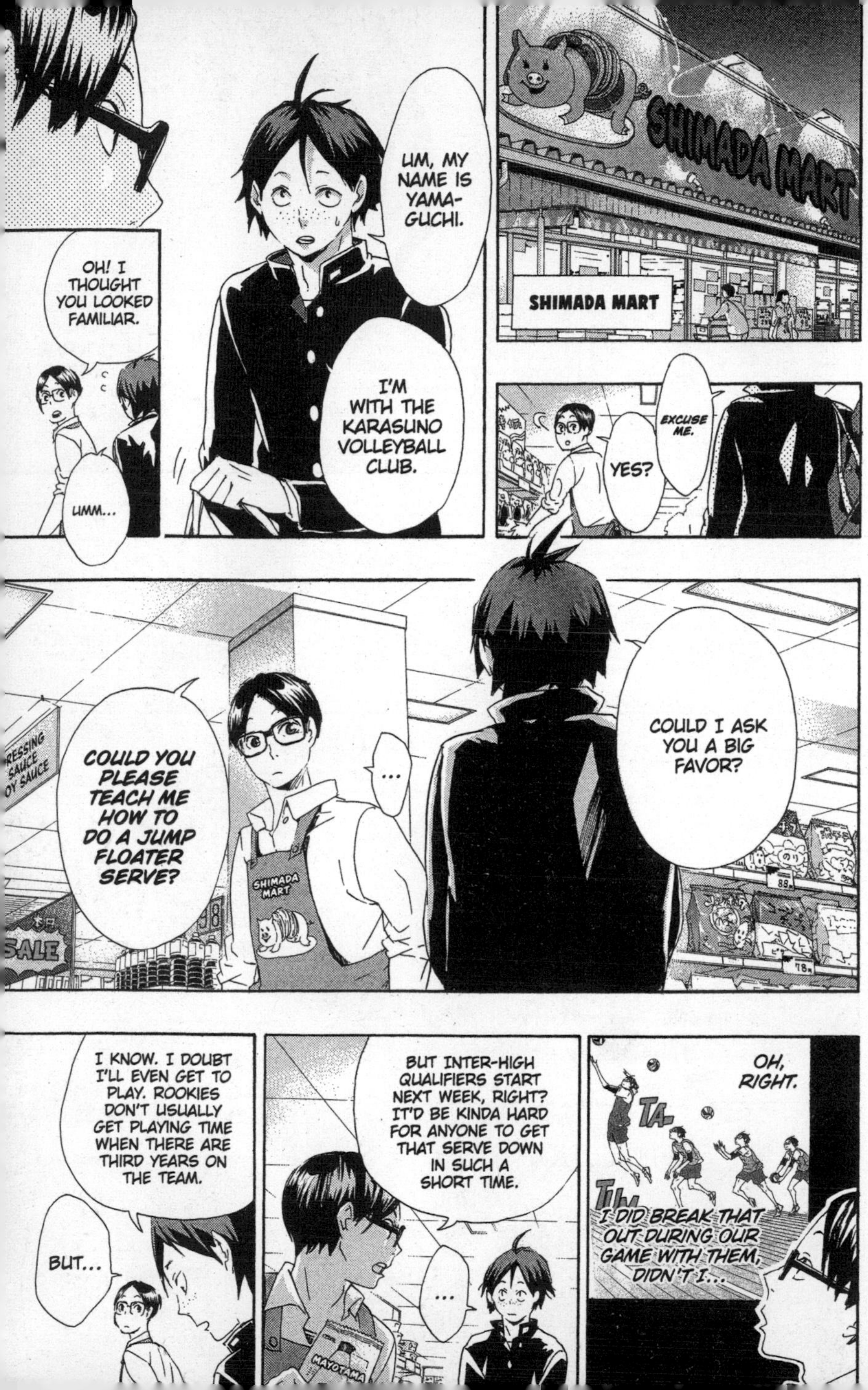
SHIMADA MART
SHIMADA MART
EXCUSE ME.
YES?
UM, MY NAME IS YAMAGUCHI.
I'M WITH THE KARASUNO VOLLEYBALL CLUB.
OH! I THOUGHT YOU LOOKED FAMILIAR.
UMM...
COULD I ASK YOU A BIG FAVOR?
...
COULD YOU PLEASE TEACH ME HOW TO DO A JUMP FLOATER SERVE?
SHIMADA MART
SALE
OH, RIGHT.
TA-
TUM
I DID BREAK THAT OUT DURING OUR GAME WITH THEM, DIDN'T I...
BUT INTER-HIGH QUALIFIERS START NEXT WEEK, RIGHT? IT'D BE KINDA HARD FOR ANYONE TO GET THAT SERVE DOWN IN SUCH A SHORT TIME.
...
I KNOW. I DOUBT I'LL EVEN GET TO PLAY. ROOKIES DON'T USUALLY GET PLAYING TIME WHEN THERE ARE THIRD YEARS ON THE TEAM.
BUT...
MAYOTAMA

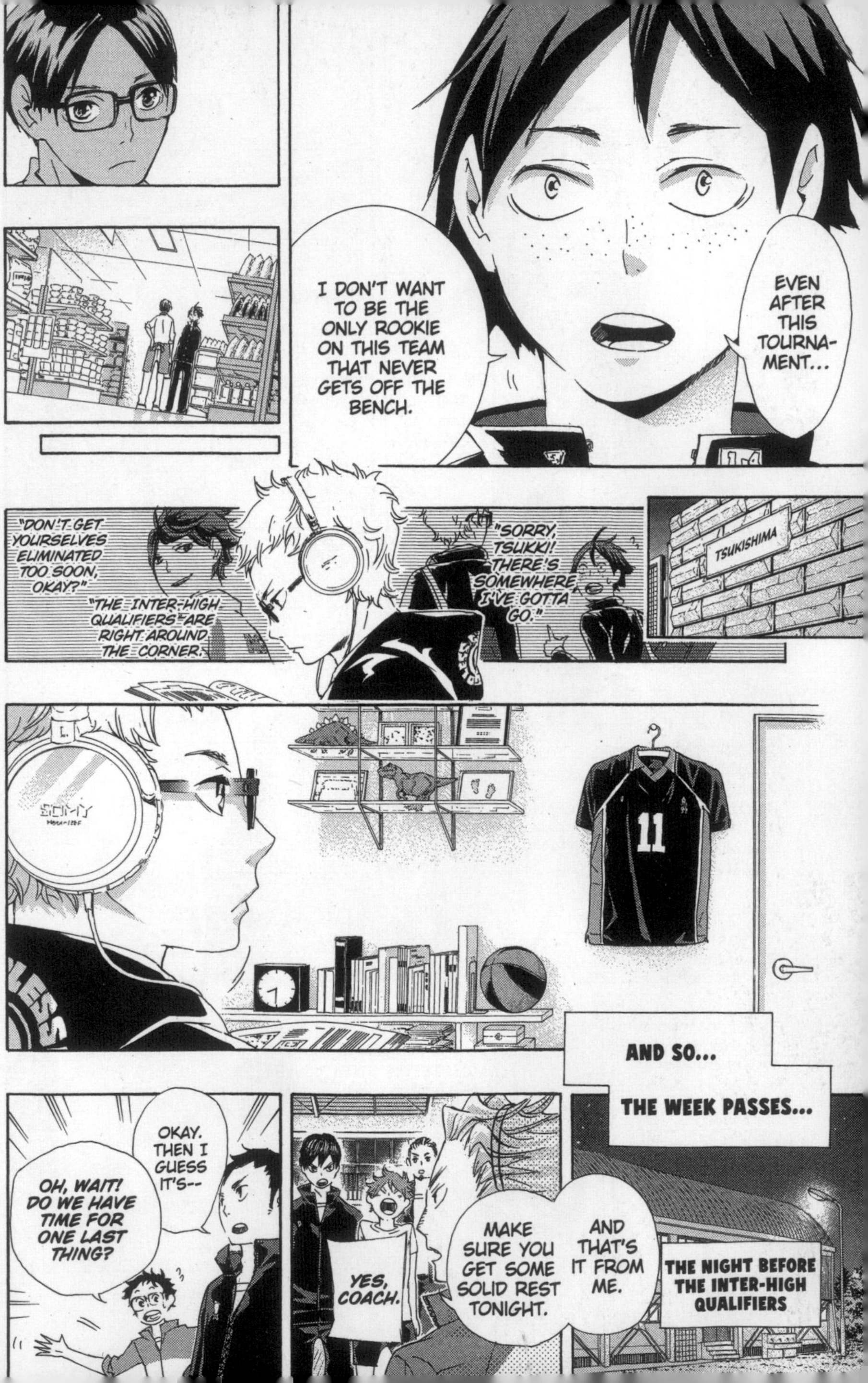
EVEN AFTER THIS TOURNAMENT...
I DON'T WANT TO BE THE ONLY ROOKIE ON THIS TEAM THAT NEVER GETS OFF THE BENCH.
TSUKISHIMA
"SORRY, TSUKKI! THERE'S SOMEWHERE I'VE GOTTA GO."
"DON'T GET YOURSELVES ELIMINATED TOO SOON, OKAY?"
"THE INTER-HIGH QUALIFIERS ARE RIGHT AROUND THE CORNER."
SONY
11
AND SO...
THE WEEK PASSES...
THE NIGHT BEFORE THE INTER-HIGH QUALIFIERS
AND THAT'S IT FROM ME.
MAKE SURE YOU GET SOME SOLID REST TONIGHT.
YES, COACH.
OKAY. THEN I GUESS IT'S--
OH, WAIT! DO WE HAVE TIME FOR ONE LAST THING?

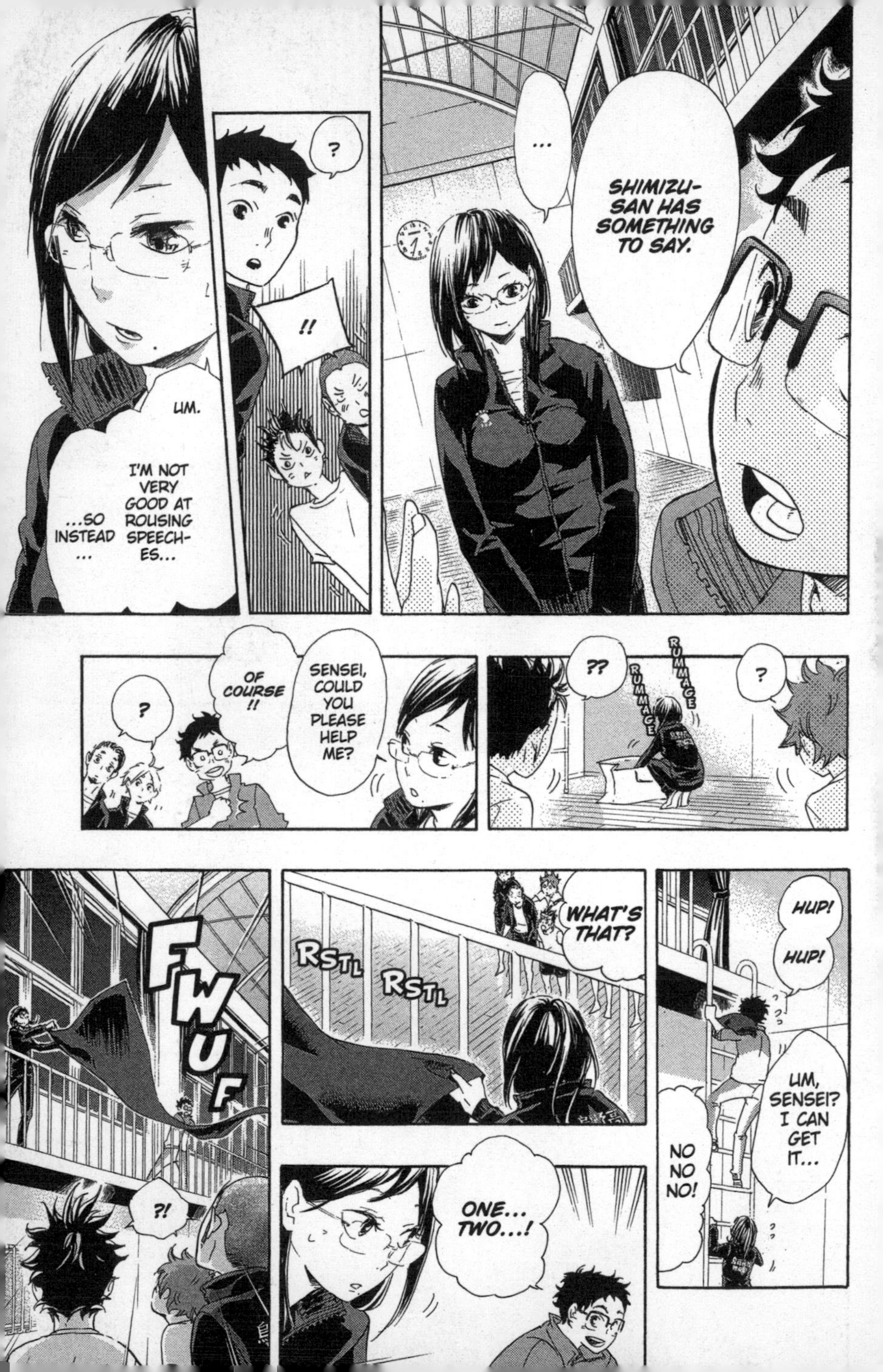
SHIMIZU-SAN HAS SOMETHING TO SAY.
...
?
!!
UM.
I'M NOT VERY GOOD AT ROUSING SPEECHES...
...SO INSTEAD...
?
??
RUMMAGE
RUMMAGE
SENSEI, COULD YOU PLEASE HELP ME?
OF COURSE!!
?
HUP!
HUP!
UM, SENSEI? I CAN GET IT...
NO NO NO!
WHAT'S THAT?
RSTL
RSTL
ONE... TWO...!
FWUF
?!

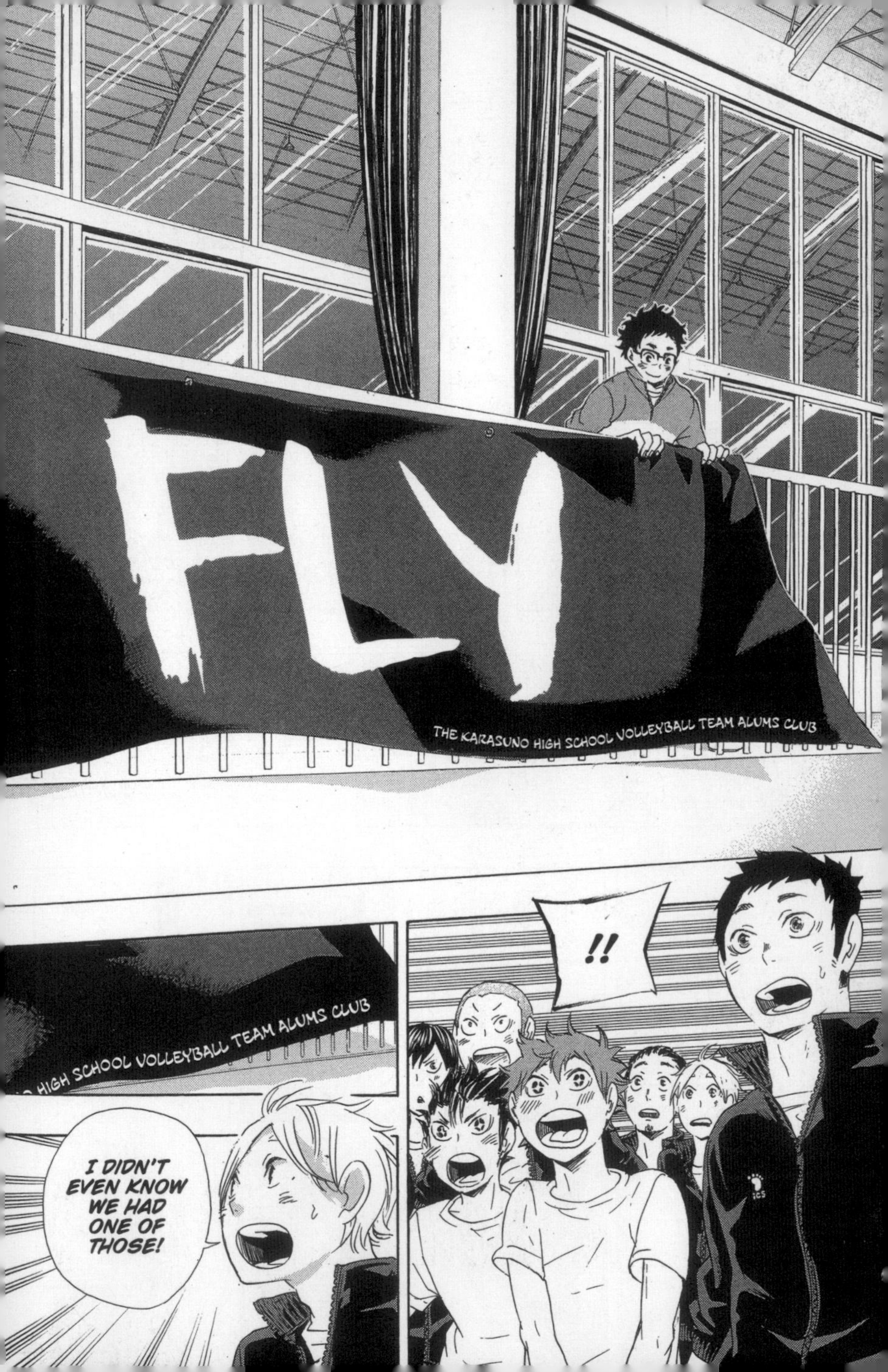
FLY
THE KARASUNO HIGH SCHOOL VOLLEYBALL TEAM ALUMS CLUB
!!
HIGH SCHOOL VOLLEYBALL TEAM ALUMS CLUB
I DIDN'T EVEN KNOW WE HAD ONE OF THOSE!

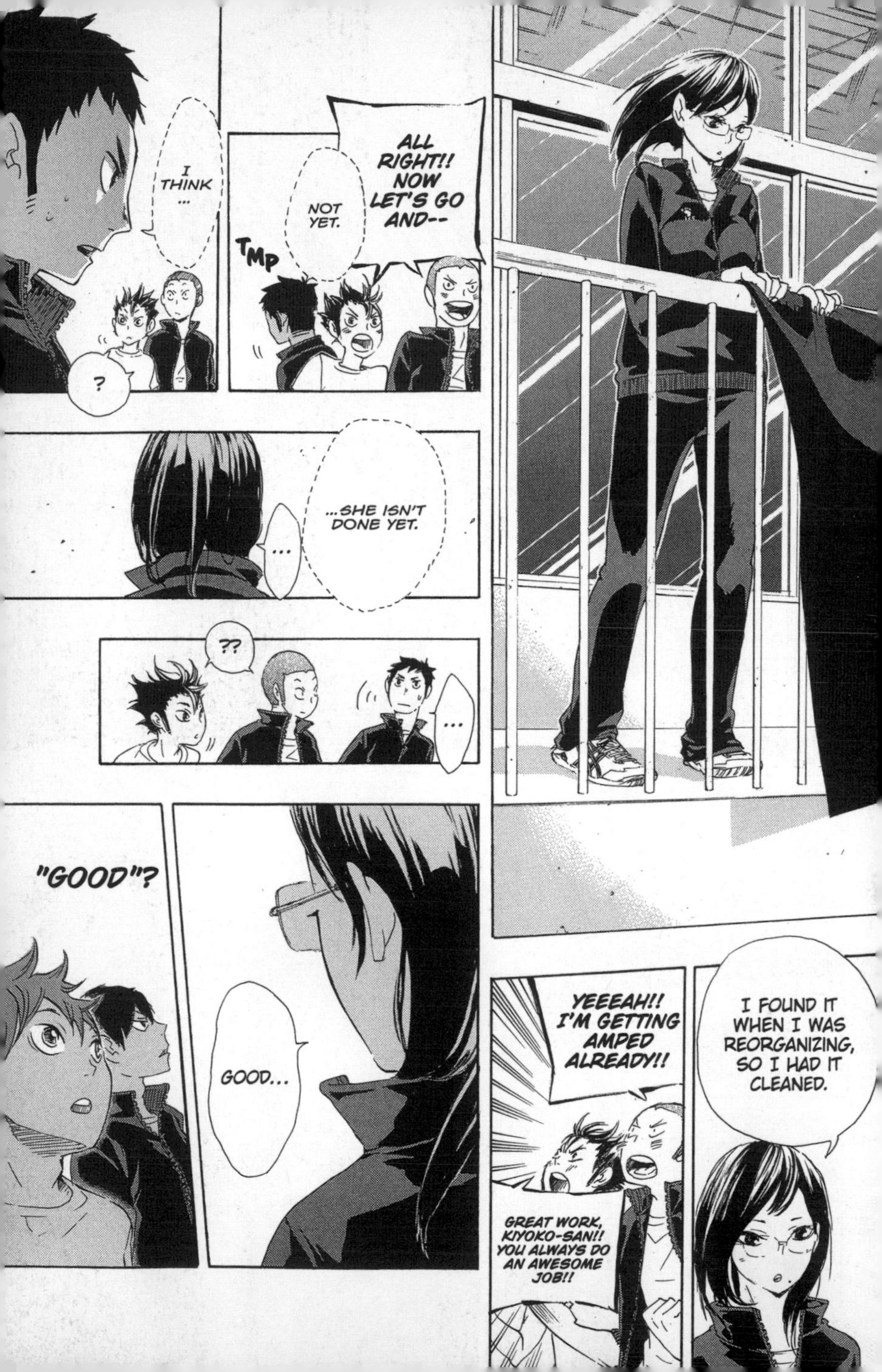
ALL RIGHT!! NOW LET'S GO AND--
TMP
NOT YET.
I THINK ...
?
...SHE ISN'T DONE YET.
...
??
...
GOOD...
"GOOD"?
I FOUND IT WHEN I WAS REORGANIZING, SO I HAD IT CLEANED.
YEEEAH!! I'M GETTING AMPED ALREADY!!
GREAT WORK, KIYOKO-SAN!! YOU ALWAYS DO AN AWESOME JOB!!

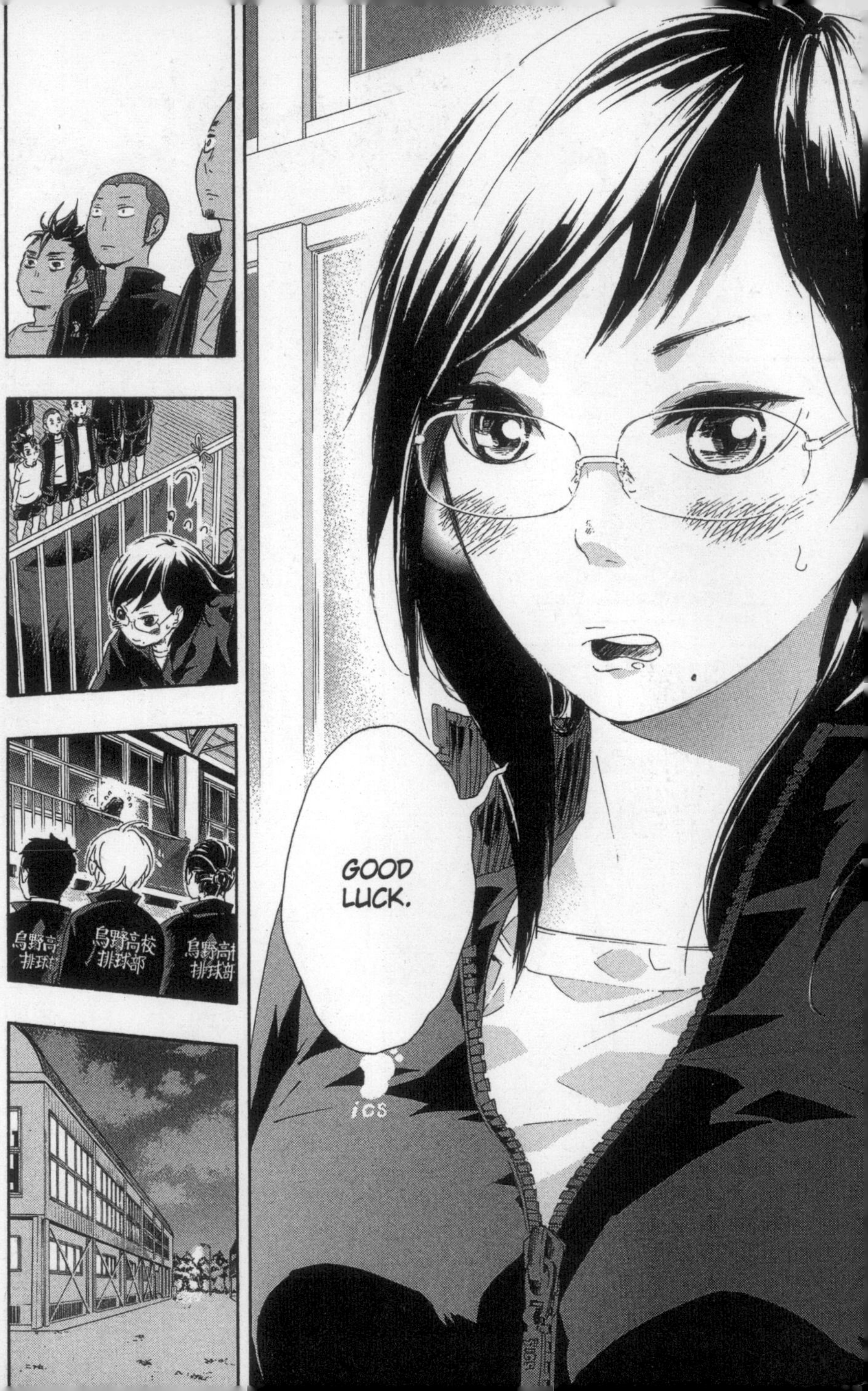
GOOD LUCK.
ics
烏野高校
排球部

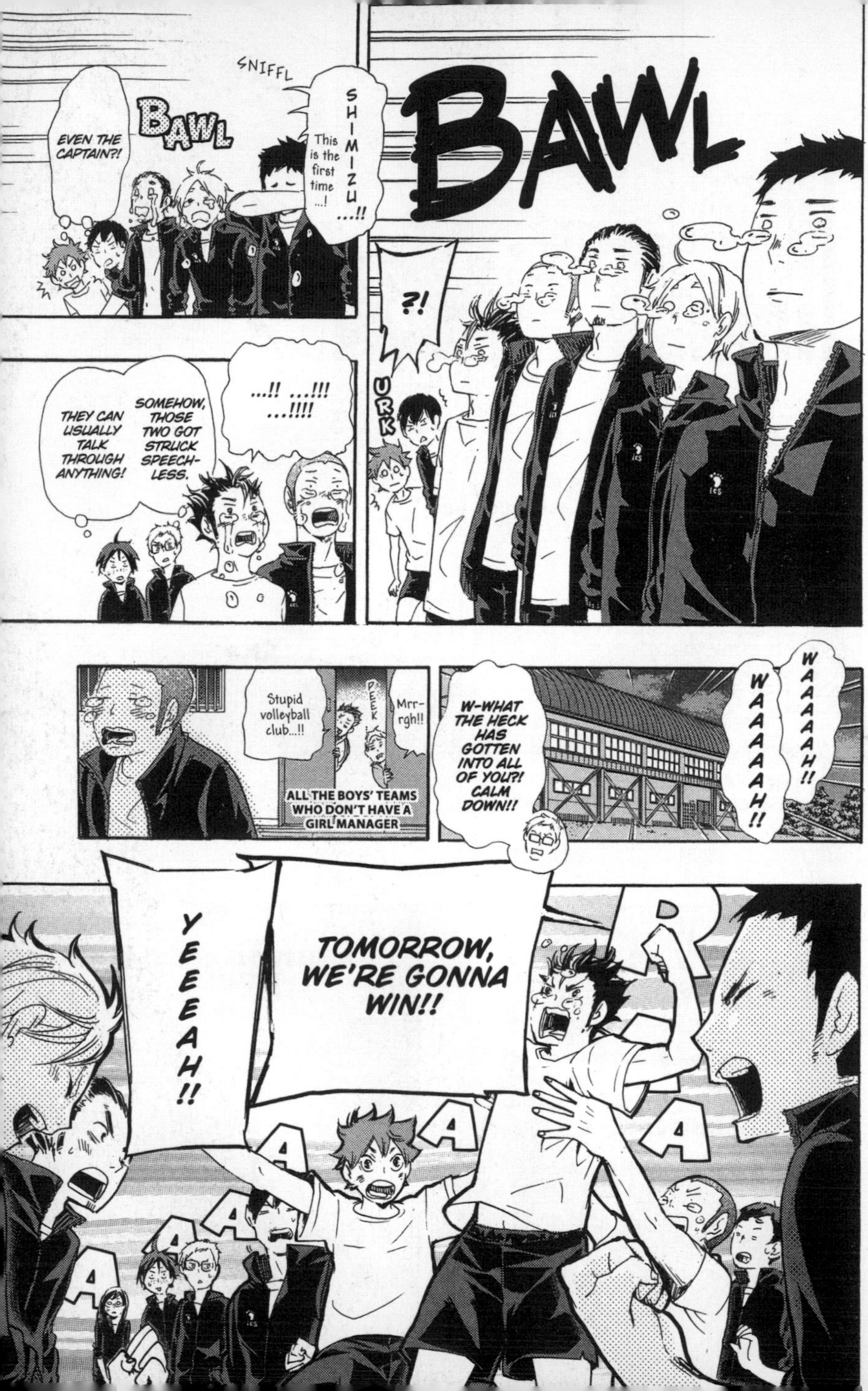
BAWL
?!
URK
SNIFFL
SHIMIZU...!!
This is the first time...!
BAWL
EVEN THE CAPTAIN?!
...!! ...!!! ...!!!!
SOMEHOW, THOSE TWO GOT STRUCK SPEECHLESS.
THEY CAN USUALLY TALK THROUGH ANYTHING!
WAAAAAH!!
WAAAAAAH!!
W-WHAT THE HECK HAS GOTTEN INTO ALL OF YOU?! CALM DOWN!!
Mrr-rgh!!
PEEK
Stupid volleyball club...!!
ALL THE BOYS' TEAMS WHO DON'T HAVE A GIRL MANAGER
RAAA
TOMORROW, WE'RE GONNA WIN!!
YEEEAH!!
AAAA

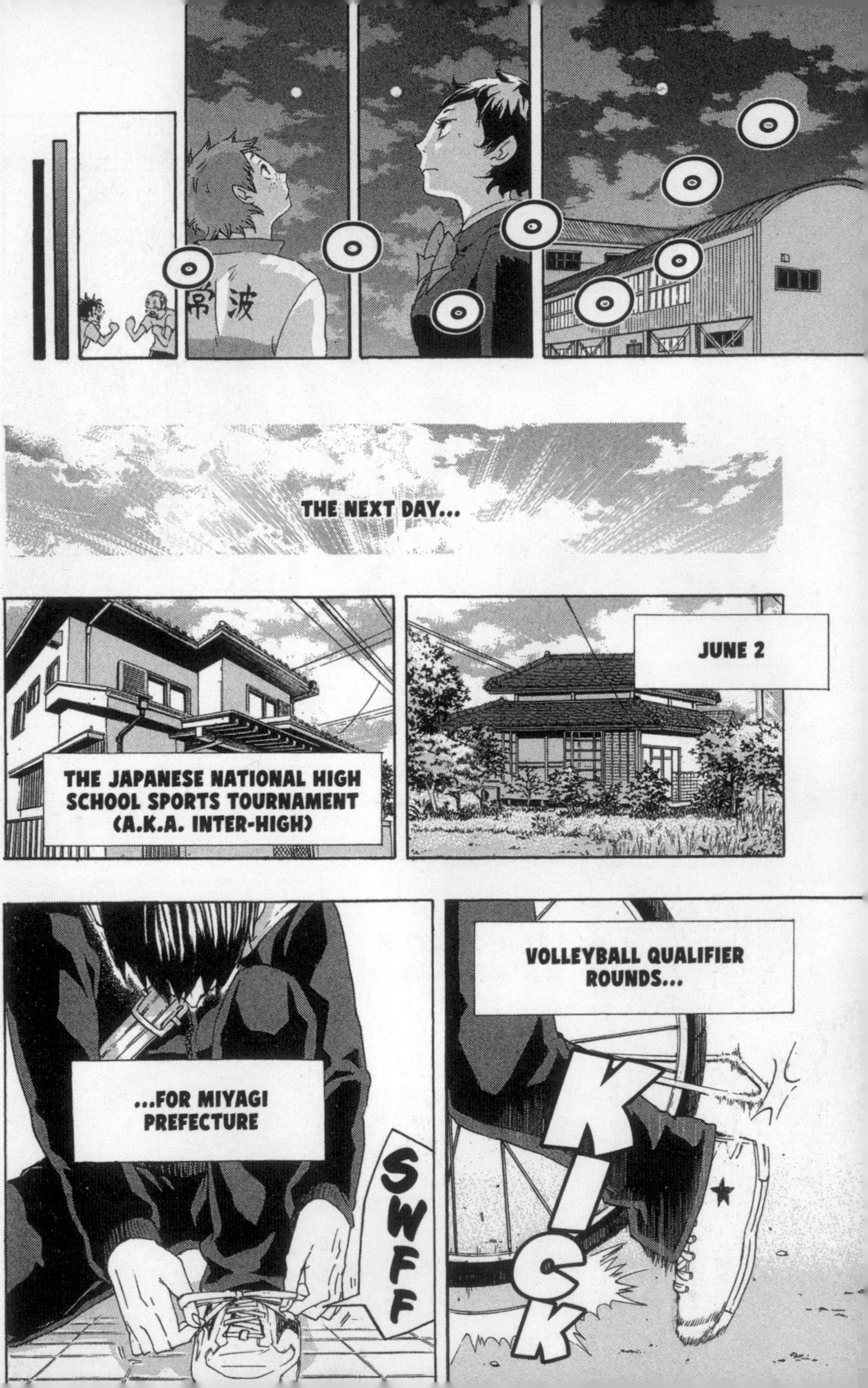
THE NEXT DAY...
JUNE 2
THE JAPANESE NATIONAL HIGH SCHOOL SPORTS TOURNAMENT (A.K.A. INTER-HIGH)
VOLLEYBALL QUALIFIER ROUNDS...
KICK
...FOR MIYAGI PREFECTURE
SWFF

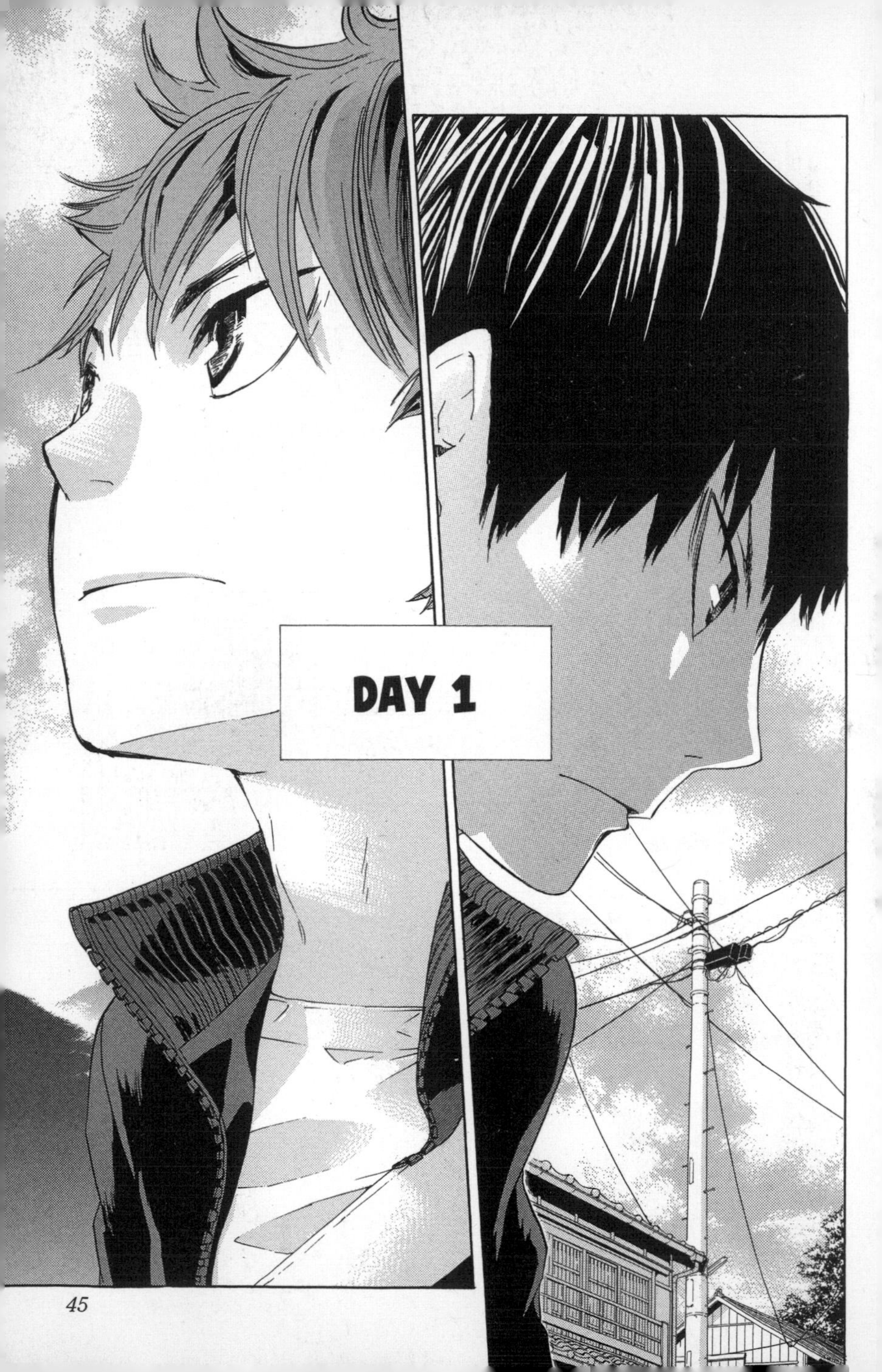
DAY 1

YUI MICHIMIYA

**KARASUNO HIGH SCHOOL
CLASS 3-1
GIRLS VOLLEYBALL CLUB
CAPTAIN**

**POSITION:
WING SPIKER**

HEIGHT: 5'3"

**WEIGHT: 112 LBS.
(AS OF APRIL, 3RD YEAR
OF HIGH SCHOOL)**

BIRTHDAY: AUGUST 1

**FAVORITE FOOD:
NATTO AND RICE**

**CURRENT WORRY:
PEOPLE SAY SHE HAS
VERY CHUNKY THIGHS.**

**ABILITY PARAMETERS
(5-POINT SCALE)**

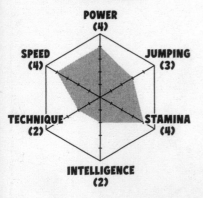

POWER
(4)

JUMPING
(3)

SPEED
(4)

STAMINA
(4)

TECHNIQUE
(2)

INTELLIGENCE
(2)

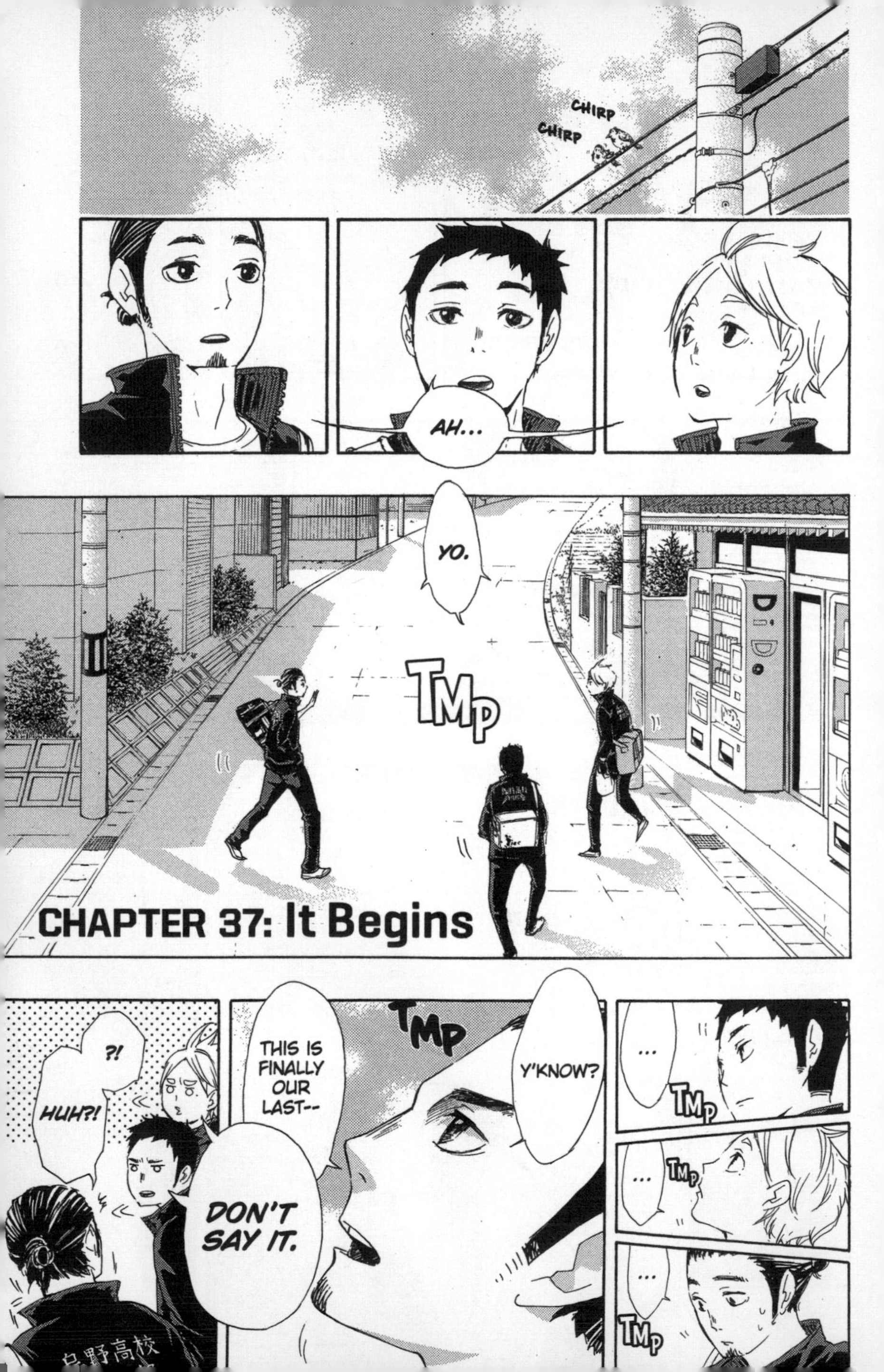
CHIRP
CHIRP
AH...
YO.
TMP
CHAPTER 37: It Begins
...
TMP
...
TMP
...
TMP
TMP
Y'KNOW?
THIS IS FINALLY OUR LAST--
DON'T SAY IT.
?!
HUH?!
烏野高校

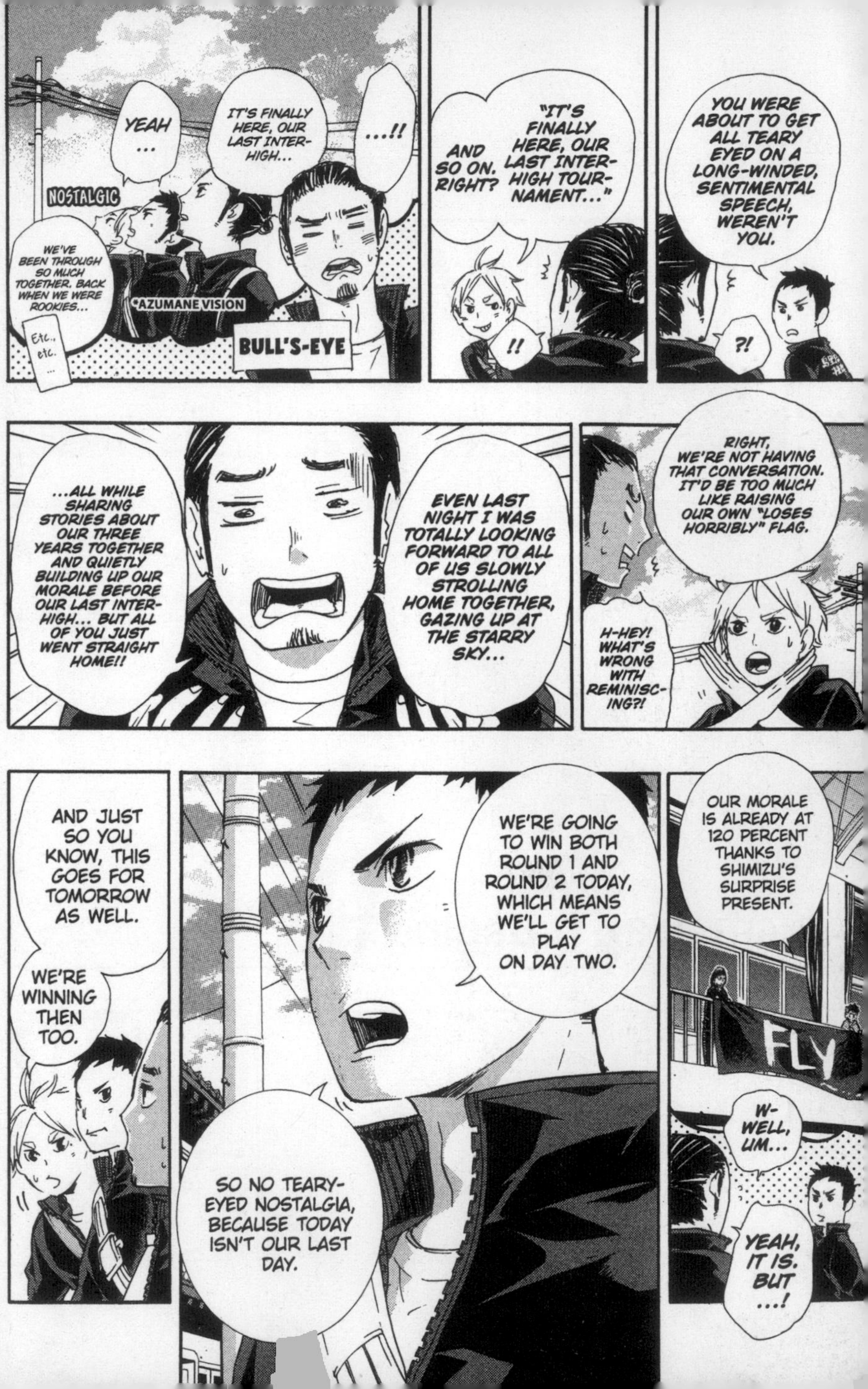
YOU WERE ABOUT TO GET ALL TEARY EYED ON A LONG-WINDED, SENTIMENTAL SPEECH, WEREN'T YOU.
?!
"IT'S FINALLY HERE, OUR LAST INTER-HIGH TOURNAMENT..."
AND SO ON. RIGHT?
!!
...!!
IT'S FINALLY HERE, OUR LAST INTER-HIGH...
YEAH ...
NOSTALGIC
WE'VE BEEN THROUGH SO MUCH TOGETHER. BACK WHEN WE WERE ROOKIES...
*AZUMANE VISION
Etc., etc. ...
BULL'S-EYE
RIGHT, WE'RE NOT HAVING THAT CONVERSATION. IT'D BE TOO MUCH LIKE RAISING OUR OWN "LOSES HORRIBLY" FLAG.
H-HEY! WHAT'S WRONG WITH REMINISCING?!
EVEN LAST NIGHT I WAS TOTALLY LOOKING FORWARD TO ALL OF US SLOWLY STROLLING HOME TOGETHER, GAZING UP AT THE STARRY SKY...
...ALL WHILE SHARING STORIES ABOUT OUR THREE YEARS TOGETHER AND QUIETLY BUILDING UP OUR MORALE BEFORE OUR LAST INTER-HIGH... BUT ALL OF YOU JUST WENT STRAIGHT HOME!!
OUR MORALE IS ALREADY AT 120 PERCENT THANKS TO SHIMIZU'S SURPRISE PRESENT.
FLY
W-WELL, UM...
YEAH, IT IS. BUT ...!
WE'RE GOING TO WIN BOTH ROUND 1 AND ROUND 2 TODAY, WHICH MEANS WE'LL GET TO PLAY ON DAY TWO.
SO NO TEARY-EYED NOSTALGIA, BECAUSE TODAY ISN'T OUR LAST DAY.
AND JUST SO YOU KNOW, THIS GOES FOR TOMORROW AS WELL.
WE'RE WINNING THEN TOO.

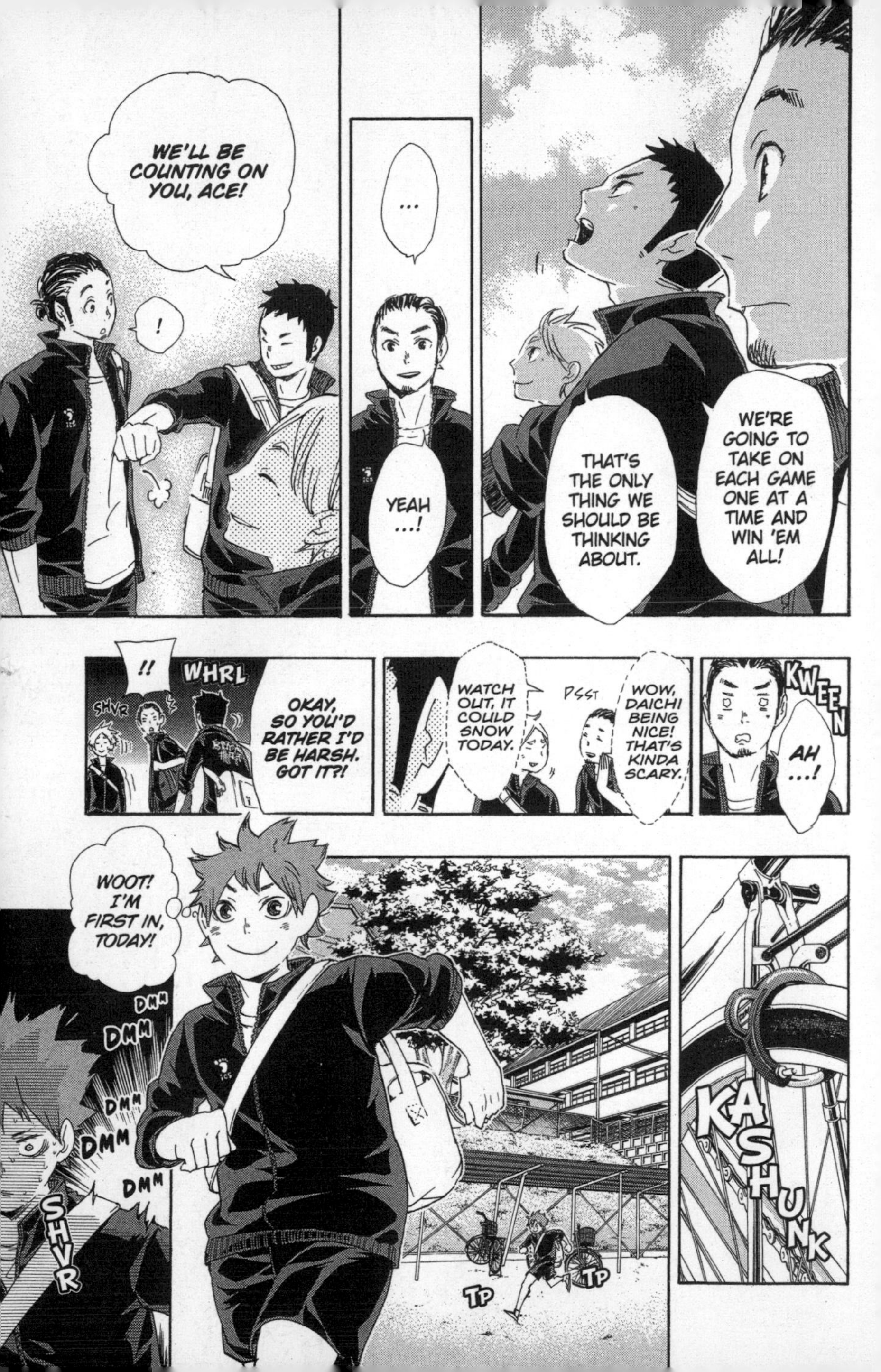
WE'RE GOING TO TAKE ON EACH GAME ONE AT A TIME AND WIN 'EM ALL!
THAT'S THE ONLY THING WE SHOULD BE THINKING ABOUT.
...
YEAH ...!
WE'LL BE COUNTING ON YOU, ACE!
!
KWEEN
AH ...!
WOW, DAICHI BEING NICE! THAT'S KINDA SCARY.
PSST
WATCH OUT, IT COULD SNOW TODAY.
OKAY, SO YOU'D RATHER I'D BE HARSH. GOT IT?!
WHRL
!!
SHVR
KASHUNK
WOOT! I'M FIRST IN, TODAY!
TP
TP
DMM
DMM
DMM
DMM
DMM
SHVR

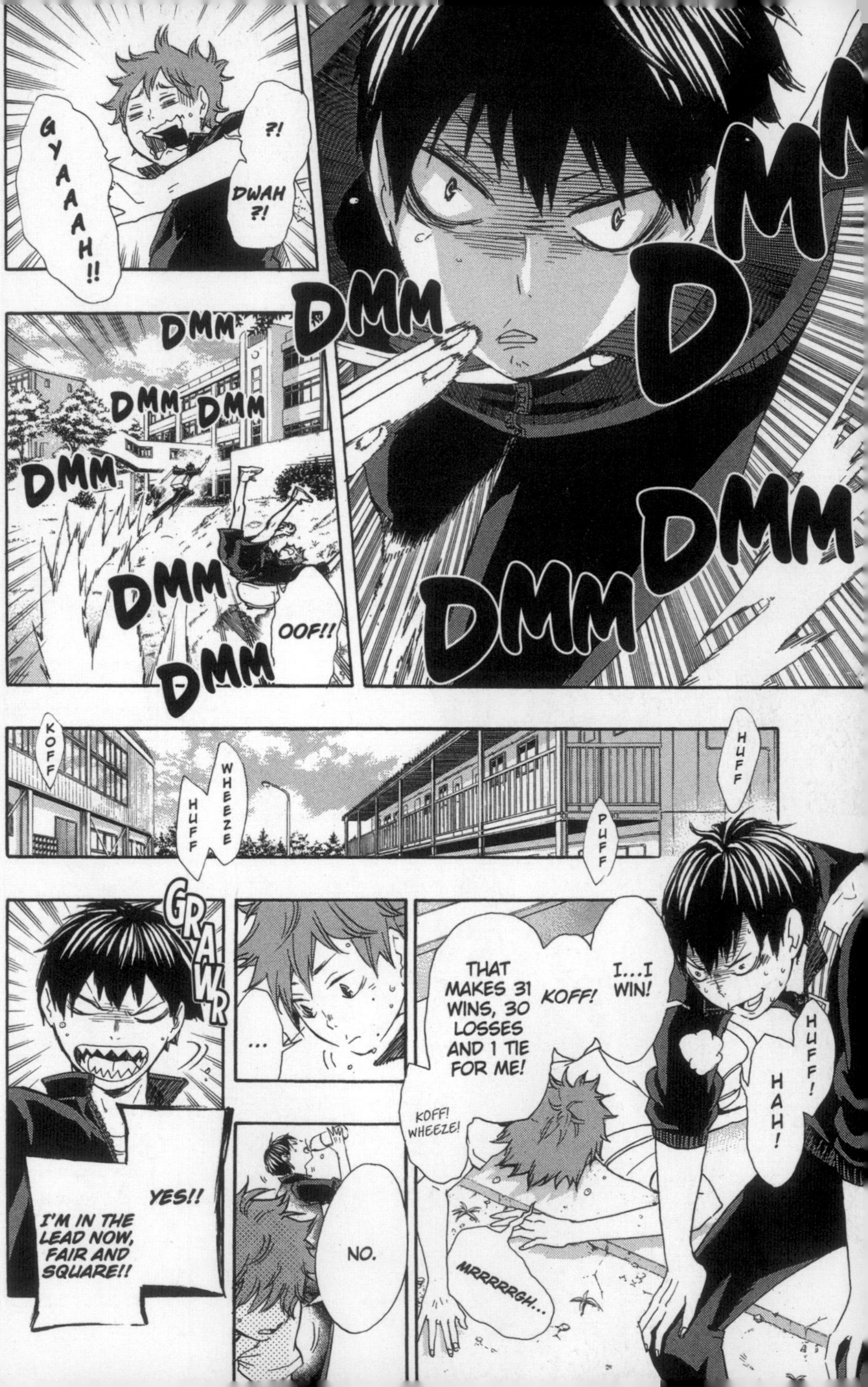
DMM
DMM
DMM
DMM
DMM
?!
DWAH?!
GYAAAH!!
DMM
DMM DMM
DMM
DMM
OOF!!
DMM
HUFF
PUFF
WHEEZE
HUFF
KOFF
I...I WIN!
HUFF!
HAH!
KOFF!
THAT MAKES 31 WINS, 30 LOSSES AND 1 TIE FOR ME!
KOFF! WHEEZE!
MRRRRRGH...
...
NO.
GRAWR
YES!!
I'M IN THE LEAD NOW, FAIR AND SQUARE!!

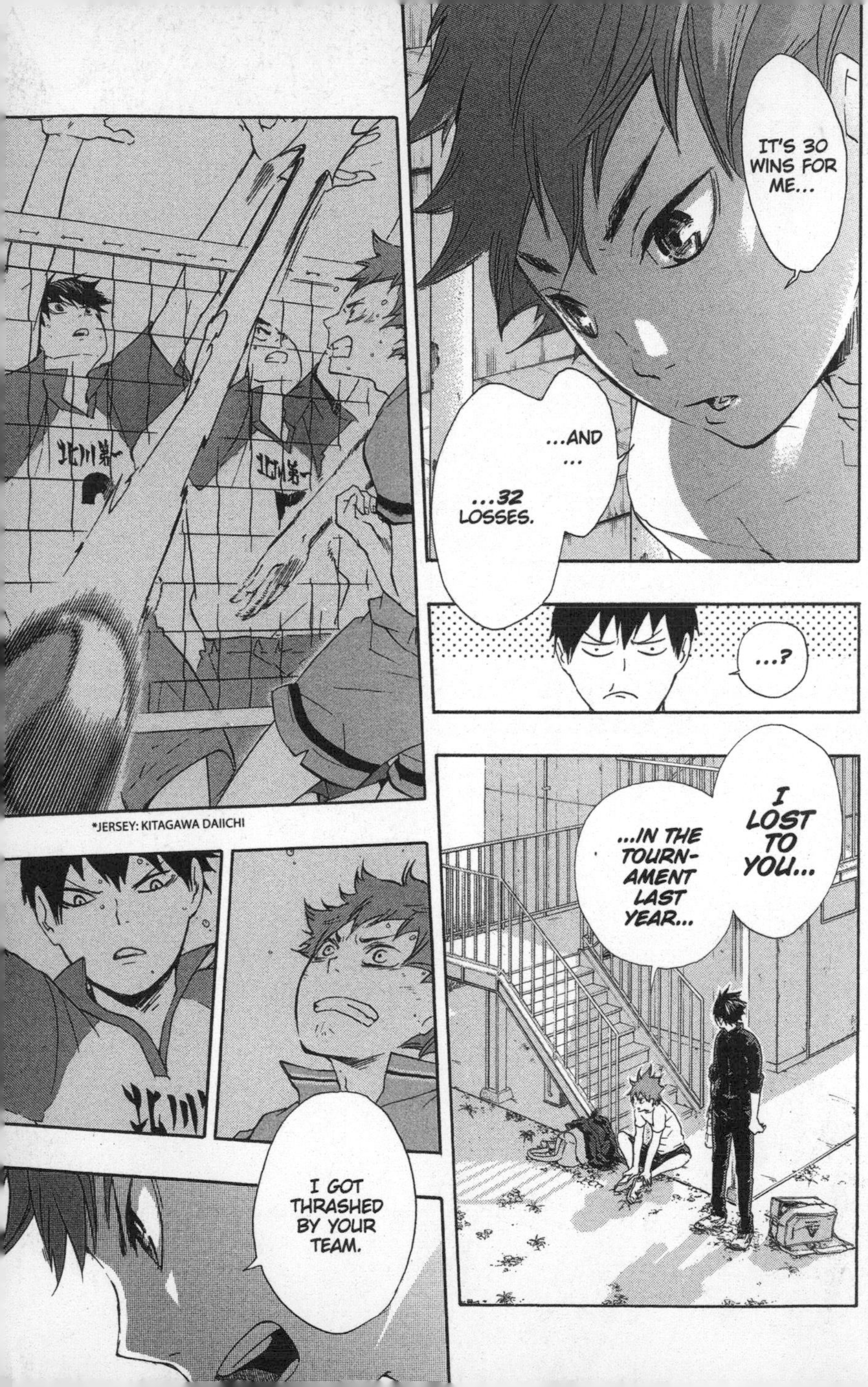
IT'S 30 WINS FOR ME...
...AND ...
...32 LOSSES.
...?
*JERSEY: KITAGAWA DAIICHI
I LOST TO YOU...
...IN THE TOURN-AMENT LAST YEAR...
I GOT THRASHED BY YOUR TEAM.

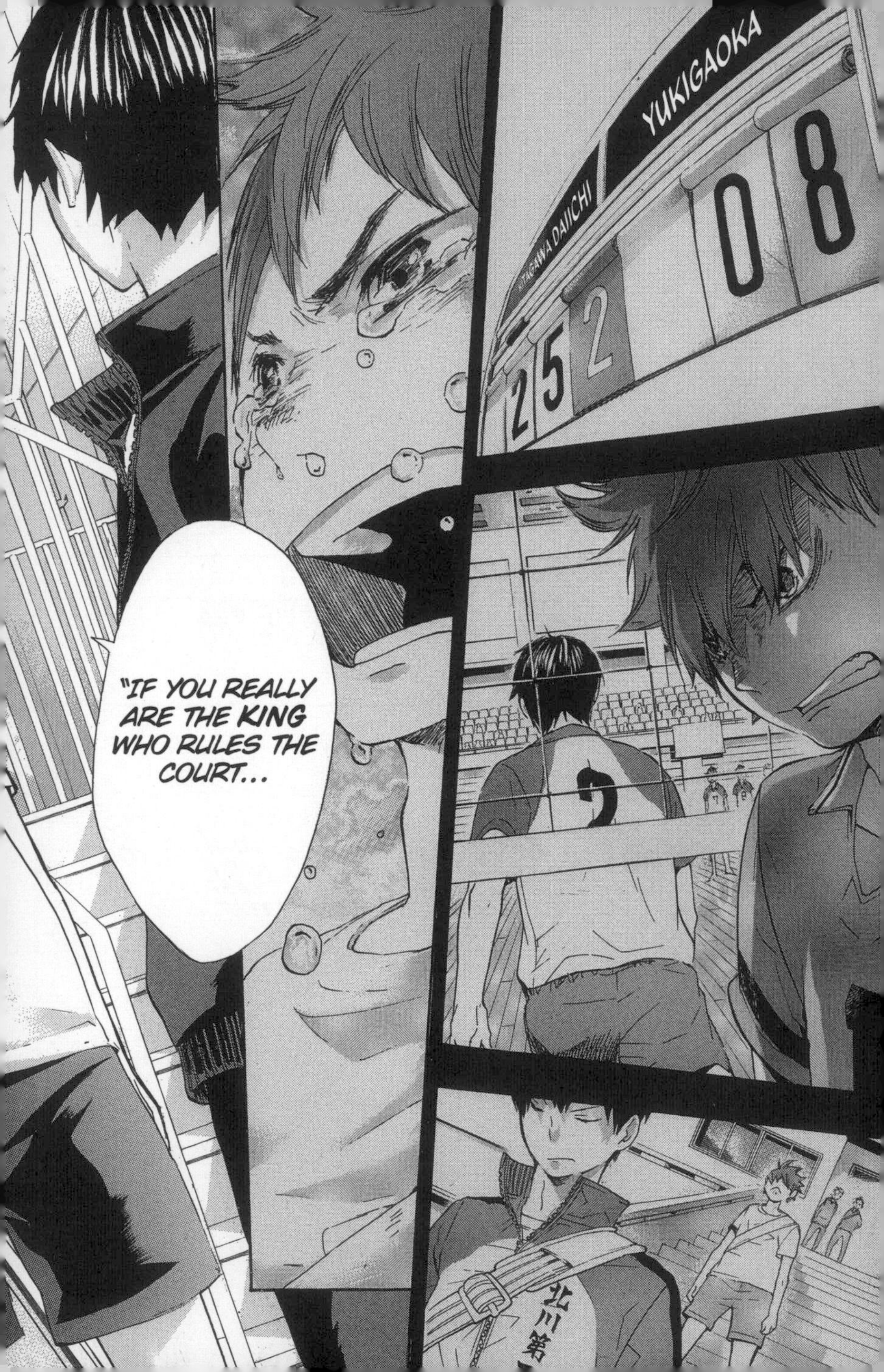
YUKIGAOKA
KITAGAWA DAIICHI
25
2
0
8
"IF YOU REALLY ARE THE KING WHO RULES THE COURT...
北川第

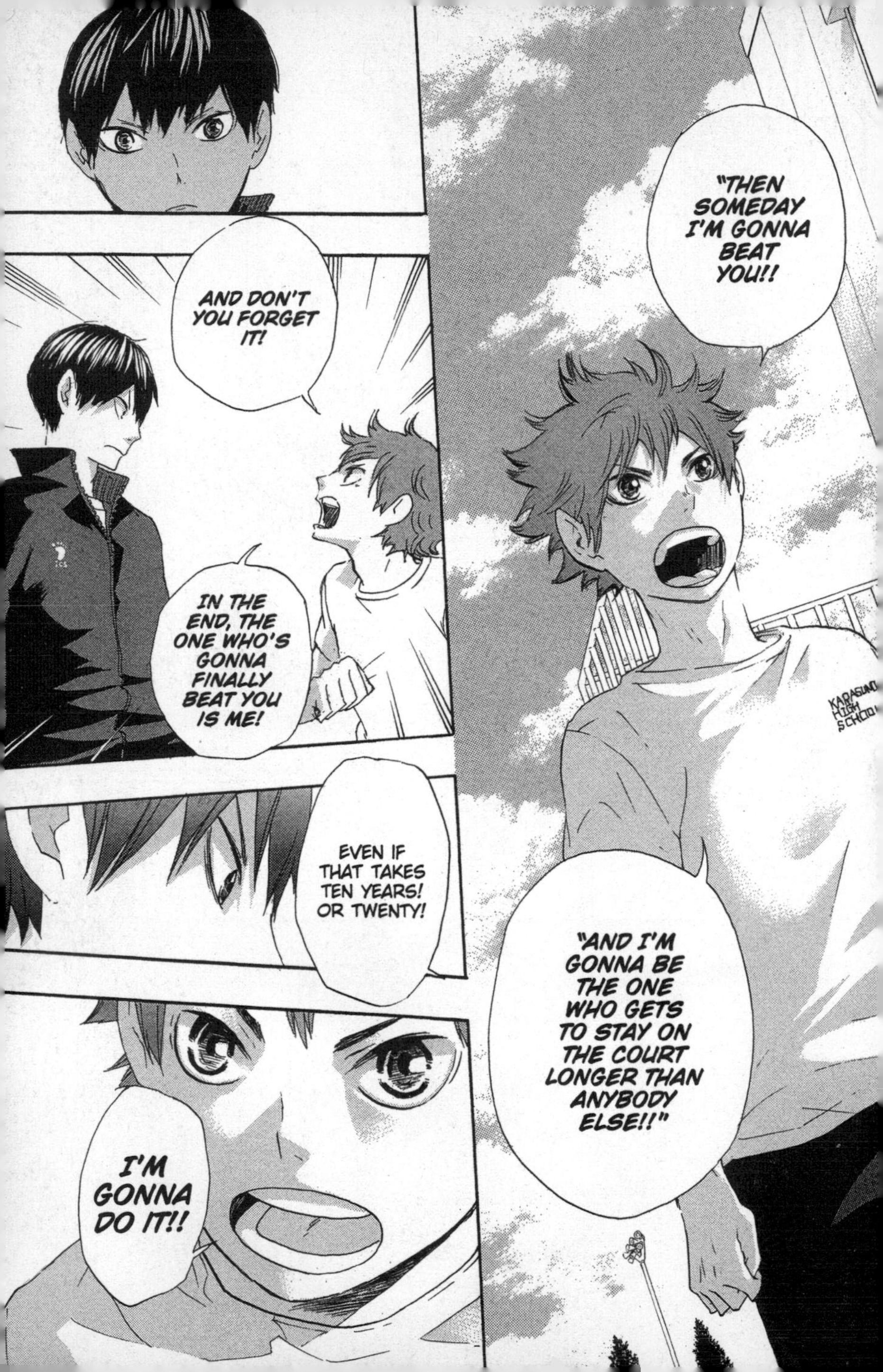
"THEN SOMEDAY I'M GONNA BEAT YOU!!
AND I'M GONNA BE THE ONE WHO GETS TO STAY ON THE COURT LONGER THAN ANYBODY ELSE!!"
AND DON'T YOU FORGET IT!
IN THE END, THE ONE WHO'S GONNA FINALLY BEAT YOU IS ME!
EVEN IF THAT TAKES TEN YEARS! OR TWENTY!
I'M GONNA DO IT!!

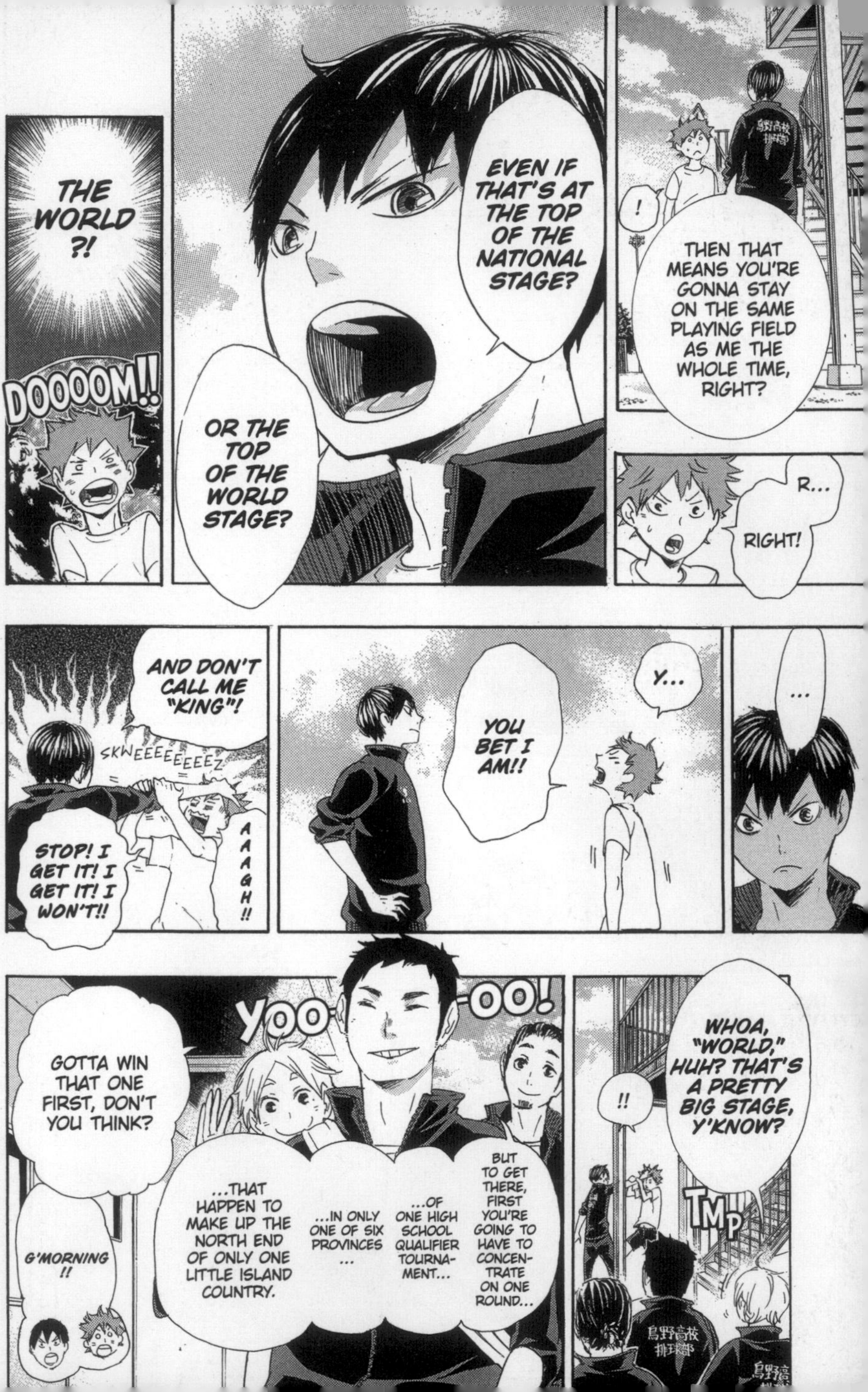

!
THEN THAT MEANS YOU'RE GONNA STAY ON THE SAME PLAYING FIELD AS ME THE WHOLE TIME, RIGHT?
R...
RIGHT!
EVEN IF THAT'S AT THE TOP OF THE NATIONAL STAGE?
OR THE TOP OF THE WORLD STAGE?
THE WORLD ?!
DOOOOM!!
...
Y...
YOU BET I AM!!
AND DON'T CALL ME "KING"!
SKWEEEEEEEEEZ
STOP! I GET IT! I GET IT! I WON'T!!
AAAAGH!!
WHOA, "WORLD," HUH? THAT'S A PRETTY BIG STAGE, Y'KNOW?
!!
TMP
烏野高校 排球部
YOO-OO!
BUT TO GET THERE, FIRST YOU'RE GOING TO HAVE TO CONCENTRATE ON ONE ROUND...
...OF ONE HIGH SCHOOL QUALIFIER TOURNAMENT...
...IN ONLY ONE OF SIX PROVINCES...
...THAT HAPPEN TO MAKE UP THE NORTH END OF ONLY ONE LITTLE ISLAND COUNTRY.
GOTTA WIN THAT ONE FIRST, DON'T YOU THINK?
G'MORNING!!

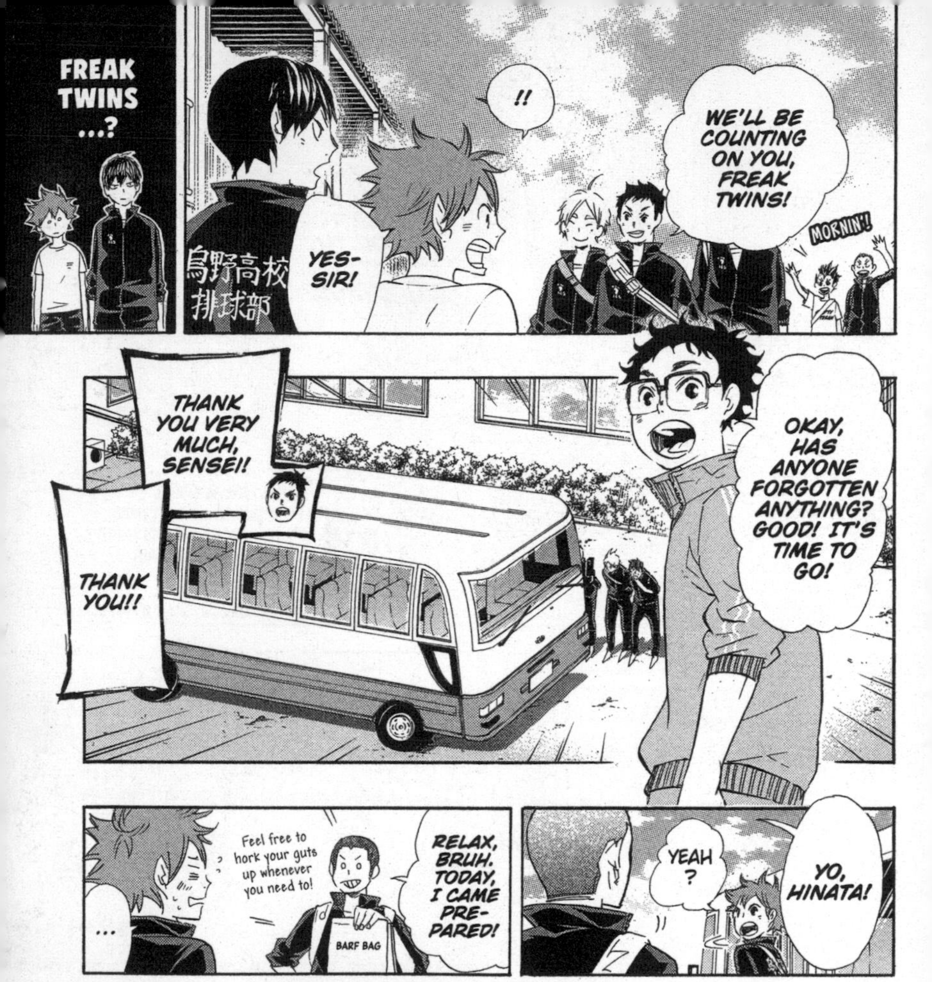
MORNIN'!
WE'LL BE COUNTING ON YOU, FREAK TWINS!
!!
烏野高校排球部
YES-SIR!
FREAK TWINS ...?
OKAY, HAS ANYONE FORGOTTEN ANYTHING? GOOD! IT'S TIME TO GO!
THANK YOU VERY MUCH, SENSEI!!
THANK YOU!!
YO, HINATA!
YEAH?
RELAX, BRUH. TODAY, I CAME PRE-PARED!
Feel free to hork your guts up whenever you need to!
BARF BAG
...

*THANK YOU TO SENDAI CITY GYMNASIUM FOR ALLOWING US TO TAKE PICTURES.

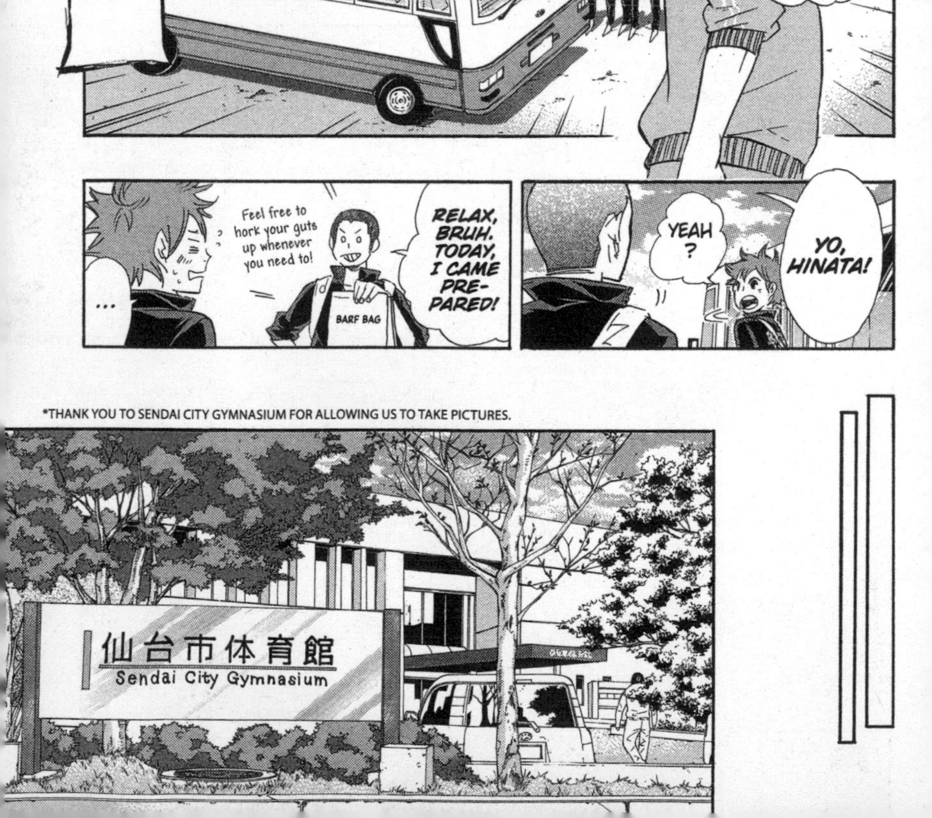
仙台市体育館
Sendai City Gymnasium

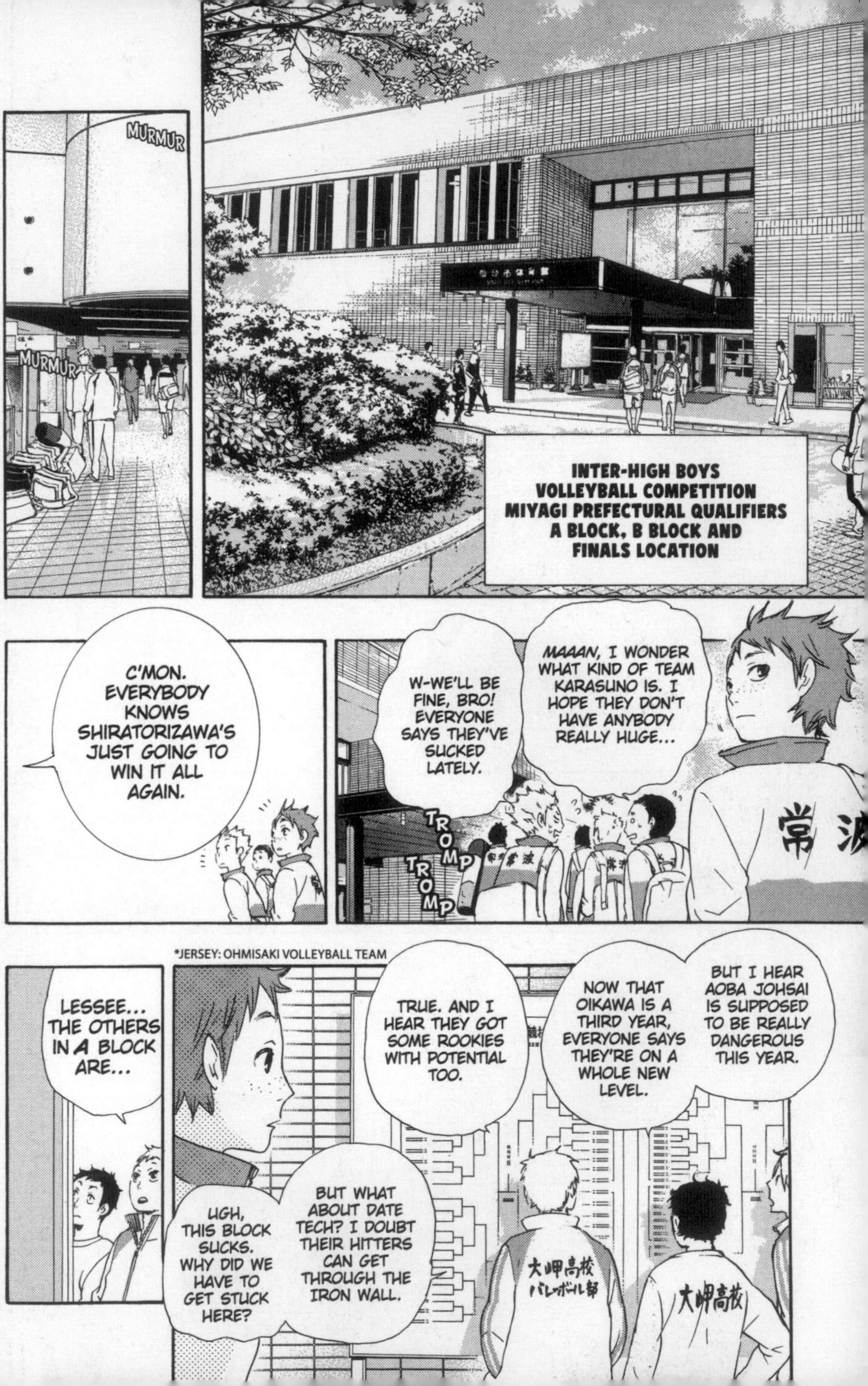
INTER-HIGH BOYS VOLLEYBALL COMPETITION MIYAGI PREFECTURAL QUALIFIERS A BLOCK, B BLOCK AND FINALS LOCATION
MURMUR
MURMUR
MAAAN, I WONDER WHAT KIND OF TEAM KARASUNO IS. I HOPE THEY DON'T HAVE ANYBODY REALLY HUGE...
W-WE'LL BE FINE, BRO! EVERYONE SAYS THEY'VE SUCKED LATELY.
常波
TROMP TROMP TROMP
C'MON. EVERYBODY KNOWS SHIRATORIZAWA'S JUST GOING TO WIN IT ALL AGAIN.
*JERSEY: OHMISAKI VOLLEYBALL TEAM
BUT I HEAR AOBA JOHSAI IS SUPPOSED TO BE REALLY DANGEROUS THIS YEAR.
NOW THAT OIKAWA IS A THIRD YEAR, EVERYONE SAYS THEY'RE ON A WHOLE NEW LEVEL.
TRUE. AND I HEAR THEY GOT SOME ROOKIES WITH POTENTIAL TOO.
大岬高校
大岬高校 バレーボール部
BUT WHAT ABOUT DATE TECH? I DOUBT THEIR HITTERS CAN GET THROUGH THE IRON WALL.
UGH, THIS BLOCK SUCKS. WHY DID WE HAVE TO GET STUCK HERE?
LESSEE... THE OTHERS IN A BLOCK ARE...

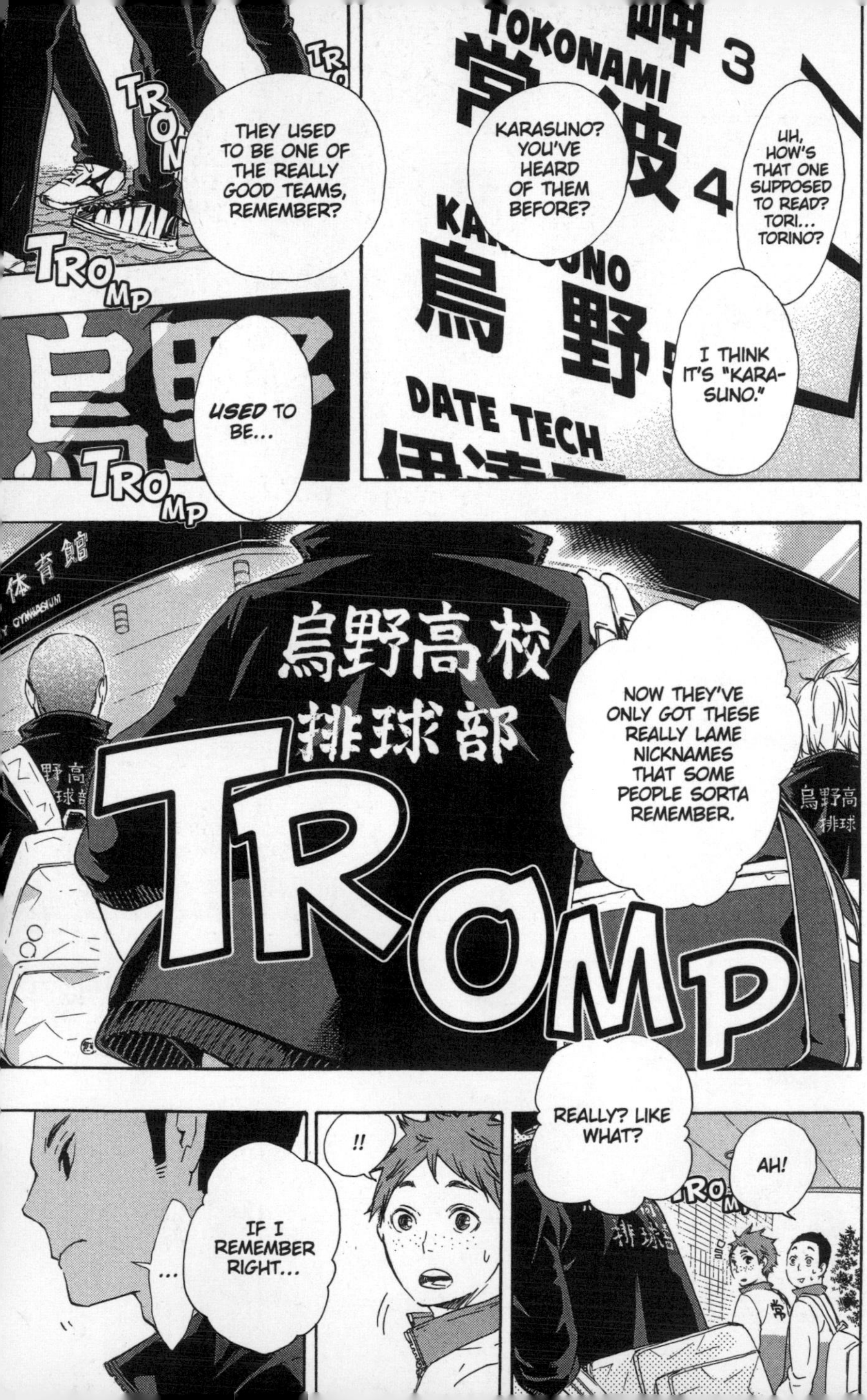

岬 3
TOKONAMI
常波 4
KARASUNO
烏野
DATE TECH
UH, HOW'S THAT ONE SUPPOSED TO READ? TORI... TORINO?
I THINK IT'S "KARASUNO."
KARASUNO? YOU'VE HEARD OF THEM BEFORE?
TROMP
THEY USED TO BE ONE OF THE REALLY GOOD TEAMS, REMEMBER?
TROMP
USED TO BE...
TROMP
体育館
烏野高校
排球部
NOW THEY'VE ONLY GOT THESE REALLY LAME NICKNAMES THAT SOME PEOPLE SORTA REMEMBER.
TROMP
AH!
REALLY? LIKE WHAT?
!!
IF I REMEMBER RIGHT...
...

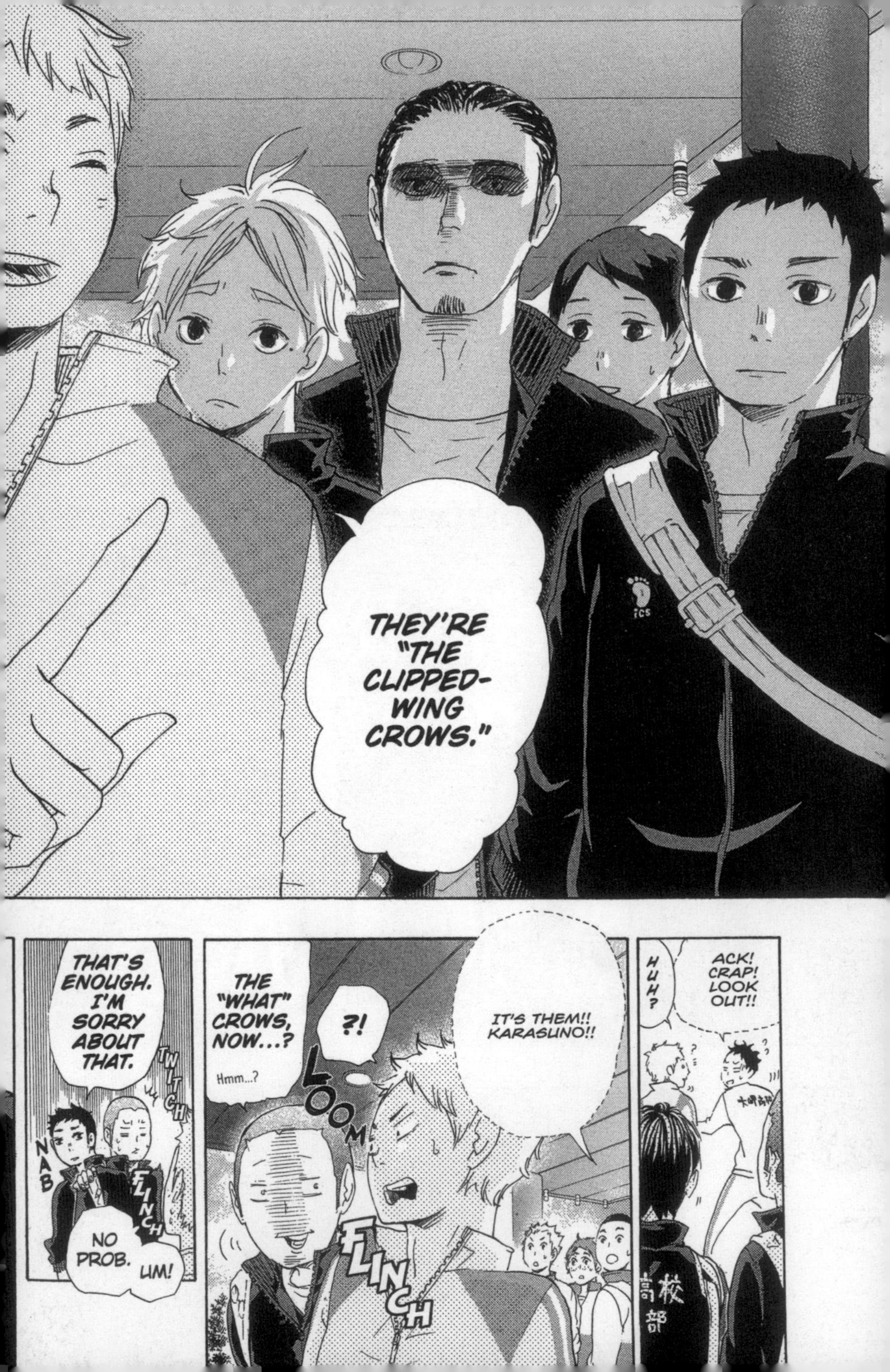

THEY'RE "THE CLIPPED-WING CROWS."
ACK! CRAP! LOOK OUT!!
HUH?
IT'S THEM!! KARASUNO!!
?!
THE "WHAT" CROWS, NOW...?
Hmm...?
LOOM
FLINCH
THAT'S ENOUGH. I'M SORRY ABOUT THAT.
TWITCH
NAB
FLINCH
NO PROB.
UM!

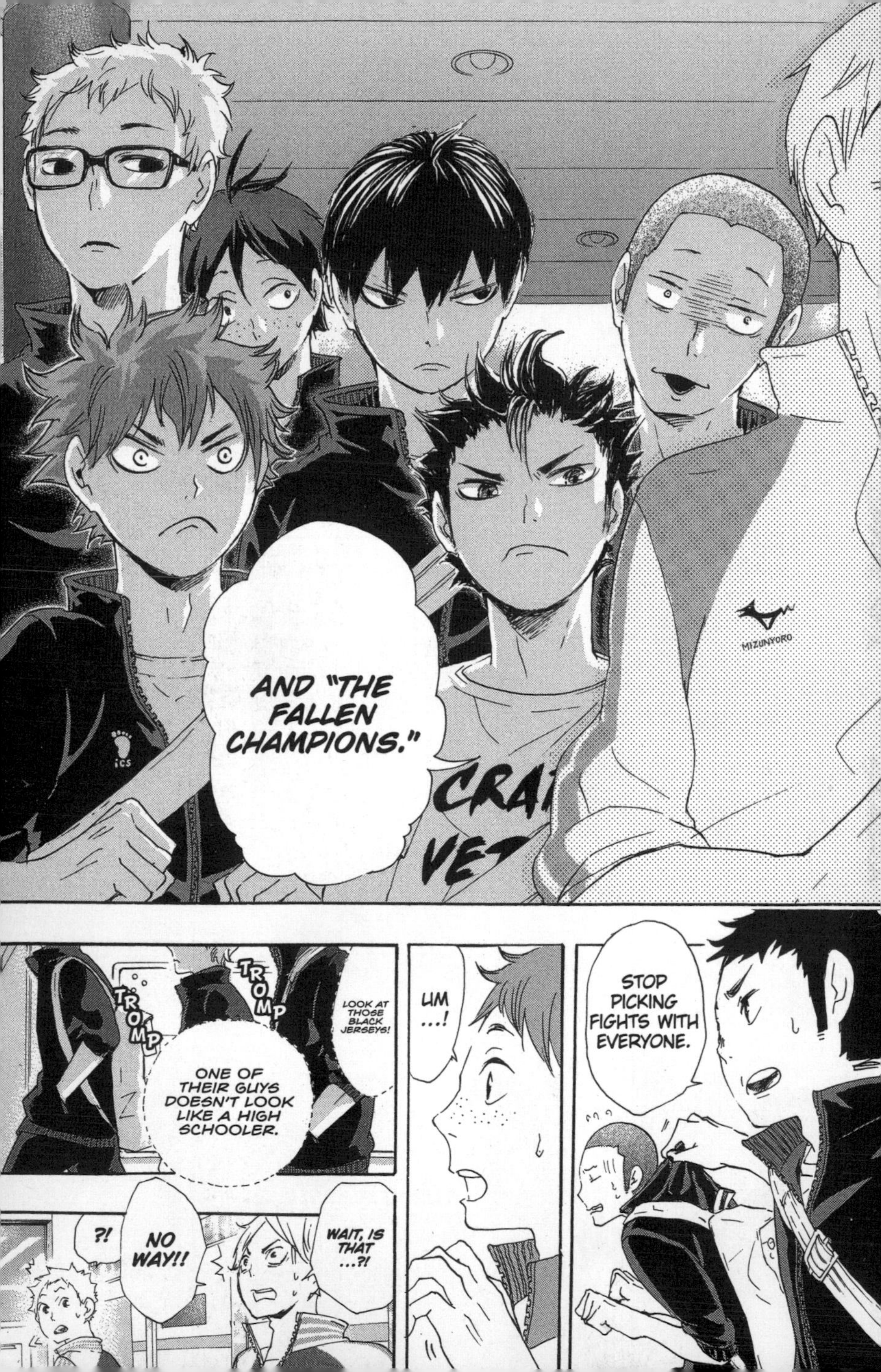
MIZUNYORO
AND "THE FALLEN CHAMPIONS."
STOP PICKING FIGHTS WITH EVERYONE.
UM ...!
TROMP
TROMP
LOOK AT THOSE BLACK JERSEYS!
ONE OF THEIR GUYS DOESN'T LOOK LIKE A HIGH SCHOOLER.
WAIT, IS THAT ...?!
NO WAY!!
?!

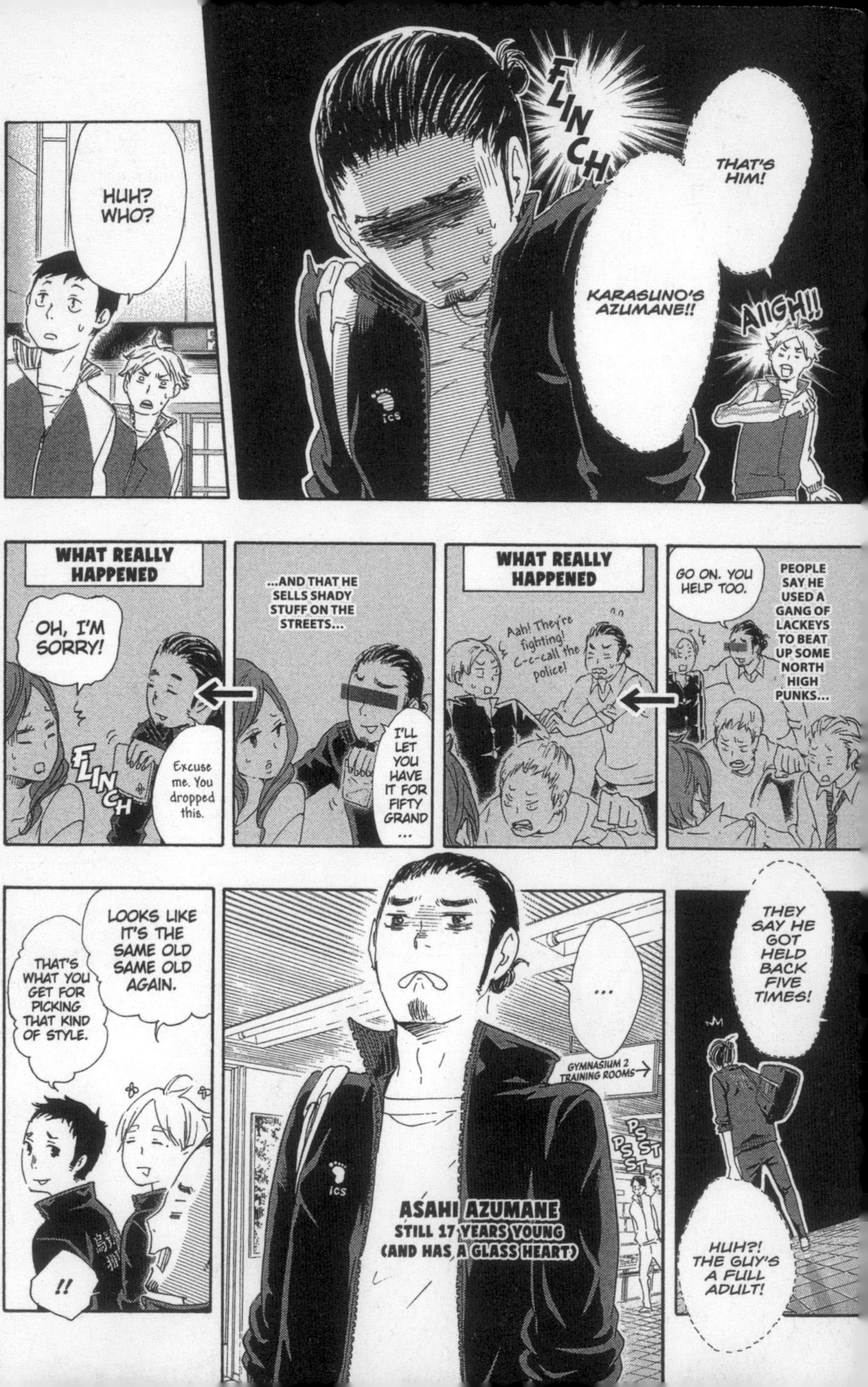
FLINCH
THAT'S HIM!
KARASUNO'S AZUMANE!!
AIIGH!!
HUH? WHO?
PEOPLE SAY HE USED A GANG OF LACKEYS TO BEAT UP SOME NORTH HIGH PUNKS...
GO ON. YOU HELP TOO.
WHAT REALLY HAPPENED
Aah! They're fighting! C-c-call the police!
...AND THAT HE SELLS SHADY STUFF ON THE STREETS...
I'LL LET YOU HAVE IT FOR FIFTY GRAND...
WHAT REALLY HAPPENED
OH, I'M SORRY!
FLINCH
Excuse me. You dropped this.
THEY SAY HE GOT HELD BACK FIVE TIMES!
HUH?! THE GUY'S A FULL ADULT!
...
GYMNASIUM 2 TRAINING ROOMS
PSST PSST
ASAHI AZUMANE
STILL 17 YEARS YOUNG
(AND HAS A GLASS HEART)
LOOKS LIKE IT'S THE SAME OLD SAME OLD AGAIN.
THAT'S WHAT YOU GET FOR PICKING THAT KIND OF STYLE.
!!

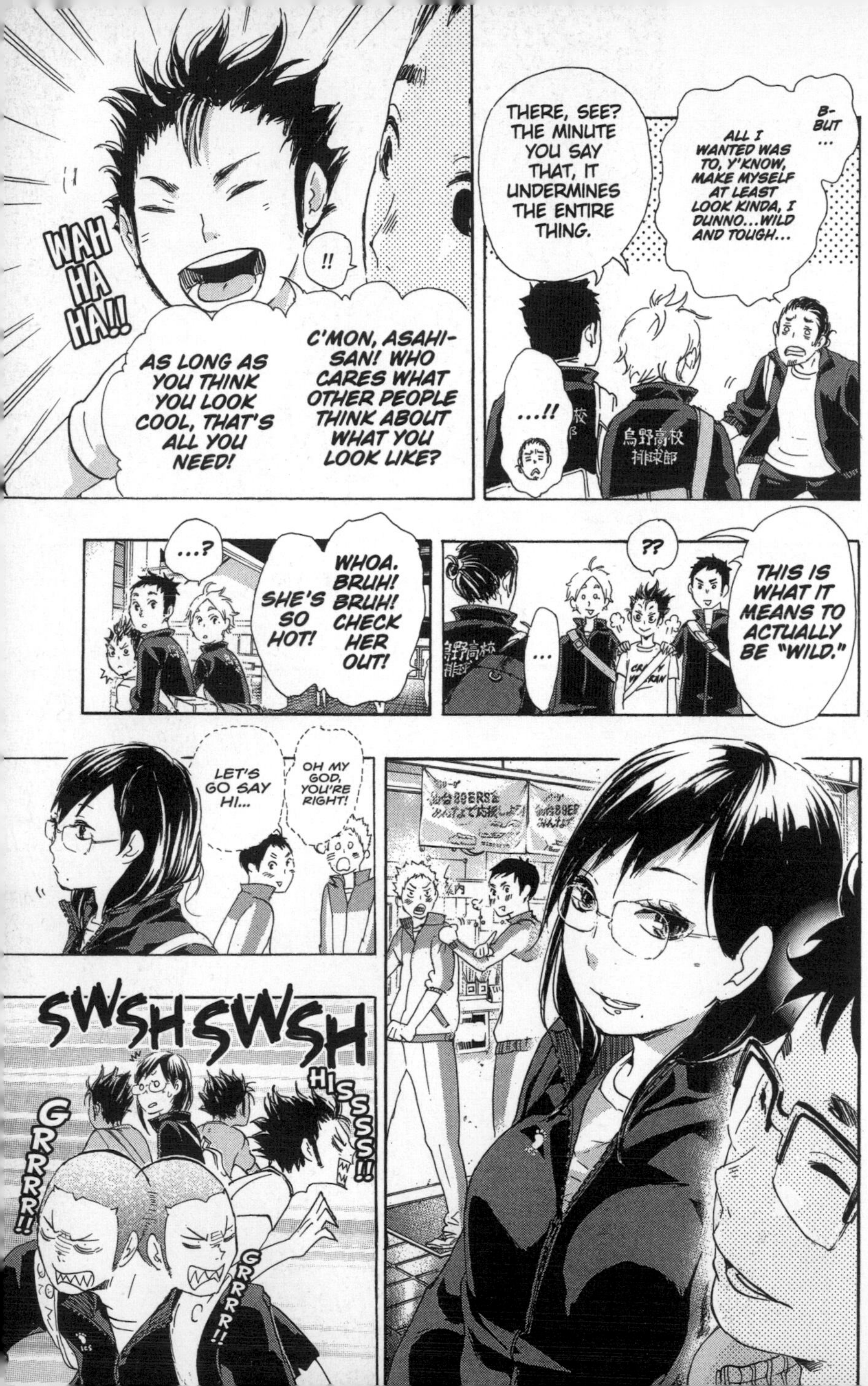
B-BUT...
ALL I WANTED WAS TO, Y'KNOW, MAKE MYSELF AT LEAST LOOK KINDA, I DUNNO...WILD AND TOUGH...
THERE, SEE? THE MINUTE YOU SAY THAT, IT UNDERMINES THE ENTIRE THING.
烏野高校 排球部
...!!
!!
WAH HA HA!!
C'MON, ASAHI-SAN! WHO CARES WHAT OTHER PEOPLE THINK ABOUT WHAT YOU LOOK LIKE?
AS LONG AS YOU THINK YOU LOOK COOL, THAT'S ALL YOU NEED!
THIS IS WHAT IT MEANS TO ACTUALLY BE "WILD."
??
...
WHOA. BRUH! BRUH! CHECK HER OUT!
SHE'S SO HOT!
...?
OH MY GOD, YOU'RE RIGHT!
LET'S GO SAY HI...
SWSH SWSH
HISSSS!!
GRRRR!!
GRRRRR!!

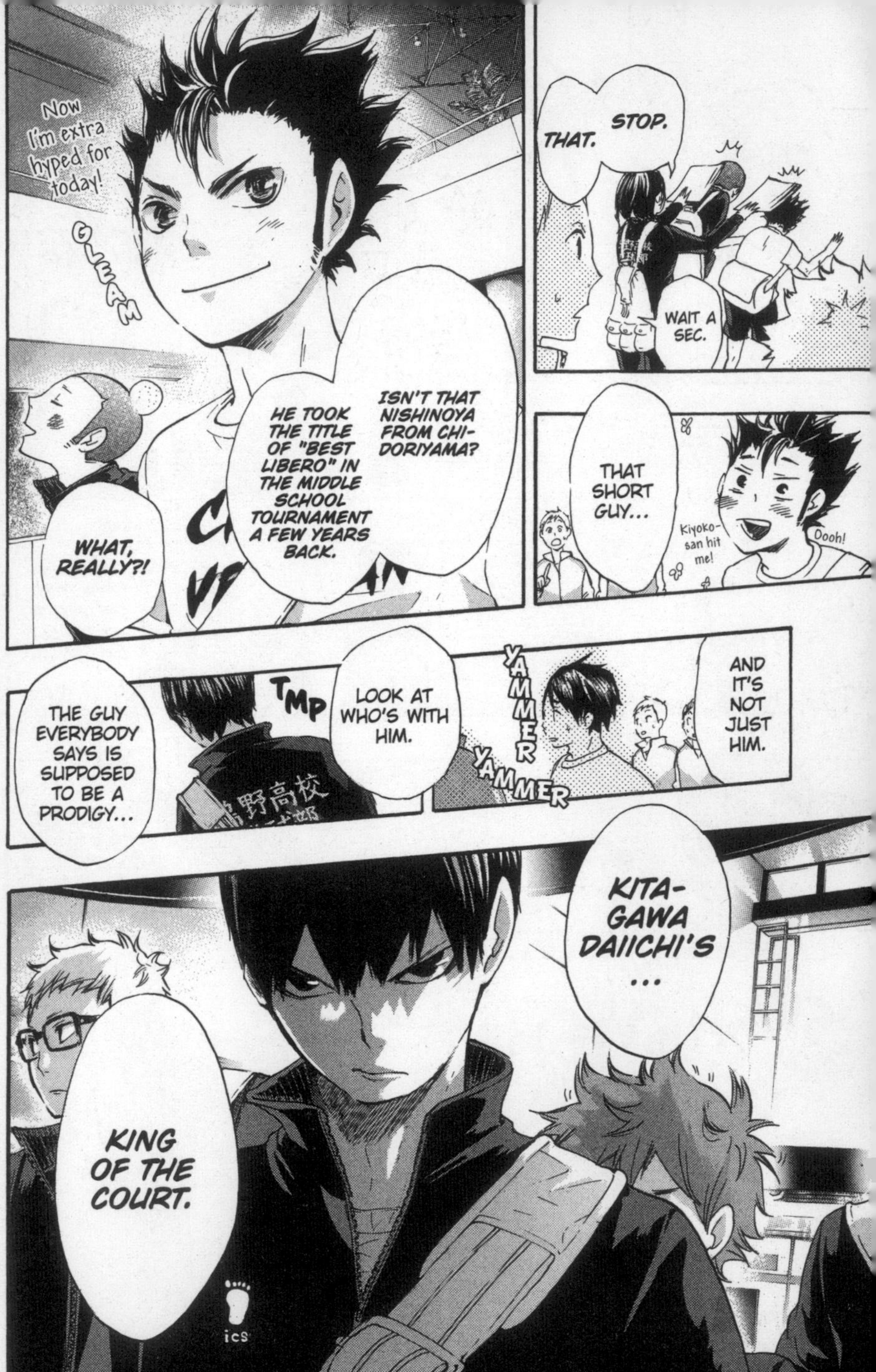
STOP. THAT.
WAIT A SEC.
Oooh!
Kiyoko-san hit me!
THAT SHORT GUY...
Now I'm extra hyped for today!
GLEAM
ISN'T THAT NISHINOYA FROM CHIDORIYAMA?
HE TOOK THE TITLE OF "BEST LIBERO" IN THE MIDDLE SCHOOL TOURNAMENT A FEW YEARS BACK.
WHAT, REALLY?!
AND IT'S NOT JUST HIM.
YAMMER
YAMMER
LOOK AT WHO'S WITH HIM.
TMP
THE GUY EVERYBODY SAYS IS SUPPOSED TO BE A PRODIGY...
KITA-GAWA DAIICHI'S...
KING OF THE COURT.

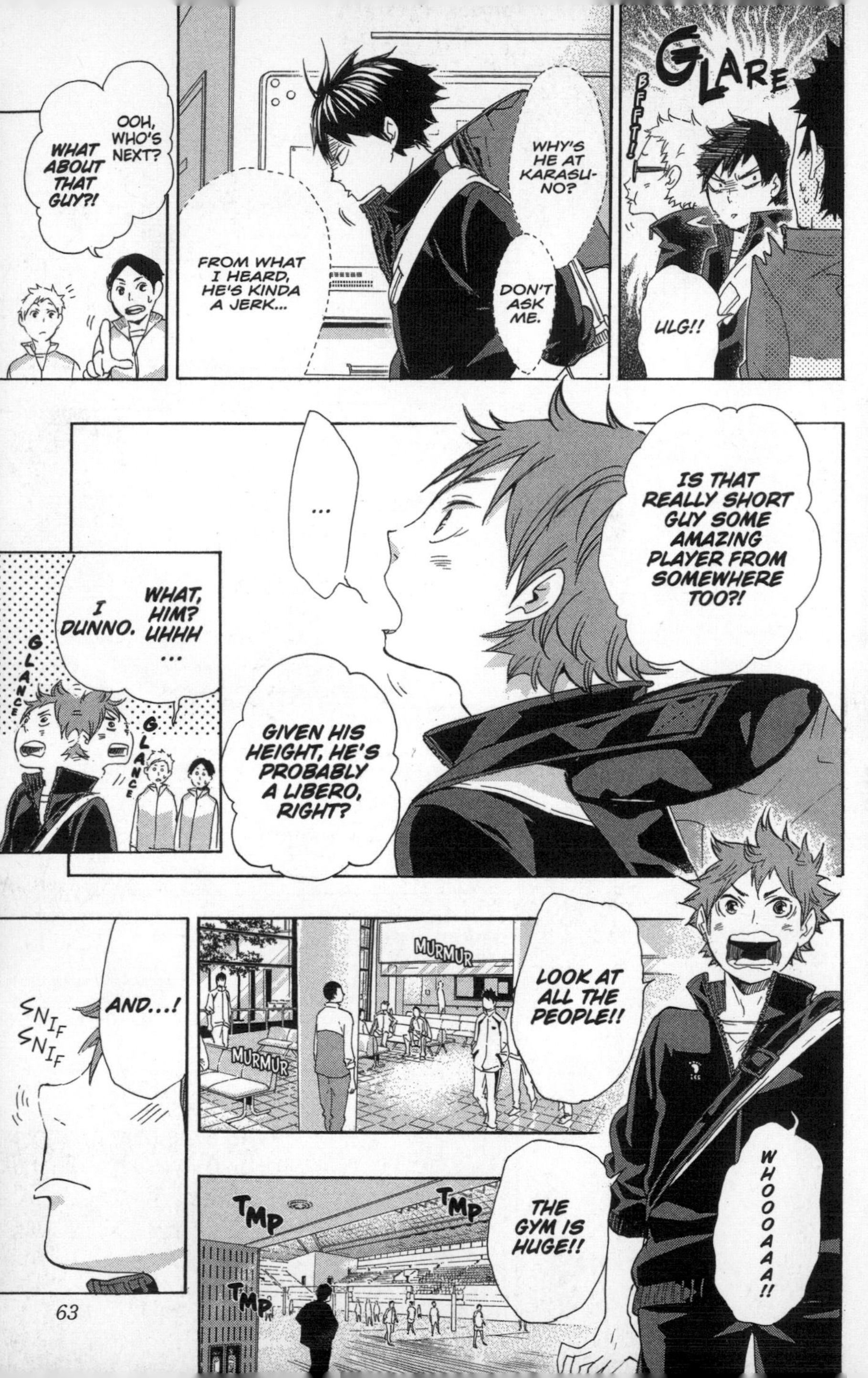
GLARE
BFFT!
ULG!!
WHY'S HE AT KARASUNO?
DON'T ASK ME.
FROM WHAT I HEARD, HE'S KINDA A JERK...
OOH, WHO'S NEXT?
WHAT ABOUT THAT GUY?!
IS THAT REALLY SHORT GUY SOME AMAZING PLAYER FROM SOMEWHERE TOO?!
...
GIVEN HIS HEIGHT, HE'S PROBABLY A LIBERO, RIGHT?
WHAT, HIM? UHHH...
I DUNNO.
GLANCE
GLANCE
WHOOOAAA!!
LOOK AT ALL THE PEOPLE!!
MURMUR
MURMUR
THE GYM IS HUGE!!
TMP
TMP
TMP
AND...!
SNIF SNIF

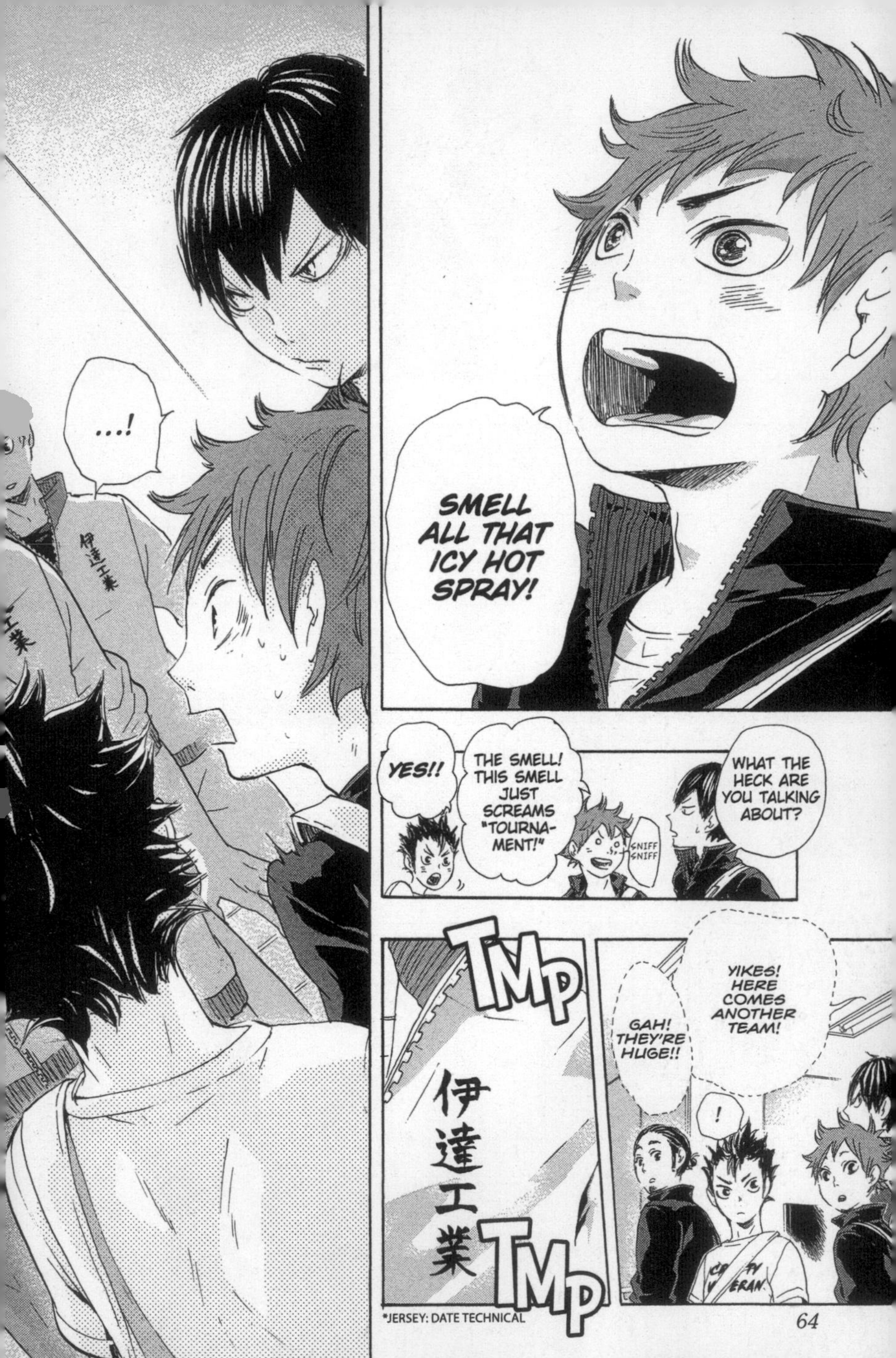
SMELL ALL THAT ICY HOT SPRAY!
WHAT THE HECK ARE YOU TALKING ABOUT?
SNIFF SNIFF
THE SMELL! THIS SMELL JUST SCREAMS "TOURNAMENT!"
YES!!
YIKES! HERE COMES ANOTHER TEAM!
GAH! THEY'RE HUGE!!
!
TMP
伊達工業
TMP
...!
伊達工業

*JERSEY: DATE TECHNICAL

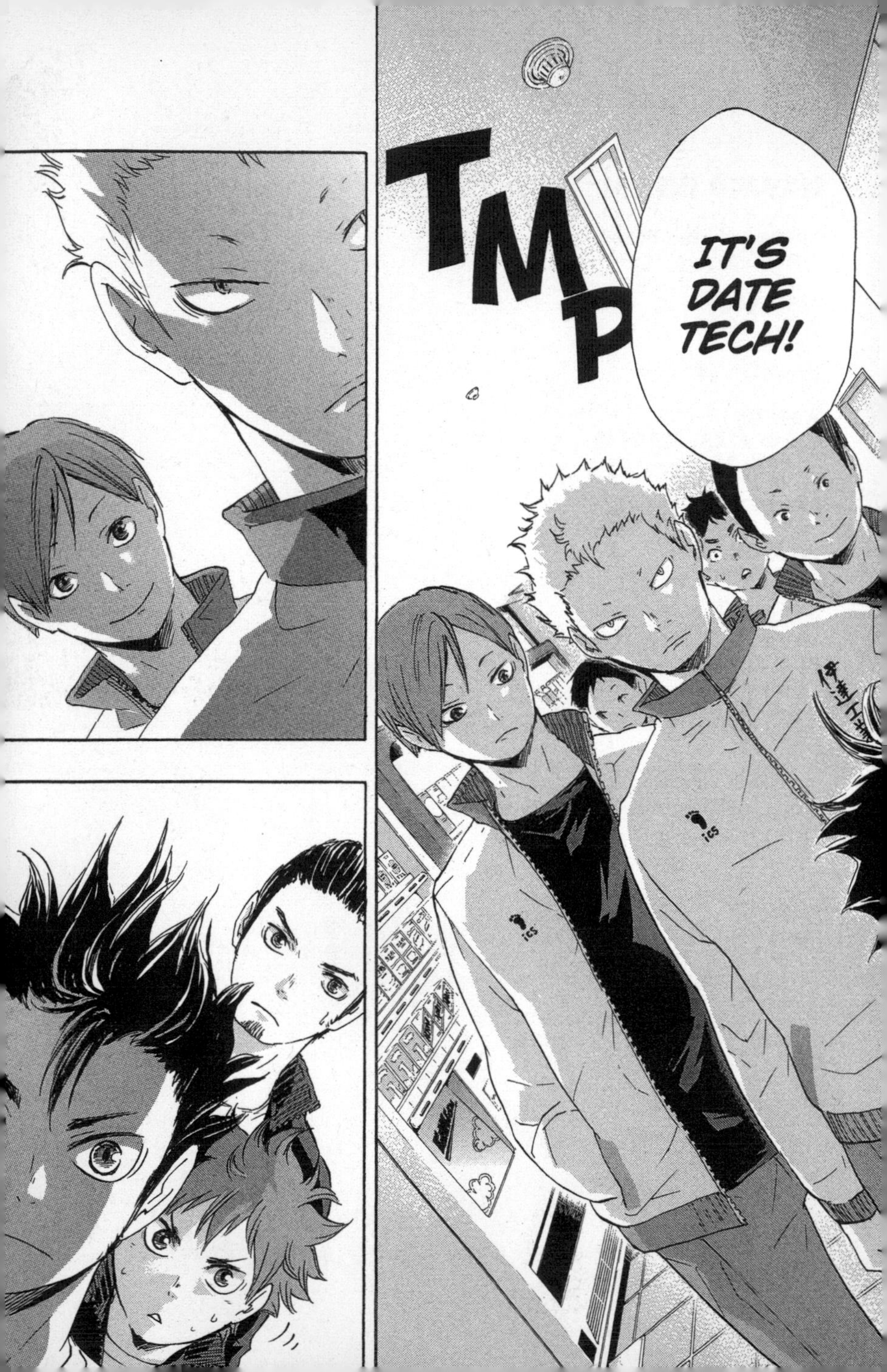
TMP
IT'S DATE TECH!

HAYATO IKEJIRI

TOKONAMI HIGH SCHOOL
CLASS 3-1

POSITION:
WING SPIKER

HEIGHT: 5'10"

WEIGHT: 149 LBS.
(AS OF APRIL, 3RD YEAR
OF HIGH SCHOOL)

BIRTHDAY: FEBRUARY 19

FAVORITE FOOD:
SOBA NOODLE OMELET

CURRENT WORRY:
WHAT TO DO AFTER
HIGH SCHOOL...

ABILITY PARAMETERS
(5-POINT SCALE)

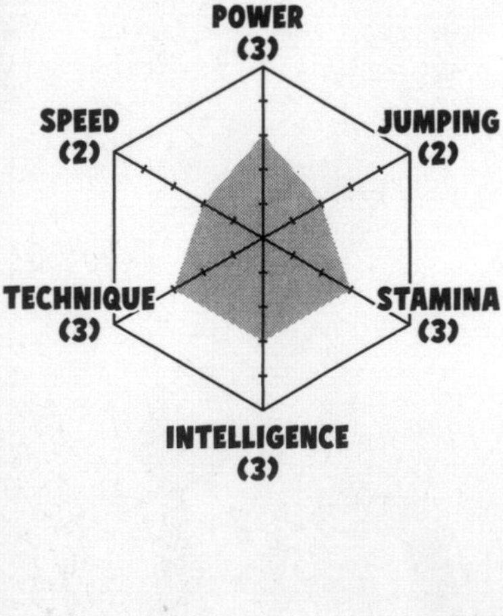
POWER
(3)
JUMPING
(2)
STAMINA
(3)
INTELLIGENCE
(3)
TECHNIQUE
(3)
SPEED
(2)

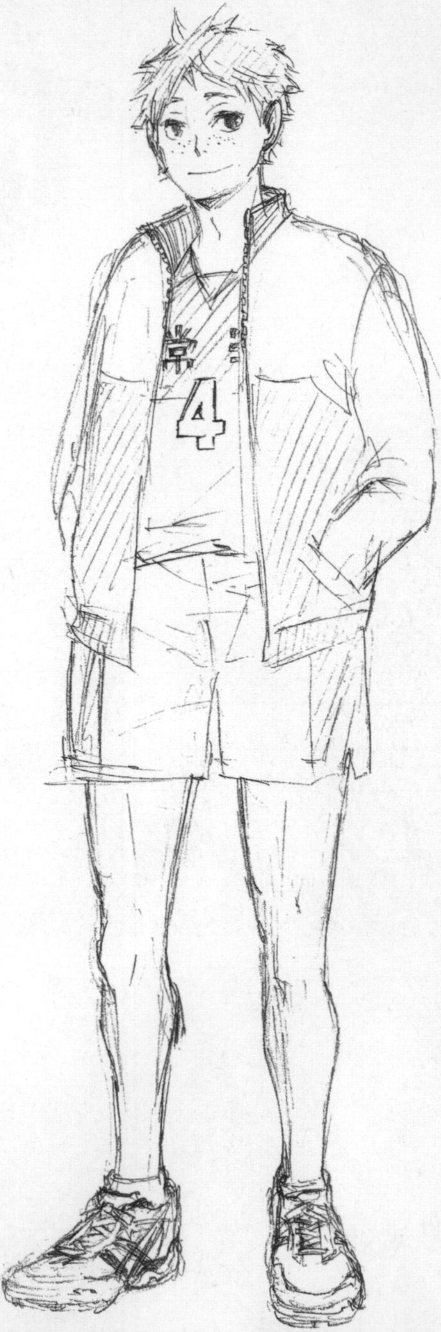
4

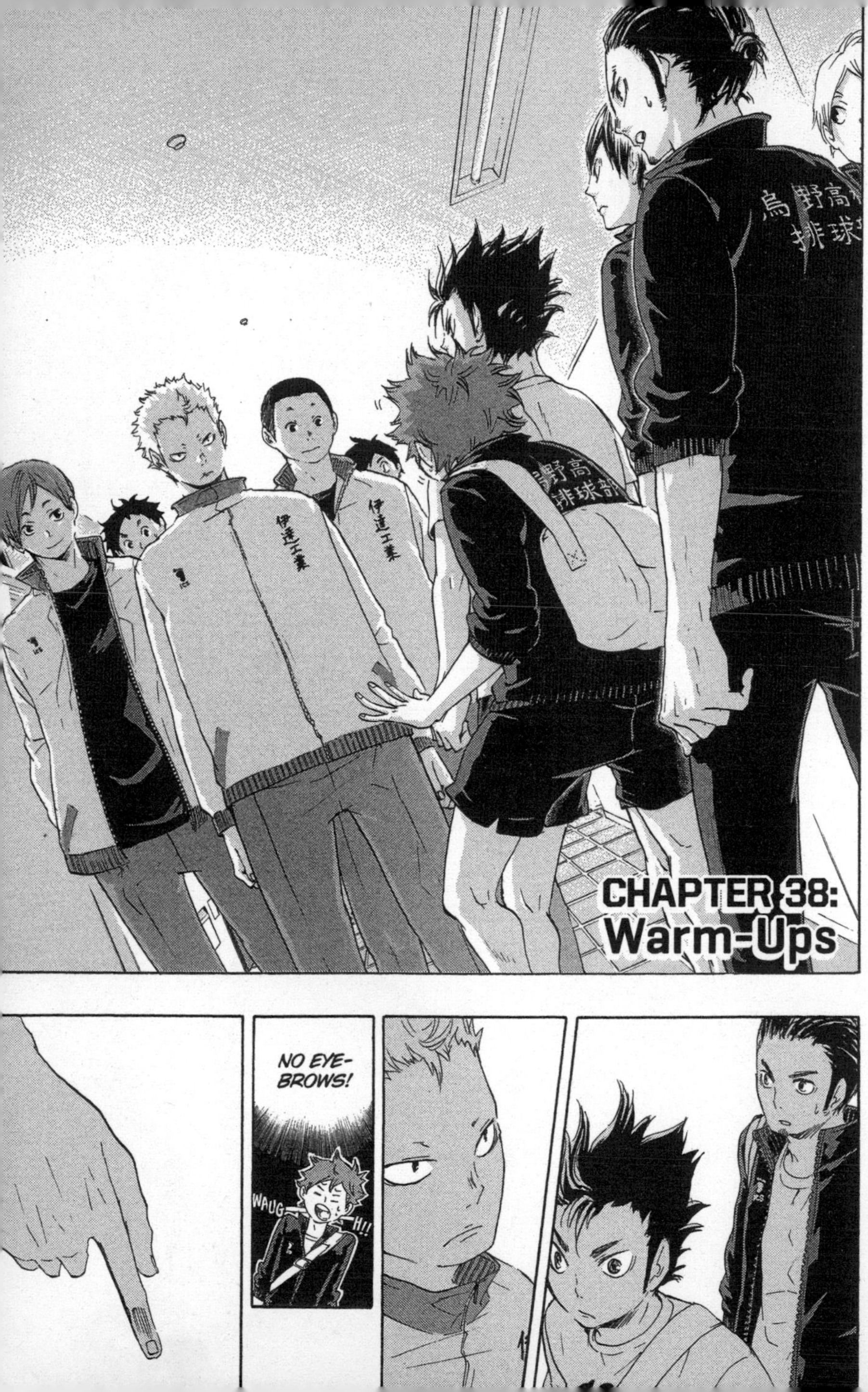
CHAPTER 38:
Warm-Ups
NO EYE-BROWS!
WAUGH!!

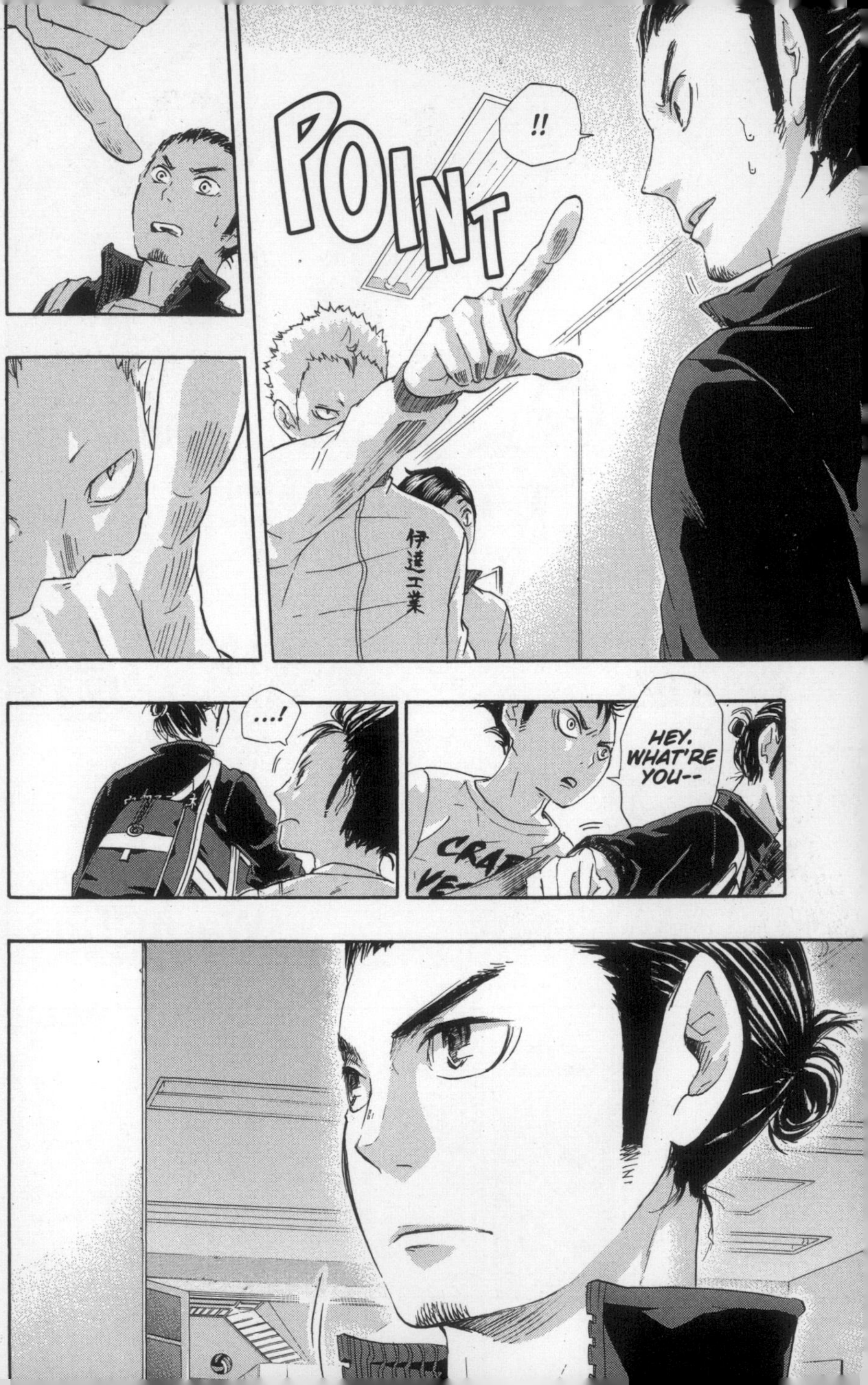
!!
POINT
伊達工業
HEY. WHAT'RE YOU--
...!

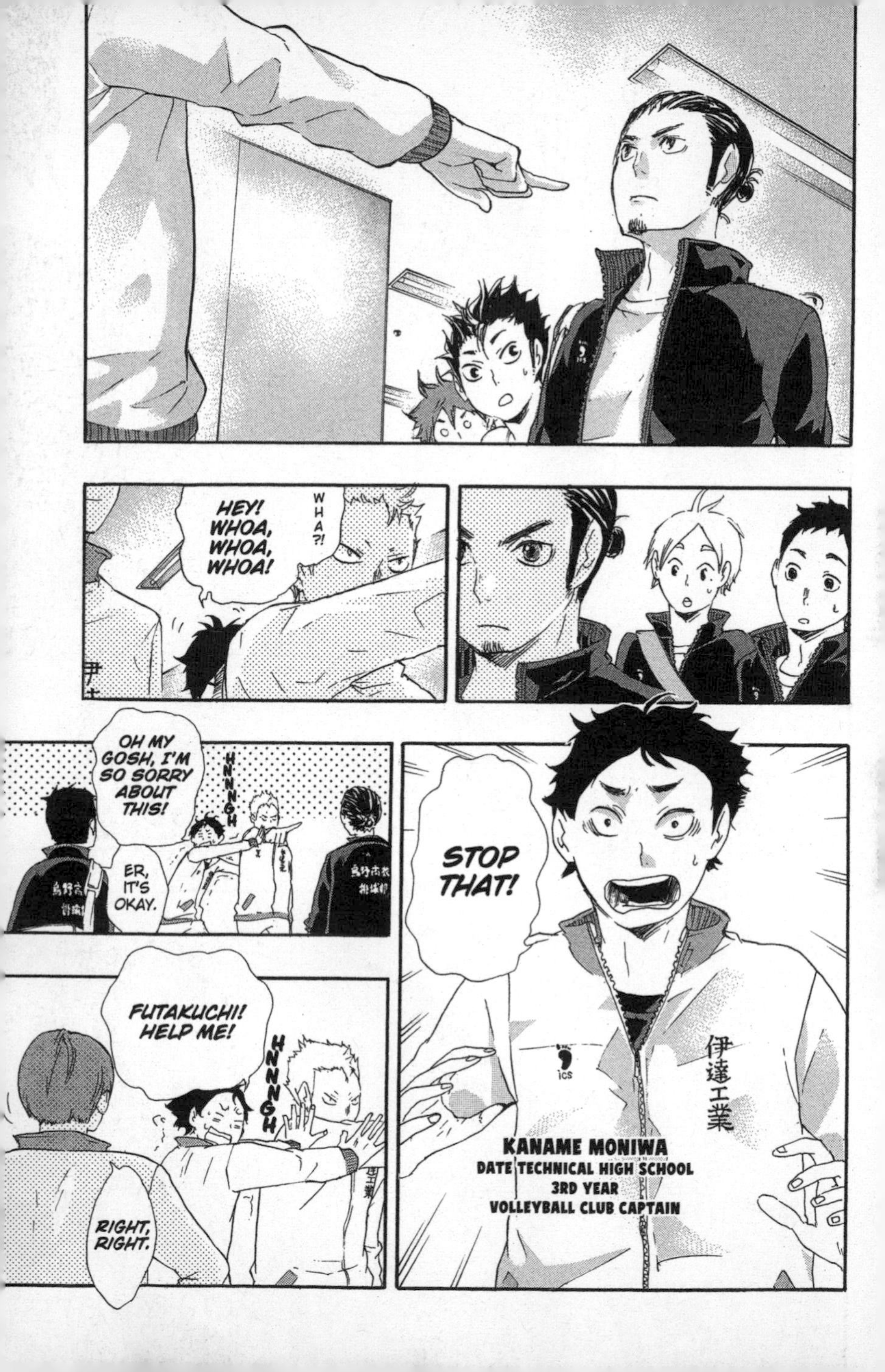
WHA?!
HEY! WHOA, WHOA, WHOA!
STOP THAT!
伊達工業
KANAME MONIWA
DATE TECHNICAL HIGH SCHOOL
3RD YEAR
VOLLEYBALL CLUB CAPTAIN
OH MY GOSH, I'M SO SORRY ABOUT THIS!
HNNNGH
ER, IT'S OKAY.
FUTAKUCHI! HELP ME!
HNNNGH
RIGHT, RIGHT.

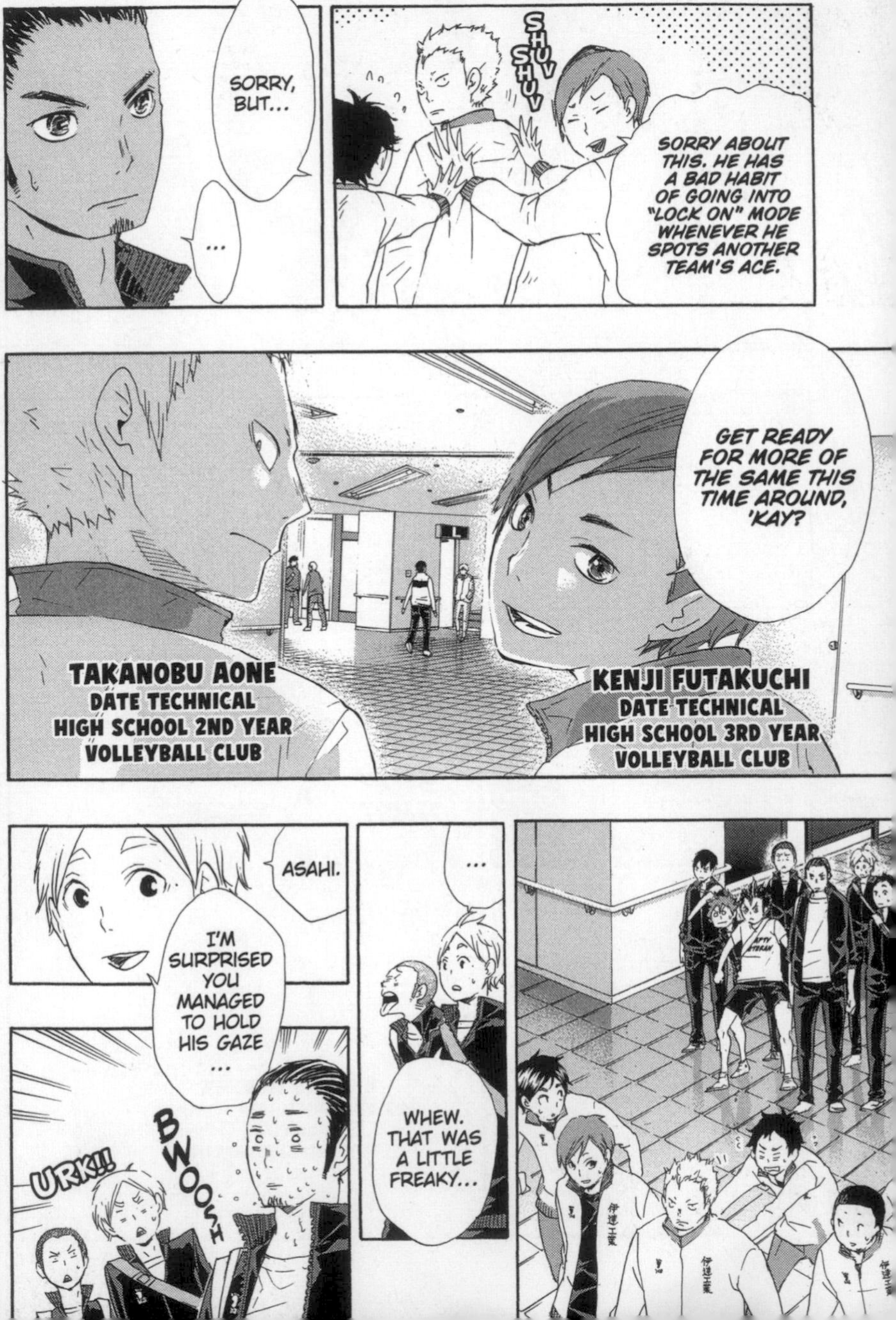
SHUV SHUV
SORRY ABOUT THIS. HE HAS A BAD HABIT OF GOING INTO "LOCK ON" MODE WHENEVER HE SPOTS ANOTHER TEAM'S ACE.
SORRY, BUT...
...
GET READY FOR MORE OF THE SAME THIS TIME AROUND, 'KAY?
KENJI FUTAKUCHI
DATE TECHNICAL HIGH SCHOOL 3RD YEAR VOLLEYBALL CLUB
TAKANOBU AONE
DATE TECHNICAL HIGH SCHOOL 2ND YEAR VOLLEYBALL CLUB
...
WHEW. THAT WAS A LITTLE FREAKY...
ASAHI.
I'M SURPRISED YOU MANAGED TO HOLD HIS GAZE...
BWOOSH
URK!!

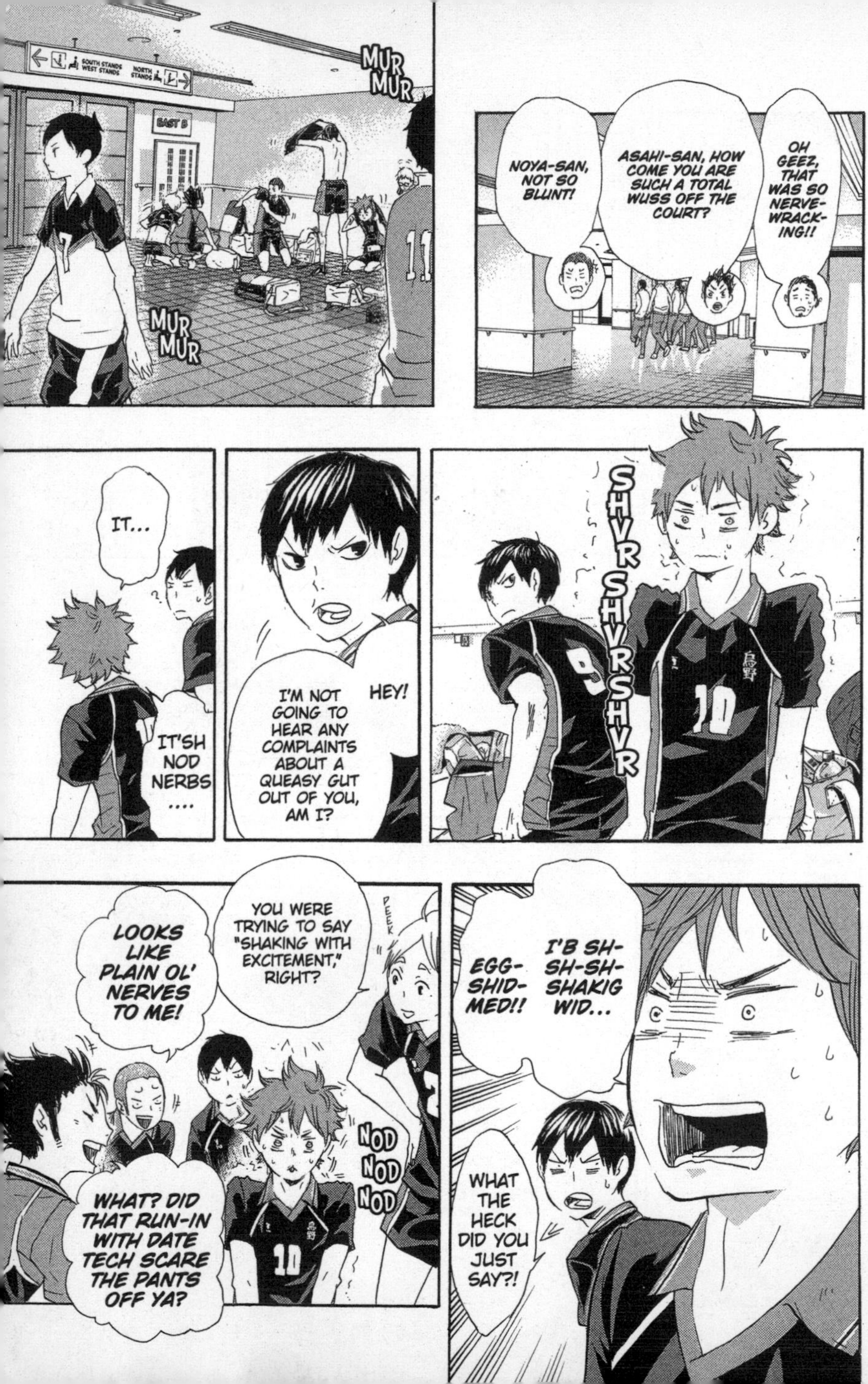
OH GEEZ, THAT WAS SO NERVE-WRACKING!!
ASAHI-SAN, HOW COME YOU ARE SUCH A TOTAL WUSS OFF THE COURT?
NOYA-SAN, NOT SO BLUNT!
SOUTH STANDS WEST STANDS
NORTH STANDS
EAST B
MUR MUR
MUR MUR
SHVR SHVR SHVR SHVR
HEY!
I'M NOT GOING TO HEAR ANY COMPLAINTS ABOUT A QUEASY GUT OUT OF YOU, AM I?
IT...
IT'SH NOD NERBS....
I'B SH-SH-SH-SHAKIG WID...
EGG-SHID-MED!!
WHAT THE HECK DID YOU JUST SAY?!
PEEK
YOU WERE TRYING TO SAY "SHAKING WITH EXCITEMENT," RIGHT?
LOOKS LIKE PLAIN OL' NERVES TO ME!
NOD NOD NOD
WHAT? DID THAT RUN-IN WITH DATE TECH SCARE THE PANTS OFF YA?

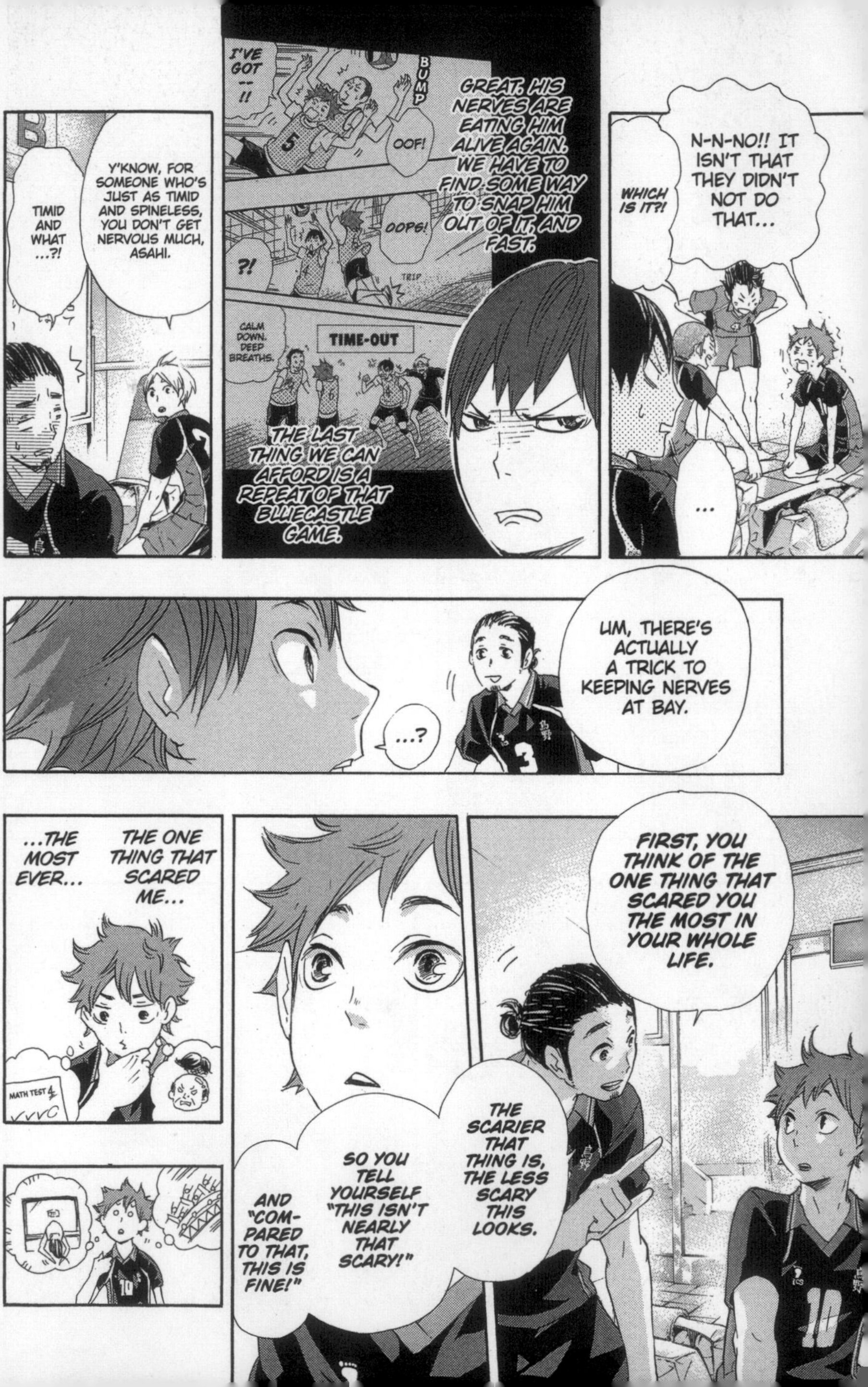
N-N-NO!! IT ISN'T THAT THEY DIDN'T NOT DO THAT...
WHICH IS IT?!
...
GREAT. HIS NERVES ARE EATING HIM ALIVE AGAIN. WE HAVE TO FIND SOME WAY TO SNAP HIM OUT OF IT, AND FAST.
BUMP
I'VE GOT--!!
OOF!
OOPS!
?!
TRIP
TIME-OUT
CALM DOWN. DEEP BREATHS.
THE LAST THING WE CAN AFFORD IS A REPEAT OF THAT BLUECASTLE GAME.
Y'KNOW, FOR SOMEONE WHO'S JUST AS TIMID AND SPINELESS, YOU DON'T GET NERVOUS MUCH, ASAHI.
TIMID AND WHAT ...?!
UM, THERE'S ACTUALLY A TRICK TO KEEPING NERVES AT BAY.
...?
FIRST, YOU THINK OF THE ONE THING THAT SCARED YOU THE MOST IN YOUR WHOLE LIFE.
THE SCARIER THAT THING IS, THE LESS SCARY THIS LOOKS.
SO YOU TELL YOURSELF "THIS ISN'T NEARLY THAT SCARY!"
AND "COMPARED TO THAT, THIS IS FINE!"
THE ONE THING THAT SCARED ME...
...THE MOST EVER...
MATH TEST 4

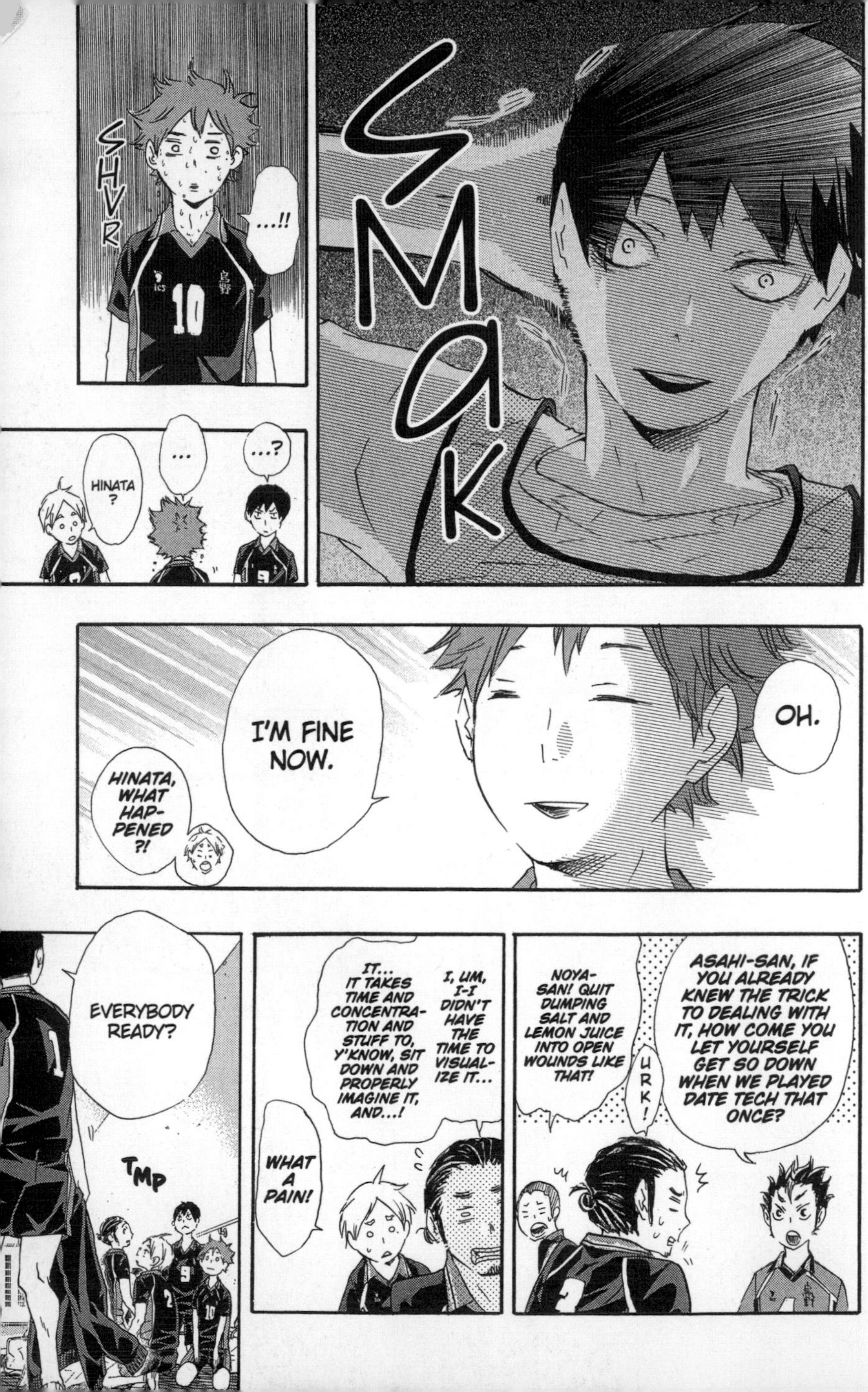
SMAK
SHVR
...!!
...?
...
HINATA?
OH.
I'M FINE NOW.
HINATA, WHAT HAPPENED?!
ASAHI-SAN, IF YOU ALREADY KNEW THE TRICK TO DEALING WITH IT, HOW COME YOU LET YOURSELF GET SO DOWN WHEN WE PLAYED DATE TECH THAT ONCE?
URK!
NOYA-SAN! QUIT DUMPING SALT AND LEMON JUICE INTO OPEN WOUNDS LIKE THAT!
I, UM, I-I DIDN'T HAVE THE TIME TO VISUALIZE IT...
IT... IT TAKES TIME AND CONCENTRATION AND STUFF TO, Y'KNOW, SIT DOWN AND PROPERLY IMAGINE IT, AND...!
WHAT A PAIN!
EVERYBODY READY?
TMP

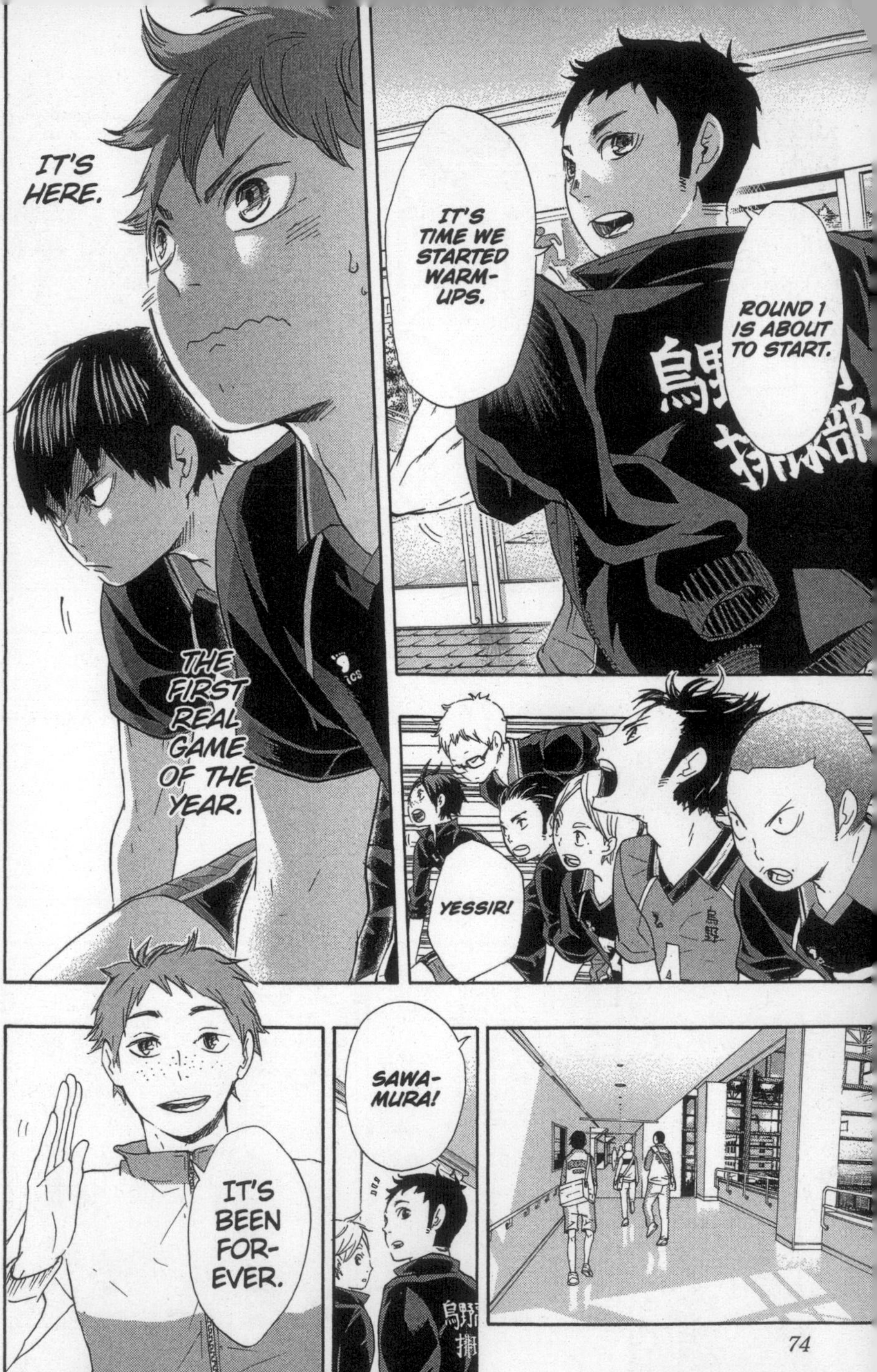
ROUND 1 IS ABOUT TO START.
IT'S TIME WE STARTED WARM-UPS.
YESSIR!
IT'S HERE.
THE FIRST REAL GAME OF THE YEAR.
SAWA-MURA!
IT'S BEEN FOR-EVER.

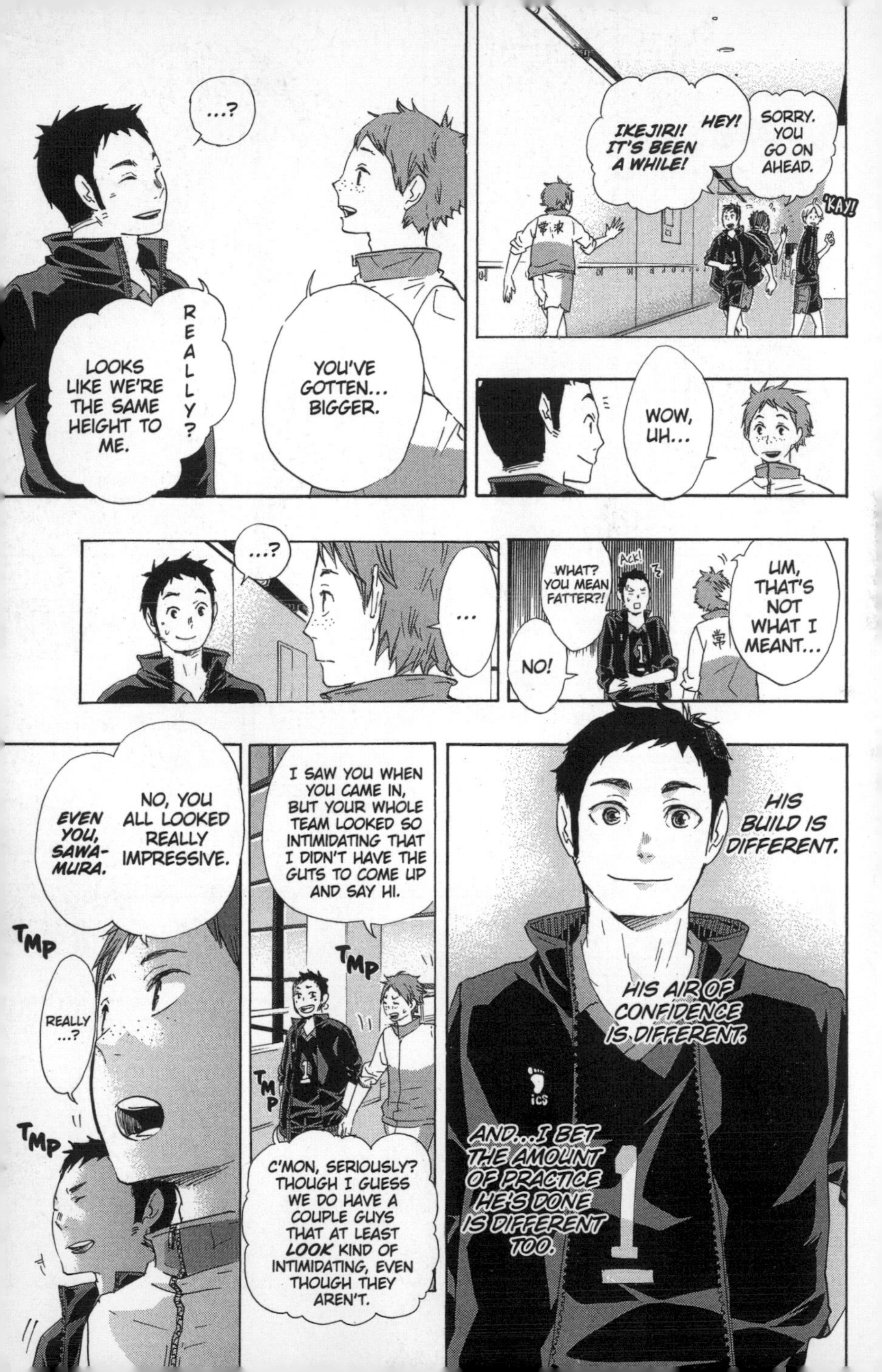
SORRY. YOU GO ON AHEAD.
'KAY!
IKEJIRI! IT'S BEEN A WHILE! HEY!
WOW, UH...
...?
YOU'VE GOTTEN... BIGGER.
REALLY? LOOKS LIKE WE'RE THE SAME HEIGHT TO ME.
UM, THAT'S NOT WHAT I MEANT...
ACK!
WHAT? YOU MEAN FATTER?!
NO!
...
...?
HIS BUILD IS DIFFERENT.
HIS AIR OF CONFIDENCE IS DIFFERENT.
AND...I BET THE AMOUNT OF PRACTICE HE'S DONE IS DIFFERENT TOO.
I SAW YOU WHEN YOU CAME IN, BUT YOUR WHOLE TEAM LOOKED SO INTIMIDATING THAT I DIDN'T HAVE THE GUTS TO COME UP AND SAY HI.
TMP
TMP
C'MON, SERIOUSLY? THOUGH I GUESS WE DO HAVE A COUPLE GUYS THAT AT LEAST LOOK KIND OF INTIMIDATING, EVEN THOUGH THEY AREN'T.
NO, YOU ALL LOOKED REALLY IMPRESSIVE.
EVEN YOU, SAWAMURA.
TMP
REALLY ...?
TMP

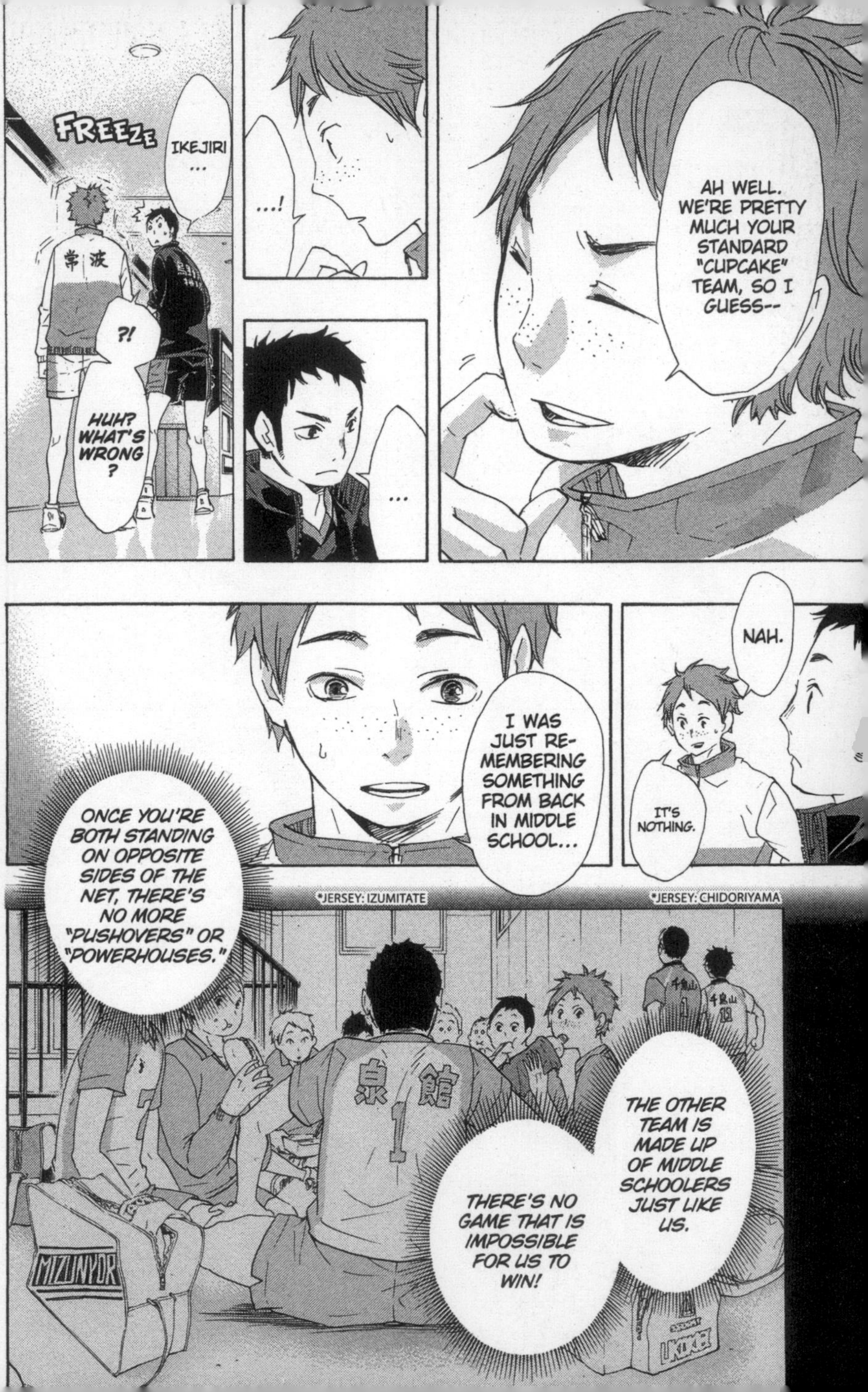
AH WELL. WE'RE PRETTY MUCH YOUR STANDARD "CUPCAKE" TEAM, SO I GUESS--
...!
...
FREEZE
IKEJIRI ...
?!
HUH? WHAT'S WRONG?
NAH.
IT'S NOTHING.
I WAS JUST RE-MEMBERING SOMETHING FROM BACK IN MIDDLE SCHOOL...
*JERSEY: CHIDORIYAMA
*JERSEY: IZUMITATE
ONCE YOU'RE BOTH STANDING ON OPPOSITE SIDES OF THE NET, THERE'S NO MORE "PUSHOVERS" OR "POWERHOUSES."
THE OTHER TEAM IS MADE UP OF MIDDLE SCHOOLERS JUST LIKE US.
THERE'S NO GAME THAT IS IMPOSSIBLE FOR US TO WIN!

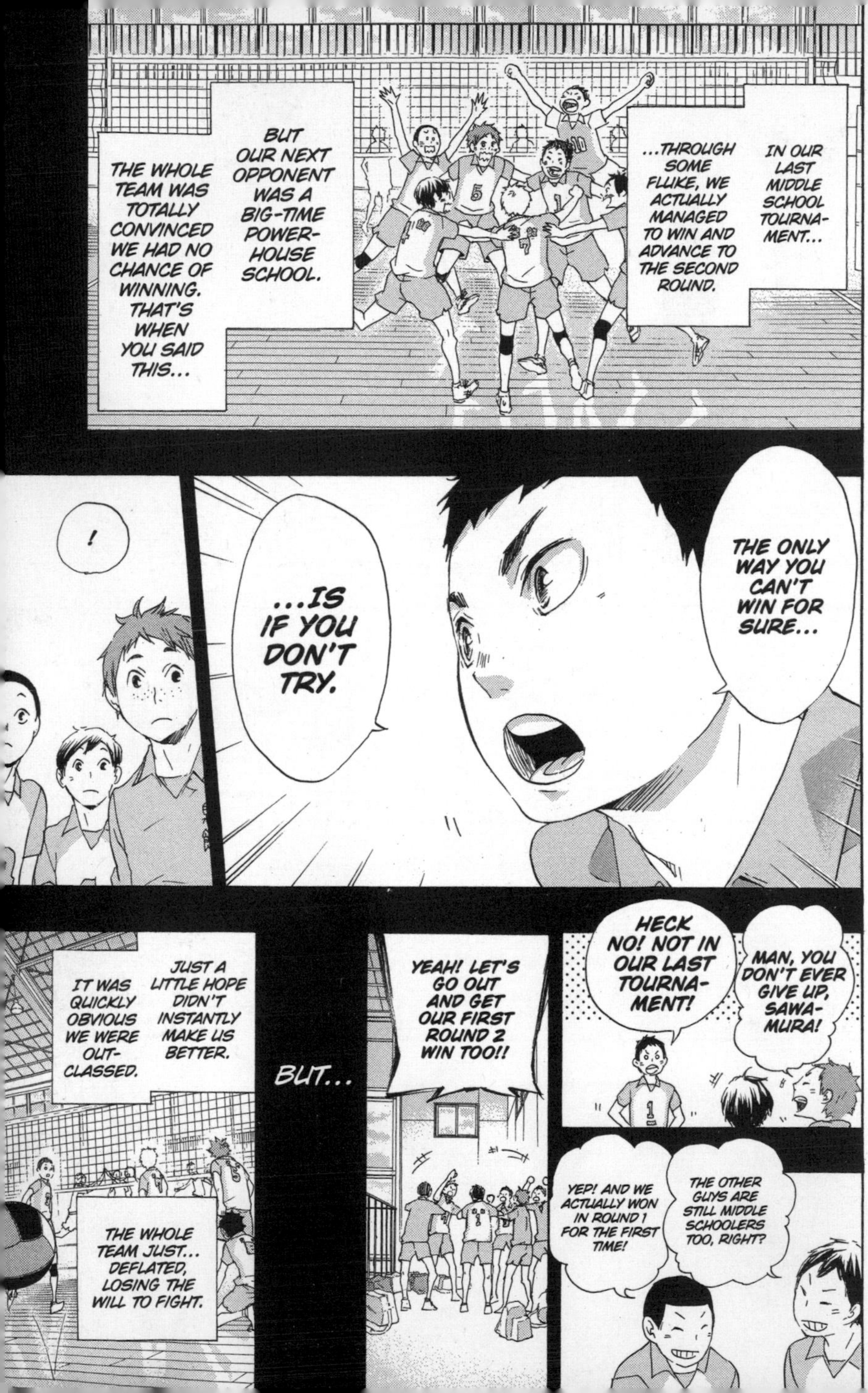
IN OUR LAST MIDDLE SCHOOL TOURNAMENT...
...THROUGH SOME FLUKE, WE ACTUALLY MANAGED TO WIN AND ADVANCE TO THE SECOND ROUND.
BUT OUR NEXT OPPONENT WAS A BIG-TIME POWERHOUSE SCHOOL.
THE WHOLE TEAM WAS TOTALLY CONVINCED WE HAD NO CHANCE OF WINNING. THAT'S WHEN YOU SAID THIS...
THE ONLY WAY YOU CAN'T WIN FOR SURE...
...IS IF YOU DON'T TRY.
!
MAN, YOU DON'T EVER GIVE UP, SAWAMURA!
HECK NO! NOT IN OUR LAST TOURNAMENT!
THE OTHER GUYS ARE STILL MIDDLE SCHOOLERS TOO, RIGHT?
YEP! AND WE ACTUALLY WON IN ROUND 1 FOR THE FIRST TIME!
YEAH! LET'S GO OUT AND GET OUR FIRST ROUND 2 WIN TOO!!
BUT...
JUST A LITTLE HOPE DIDN'T INSTANTLY MAKE US BETTER.
IT WAS QUICKLY OBVIOUS WE WERE OUTCLASSED.
THE WHOLE TEAM JUST... DEFLATED, LOSING THE WILL TO FIGHT.

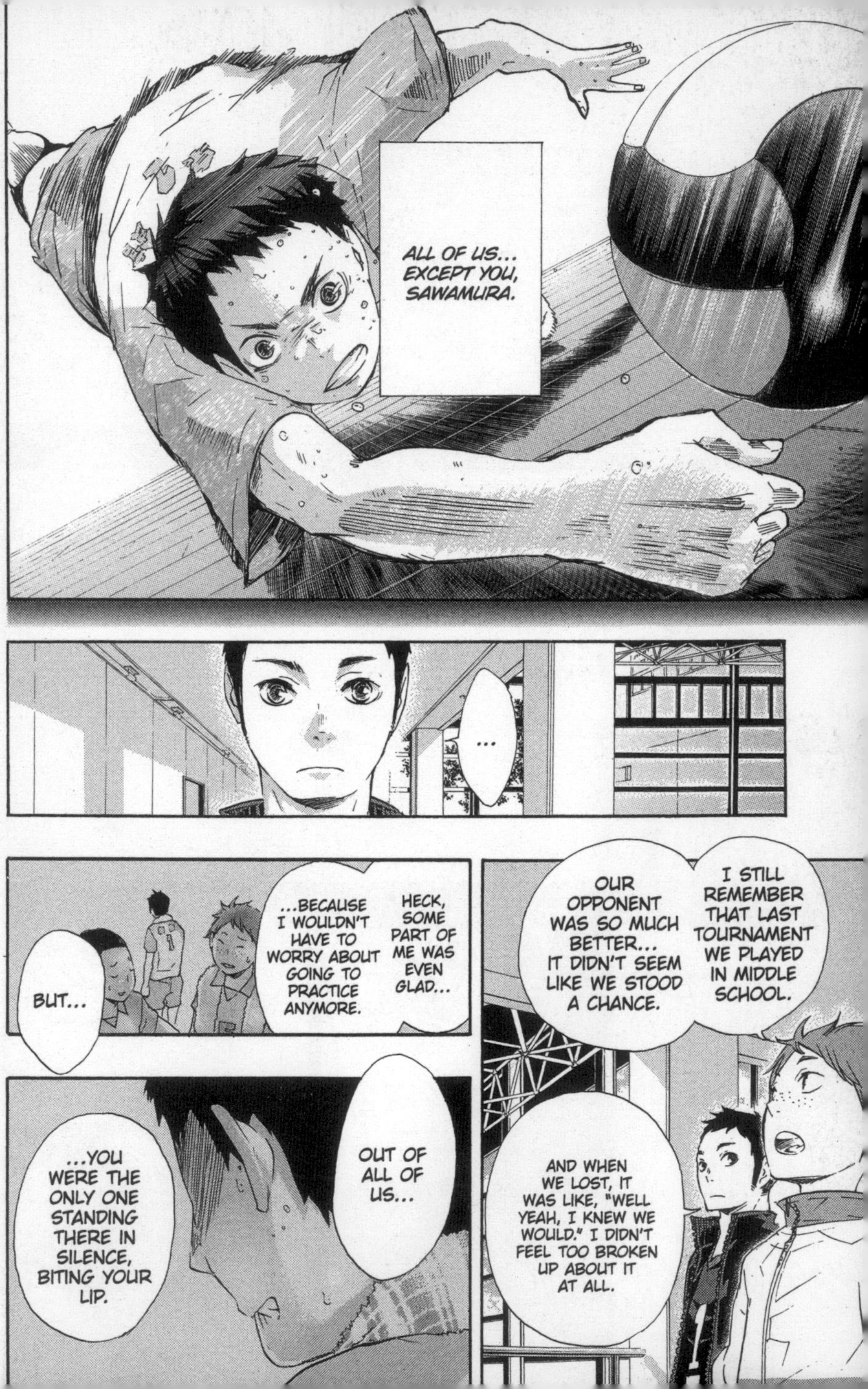
ALL OF US... EXCEPT YOU, SAWAMURA.
...
I STILL REMEMBER THAT LAST TOURNAMENT WE PLAYED IN MIDDLE SCHOOL.
OUR OPPONENT WAS SO MUCH BETTER... IT DIDN'T SEEM LIKE WE STOOD A CHANCE.
AND WHEN WE LOST, IT WAS LIKE, "WELL YEAH, I KNEW WE WOULD." I DIDN'T FEEL TOO BROKEN UP ABOUT IT AT ALL.
HECK, SOME PART OF ME WAS EVEN GLAD...
...BECAUSE I WOULDN'T HAVE TO WORRY ABOUT GOING TO PRACTICE ANYMORE.
BUT...
OUT OF ALL OF US...
...YOU WERE THE ONLY ONE STANDING THERE IN SILENCE, BITING YOUR LIP.

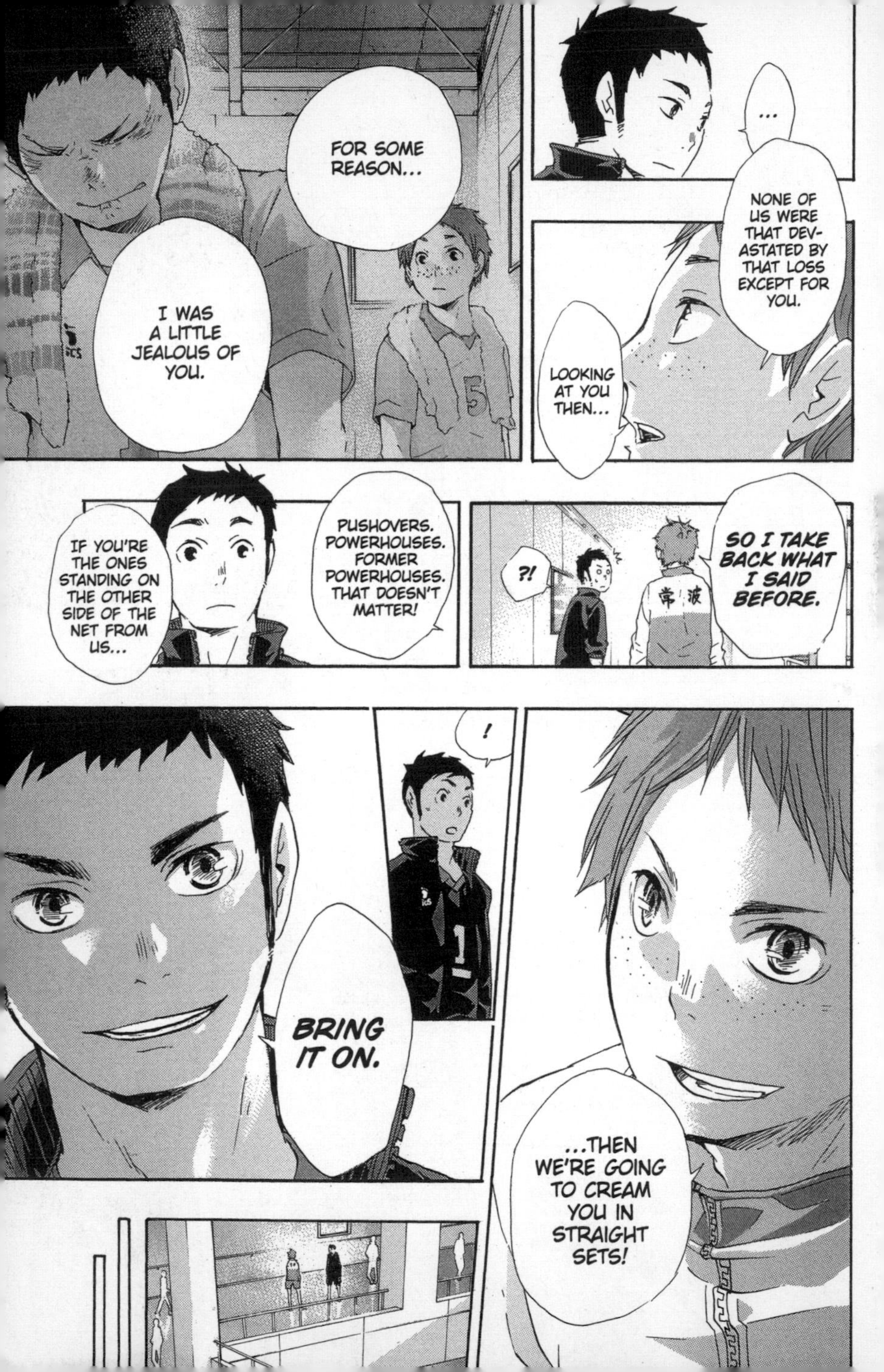
...
NONE OF US WERE THAT DEV-ASTATED BY THAT LOSS EXCEPT FOR YOU.
LOOKING AT YOU THEN...
FOR SOME REASON...
I WAS A LITTLE JEALOUS OF YOU.
SO I TAKE BACK WHAT I SAID BEFORE.
?!
PUSHOVERS. POWERHOUSES. FORMER POWERHOUSES. THAT DOESN'T MATTER!
IF YOU'RE THE ONES STANDING ON THE OTHER SIDE OF THE NET FROM US...
...THEN WE'RE GOING TO CREAM YOU IN STRAIGHT SETS!
!
BRING IT ON.

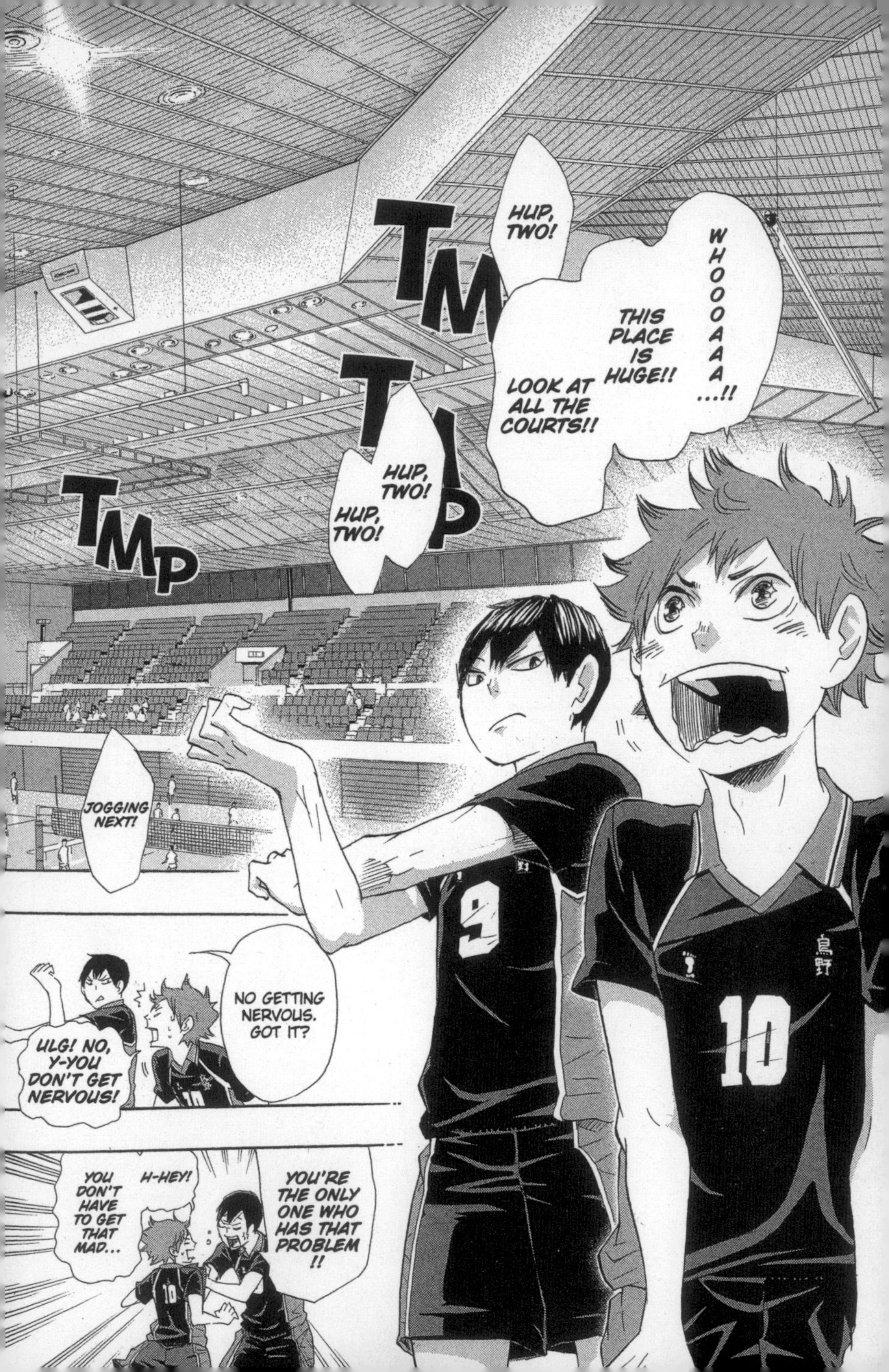
WHOOOOAAA...!!
THIS PLACE IS HUGE!!
LOOK AT ALL THE COURTS!!
TMP
HUP, TWO!
TMP
HUP, TWO!
HUP, TWO!
TMP
JOGGING NEXT!
NO GETTING NERVOUS. GOT IT?
ULG! NO, Y-YOU DON'T GET NERVOUS!
YOU'RE THE ONLY ONE WHO HAS THAT PROBLEM!!
H-HEY!
YOU DON'T HAVE TO GET THAT MAD...

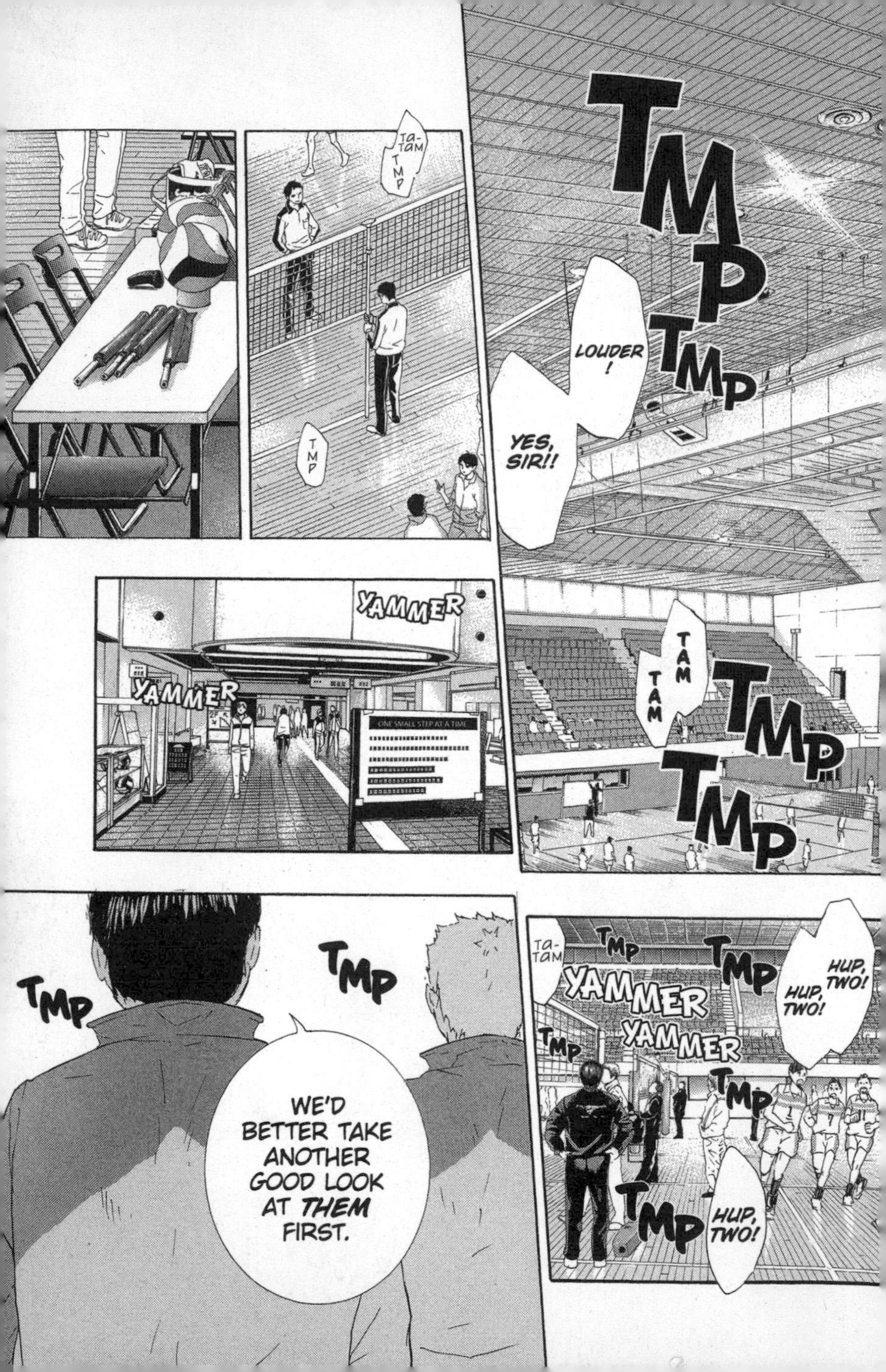
TMP
TMP
TMP
LOUDER!
YES, SIR!!
TA-TAM TMP
TMP
TAM TAM
TMP
TMP
YAMMER
YAMMER
ONE SMALL STEP AT A TIME
TA-TAM
TMP
TMP
YAMMER
YAMMER
HUP, TWO!
HUP, TWO!
TMP
TMP
TMP
HUP, TWO!
TMP
TMP
WE'D BETTER TAKE ANOTHER GOOD LOOK AT *THEM* FIRST.

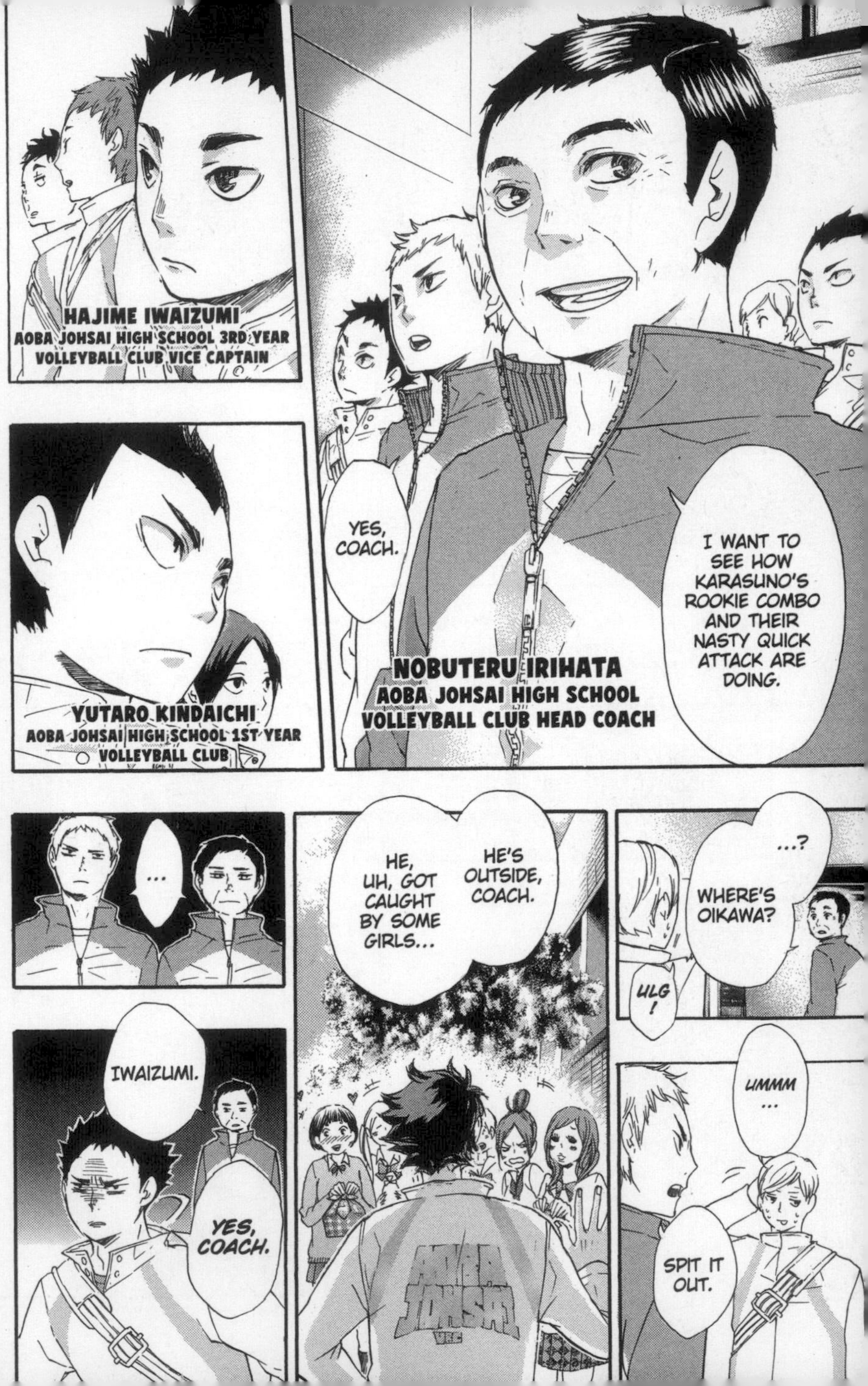
I WANT TO SEE HOW KARASUNO'S ROOKIE COMBO AND THEIR NASTY QUICK ATTACK ARE DOING.
YES, COACH.
NOBUTERU IRIHATA
AOBA JOHSAI HIGH SCHOOL
VOLLEYBALL CLUB HEAD COACH
HAJIME IWAIZUMI
AOBA JOHSAI HIGH SCHOOL 3RD YEAR
VOLLEYBALL CLUB VICE CAPTAIN
YUTARO KINDAICHI
AOBA JOHSAI HIGH SCHOOL 1ST YEAR
VOLLEYBALL CLUB
...?
WHERE'S OIKAWA?
ULG!
UMMM ...
SPIT IT OUT.
HE'S OUTSIDE, COACH.
HE, UH, GOT CAUGHT BY SOME GIRLS...
...
IWAIZUMI.
YES, COACH.

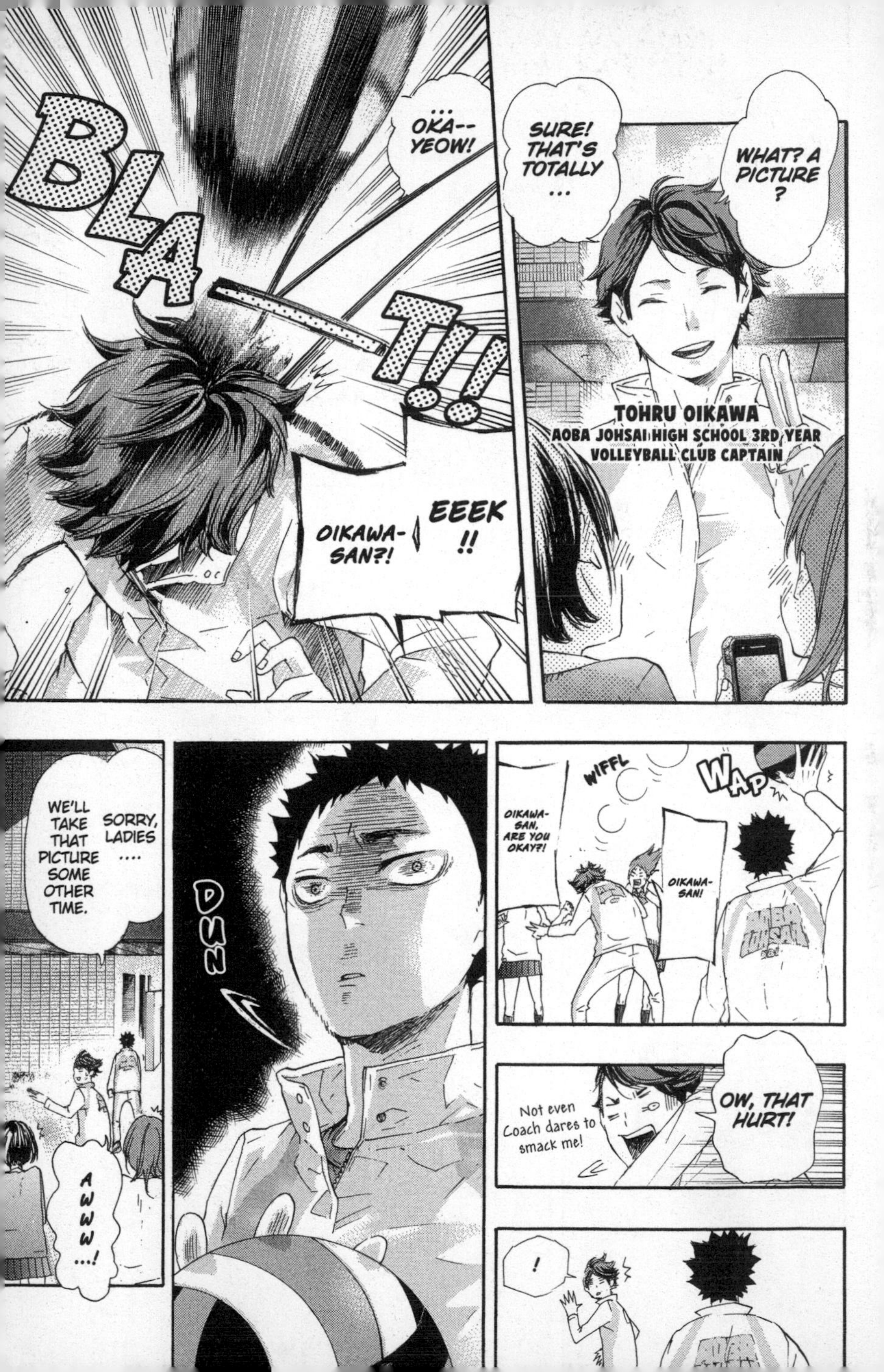
WHAT? A PICTURE ?
SURE! THAT'S TOTALLY ...
TOHRU OIKAWA
AOBA JOHSAI HIGH SCHOOL 3RD YEAR
VOLLEYBALL CLUB CAPTAIN
... OKA-- YEOW!
BLAT!!
EEEK !!
OIKAWA-SAN?!
WAP
WIFFL
OIKAWA-SAN, ARE YOU OKAY?!
OIKAWA-SAN!
OW, THAT HURT!
Not even Coach dares to smack me!
!
DUN
SORRY, LADIES ....
WE'LL TAKE THAT PICTURE SOME OTHER TIME.
AWWW ...!

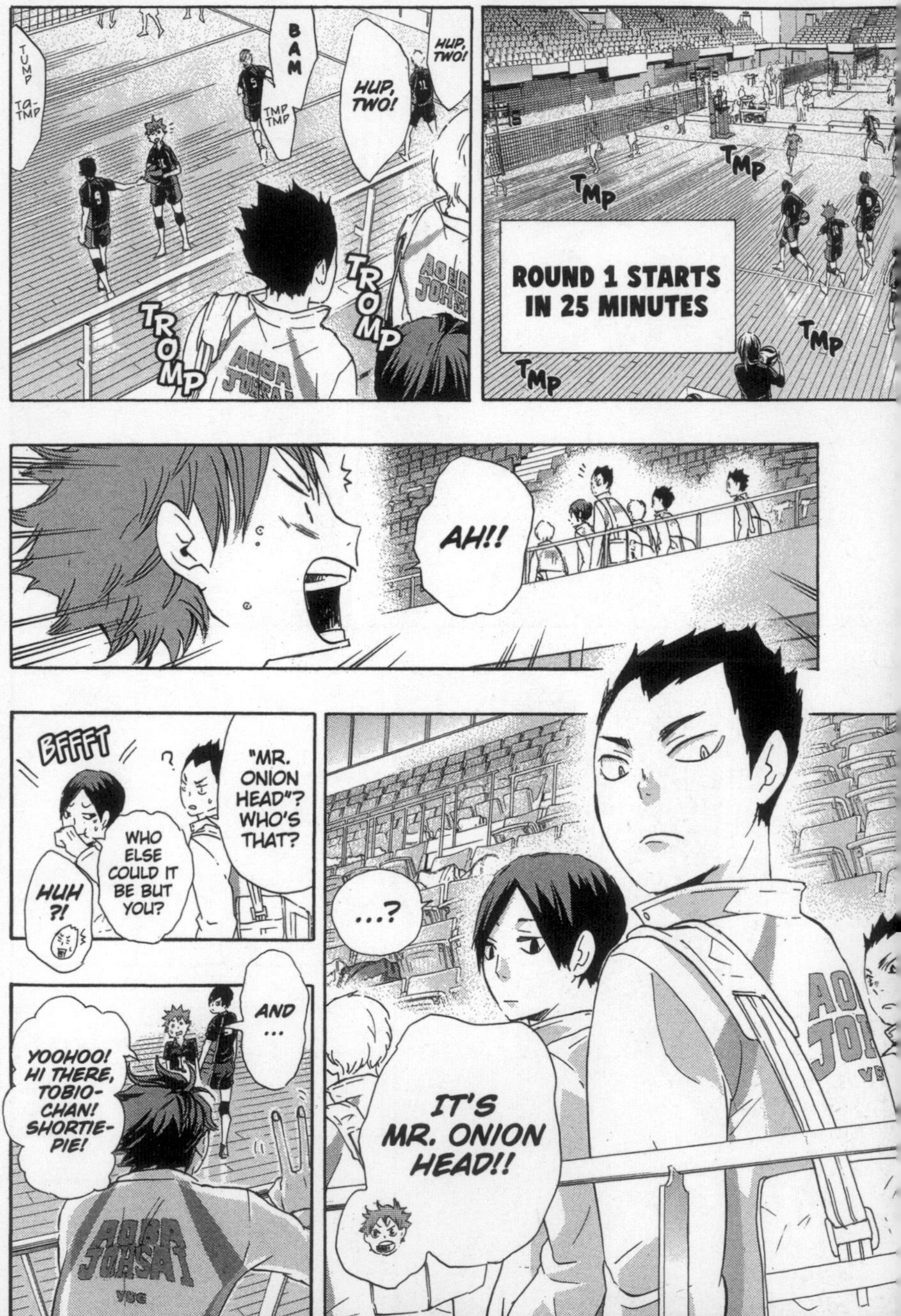
ROUND 1 STARTS IN 25 MINUTES
TMP
TMP
TMP
TMP
HUP, TWO!
HUP, TWO!
BAM
TMP TMP
TUMP
ta-TMP
TROMP
TROMP
AH!!
...?
IT'S MR. ONION HEAD!!
"MR. ONION HEAD"? WHO'S THAT?
WHO ELSE COULD IT BE BUT YOU?
HUH?!
BFFFT
AND...
YOOHOO! HI THERE, TOBIO-CHAN! SHORTIE-PIE!

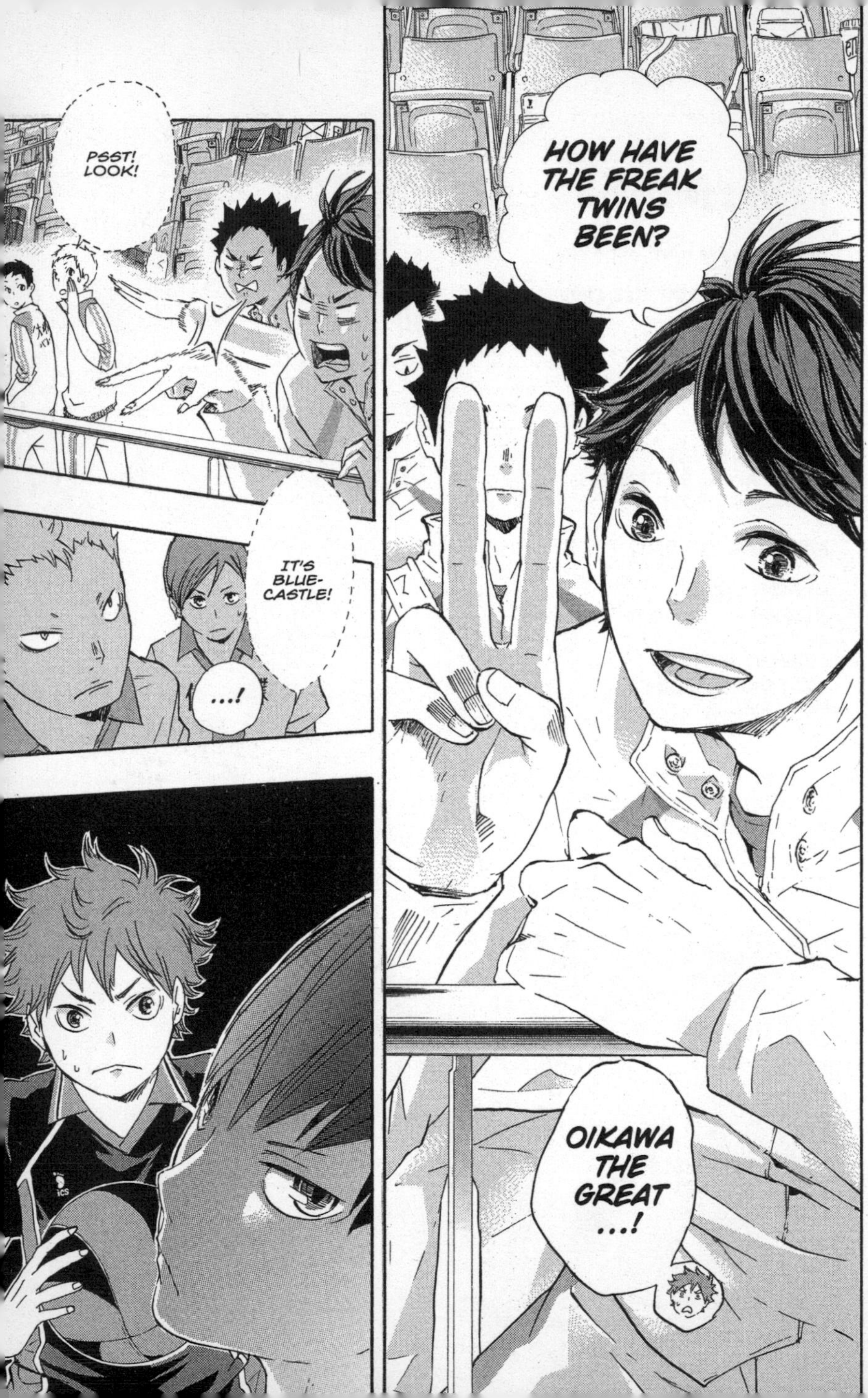
PSST! LOOK!
IT'S BLUE-CASTLE!
...!
HOW HAVE THE FREAK TWINS BEEN?
OIKAWA THE GREAT ...!

HAJIME IWAIZUMI

AOBA JOHSAI HIGH SCHOOL
CLASS 3-5
VOLLEYBALL CLUB VICE CAPTAIN

POSITION:
WING SPIKER

HEIGHT: 5'11"

WEIGHT: 155 LBS.
(AS OF APRIL, 3RD YEAR
OF HIGH SCHOOL)

BIRTHDAY: JUNE 10

FAVORITE FOOD:
***AGEDASHI* DEEP-FRIED TOFU**

CURRENT WORRY:
JUST ONE MORE INCH...
NOT EVEN...!

ABILITY PARAMETERS
(5-POINT SCALE)

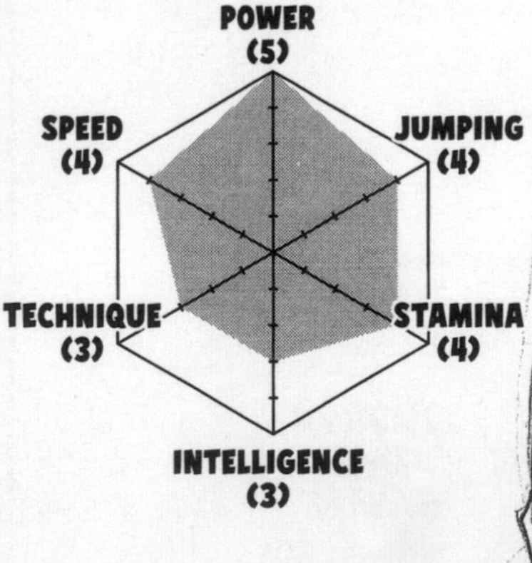
POWER (5)
JUMPING (4)
STAMINA (4)
INTELLIGENCE (3)
TECHNIQUE (3)
SPEED (4)

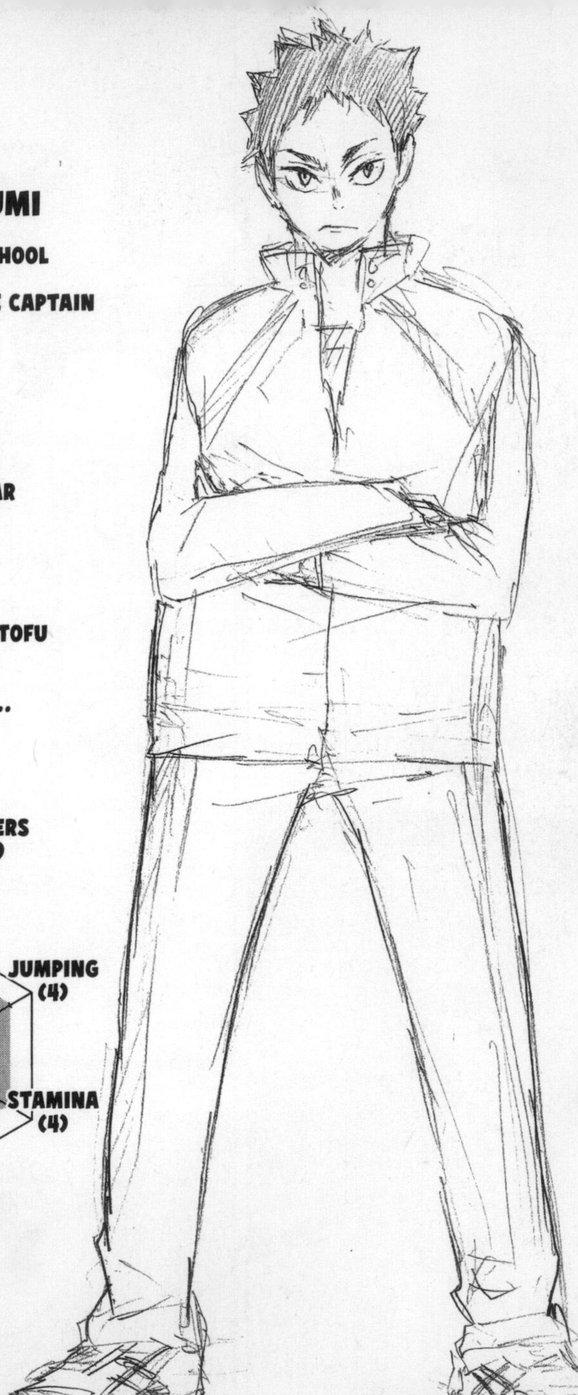

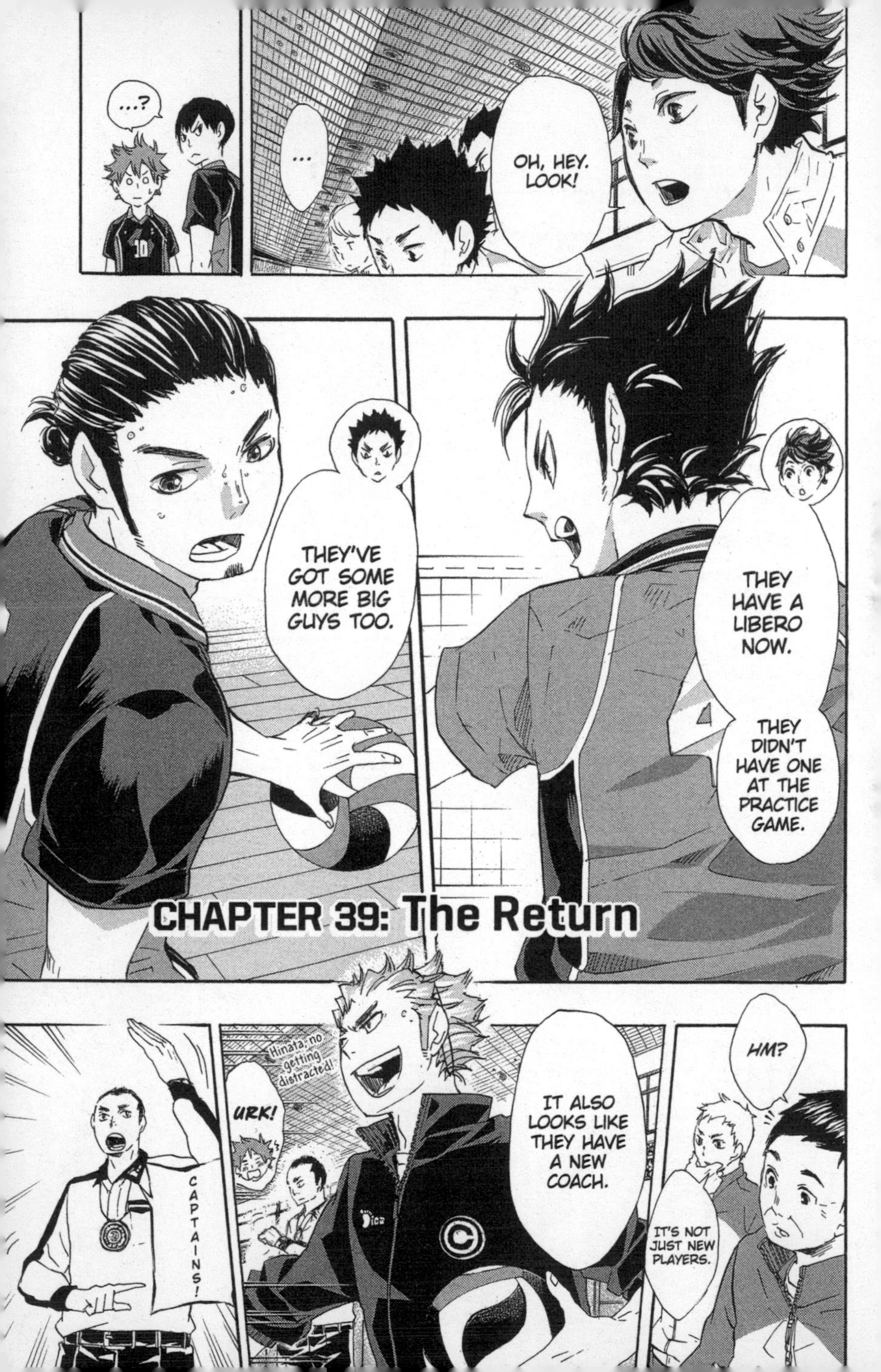
OH, HEY. LOOK!
...
...?
THEY HAVE A LIBERO NOW.
THEY DIDN'T HAVE ONE AT THE PRACTICE GAME.
THEY'VE GOT SOME MORE BIG GUYS TOO.
CHAPTER 39: The Return
HM?
IT'S NOT JUST NEW PLAYERS.
IT ALSO LOOKS LIKE THEY HAVE A NEW COACH.
Hinata, no getting distracted!
URK!
CAPTAINS!

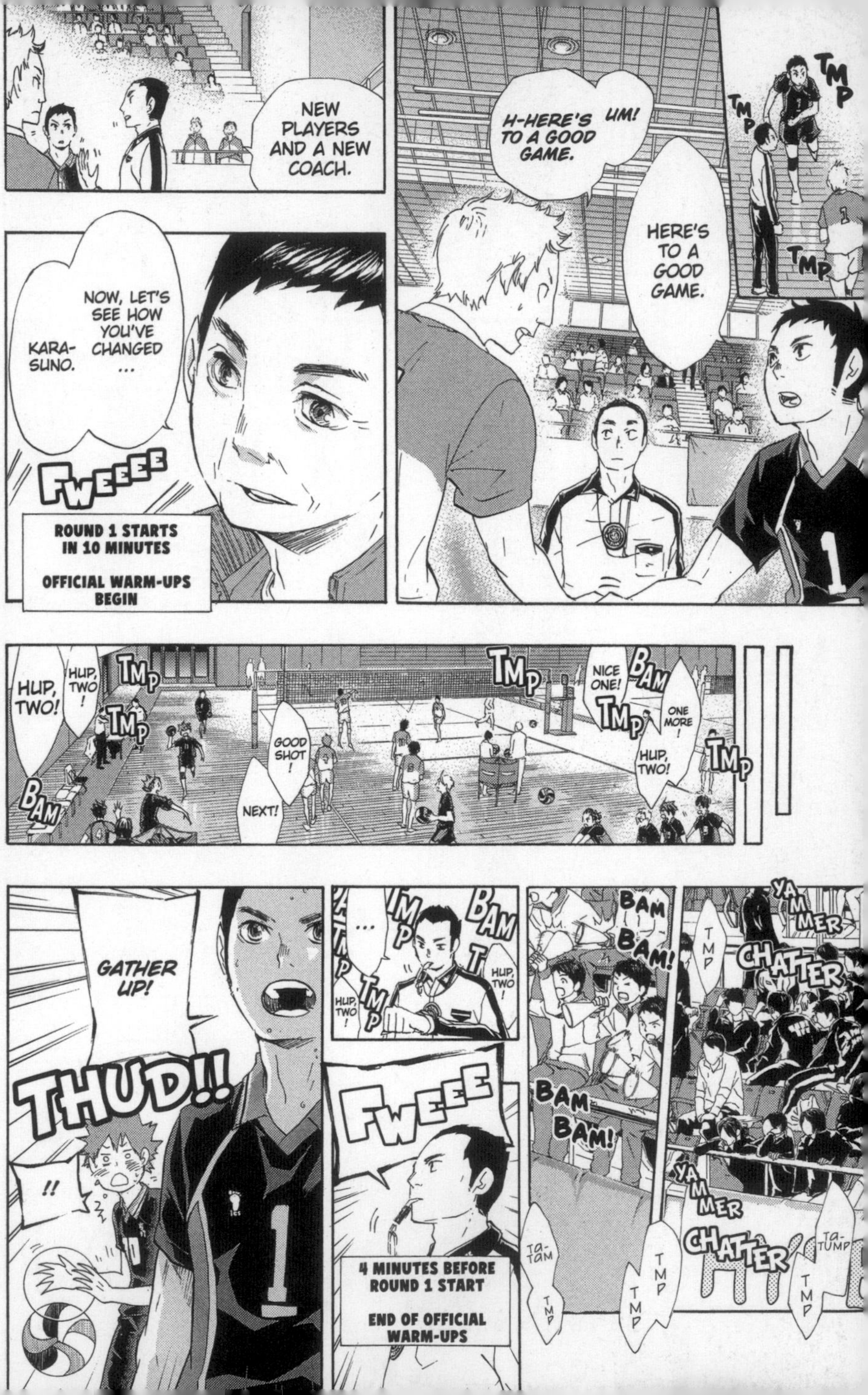
TMP
TMP
TMP
UM!
H-HERE'S TO A GOOD GAME.
HERE'S TO A GOOD GAME.
NEW PLAYERS AND A NEW COACH.
NOW, LET'S SEE HOW YOU'VE CHANGED ...
KARA-SUNO.
FWEEEE
ROUND 1 STARTS IN 10 MINUTES
OFFICIAL WARM-UPS BEGIN
TMP
HUP, TWO!
ONE MORE!
BAM
NICE ONE!
TMP
TMP
GOOD SHOT!
NEXT!
TMP
TMP
HUP, TWO!
HUP, TWO!
BAM
YAMMER
CHATTER
TMP
BAM BAM!
BAM BAM!
YAMMER
CHATTER
TA-TUMP
TMP
TMP
TMP
TA-TAM
TMP
BAM
T
HUP, TWO!
TMP
...
HUP, TWO!
TMP
FWEEE
4 MINUTES BEFORE ROUND 1 START
END OF OFFICIAL WARM-UPS
GATHER UP!
THUD!!
!!

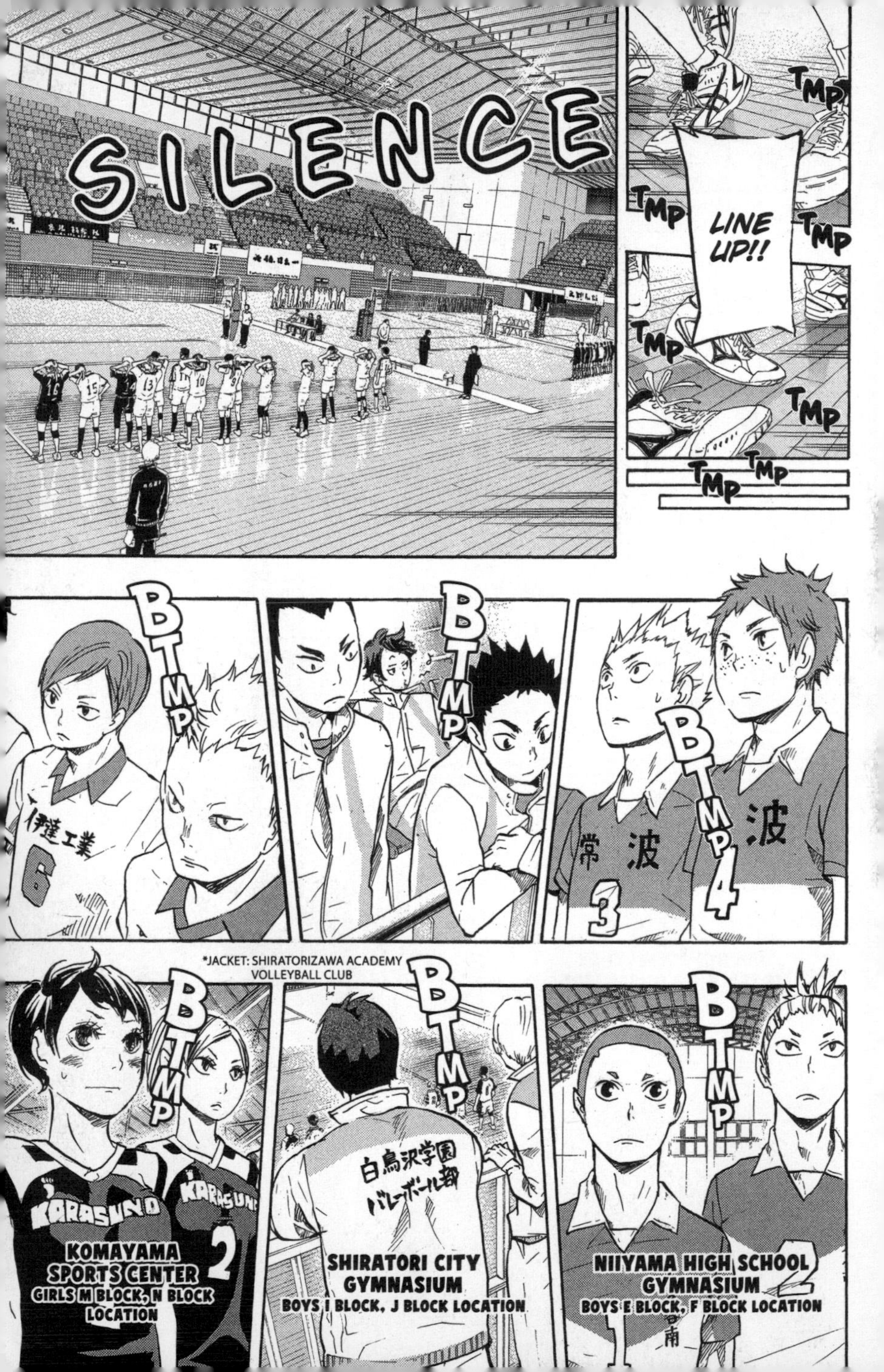
TMP
TMP
TMP
LINE UP!!
TMP
TMP
TMP
TMP
TMP
SILENCE
BTMP
常波
3
波
4
BTMP
伊達工業
6
NIIYAMA HIGH SCHOOL GYMNASIUM
BOYS E BLOCK, F BLOCK LOCATION
BTMP
白鳥沢学園 バレーボール部
*JACKET: SHIRATORIZAWA ACADEMY VOLLEYBALL CLUB
SHIRATORI CITY GYMNASIUM
BOYS I BLOCK, J BLOCK LOCATION
BTMP
KARASUNO
KARASUNO
2
KOMAYAMA SPORTS CENTER
GIRLS M BLOCK, N BLOCK LOCATION

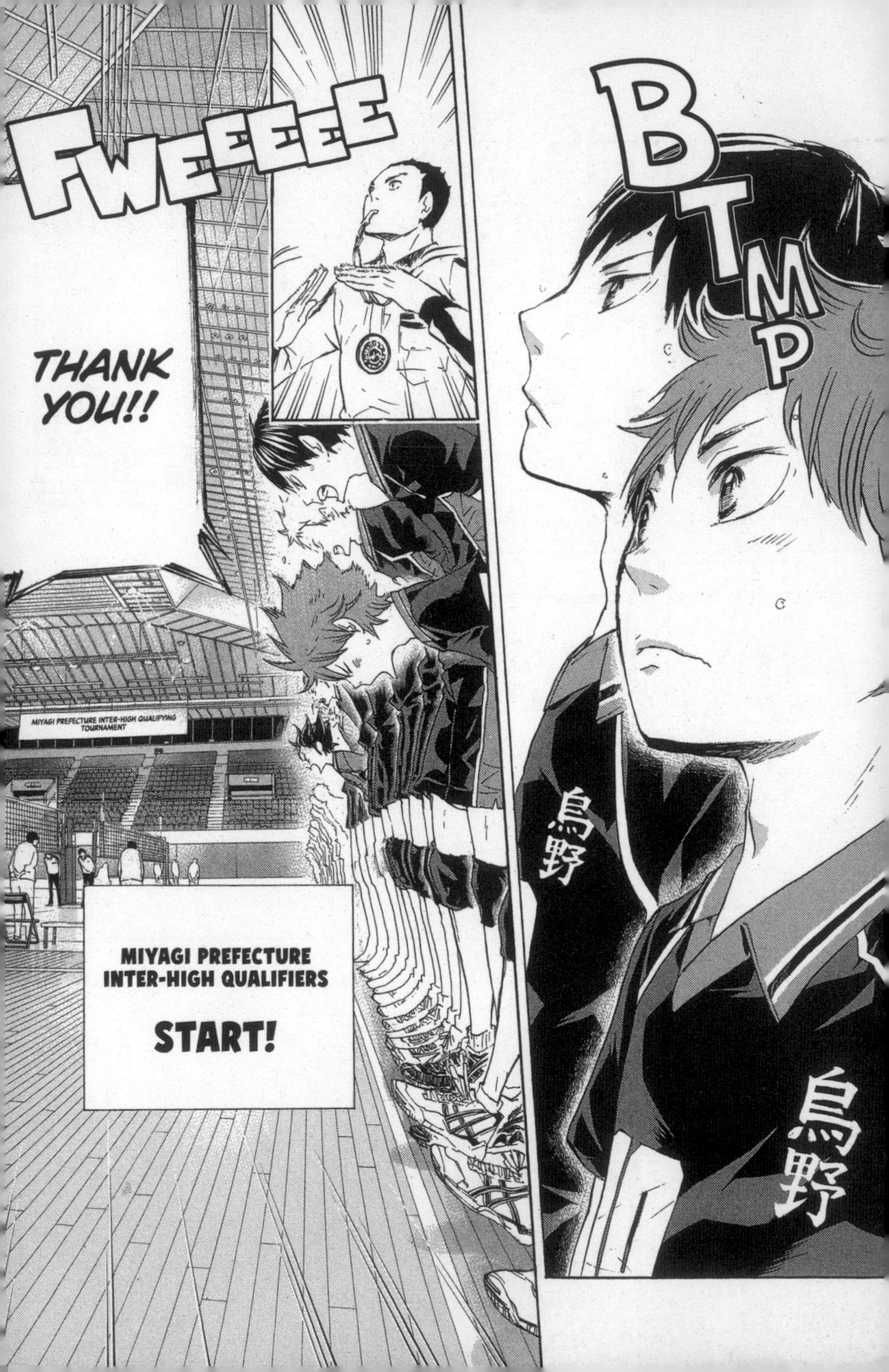
BTMP
烏野
烏野
FWEEEEE
THANK YOU!!
MIYAGI PREFECTURE INTER-HIGH QUALIFYING TOURNAMENT
MIYAGI PREFECTURE INTER-HIGH QUALIFIERS START!

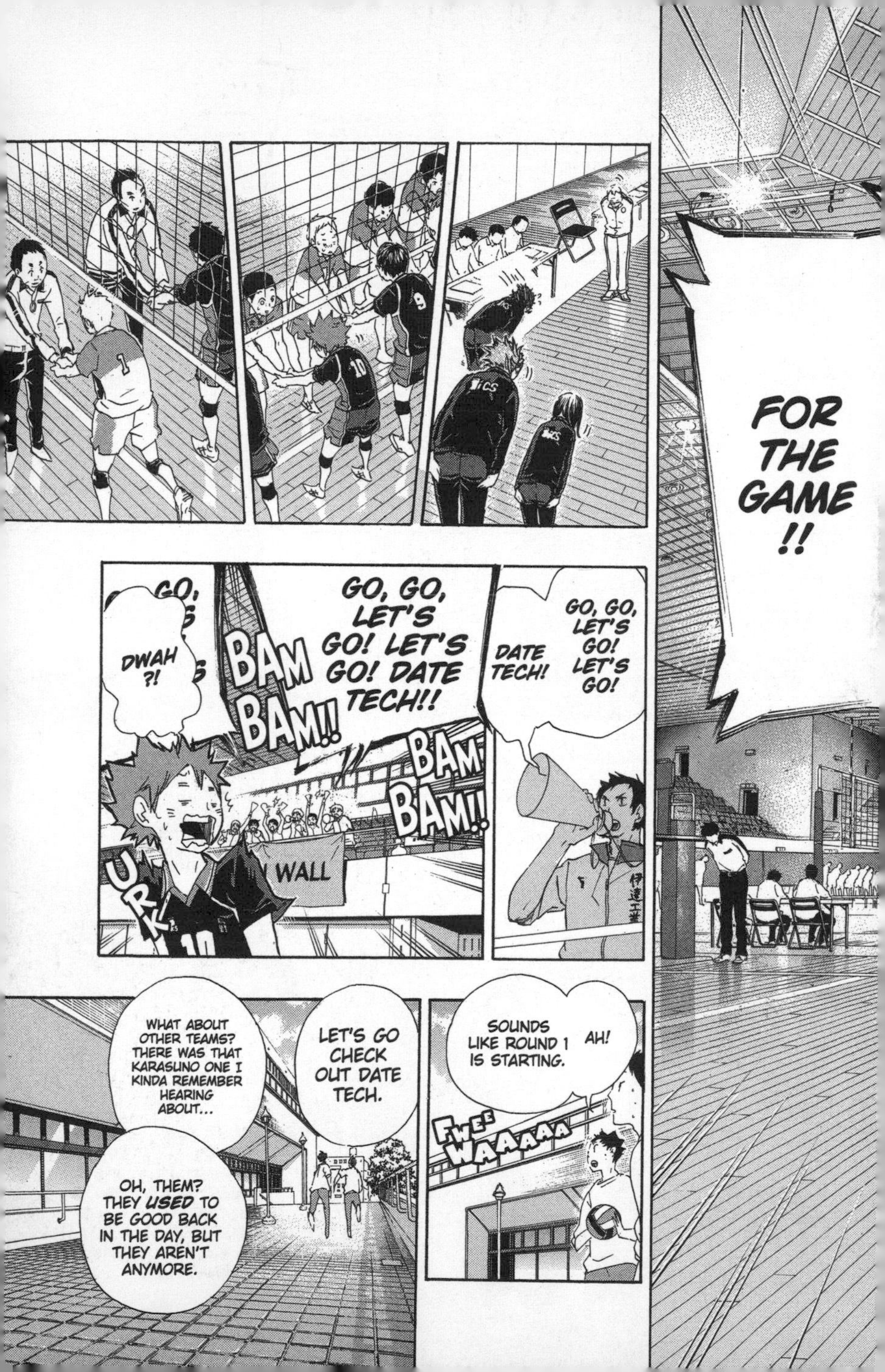
FOR THE GAME!!
GO, GO, LET'S GO! LET'S GO!
DATE TECH!
GO, GO, LET'S GO! LET'S GO! DATE TECH!!
BAM BAM!!
BAM BAM!!
DWAH ?!
URK
WALL
AH!
SOUNDS LIKE ROUND 1 IS STARTING.
FWEE WAAAAAA
LET'S GO CHECK OUT DATE TECH.
WHAT ABOUT OTHER TEAMS? THERE WAS THAT KARASUNO ONE I KINDA REMEMBER HEARING ABOUT...
OH, THEM? THEY *USED* TO BE GOOD BACK IN THE DAY, BUT THEY AREN'T ANYMORE.

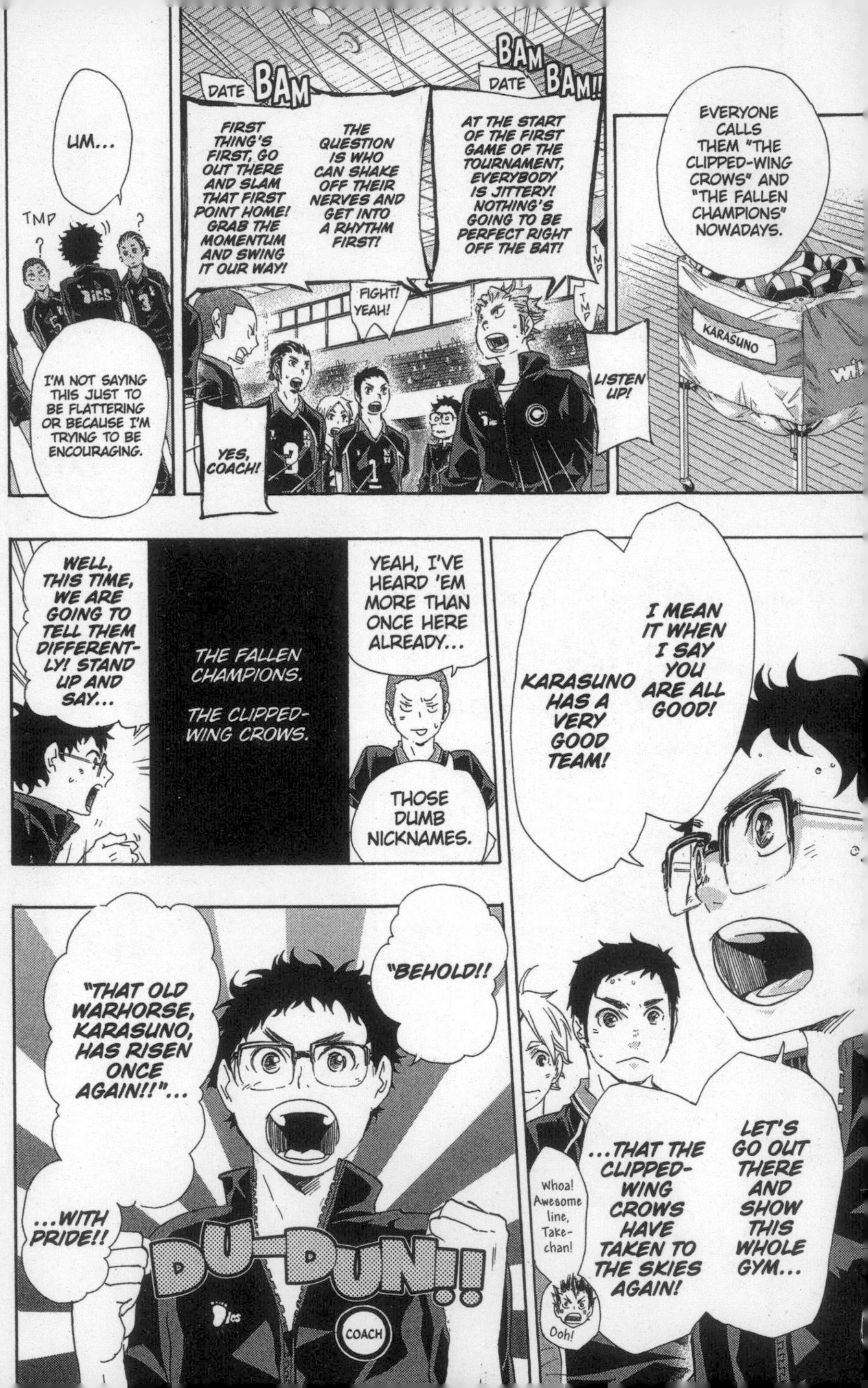
EVERYONE CALLS THEM "THE CLIPPED-WING CROWS" AND "THE FALLEN CHAMPIONS" NOWADAYS.
KARASUNO
BAM BAM!!
DATE
AT THE START OF THE FIRST GAME OF THE TOURNAMENT, EVERYBODY IS JITTERY! NOTHING'S GOING TO BE PERFECT RIGHT OFF THE BAT!
TMP
TMP
LISTEN UP!
FIGHT! YEAH!
THE QUESTION IS WHO CAN SHAKE OFF THEIR NERVES AND GET INTO A RHYTHM FIRST!
DATE
BAM
FIRST THING'S FIRST, GO OUT THERE AND SLAM THAT FIRST POINT HOME! GRAB THE MOMENTUM AND SWING IT OUR WAY!
YES, COACH!
UM...
TMP
?
?
I'M NOT SAYING THIS JUST TO BE FLATTERING OR BECAUSE I'M TRYING TO BE ENCOURAGING.
I MEAN IT WHEN I SAY YOU ARE ALL GOOD!
KARASUNO HAS A VERY GOOD TEAM!
LET'S GO OUT THERE AND SHOW THIS WHOLE GYM...
...THAT THE CLIPPED-WING CROWS HAVE TAKEN TO THE SKIES AGAIN!
Whoa! Awesome line, Take-chan!
Ooh!
YEAH, I'VE HEARD 'EM MORE THAN ONCE HERE ALREADY...
THOSE DUMB NICKNAMES.
THE FALLEN CHAMPIONS.
THE CLIPPED-WING CROWS.
WELL, THIS TIME, WE ARE GOING TO TELL THEM DIFFERENTLY! STAND UP AND SAY...
"BEHOLD!!
"THAT OLD WARHORSE, KARASUNO, HAS RISEN ONCE AGAIN!!"...
...WITH PRIDE!!
DU-DUN!!
COACH

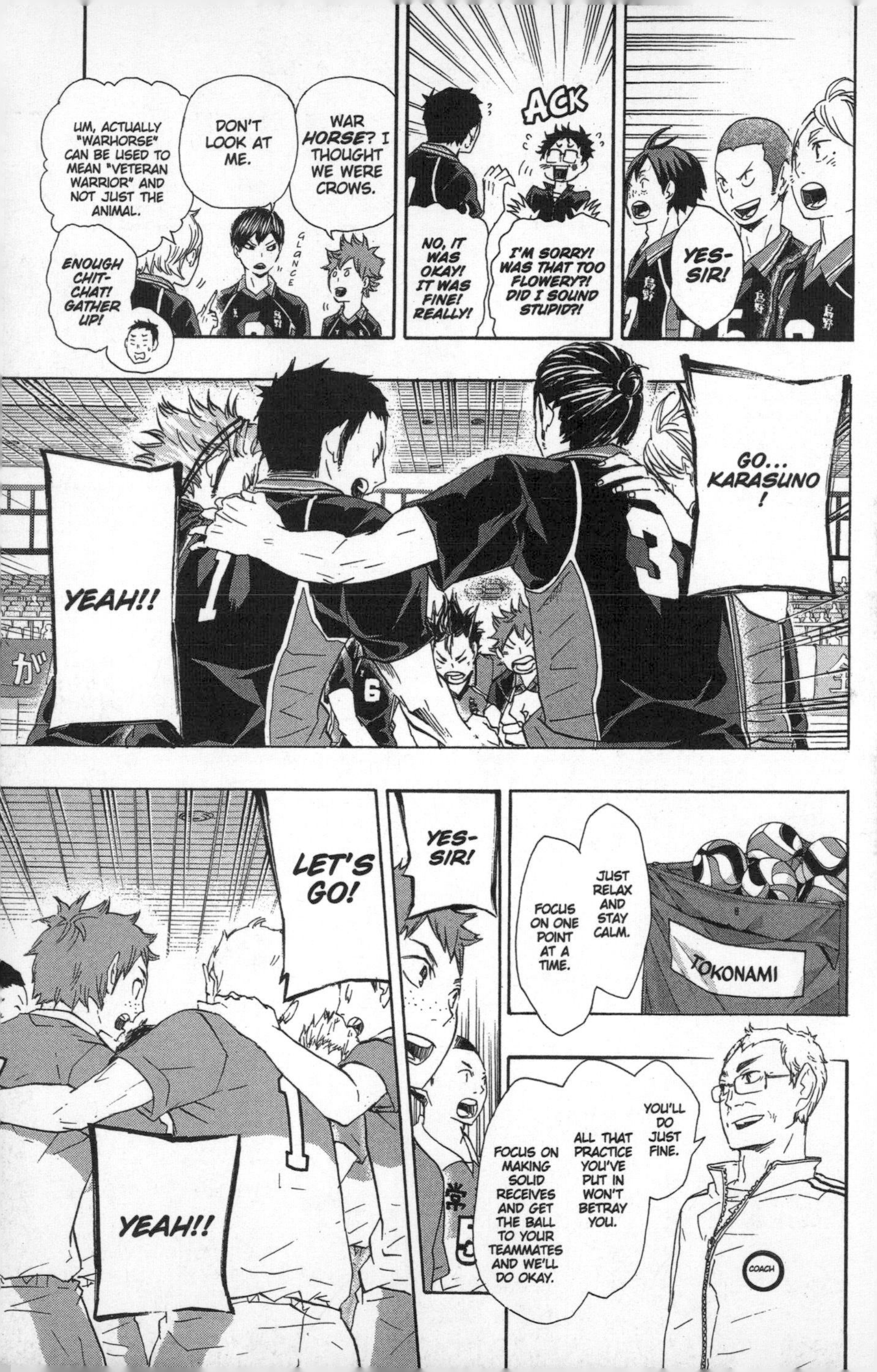
YES-SIR!
ACK
I'M SORRY! WAS THAT TOO FLOWERY?! DID I SOUND STUPID?!
NO, IT WAS OKAY! IT WAS FINE! REALLY!
WAR HORSE? I THOUGHT WE WERE CROWS.
GLANCE
DON'T LOOK AT ME.
UM, ACTUALLY "WARHORSE" CAN BE USED TO MEAN "VETERAN WARRIOR" AND NOT JUST THE ANIMAL.
ENOUGH CHIT-CHAT! GATHER UP!
GO... KARASUNO!
YEAH!!
JUST RELAX AND STAY CALM.
FOCUS ON ONE POINT AT A TIME.
TOKONAMI
YOU'LL DO JUST FINE.
ALL THAT PRACTICE YOU'VE PUT IN WON'T BETRAY YOU.
FOCUS ON MAKING SOLID RECEIVES AND GET THE BALL TO YOUR TEAMMATES AND WE'LL DO OKAY.
COACH
YES-SIR!
LET'S GO!
YEAH!!

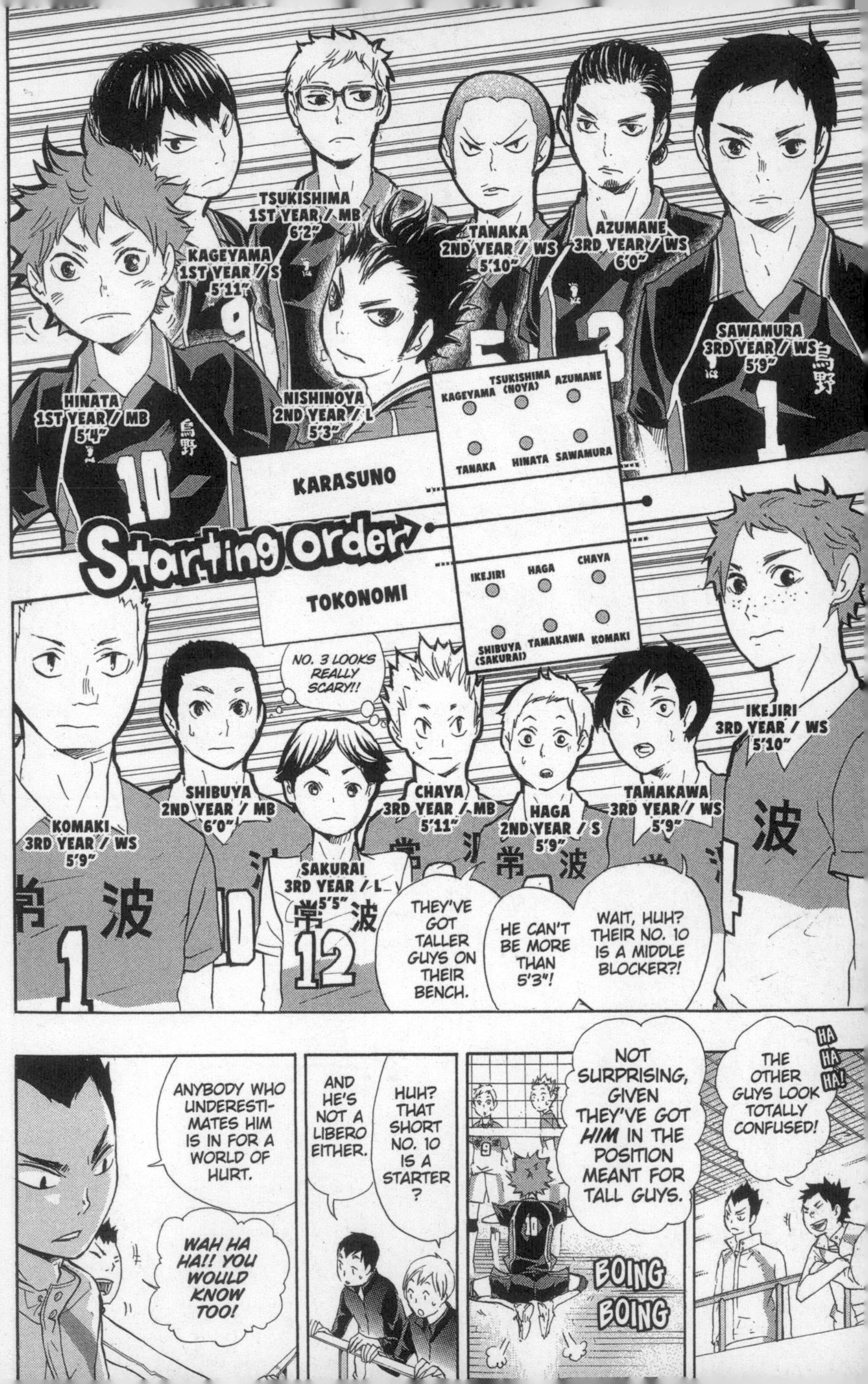
SAWAMURA
3RD YEAR / WS
5'9"
AZUMANE
3RD YEAR / WS
6'0"
TANAKA
2ND YEAR / WS
5'10"
TSUKISHIMA
1ST YEAR / MB
6'2"
KAGEYAMA
1ST YEAR / S
5'11"
NISHINOYA
2ND YEAR / L
5'3"
HINATA
1ST YEAR / MB
5'4"
KARASUNO
KAGEYAMA TSUKISHIMA (NOYA) AZUMANE
TANAKA HINATA SAWAMURA
Starting order
TOKONOMI
IKEJIRI HAGA CHAYA
SHIBUYA (SAKURAI) TAMAKAWA KOMAKI
IKEJIRI
3RD YEAR / WS
5'10"
TAMAKAWA
3RD YEAR / WS
5'9"
HAGA
2ND YEAR / S
5'9"
CHAYA
3RD YEAR / MB
5'11"
NO. 3 LOOKS REALLY SCARY!!
SHIBUYA
2ND YEAR / MB
6'0"
KOMAKI
3RD YEAR / WS
5'9"
SAKURAI
3RD YEAR / L
5'5"
WAIT, HUH? THEIR NO. 10 IS A MIDDLE BLOCKER?!
HE CAN'T BE MORE THAN 5'3"!
THEY'VE GOT TALLER GUYS ON THEIR BENCH.
HA HA HA!
THE OTHER GUYS LOOK TOTALLY CONFUSED!
NOT SURPRISING, GIVEN THEY'VE GOT *HIM* IN THE POSITION MEANT FOR TALL GUYS.
BOING BOING
HUH? THAT SHORT NO. 10 IS A STARTER?
AND HE'S NOT A LIBERO EITHER.
ANYBODY WHO UNDERESTIMATES HIM IS IN FOR A WORLD OF HURT.
WAH HA HA!! YOU WOULD KNOW TOO!

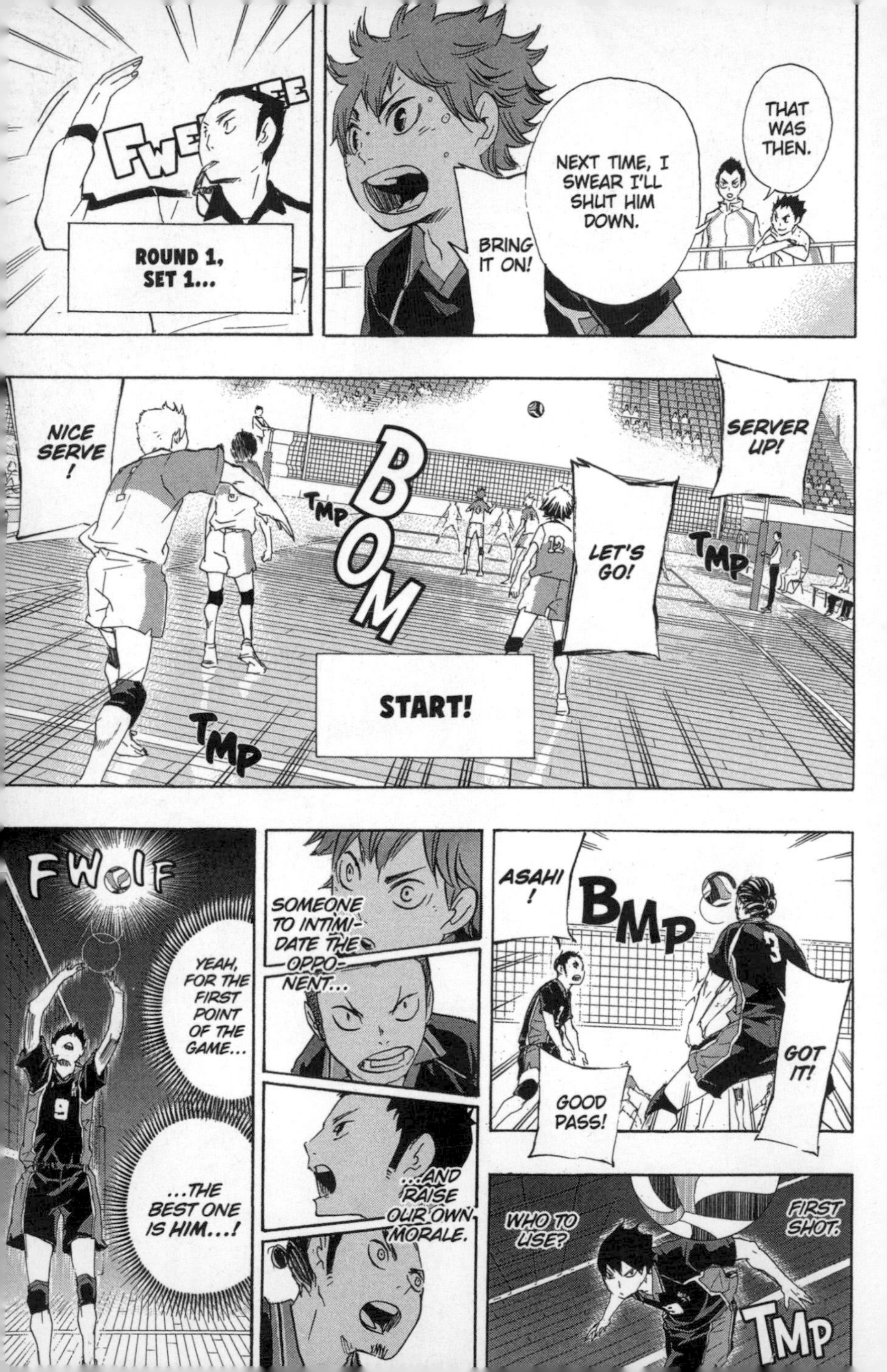
THAT WAS THEN.
NEXT TIME, I SWEAR I'LL SHUT HIM DOWN.
BRING IT ON!
ROUND 1, SET 1...
SERVER UP!
LET'S GO!
TMP
BOM
TMP
NICE SERVE!
START!
TMP
BMP
ASAHI!
GOT IT!
GOOD PASS!
FIRST SHOT.
WHO TO USE?
TMP
SOMEONE TO INTIMIDATE THE OPPONENT...
...AND RAISE OUR OWN MORALE.
FWIF
YEAH, FOR THE FIRST POINT OF THE GAME...
...THE BEST ONE IS HIM...!

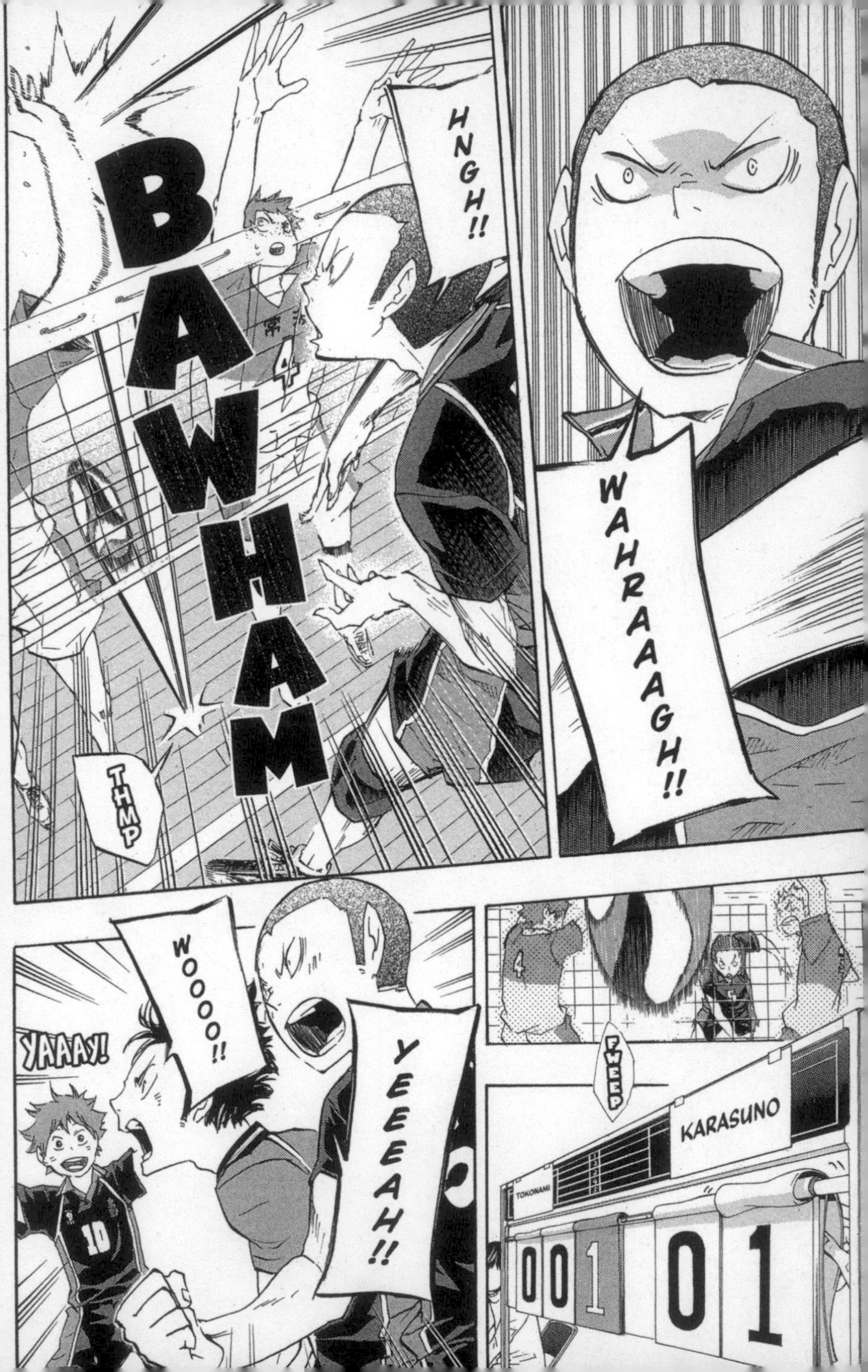
WAHRAAAAGH!!
HNGH!!
BAWHAM
THMP
FWEEP
KARASUNO
TOKONAMI
001
01
YEEEAH!!
WOOOOO!!
YAAAY!

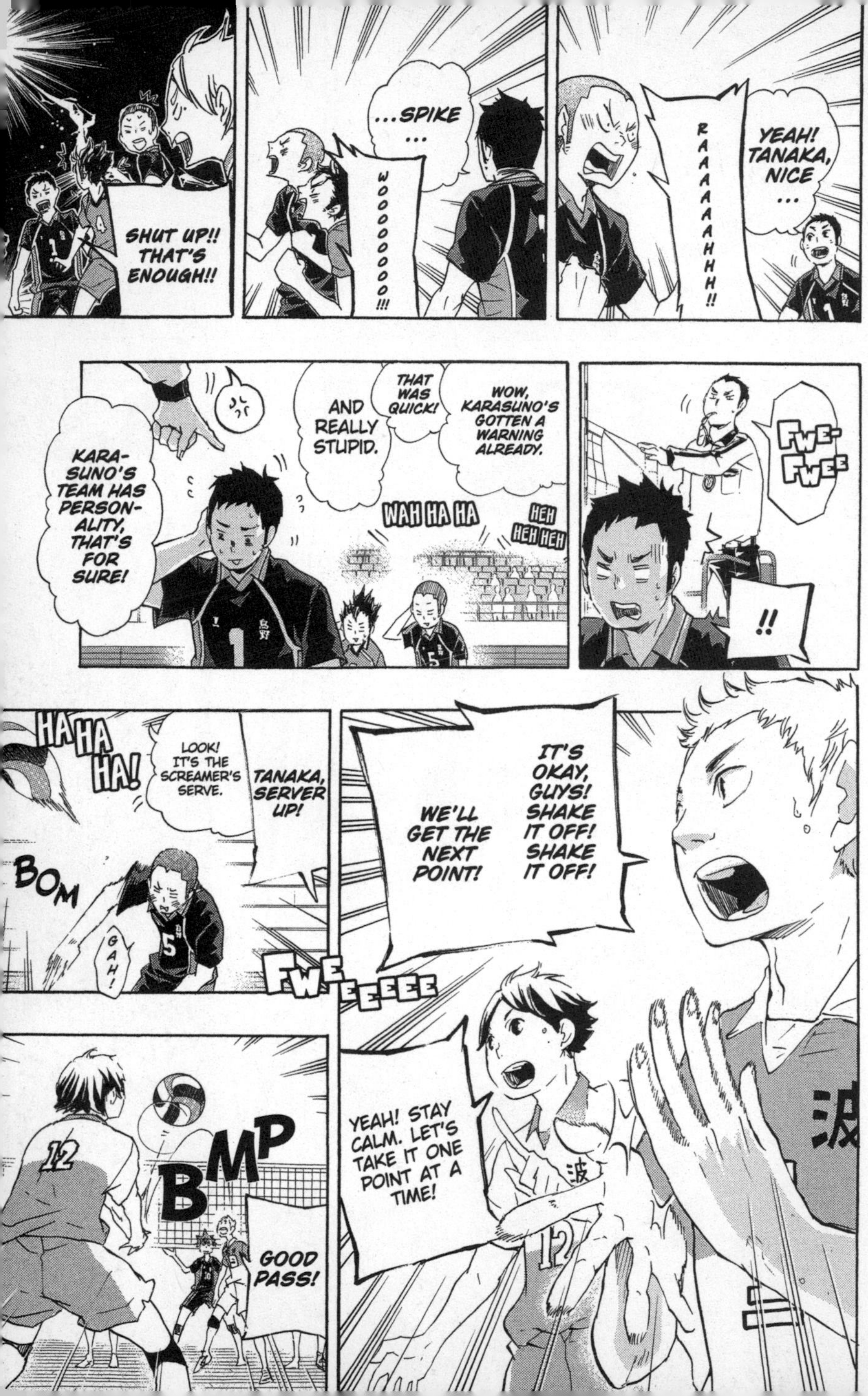
YEAH! TANAKA, NICE ...
RAAAAAAAHHH!!
...SPIKE ...
WOOOOOOOOO!!!
SHUT UP!! THAT'S ENOUGH!!
FWE-FWEE
!!
WOW, KARASUNO'S GOTTEN A WARNING ALREADY.
THAT WAS QUICK!
AND REALLY STUPID.
HEH HEH HEH
WAH HA HA
KARA-SUNO'S TEAM HAS PERSON-ALITY, THAT'S FOR SURE!
IT'S OKAY, GUYS! SHAKE IT OFF! SHAKE IT OFF!
WE'LL GET THE NEXT POINT!
YEAH! STAY CALM. LET'S TAKE IT ONE POINT AT A TIME!
TANAKA, SERVER UP!
LOOK! IT'S THE SCREAMER'S SERVE.
HA HA HA!
BOM
GAH!
FWEEEEEE
BMP
GOOD PASS!

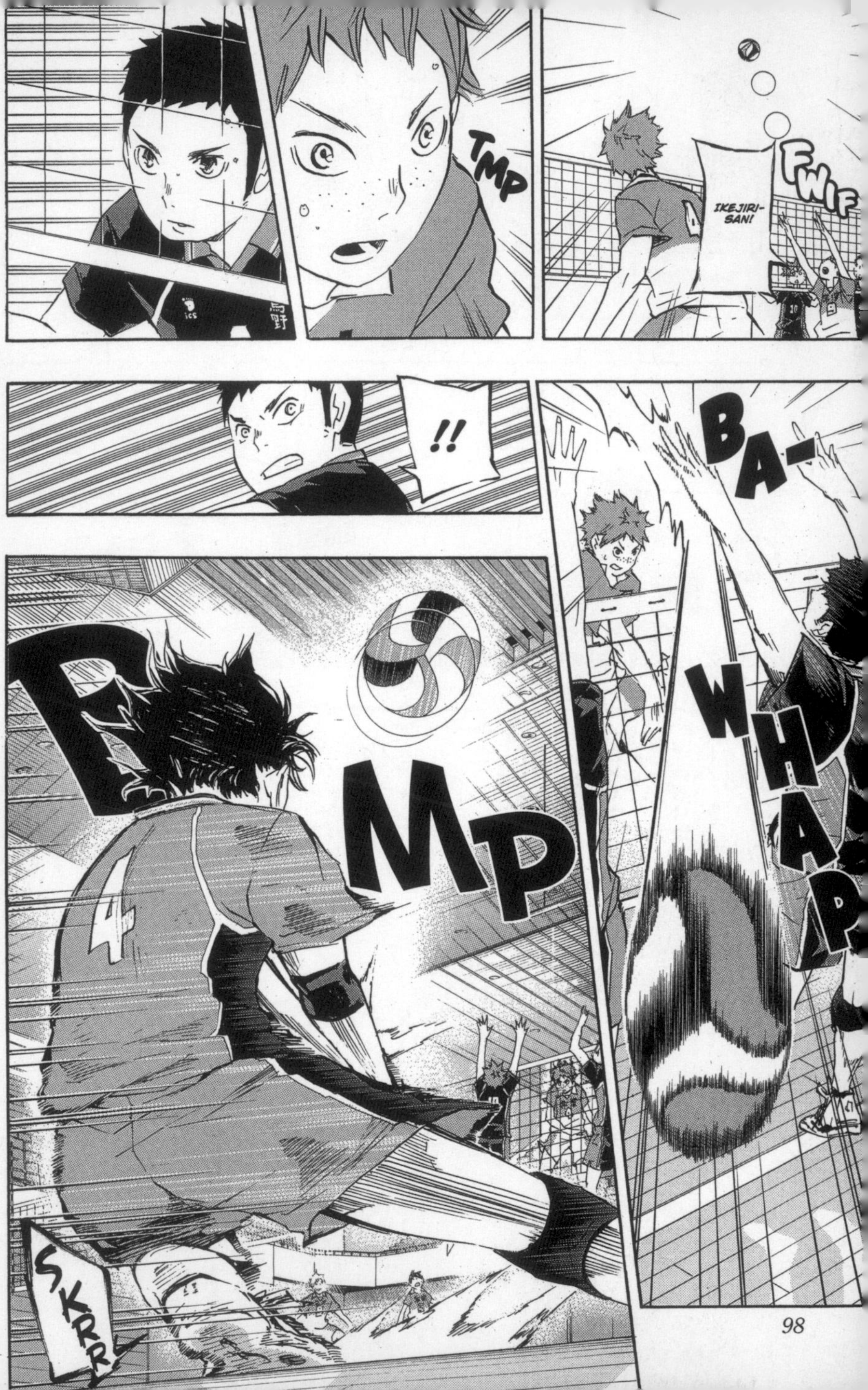
FWIF
IKEJIRI-SAN!
TMP
BA-
WHAP
!!
MP
SKRR

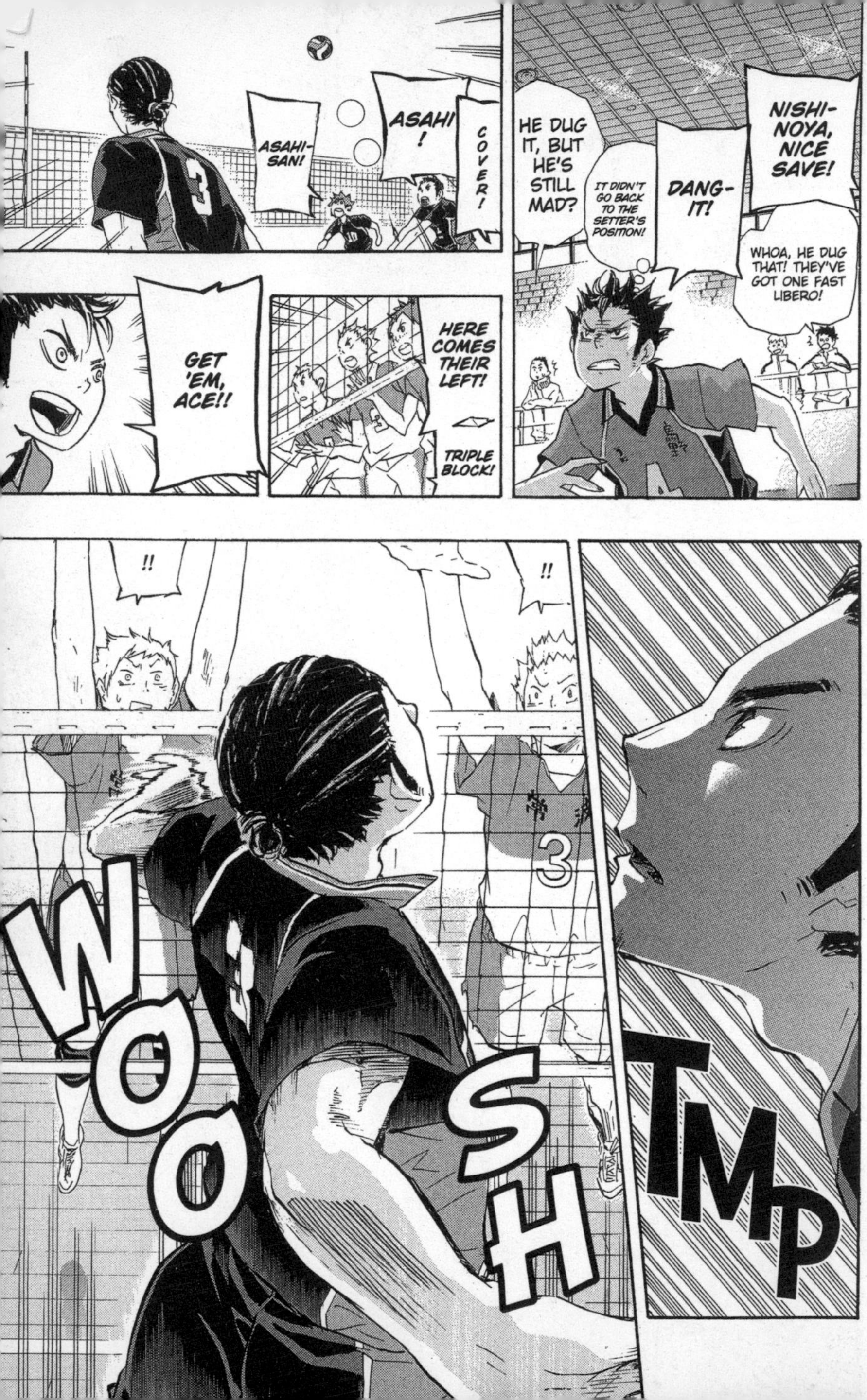
NISHI-NOYA, NICE SAVE!
DANG-IT!
HE DUG IT, BUT HE'S STILL MAD?
IT DIDN'T GO BACK TO THE SETTER'S POSITION!
WHOA, HE DUG THAT! THEY'VE GOT ONE FAST LIBERO!
COVER!
ASAHI!
ASAHI-SAN!
HERE COMES THEIR LEFT!
TRIPLE BLOCK!
GET 'EM, ACE!!
TMP
!!
!!
WOOSH

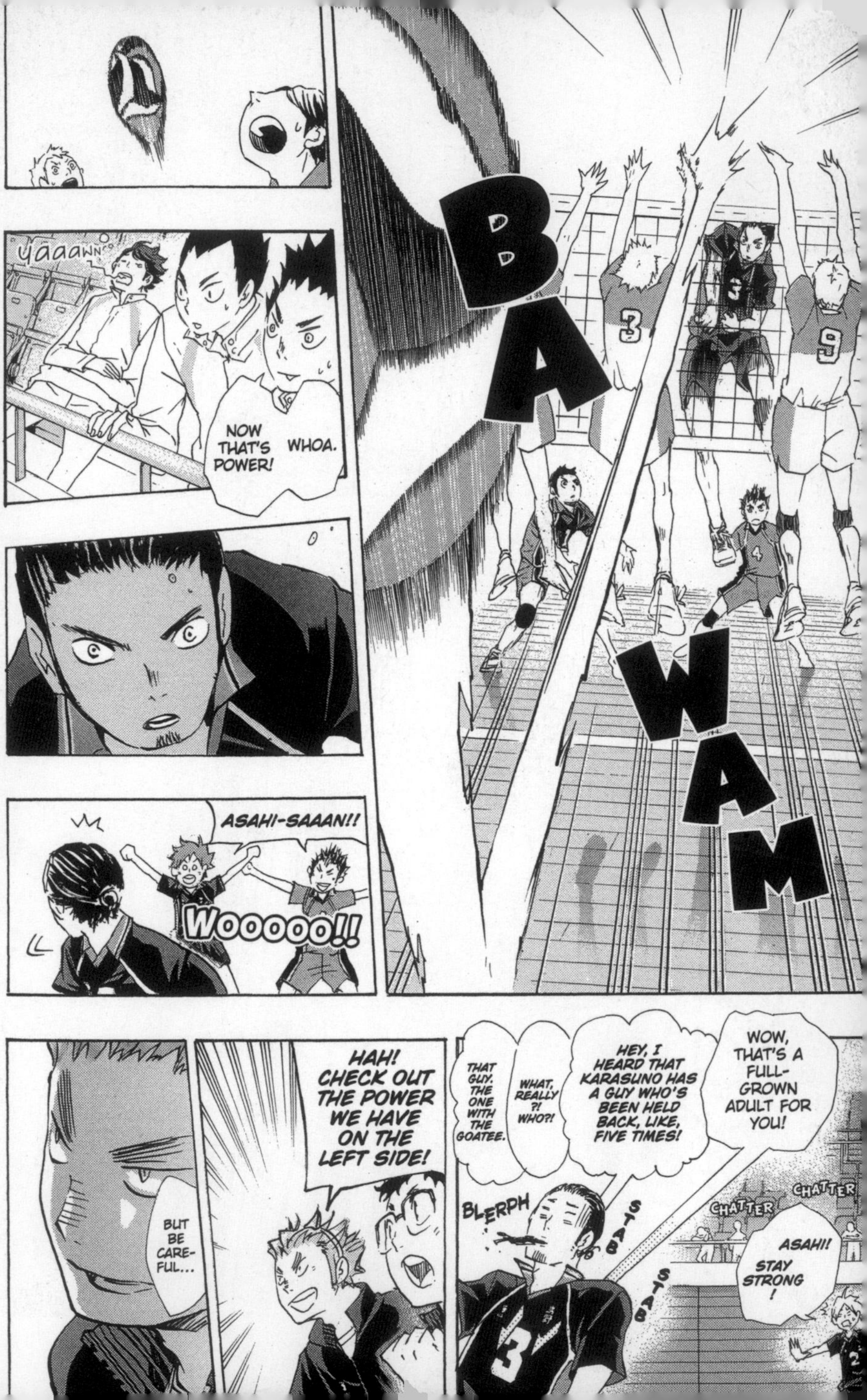
BA
WAM
yaaawn
WHOA.
NOW THAT'S POWER!
ASAHI-SAAAN!!
Wooooo!!
WOW, THAT'S A FULL-GROWN ADULT FOR YOU!
HEY, I HEARD THAT KARASUNO HAS A GUY WHO'S BEEN HELD BACK, LIKE, FIVE TIMES!
WHAT, REALLY?! WHO?!
THAT GUY. THE ONE WITH THE GOATEE.
CHATTER
CHATTER
ASAHI! STAY STRONG!
STAB
STAB
BLERPH
HAH! CHECK OUT THE POWER WE HAVE ON THE LEFT SIDE!
BUT BE CARE-FUL...

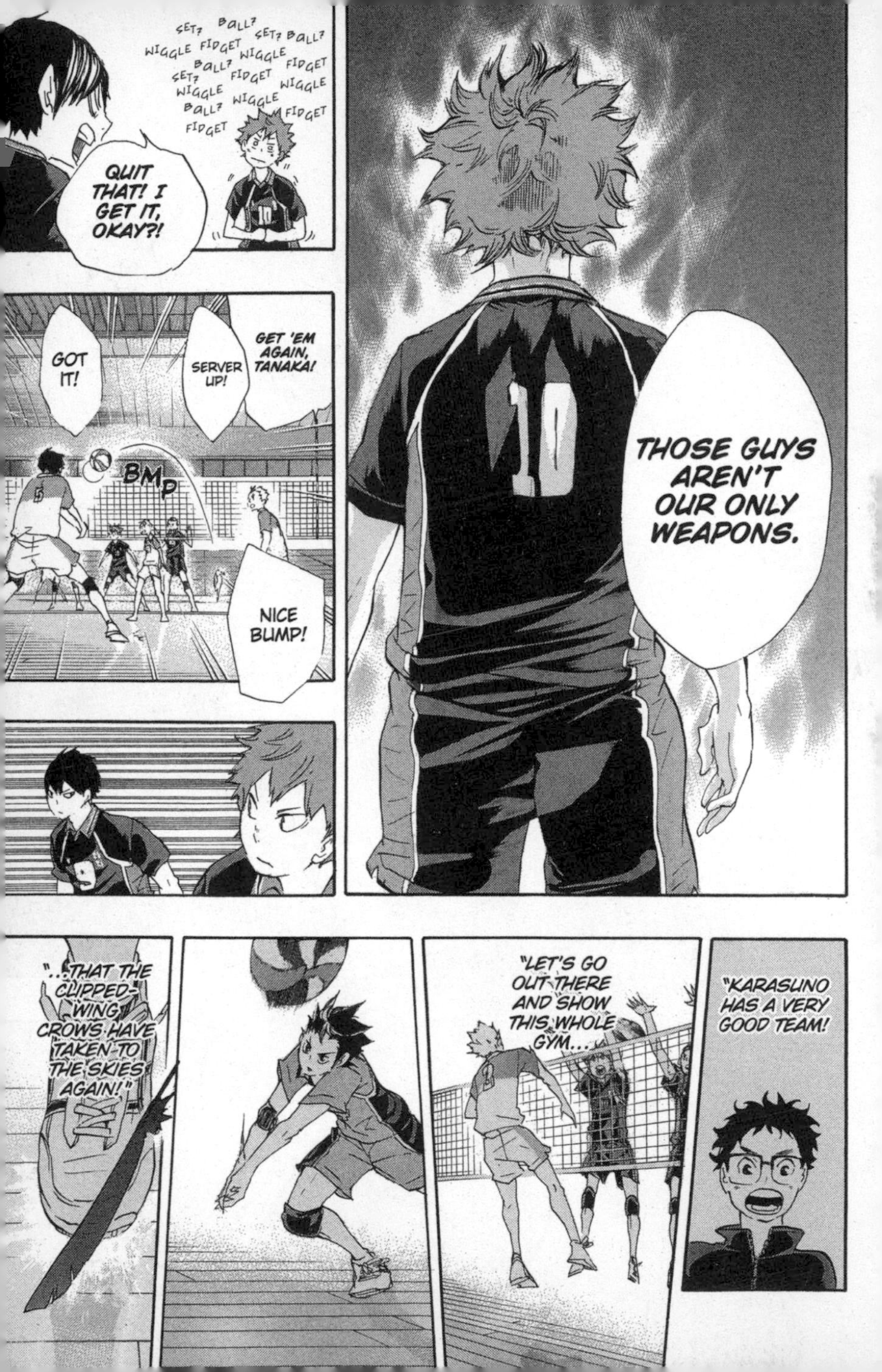
THOSE GUYS AREN'T OUR ONLY WEAPONS.
SET? BALL? WIGGLE FIDGET SET? BALL? WIGGLE BALL? WIGGLE FIDGET SET? FIDGET WIGGLE BALL? WIGGLE WIGGLE FIDGET FIDGET
QUIT THAT! I GET IT, OKAY?!
GET 'EM AGAIN, TANAKA!
SERVER UP!
GOT IT!
BMP
NICE BUMP!
"KARASUNO HAS A VERY GOOD TEAM!
"LET'S GO OUT THERE AND SHOW THIS WHOLE GYM...
"...THAT THE CLIPPED-WING CROWS HAVE TAKEN TO THE SKIES AGAIN!"

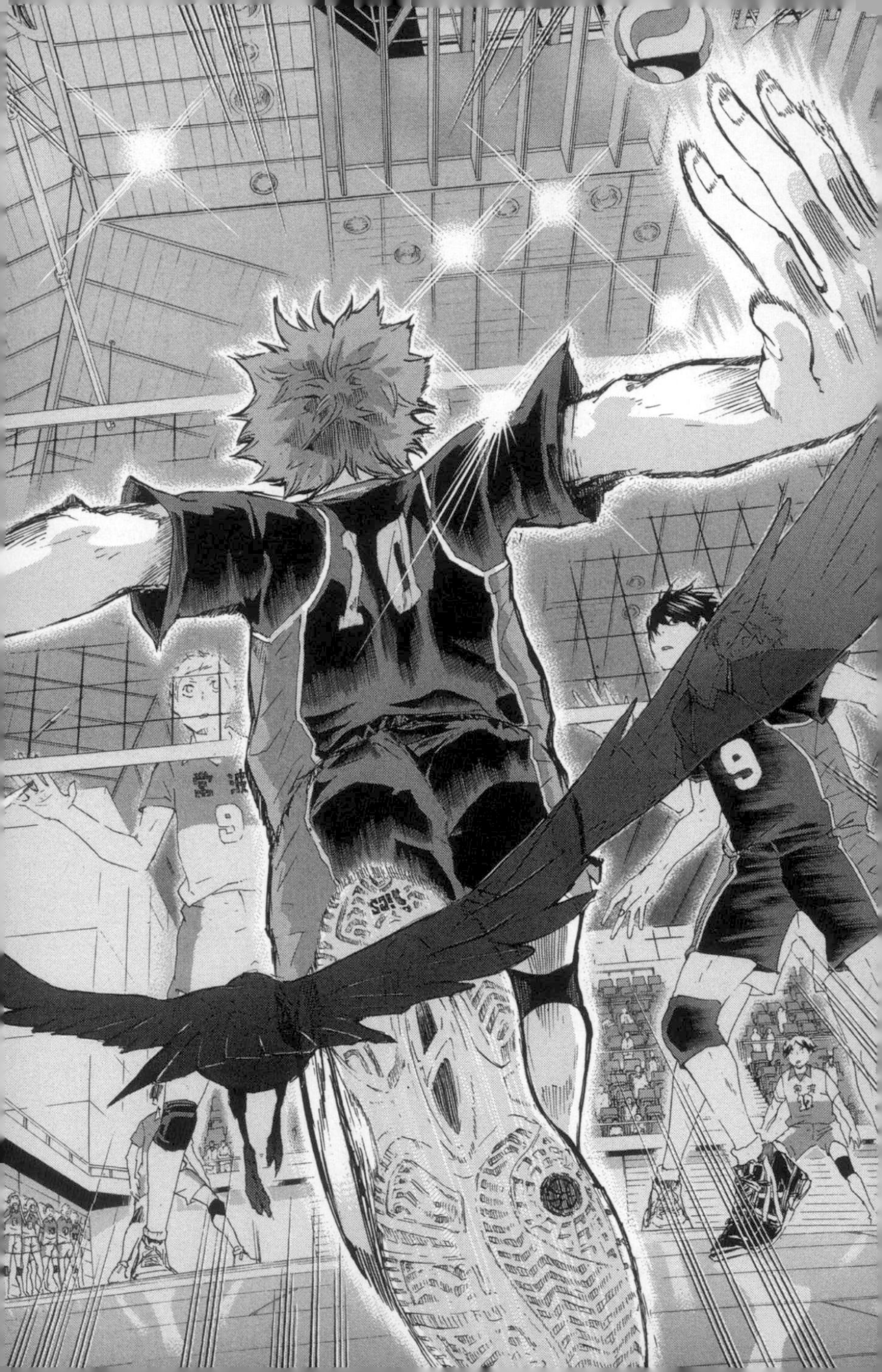

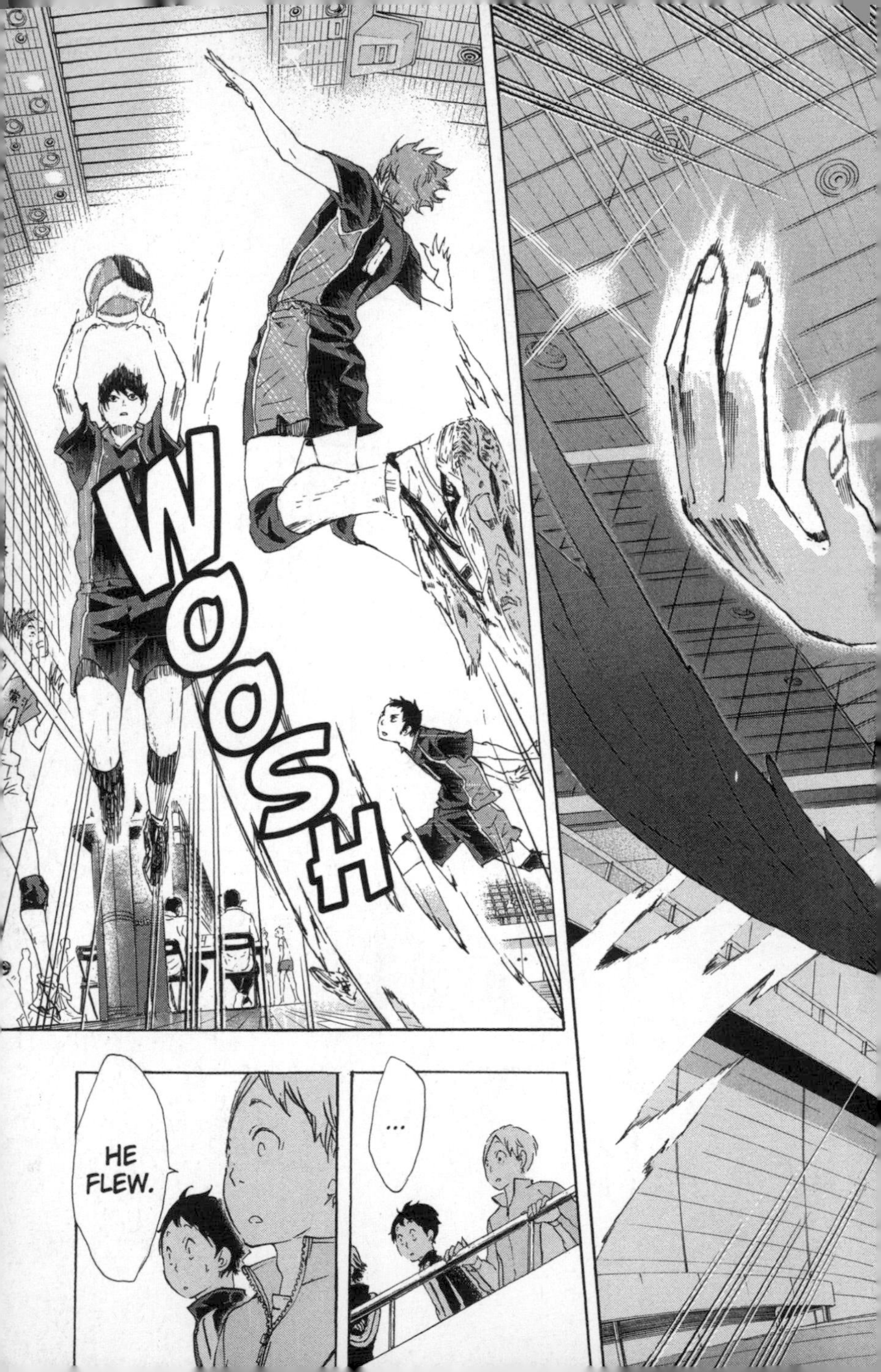
WOOSH
...
HE FLEW.

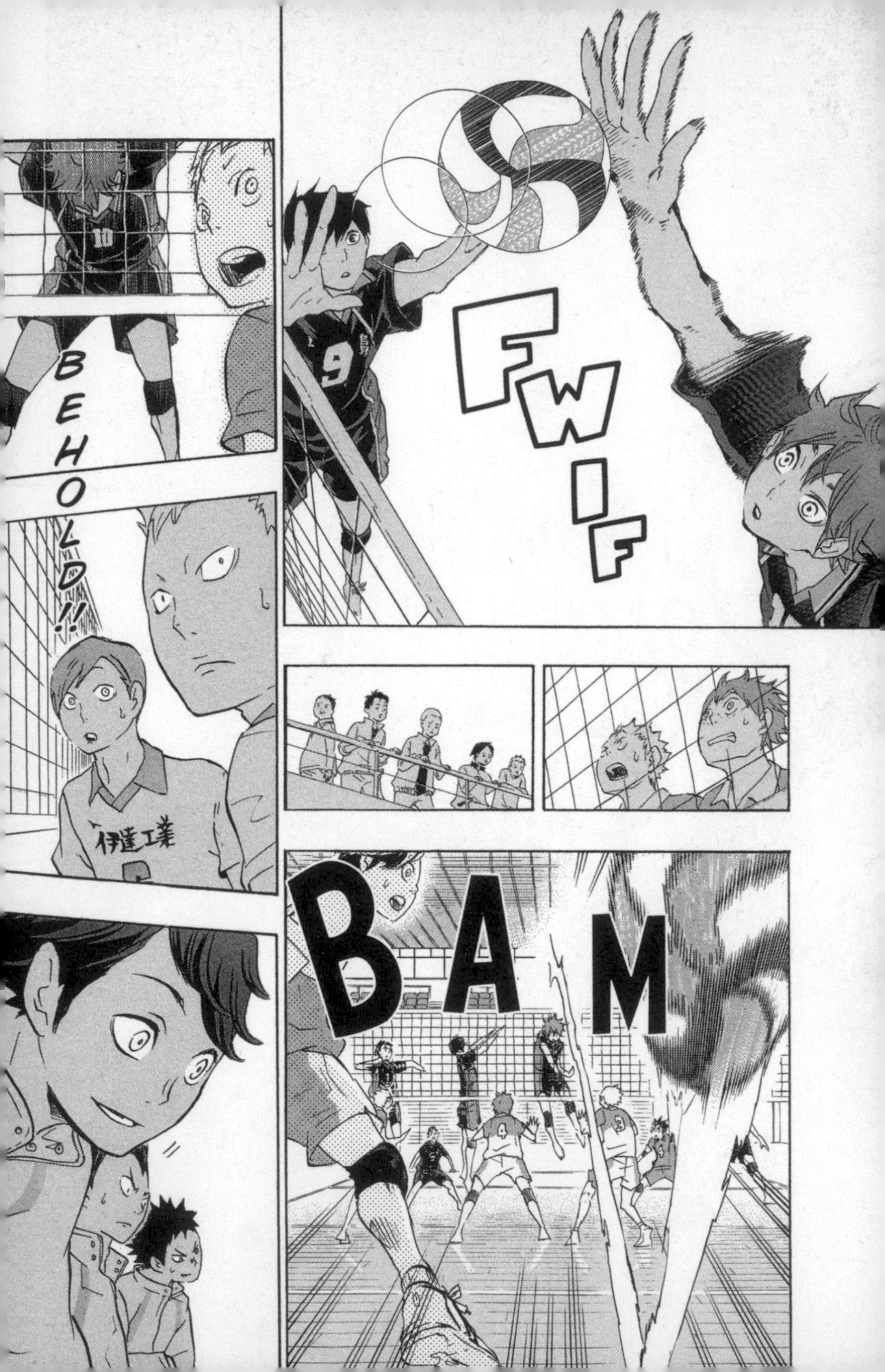
FWIF
BAM
BEHOLD!!
伊達工業

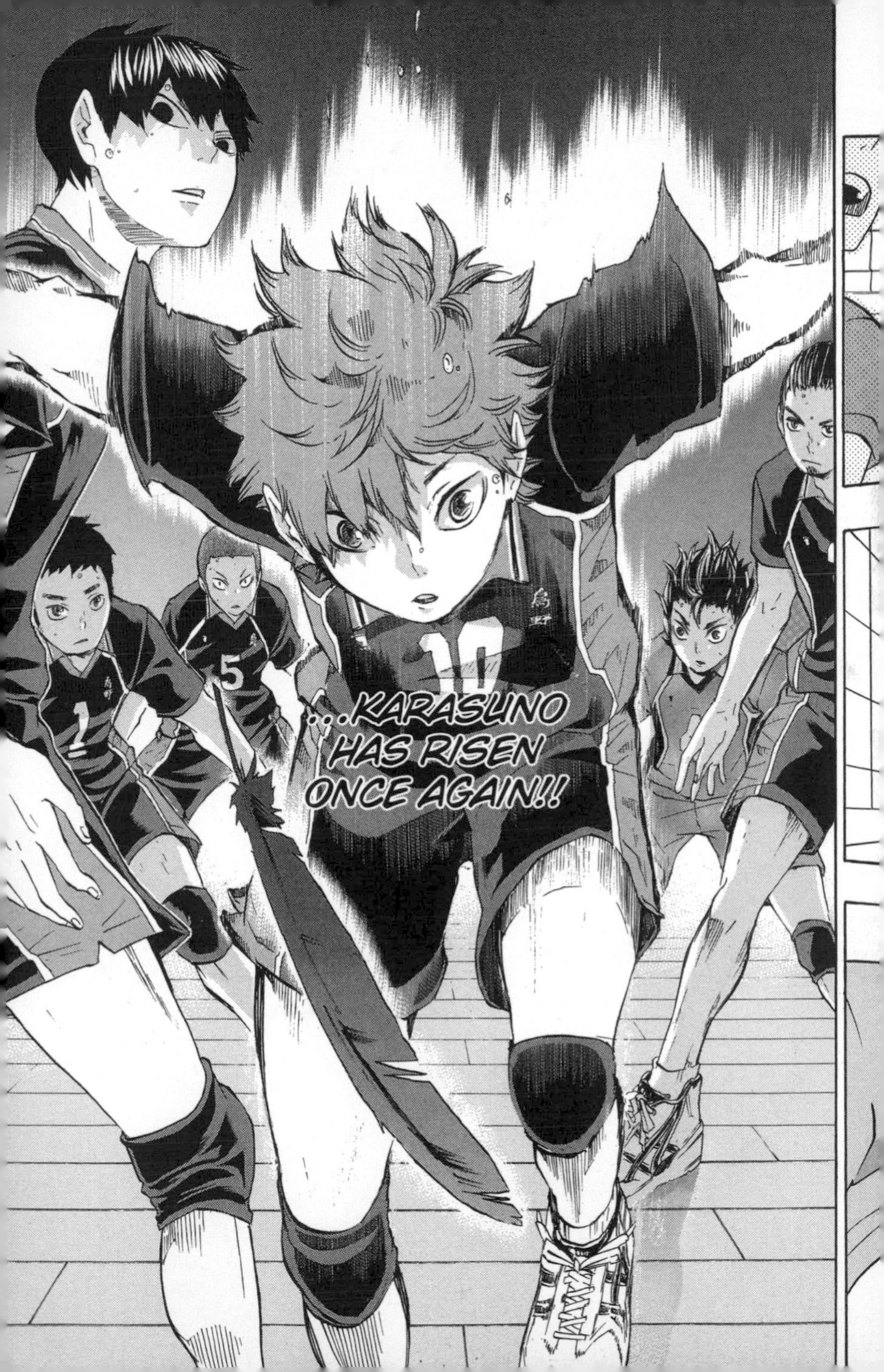
...KARASUNO HAS RISEN ONCE AGAIN!!

← Three pages have been added to the following chapter (chapter 40) since it originally ran in *Weekly Shonen Jump*. The content of the chapter hasn't changed significantly, but due to page constraints, I had to trim a few things out from the original run. I later went back and added a little back in.

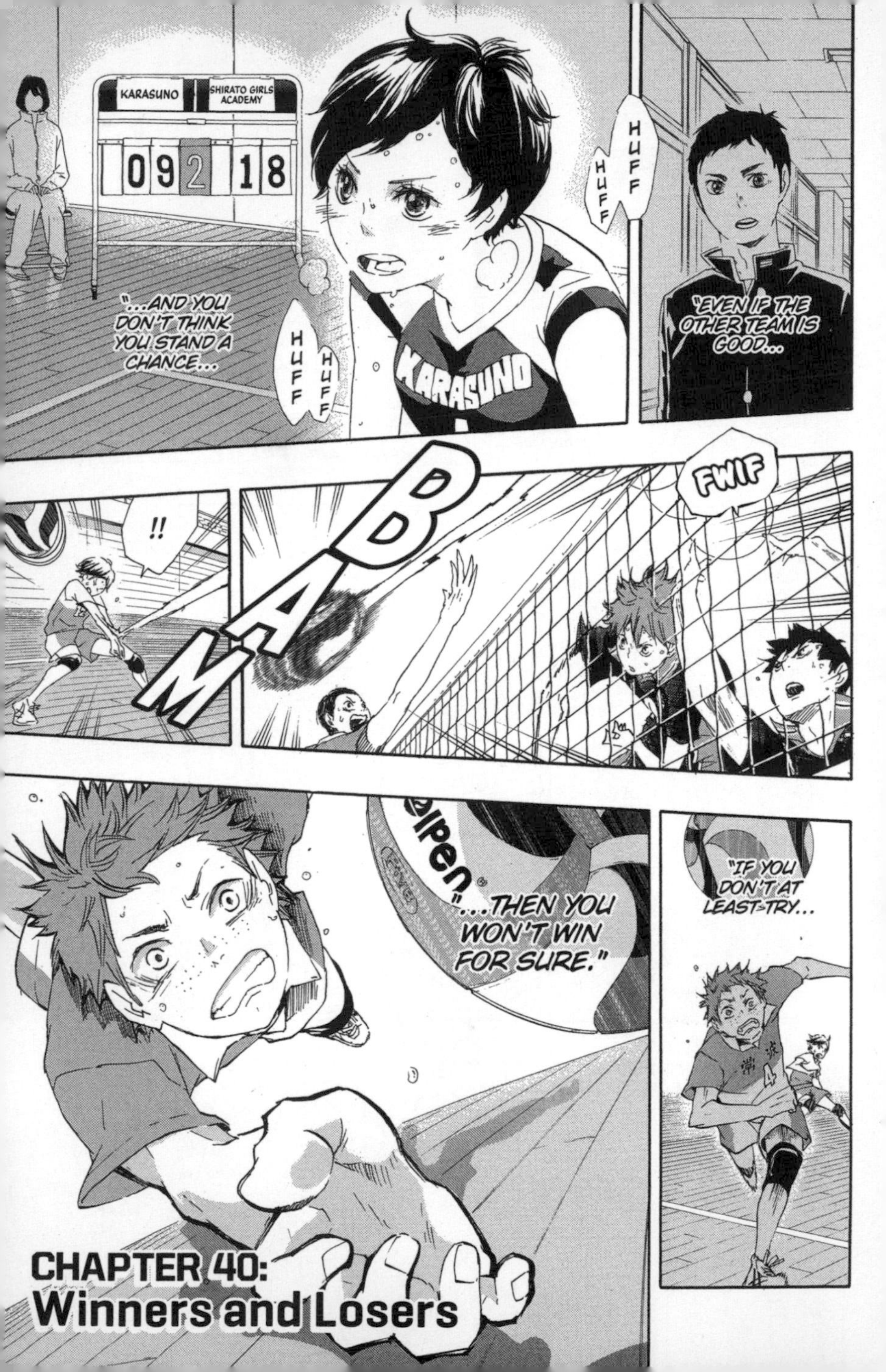
"EVEN IF THE OTHER TEAM IS GOOD...
HUFF HUFF
KARASUNO
SHIRATO GIRLS ACADEMY
09 2 18
KARASUNO
HUFF HUFF
"...AND YOU DON'T THINK YOU STAND A CHANCE...
FWIF
BAM
!!
"IF YOU DON'T AT LEAST TRY...
"...THEN YOU WON'T WIN FOR SURE."

CHAPTER 40: Winners and Losers

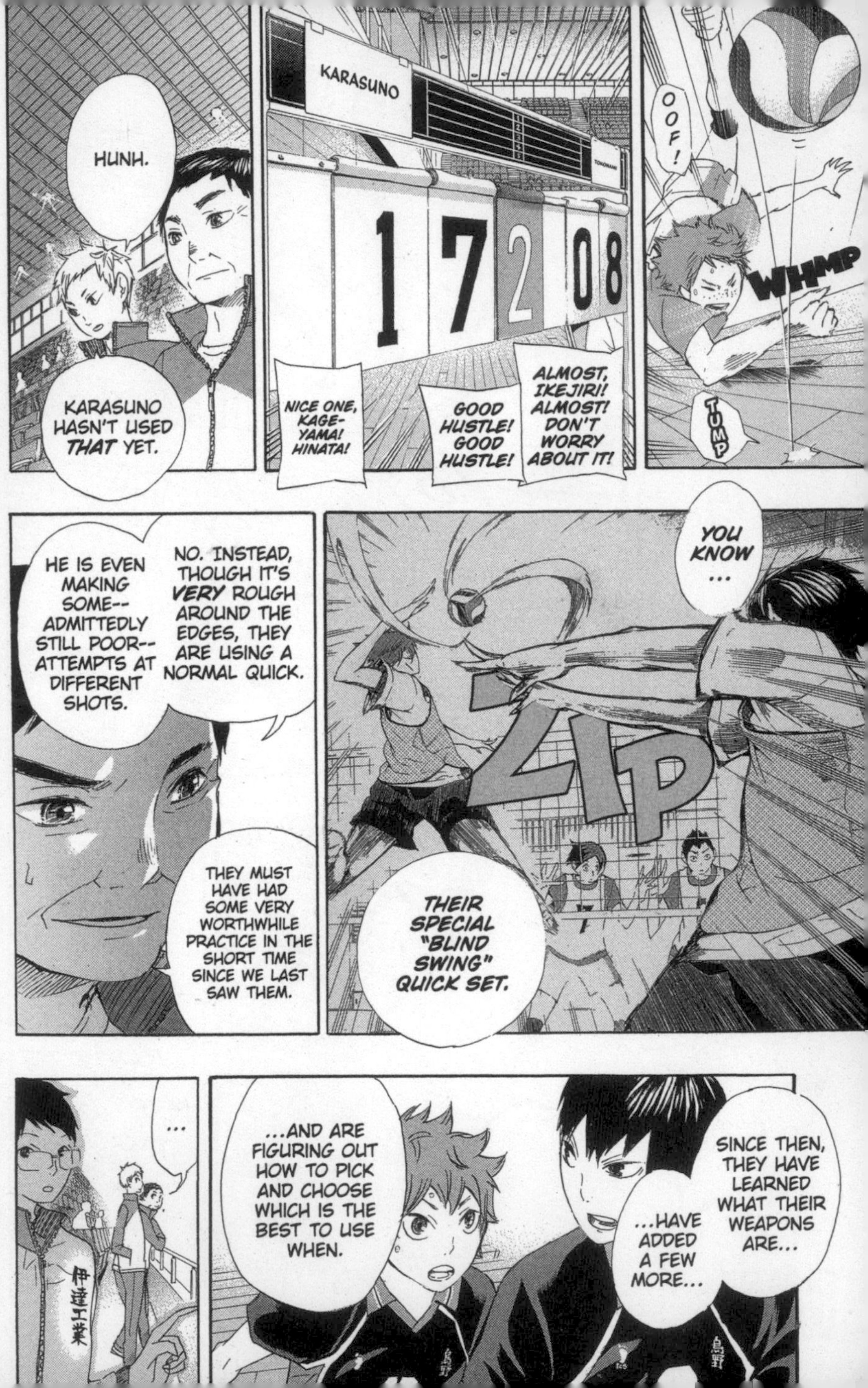
OOF!
WHMP
TUMP
KARASUNO
ALMOST, IKEJIRI! ALMOST! DON'T WORRY ABOUT IT!
GOOD HUSTLE! GOOD HUSTLE!
NICE ONE, KAGE-YAMA! HINATA!
HUNH.
KARASUNO HASN'T USED THAT YET.
YOU KNOW...
ZIP
THEIR SPECIAL "BLIND SWING" QUICK SET.
NO. INSTEAD, THOUGH IT'S VERY ROUGH AROUND THE EDGES, THEY ARE USING A NORMAL QUICK.
HE IS EVEN MAKING SOME--ADMITTEDLY STILL POOR--ATTEMPTS AT DIFFERENT SHOTS.
THEY MUST HAVE HAD SOME VERY WORTHWHILE PRACTICE IN THE SHORT TIME SINCE WE LAST SAW THEM.
SINCE THEN, THEY HAVE LEARNED WHAT THEIR WEAPONS ARE...
...HAVE ADDED A FEW MORE...
...AND ARE FIGURING OUT HOW TO PICK AND CHOOSE WHICH IS THE BEST TO USE WHEN.
...
伊達工業

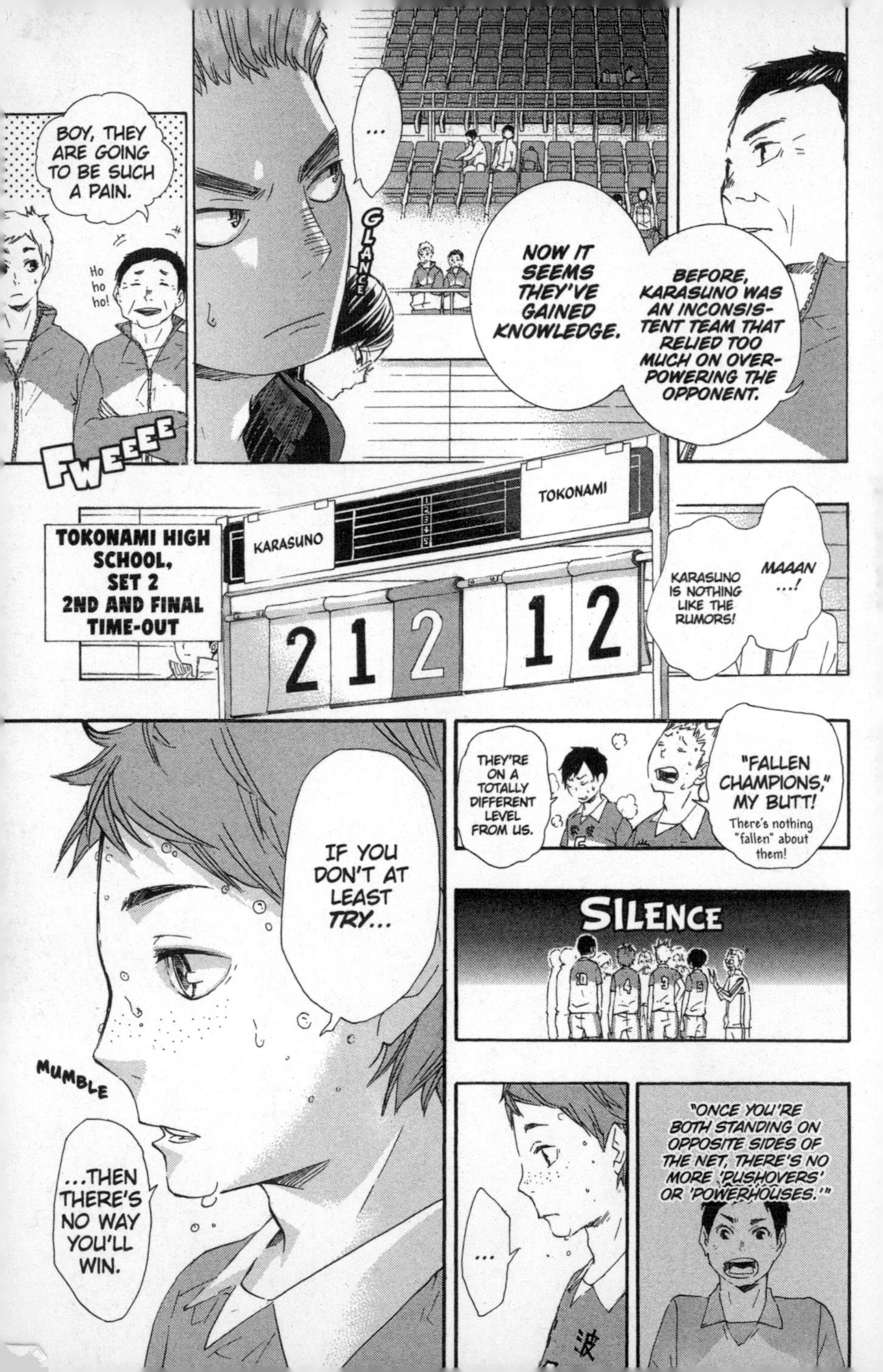
BEFORE, KARASUNO WAS AN INCONSISTENT TEAM THAT RELIED TOO MUCH ON OVERPOWERING THE OPPONENT.
NOW IT SEEMS THEY'VE GAINED KNOWLEDGE.
...
GLANCE
BOY, THEY ARE GOING TO BE SUCH A PAIN.
Ho ho ho!
FWEEEE
MAAAN ...!
KARASUNO IS NOTHING LIKE THE RUMORS!
TOKONAMI
KARASUNO
21 2 12
TOKONAMI HIGH SCHOOL, SET 2 2ND AND FINAL TIME-OUT
"FALLEN CHAMPIONS," MY BUTT!
There's nothing "fallen" about them!
THEY'RE ON A TOTALLY DIFFERENT LEVEL FROM US.
SILENCE
"ONCE YOU'RE BOTH STANDING ON OPPOSITE SIDES OF THE NET, THERE'S NO MORE 'PUSHOVERS' OR 'POWERHOUSES.'"
...
IF YOU DON'T AT LEAST TRY...
MUMBLE
...THEN THERE'S NO WAY YOU'LL WIN.

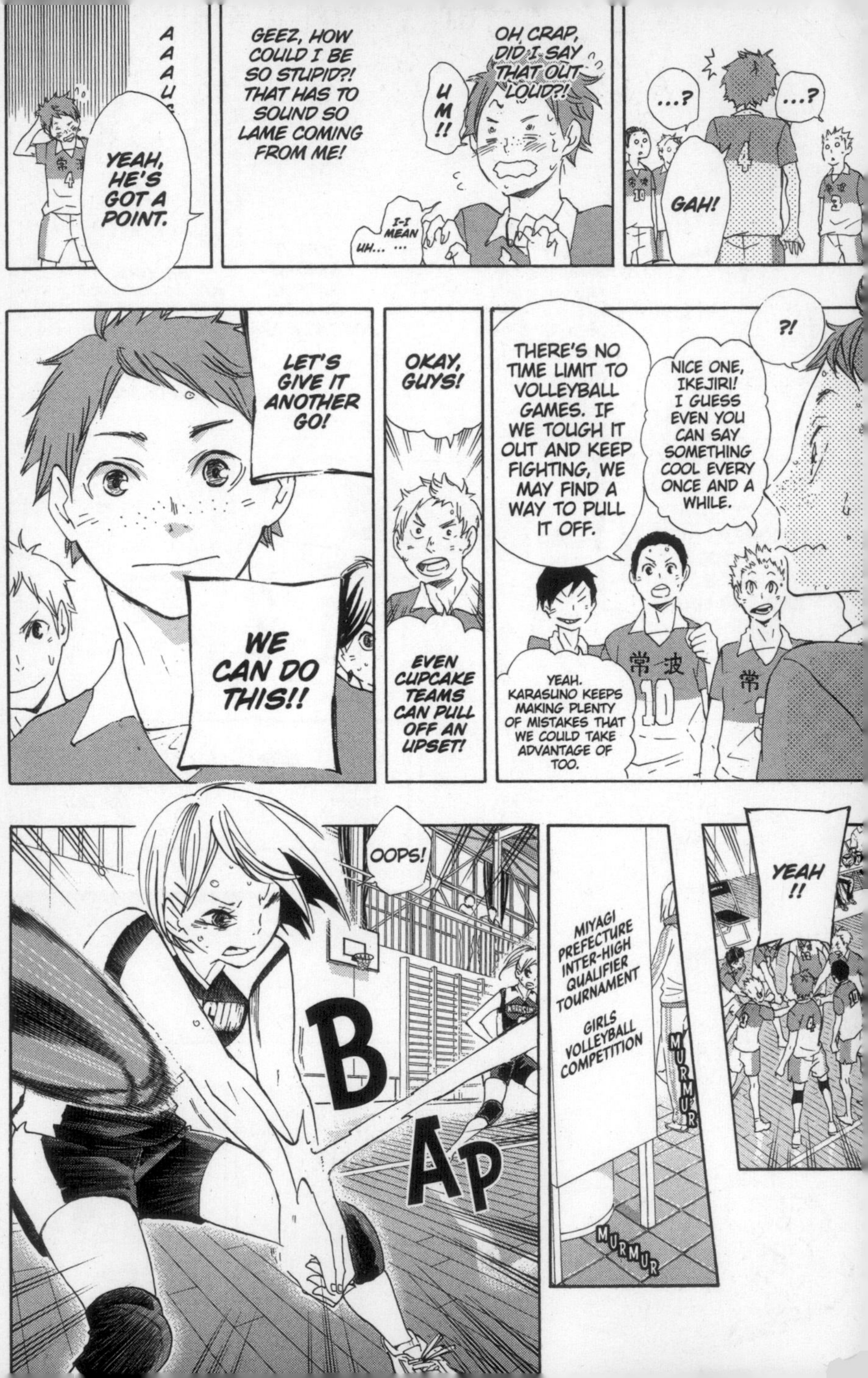
...?
...?
GAH!
OH, CRAP, DID I SAY THAT OUT LOUD?!
UM!!
I-I MEAN ...
UH...
GEEZ, HOW COULD I BE SO STUPID?! THAT HAS TO SOUND SO LAME COMING FROM ME!
YEAH, HE'S GOT A POINT.
?!
NICE ONE, IKEJIRI! I GUESS EVEN YOU CAN SAY SOMETHING COOL EVERY ONCE AND A WHILE.
THERE'S NO TIME LIMIT TO VOLLEYBALL GAMES. IF WE TOUGH IT OUT AND KEEP FIGHTING, WE MAY FIND A WAY TO PULL IT OFF.
YEAH. KARASUNO KEEPS MAKING PLENTY OF MISTAKES THAT WE COULD TAKE ADVANTAGE OF TOO.
OKAY, GUYS!
EVEN CUPCAKE TEAMS CAN PULL OFF AN UPSET!
LET'S GIVE IT ANOTHER GO!
WE CAN DO THIS!!
YEAH!!
MIYAGI PREFECTURE INTER-HIGH QUALIFIER TOURNAMENT
GIRLS VOLLEYBALL COMPETITION
MURMUR
MURMUR
OOPS!
BAP

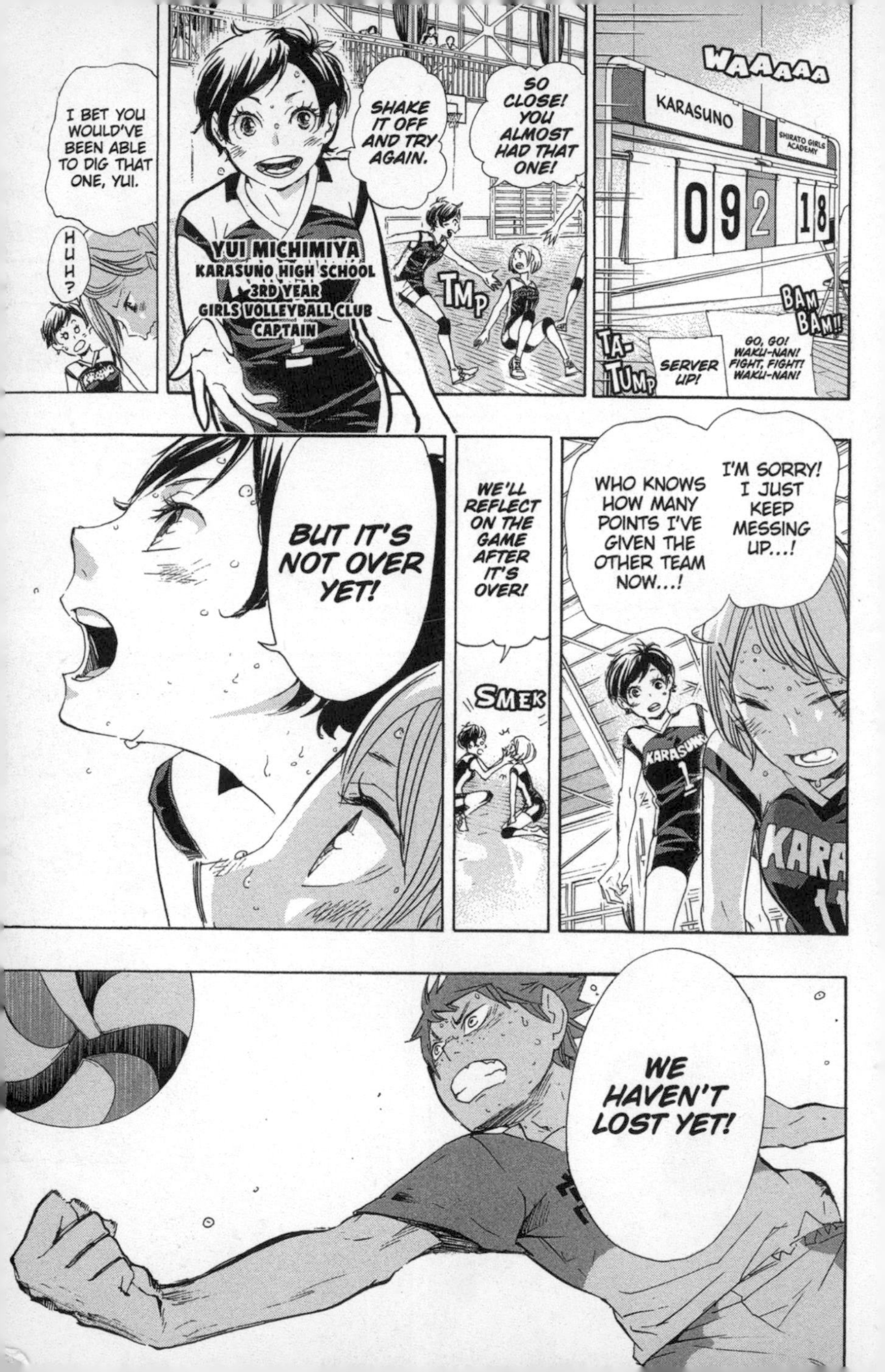
WAAAAA
KARASUNO
SHIRATO GIRLS ACADEMY
09 2 18
BAM BAM!!
GO, GO! WAKU-NAN! FIGHT, FIGHT! WAKU-NAN!
SERVER UP!
TA-TUMP
SO CLOSE! YOU ALMOST HAD THAT ONE!
SHAKE IT OFF AND TRY AGAIN.
TMP
YUI MICHIMIYA
KARASUNO HIGH SCHOOL
3RD YEAR
GIRLS VOLLEYBALL CLUB
CAPTAIN
I BET YOU WOULD'VE BEEN ABLE TO DIG THAT ONE, YUI.
HUH?
I'M SORRY! I JUST KEEP MESSING UP...!
WHO KNOWS HOW MANY POINTS I'VE GIVEN THE OTHER TEAM NOW...!
KARASUNO
WE'LL REFLECT ON THE GAME AFTER IT'S OVER!
SMEK
BUT IT'S NOT OVER YET!
WE HAVEN'T LOST YET!

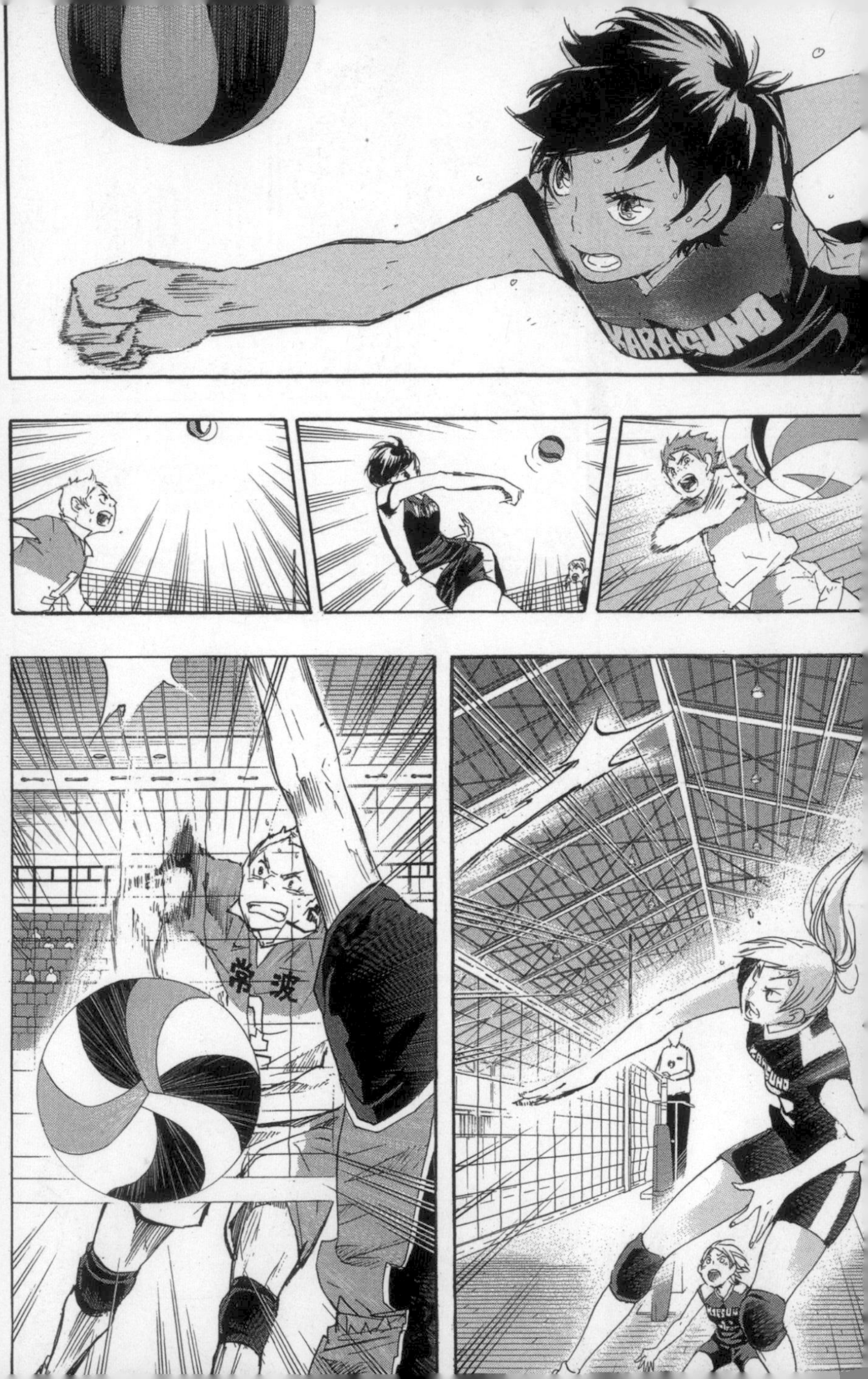
KARASUNO
常波

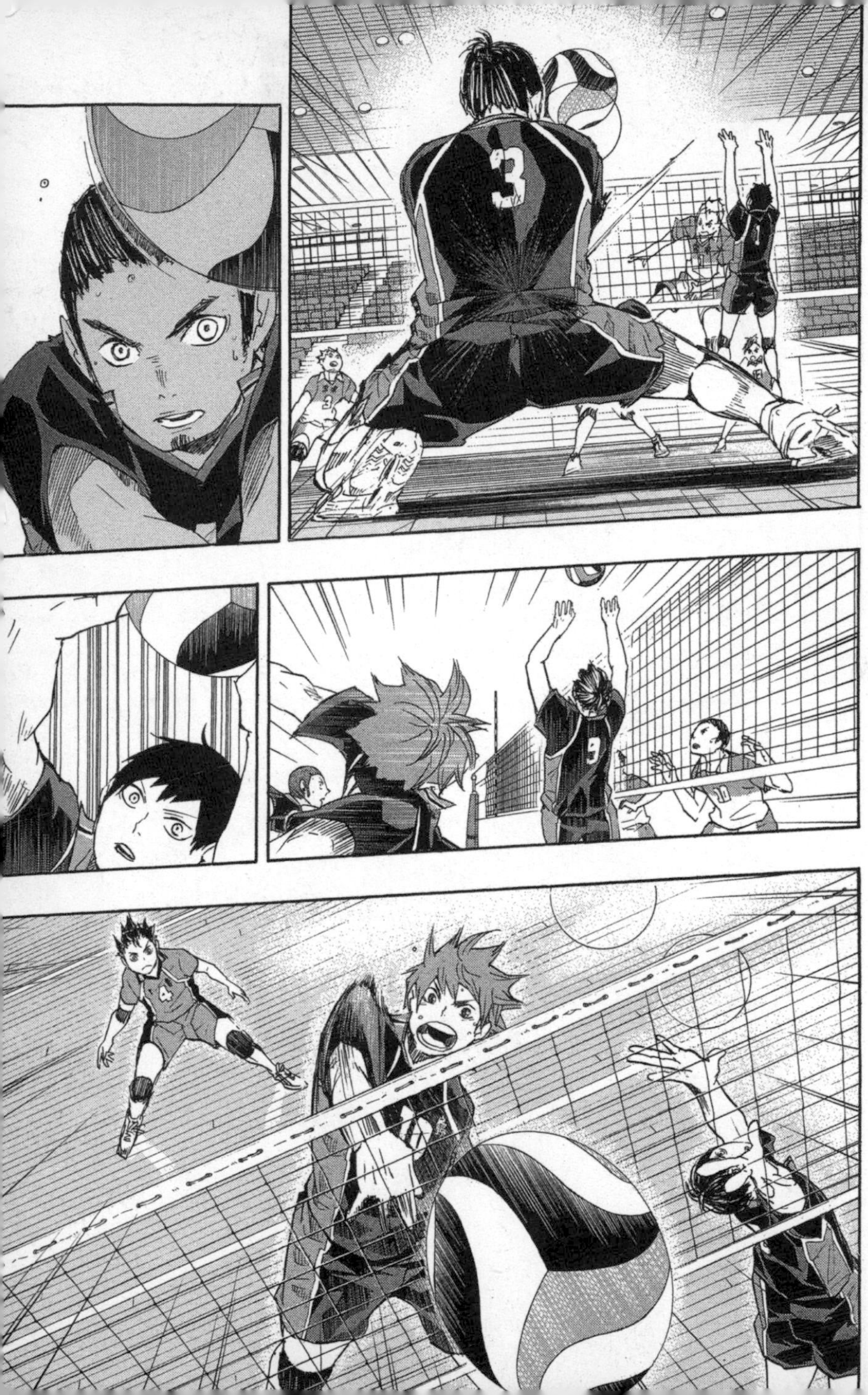

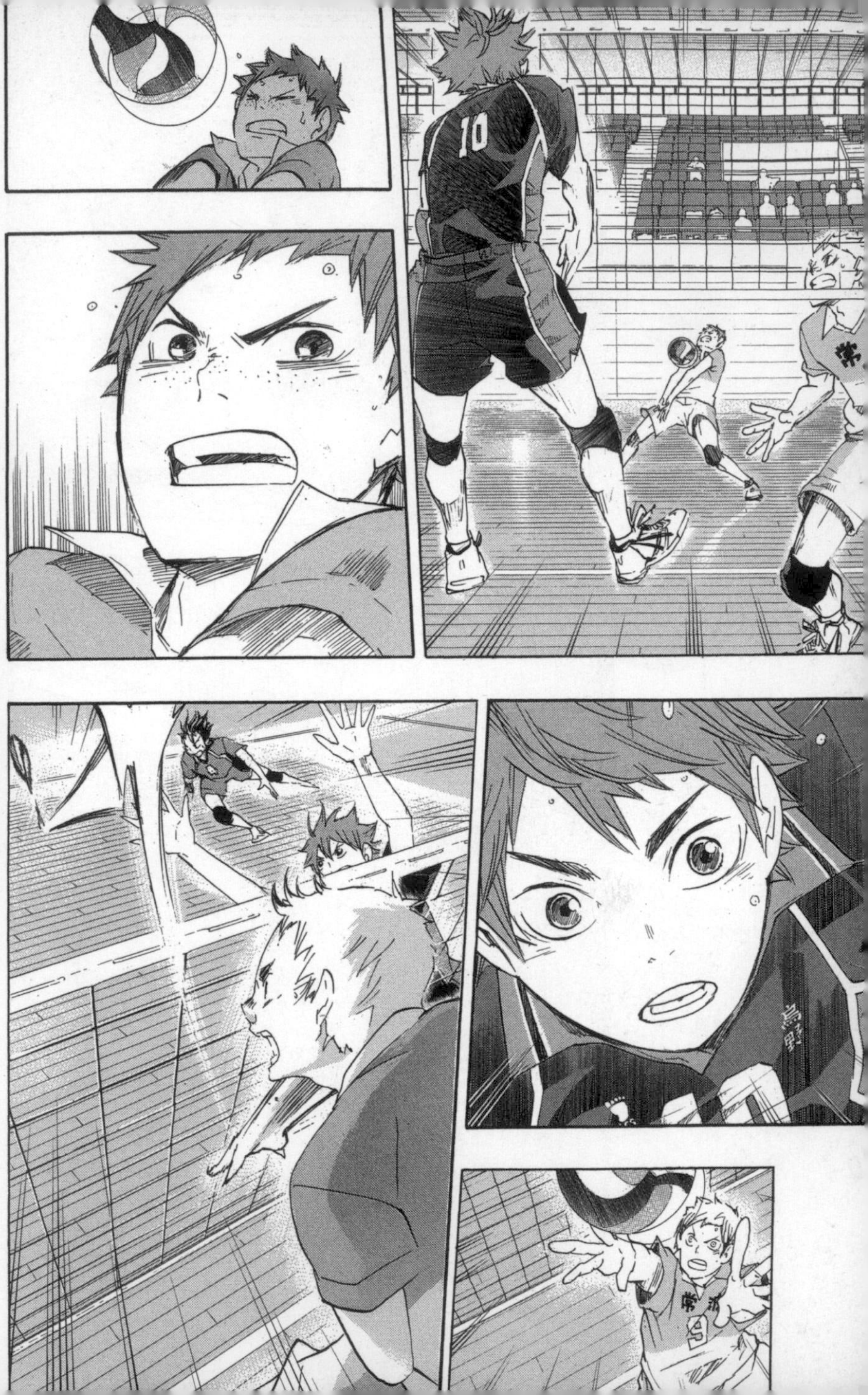

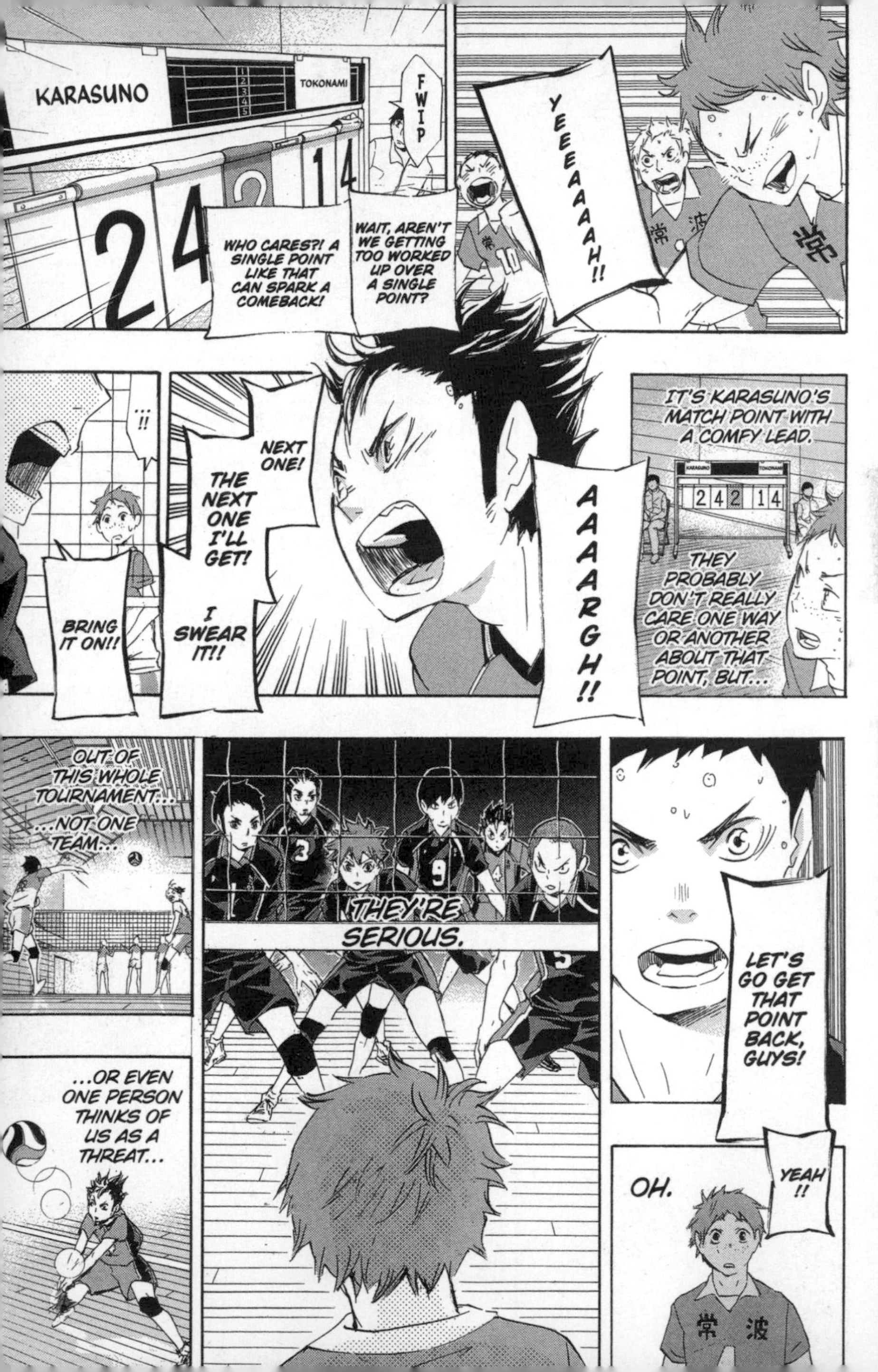
YEEEAAAAAH!!
FWIP
KARASUNO
TOKONAMI
24 2 14
WAIT, AREN'T WE GETTING TOO WORKED UP OVER A SINGLE POINT?
WHO CARES?! A SINGLE POINT LIKE THAT CAN SPARK A COMEBACK!
IT'S KARASUNO'S MATCH POINT WITH A COMFY LEAD.
THEY PROBABLY DON'T REALLY CARE ONE WAY OR ANOTHER ABOUT THAT POINT, BUT...
AAAAARGH!!
NEXT ONE!
THE NEXT ONE I'LL GET!
I SWEAR IT!!
...!!
BRING IT ON!!
LET'S GO GET THAT POINT BACK, GUYS!
YEAH!!
OH.
THEY'RE SERIOUS.
OUT OF THIS WHOLE TOURNAMENT...
...NOT ONE TEAM...
...OR EVEN ONE PERSON THINKS OF US AS A THREAT...

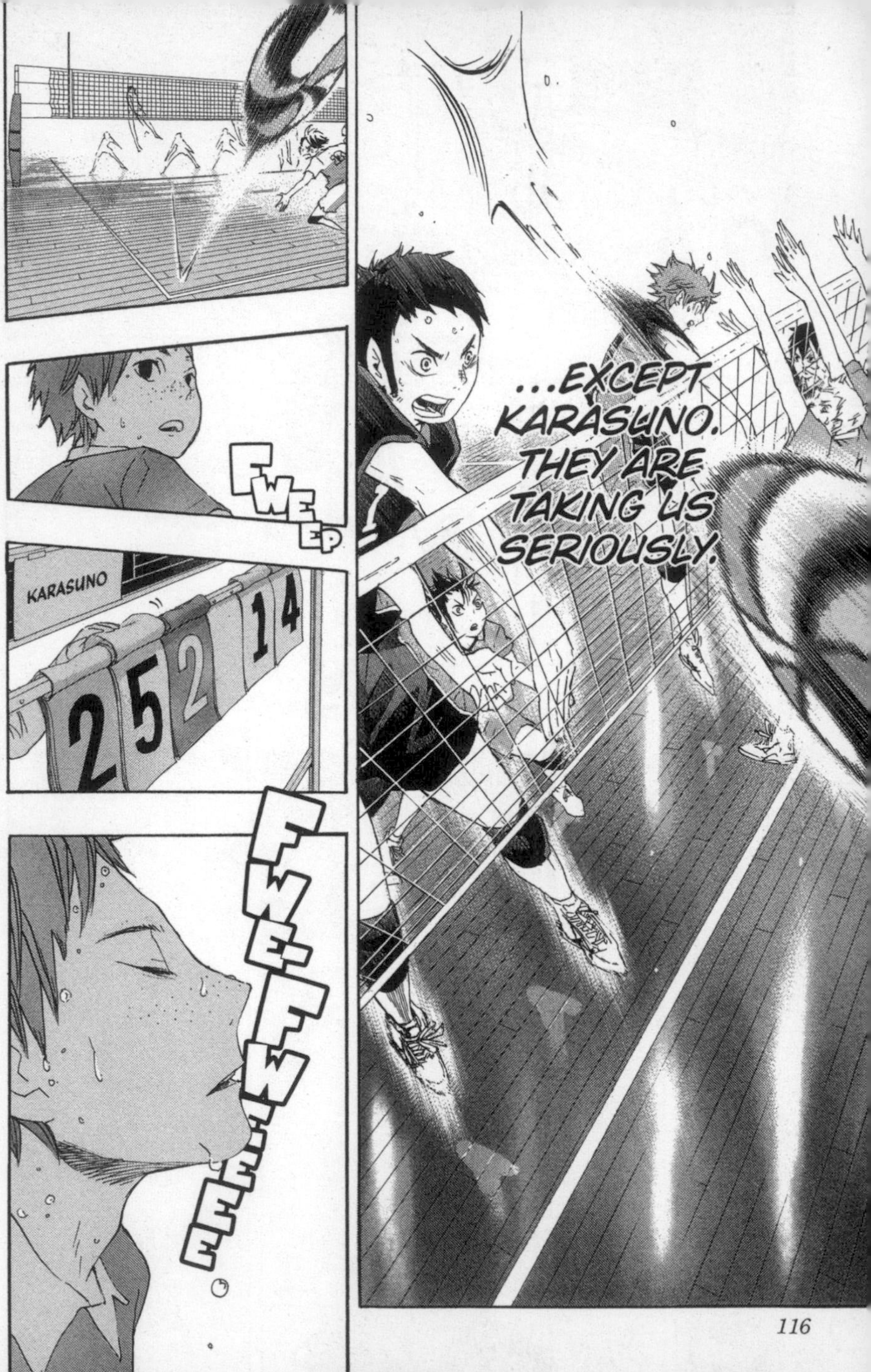
...EXCEPT KARASUNO. THEY ARE TAKING US SERIOUSLY.
FWEEP
KARASUNO
25
2
14
FWE-FWEEEE

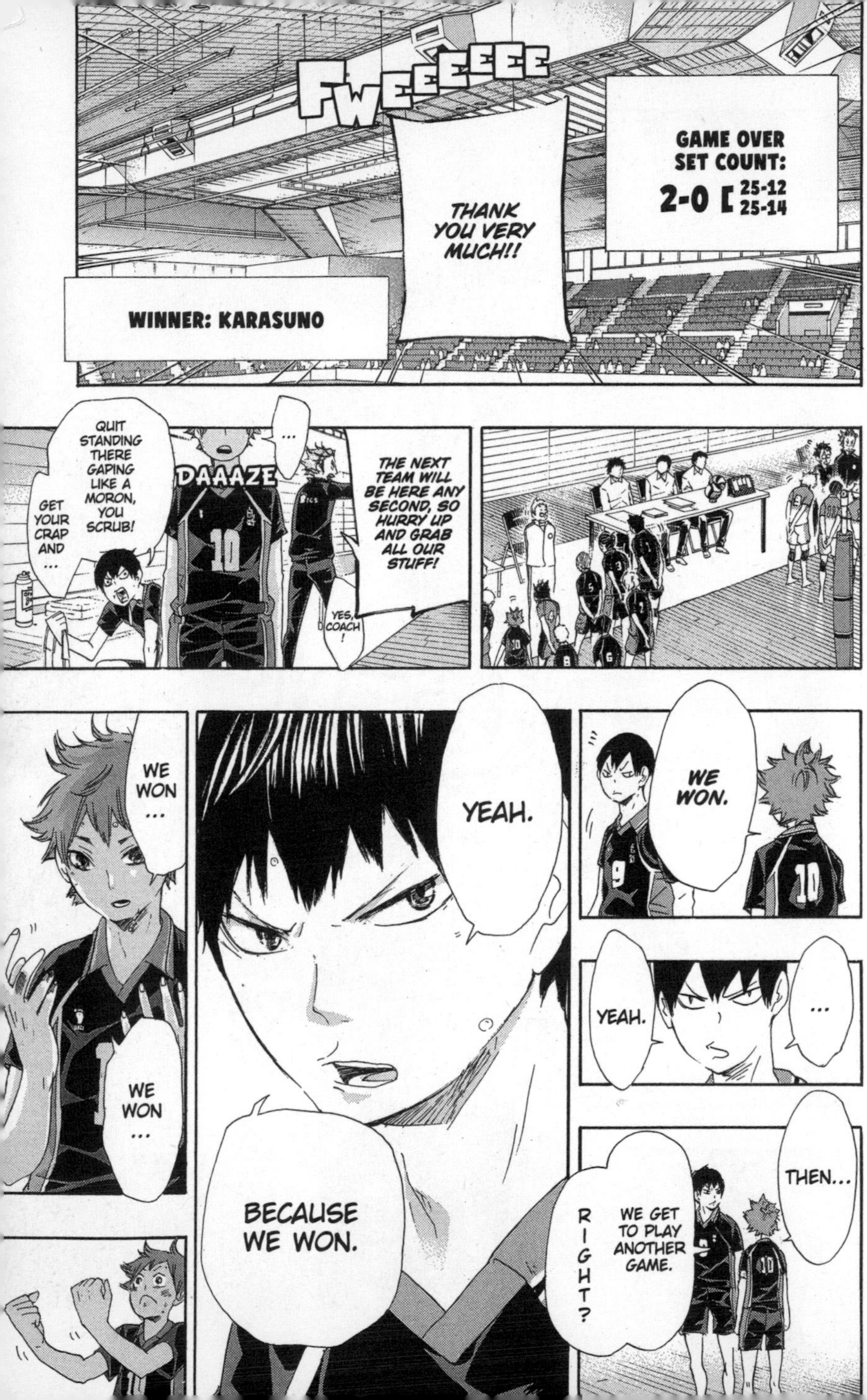
FWEEEEEE
GAME OVER
SET COUNT:
2-0 [25-12 25-14
THANK YOU VERY MUCH!!
WINNER: KARASUNO
THE NEXT TEAM WILL BE HERE ANY SECOND, SO HURRY UP AND GRAB ALL OUR STUFF!
YES, COACH!
...
DAAAZE
QUIT STANDING THERE GAPING LIKE A MORON, YOU SCRUB!
GET YOUR CRAP AND ...
WE WON.
...
YEAH.
THEN...
WE GET TO PLAY ANOTHER GAME.
RIGHT?
YEAH.
BECAUSE WE WON.
WE WON ...
WE WON ...

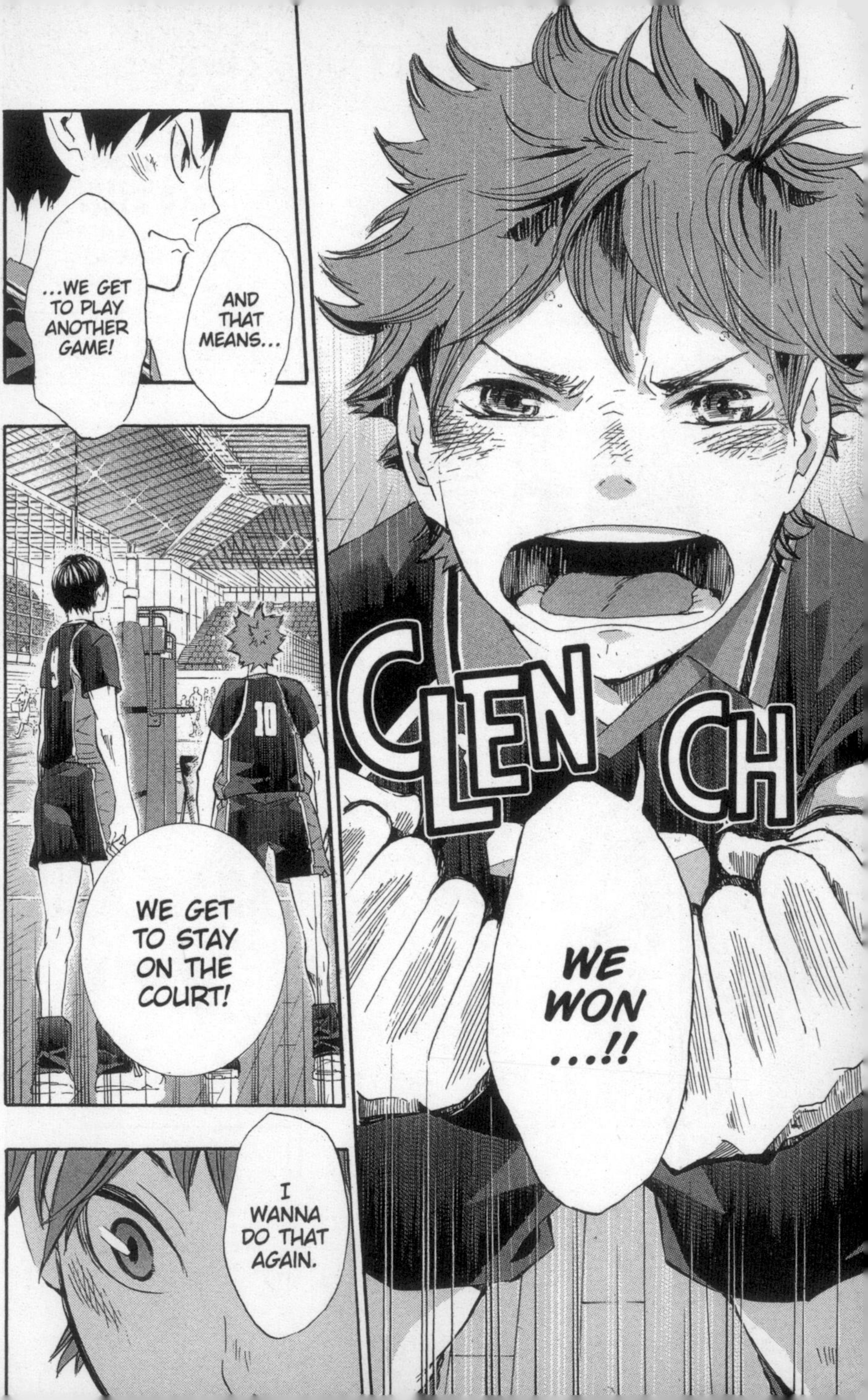
CLENCH
WE WON ...!!
AND THAT MEANS...
...WE GET TO PLAY ANOTHER GAME!
WE GET TO STAY ON THE COURT!
I WANNA DO THAT AGAIN.

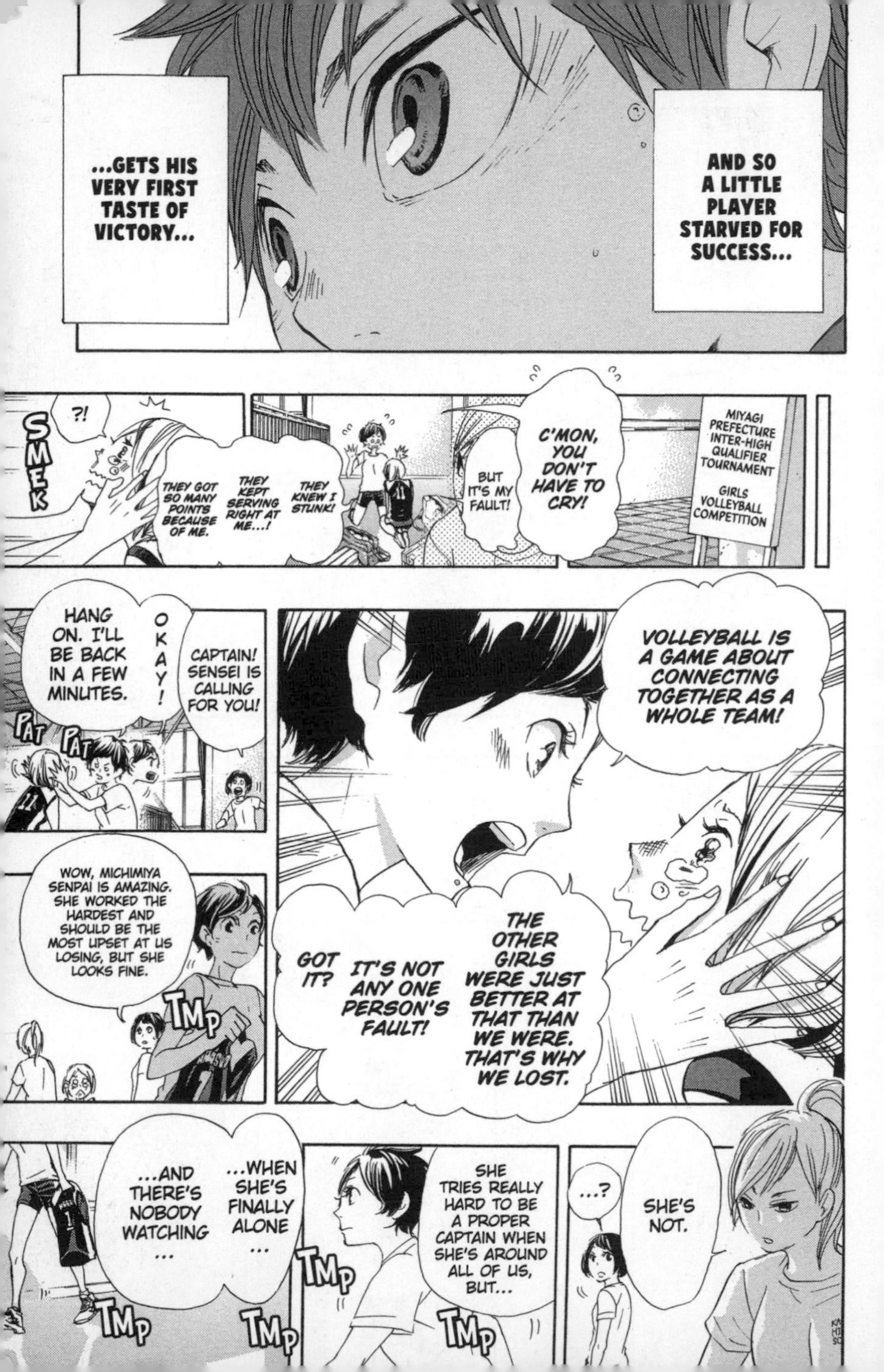
AND SO A LITTLE PLAYER STARVED FOR SUCCESS...
...GETS HIS VERY FIRST TASTE OF VICTORY...
MIYAGI PREFECTURE INTER-HIGH QUALIFIER TOURNAMENT
GIRLS VOLLEYBALL COMPETITION
C'MON, YOU DON'T HAVE TO CRY!
BUT IT'S MY FAULT!
THEY KNEW I STUNK!
THEY KEPT SERVING RIGHT AT ME...!
THEY GOT SO MANY POINTS BECAUSE OF ME.
?!
SMEK
VOLLEYBALL IS A GAME ABOUT CONNECTING TOGETHER AS A WHOLE TEAM!
THE OTHER GIRLS WERE JUST BETTER AT THAT THAN WE WERE. THAT'S WHY WE LOST.
IT'S NOT ANY ONE PERSON'S FAULT!
GOT IT?
CAPTAIN! SENSEI IS CALLING FOR YOU!
OKAY!
HANG ON. I'LL BE BACK IN A FEW MINUTES.
PAT PAT
WOW, MICHIMIYA SENPAI IS AMAZING. SHE WORKED THE HARDEST AND SHOULD BE THE MOST UPSET AT US LOSING, BUT SHE LOOKS FINE.
TMP
SHE'S NOT.
...?
SHE TRIES REALLY HARD TO BE A PROPER CAPTAIN WHEN SHE'S AROUND ALL OF US, BUT...
TMP
TMP
...WHEN SHE'S FINALLY ALONE...
...AND THERE'S NOBODY WATCHING...
TMP
TMP

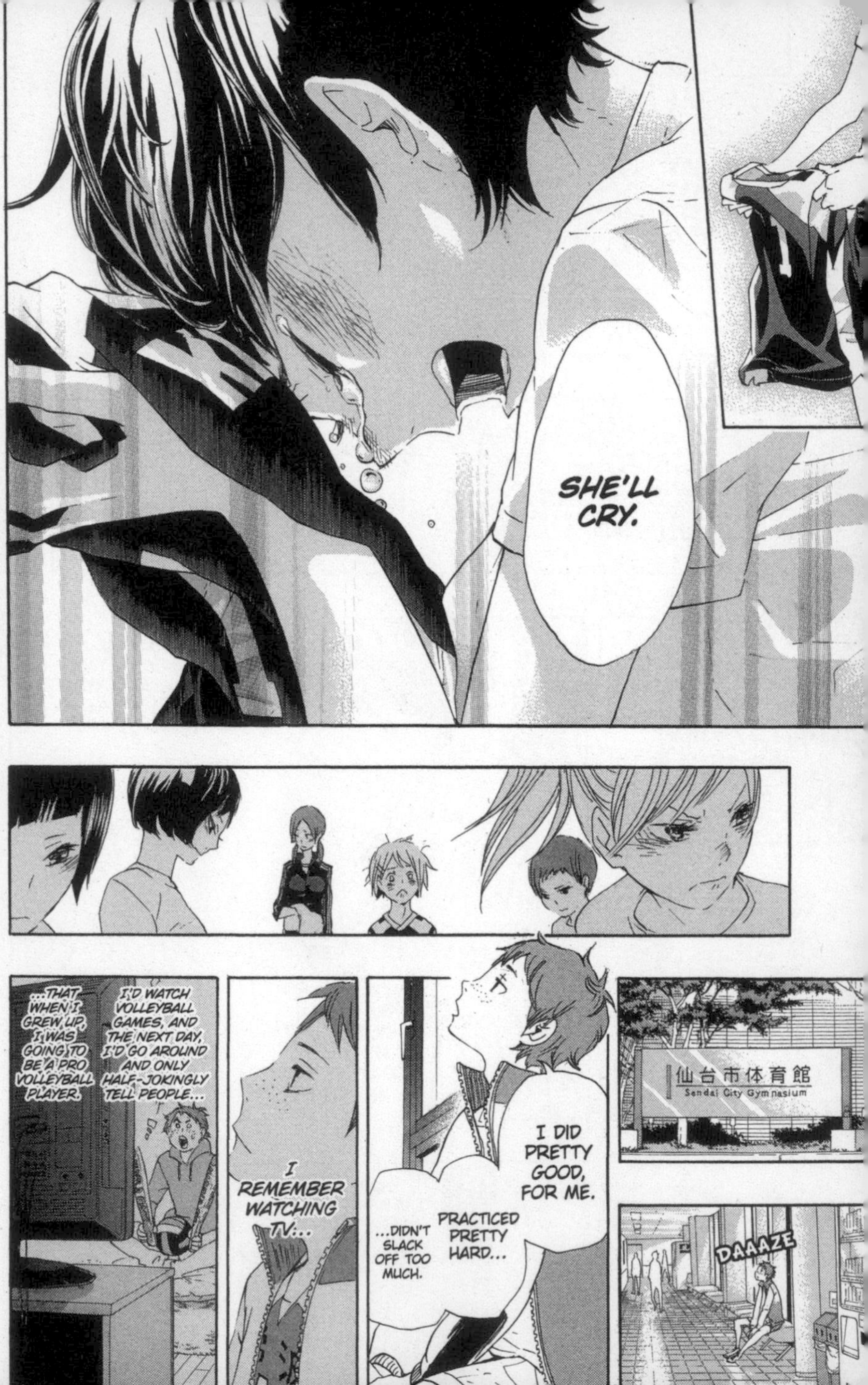
SHE'LL CRY.
仙台市体育館
Sendai City Gymnasium
DAAAZE
I DID PRETTY GOOD, FOR ME.
PRACTICED PRETTY HARD...
...DIDN'T SLACK OFF TOO MUCH.
I REMEMBER WATCHING TV...
I'D WATCH VOLLEYBALL GAMES, AND THE NEXT DAY, I'D GO AROUND AND ONLY HALF-JOKINGLY TELL PEOPLE...
...THAT WHEN I GREW UP, I WAS GOING TO BE A PRO VOLLEYBALL PLAYER.

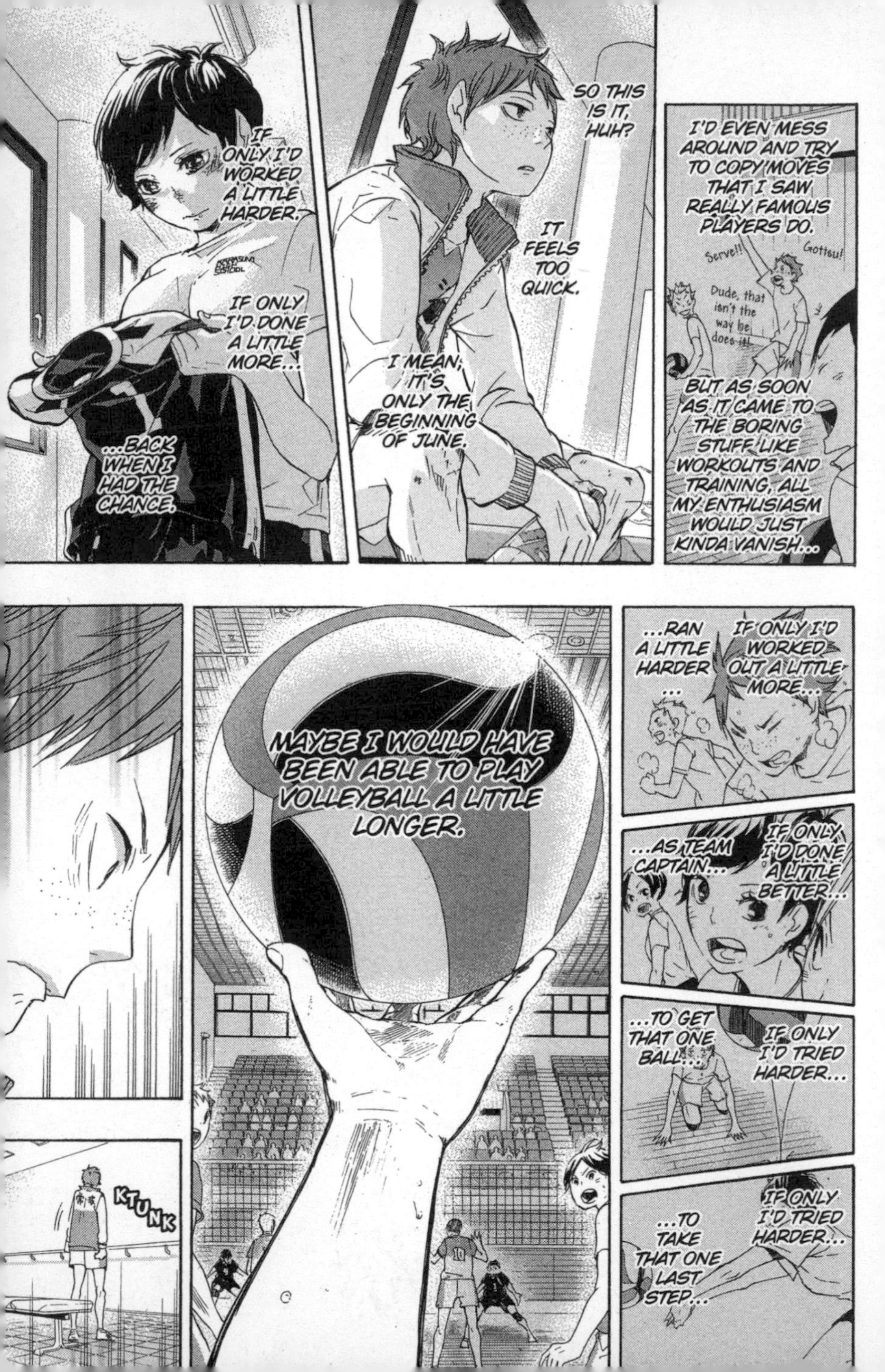
I'D EVEN MESS AROUND AND TRY TO COPY MOVES THAT I SAW REALLY FAMOUS PLAYERS DO.
Gottsu!
Serve!!
Dude, that isn't the way he does it!
BUT AS SOON AS IT CAME TO THE BORING STUFF LIKE WORKOUTS AND TRAINING, ALL MY ENTHUSIASM WOULD JUST KINDA VANISH...
SO THIS IS IT, HUH?
IT FEELS TOO QUICK.
I MEAN, IT'S ONLY THE BEGINNING OF JUNE.
IF ONLY I'D WORKED A LITTLE HARDER.
IF ONLY I'D DONE A LITTLE MORE...
...BACK WHEN I HAD THE CHANCE.
IF ONLY I'D WORKED OUT A LITTLE MORE...
...RAN A LITTLE HARDER...
IF ONLY I'D DONE A LITTLE BETTER...
...AS TEAM CAPTAIN...
IF ONLY I'D TRIED HARDER...
...TO GET THAT ONE BALL...
IF ONLY I'D TRIED HARDER...
...TO TAKE THAT ONE LAST STEP...
MAYBE I WOULD HAVE BEEN ABLE TO PLAY VOLLEYBALL A LITTLE LONGER.
KTUNK

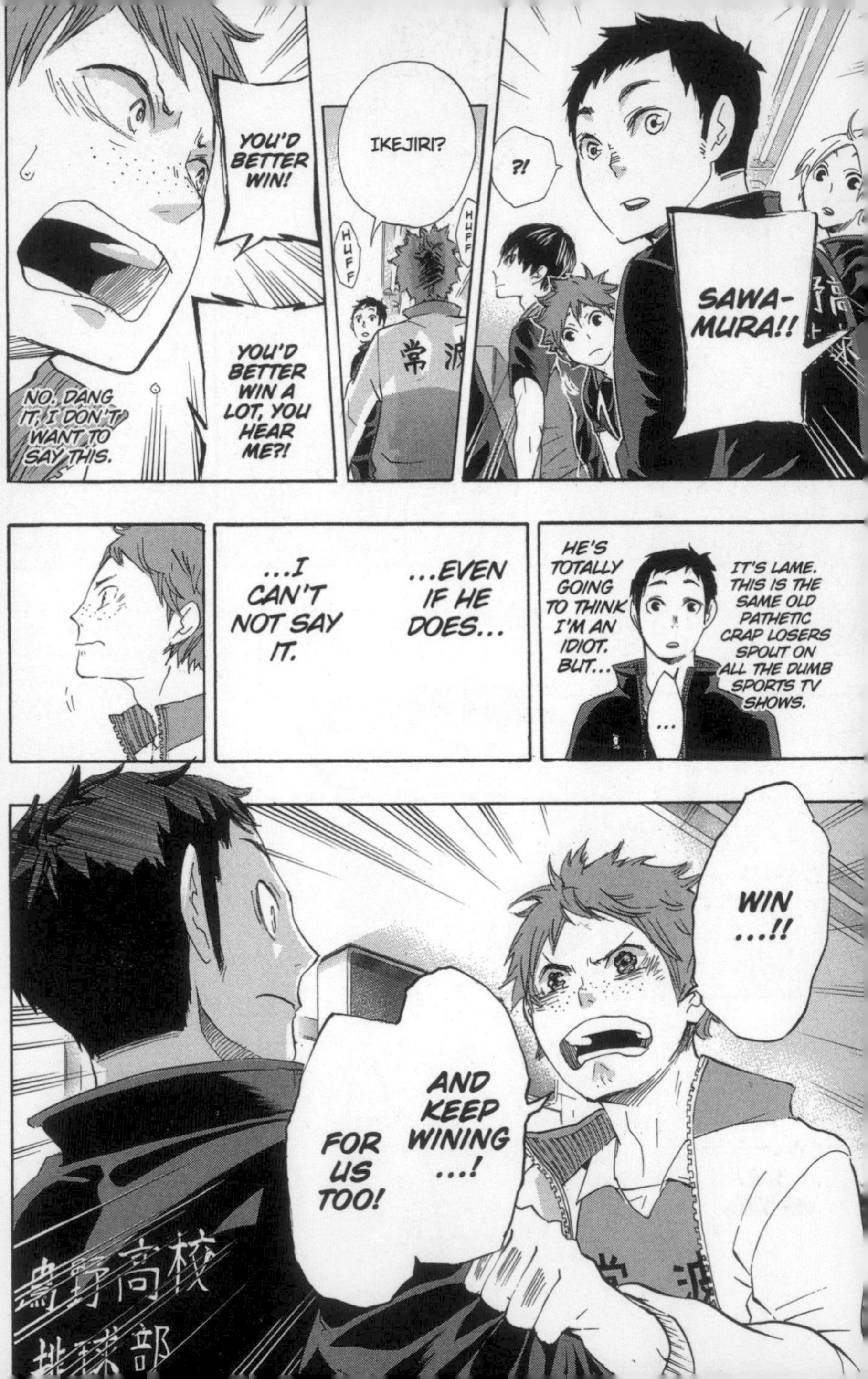
?!
SAWA-MURA!!
IKEJIRI?
HUFF
HUFF
YOU'D BETTER WIN!
YOU'D BETTER WIN A LOT, YOU HEAR ME?!
NO, DANG IT, I DON'T WANT TO SAY THIS.
IT'S LAME. THIS IS THE SAME OLD PATHETIC CRAP LOSERS SPOUT ON ALL THE DUMB SPORTS TV SHOWS.
HE'S TOTALLY GOING TO THINK I'M AN IDIOT. BUT...
...
...EVEN IF HE DOES...
...I CAN'T NOT SAY IT.
WIN ...!!
AND KEEP WINING ...!
FOR US TOO!
烏野高校
排球部

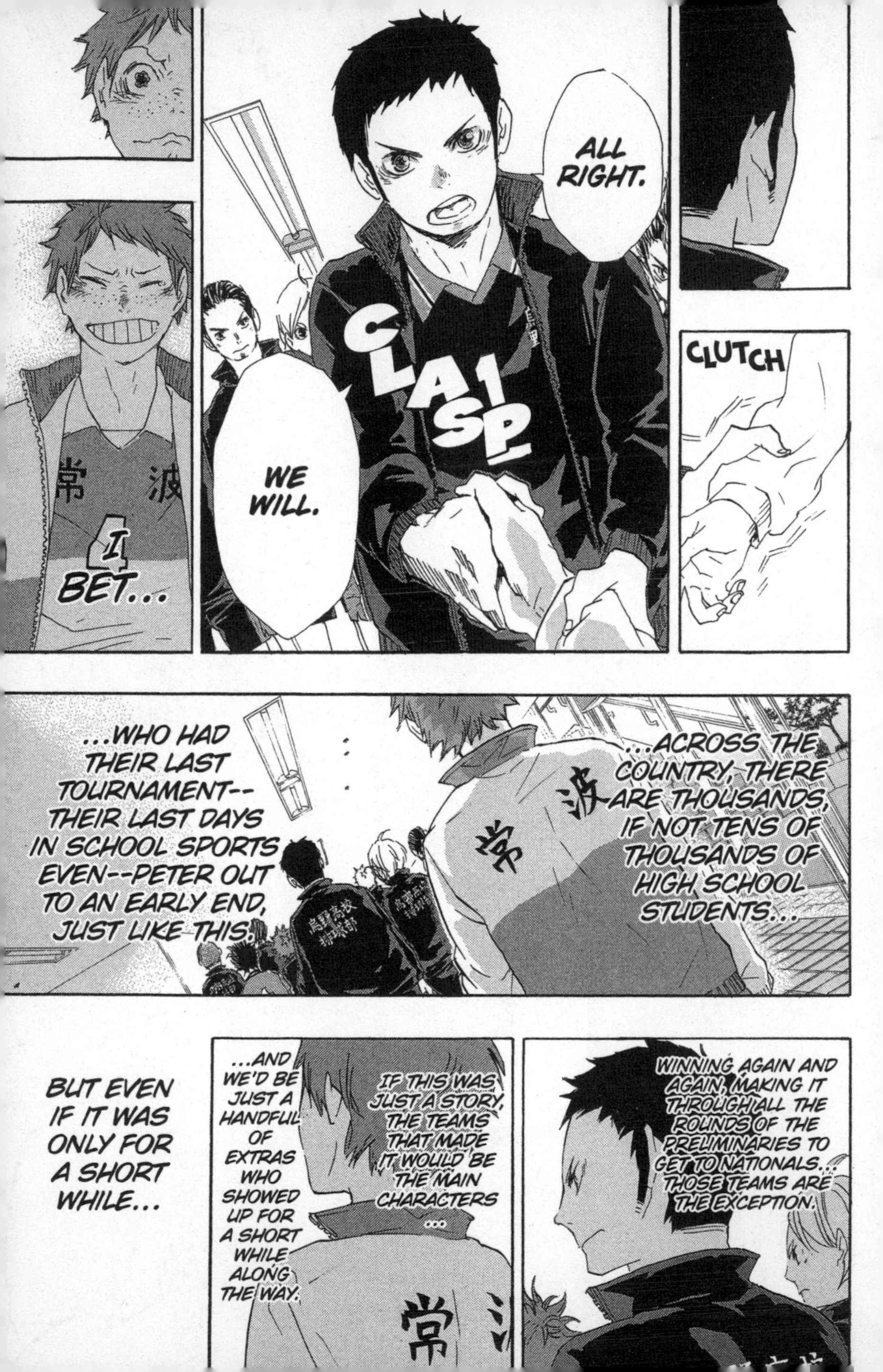
CLUTCH
ALL RIGHT.
WE WILL.
I BET...
...ACROSS THE COUNTRY, THERE ARE THOUSANDS, IF NOT TENS OF THOUSANDS OF HIGH SCHOOL STUDENTS...
...WHO HAD THEIR LAST TOURNAMENT--THEIR LAST DAYS IN SCHOOL SPORTS EVEN--PETER OUT TO AN EARLY END, JUST LIKE THIS.
WINNING AGAIN AND AGAIN, MAKING IT THROUGH ALL THE ROUNDS OF THE PRELIMINARIES TO GET TO NATIONALS... THOSE TEAMS ARE THE EXCEPTION.
IF THIS WAS JUST A STORY, THE TEAMS THAT MADE IT WOULD BE THE MAIN CHARACTERS...
...AND WE'D BE JUST A HANDFUL OF EXTRAS WHO SHOWED UP FOR A SHORT WHILE ALONG THE WAY.
BUT EVEN IF IT WAS ONLY FOR A SHORT WHILE...

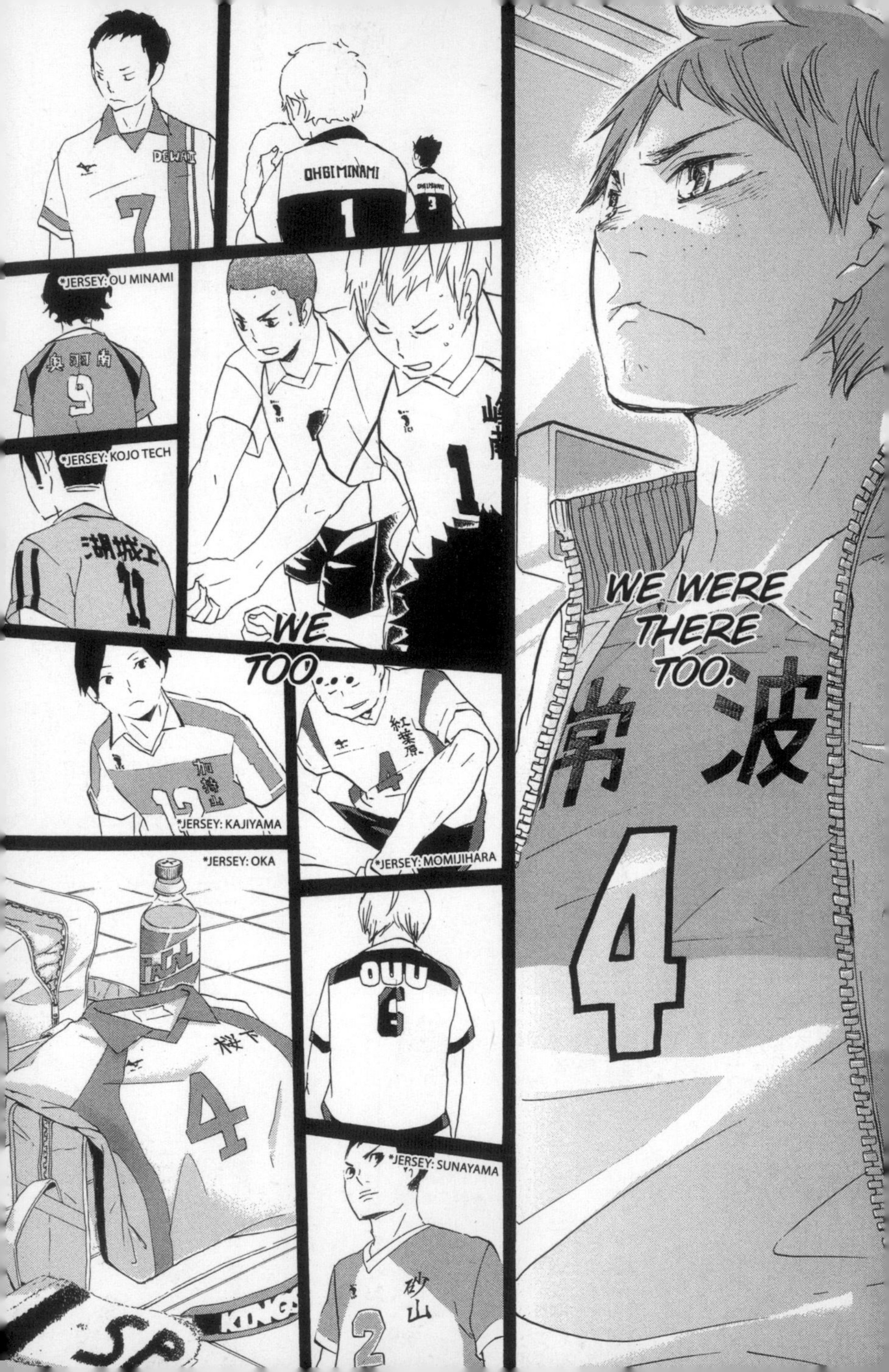
WE WERE THERE TOO.
OHBI MINAMI
DEWAI
WE TOO...
*JERSEY: OU MINAMI
*JERSEY: KOJO TECH
*JERSEY: MOMIJIHARA
*JERSEY: KAJIYAMA
OUU
*JERSEY: SUNAYAMA
*JERSEY: OKA
KINGS

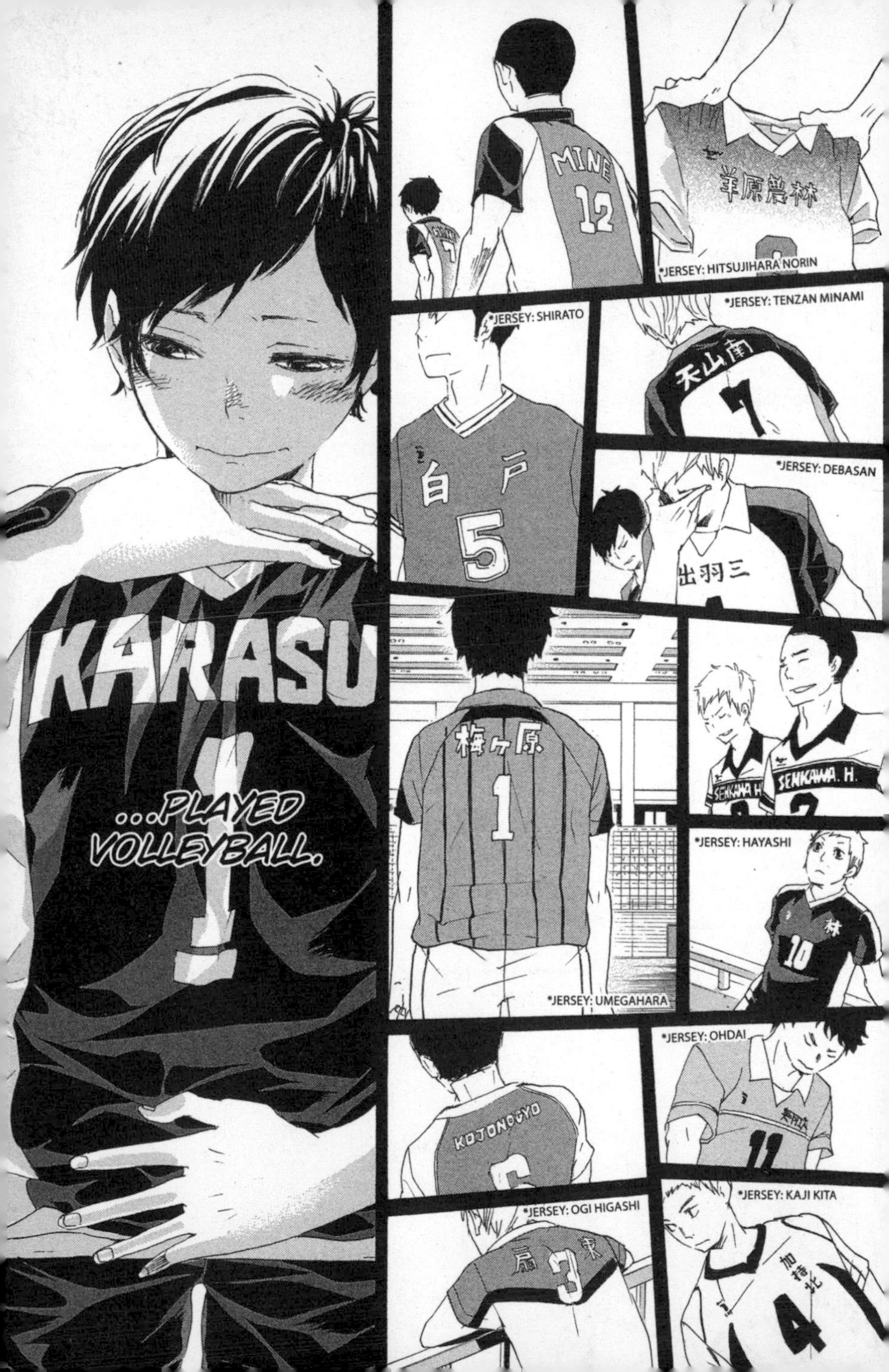
*JERSEY: HITSUJIHARA NORIN
羊原農林
MINE
*JERSEY: TENZAN MINAMI
天山南
*JERSEY: DEBASAN
出羽三
*JERSEY: SHIRATO
白戸
SENKAWA. H.
*JERSEY: HAYASHI
*JERSEY: UMEGAHARA
梅ヶ原
*JERSEY: OHDAI
KOJONOGYO
*JERSEY: KAJI KITA
加持北
*JERSEY: OGI HIGASHI
扇東
KARASU
...PLAYED VOLLEYBALL.

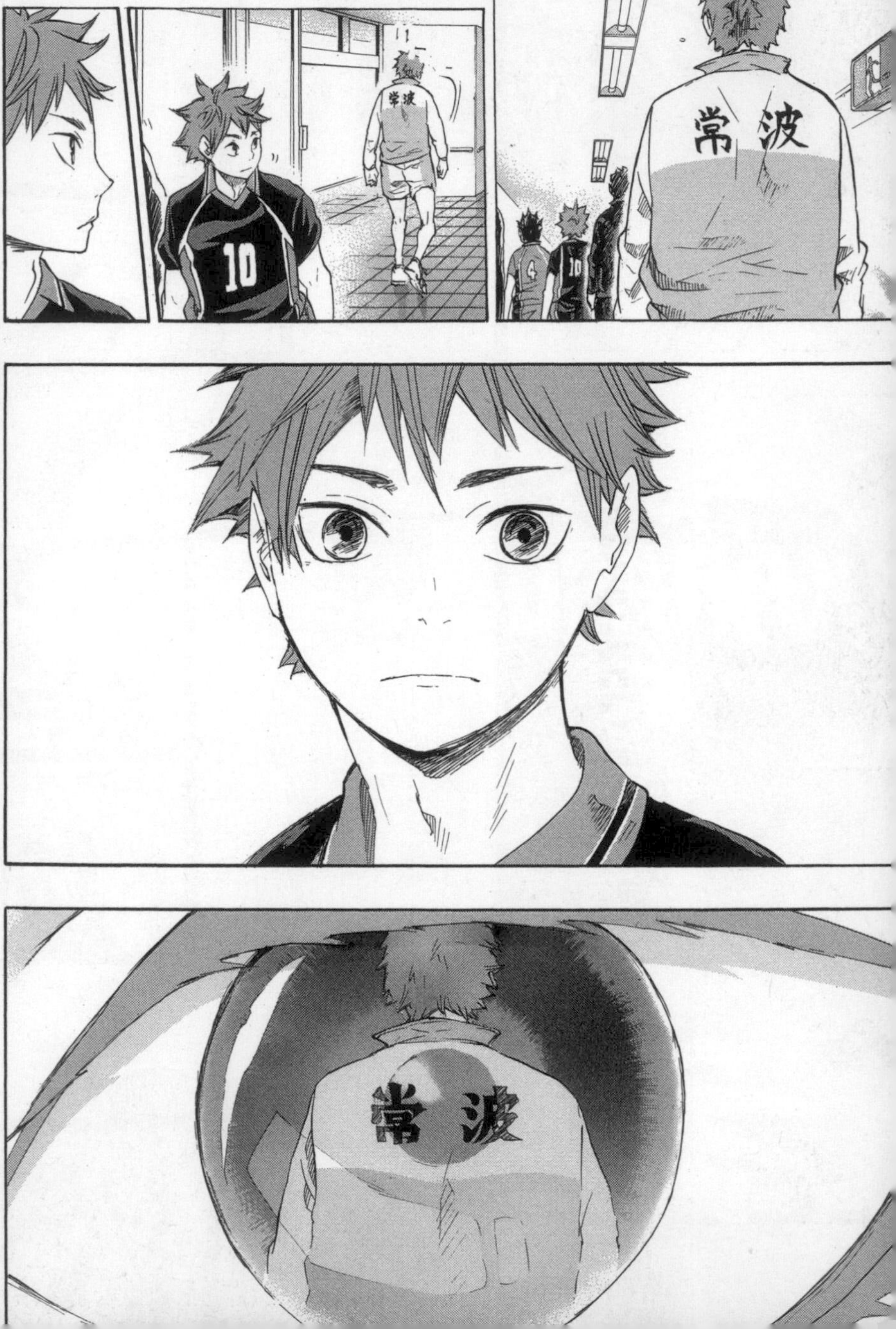
常波
常波
常波

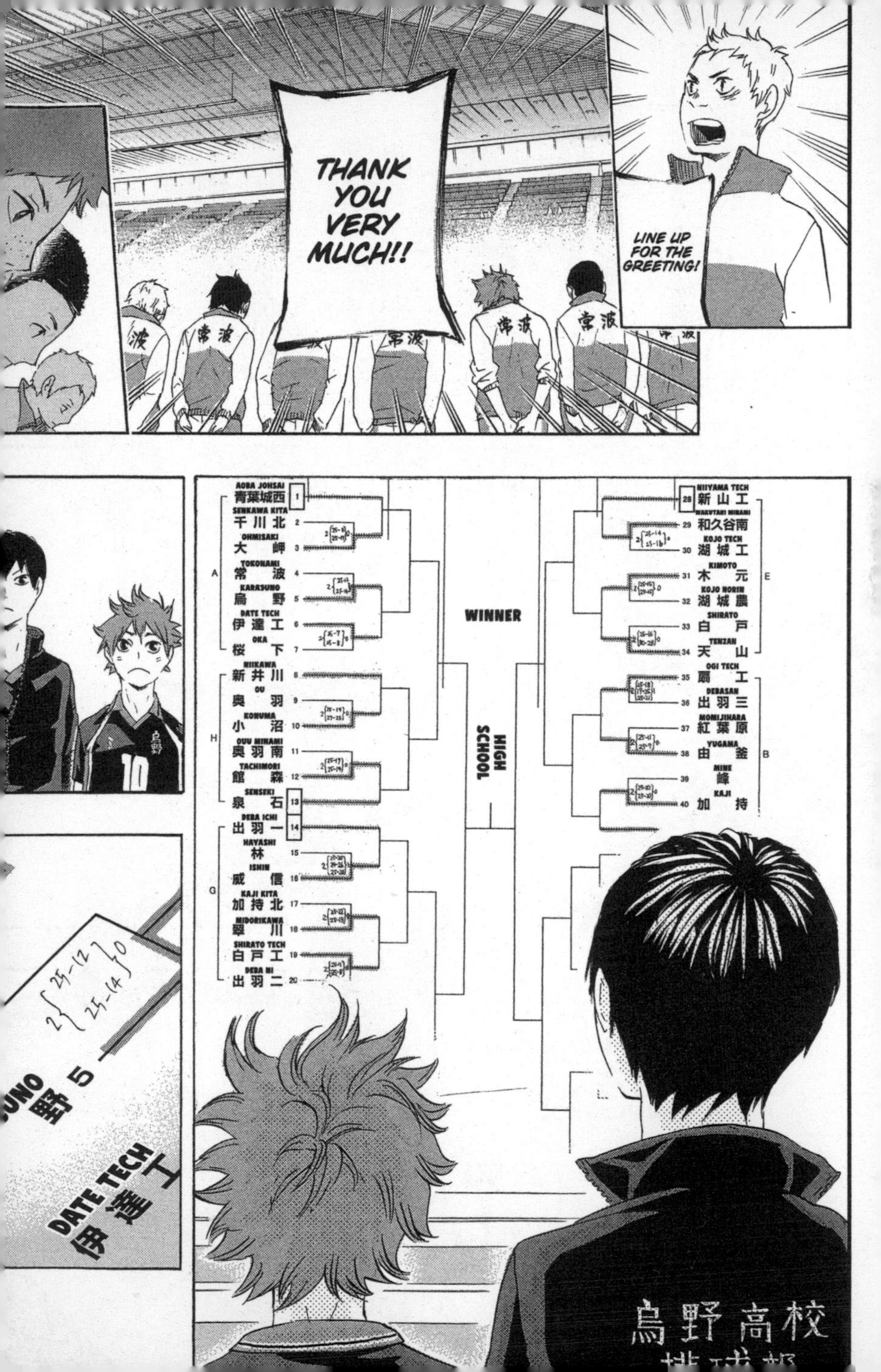
LINE UP FOR THE GREETING!
THANK YOU VERY MUCH!!
AOBA JOHSAI
青葉城西 1
SENKAWA KITA
千川北 2
OHMISAKI
大岬 3
TOKONAMI
常波 4
KARASUNO
烏野 5
DATE TECH
伊達工 6
OKA
桜下 7
NIIKAWA
新井川 8
OU
奥羽 9
KONUMA
小沼 10
OUU MINAMI
奥羽南 11
TACHIMORI
館森 12
SENSEKI
泉石 13
DEBA ICHI
出羽一 14
HAYASHI
林 15
ISHIN
威信 16
KAJI KITA
加持北 17
MIDORIKAWA
翠川 18
SHIRATO TECH
白戸工 19
DEBA NI
出羽二 20
A
H
G
WINNER
HIGH SCHOOL
NIIYAMA TECH
28 新山工
WAKUTANI MINAMI
29 和久谷南
KOJO TECH
30 湖城工
KIMOTO
31 木元
KOJO NORIN
32 湖城農
SHIRATO
33 白戸
TENZAN
34 天山
OGI TECH
35 扇工
DEBASAN
36 出羽三
MOMIJIHARA
37 紅葉原
YUGAMA
38 由釜
MINE
39 峰
KAJI
40 加持
E
B
2 25-12 25-14 0
UNO 野 5
DATE TECH 伊達工
烏野高校

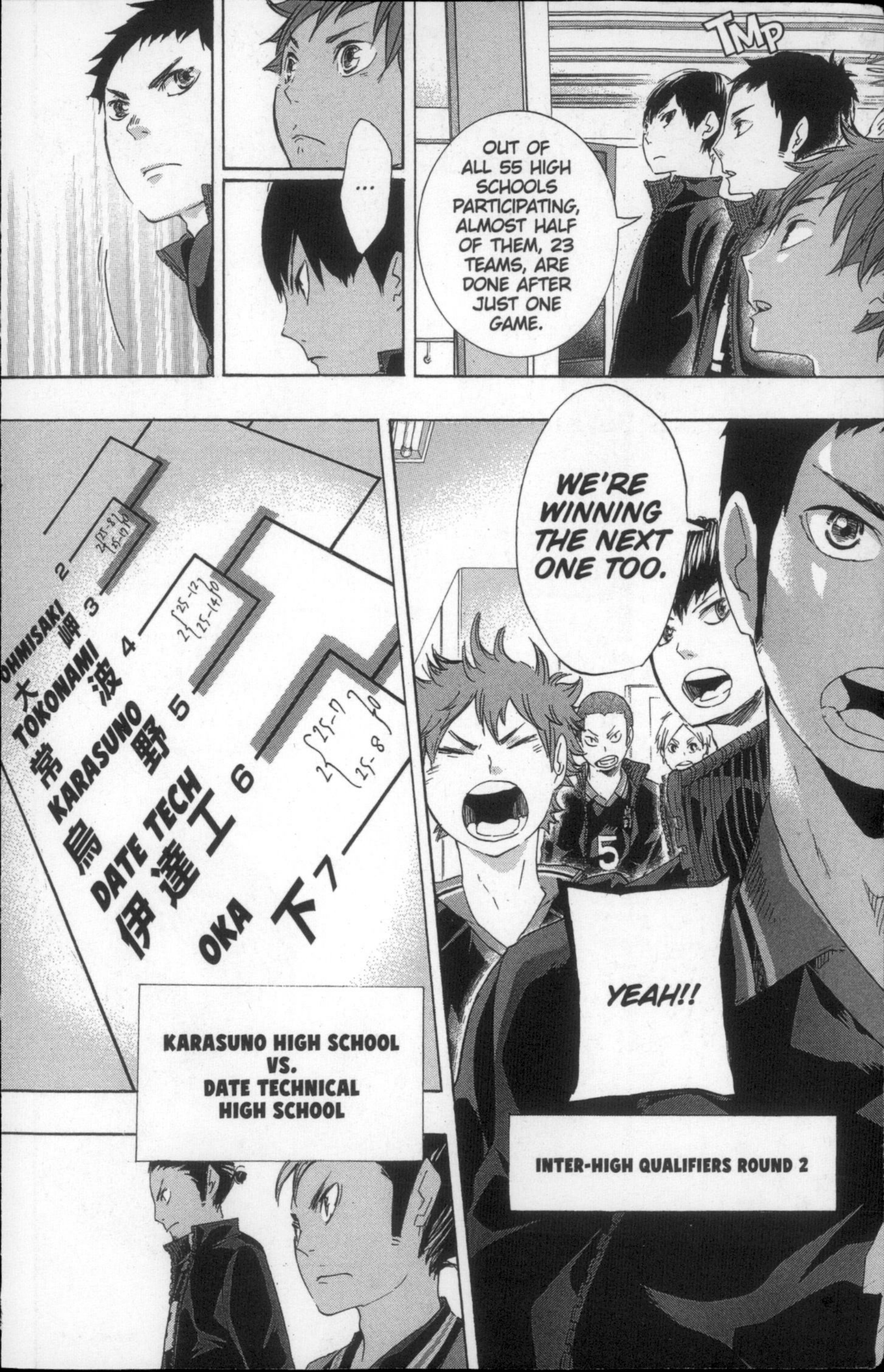
TMP
OUT OF ALL 55 HIGH SCHOOLS PARTICIPATING, ALMOST HALF OF THEM, 23 TEAMS, ARE DONE AFTER JUST ONE GAME.
...
WE'RE WINNING THE NEXT ONE TOO.
YEAH!!
INTER-HIGH QUALIFIERS ROUND 2
OHMISAKI 大岬
TOKONAMI 常波
KARASUNO 烏野
DATE TECH 伊達工
OKA 下
KARASUNO HIGH SCHOOL VS. DATE TECHNICAL HIGH SCHOOL

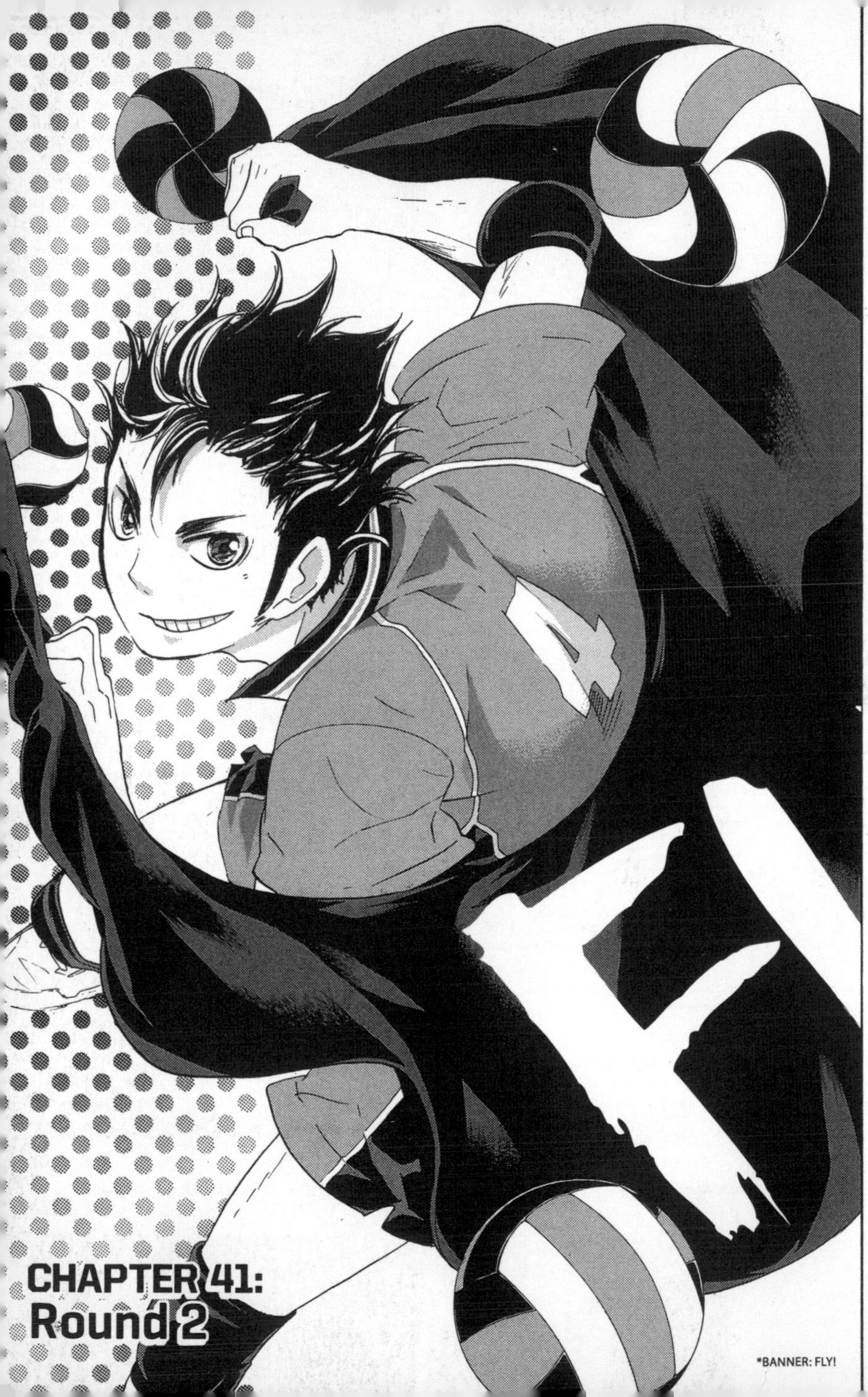

CHAPTER 41: Round 2

*BANNER: FLY!

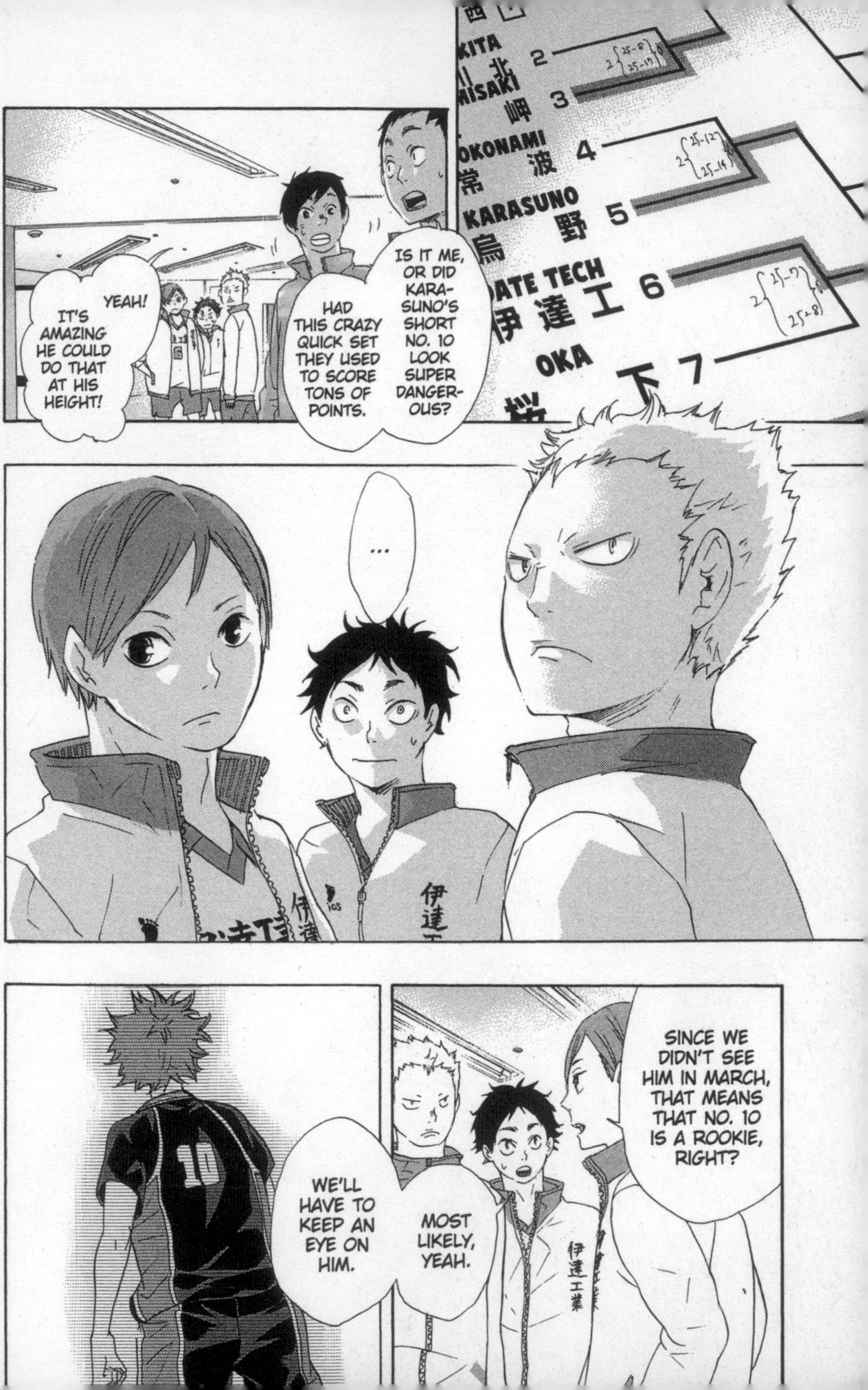

KITA
北 2
MISAKI
岬 3
OKONAMI
常波 4
KARASUNO
烏野 5
DATE TECH
伊達工 6
OKA
下 7
IS IT ME, OR DID KARASUNO'S SHORT NO. 10 LOOK SUPER DANGEROUS?
HAD THIS CRAZY QUICK SET THEY USED TO SCORE TONS OF POINTS.
YEAH! IT'S AMAZING HE COULD DO THAT AT HIS HEIGHT!
...
SINCE WE DIDN'T SEE HIM IN MARCH, THAT MEANS THAT NO. 10 IS A ROOKIE, RIGHT?
MOST LIKELY, YEAH.
WE'LL HAVE TO KEEP AN EYE ON HIM.

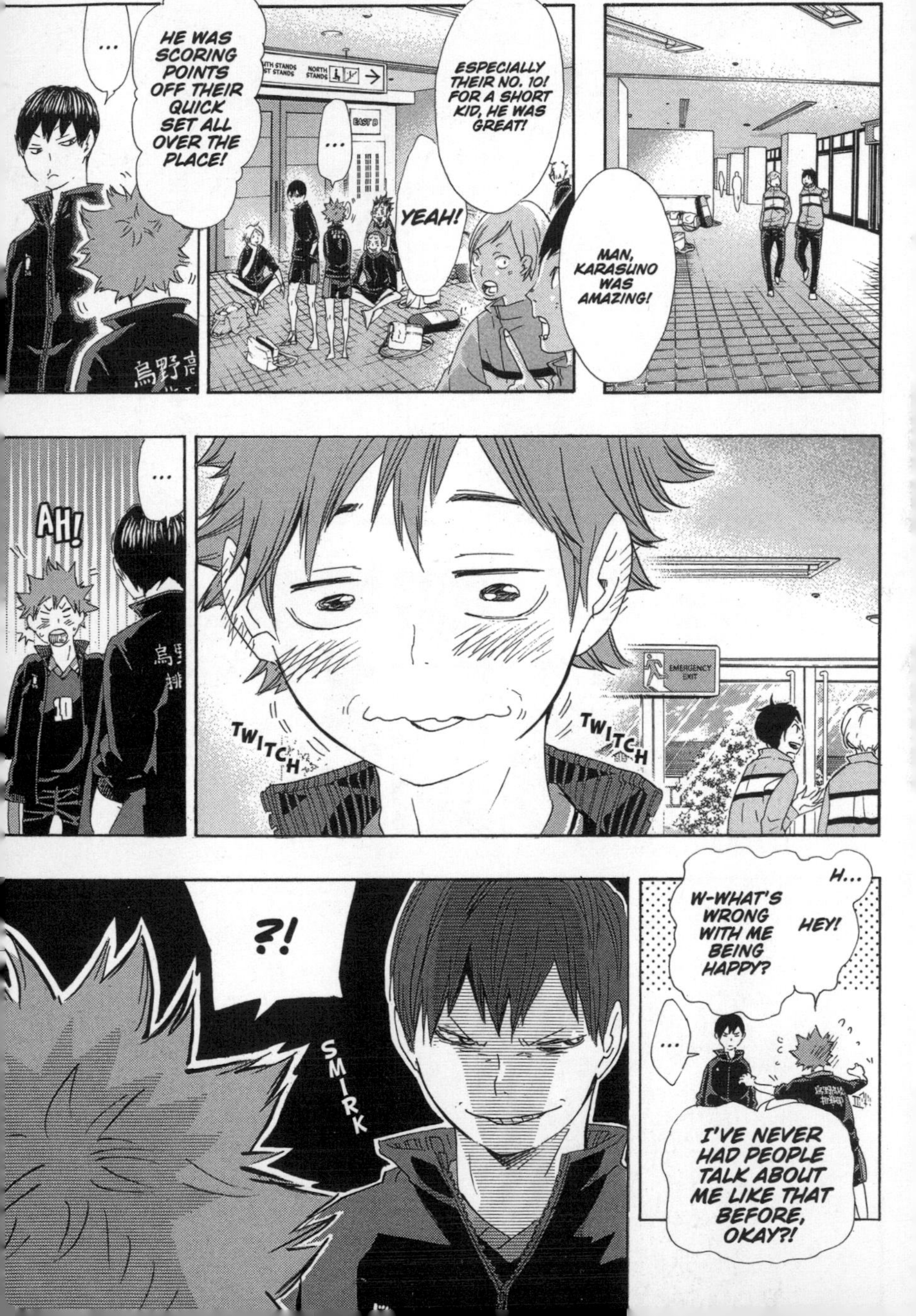
MAN, KARASUNO WAS AMAZING!
ESPECIALLY THEIR NO. 10! FOR A SHORT KID, HE WAS GREAT!
YEAH!
...
HE WAS SCORING POINTS OFF THEIR QUICK SET ALL OVER THE PLACE!
...
EMERGENCY EXIT
TWITCH
TWITCH
...
AH!
H...
HEY!
W-WHAT'S WRONG WITH ME BEING HAPPY?
...
I'VE NEVER HAD PEOPLE TALK ABOUT ME LIKE THAT BEFORE, OKAY?!
?!
SMIRK

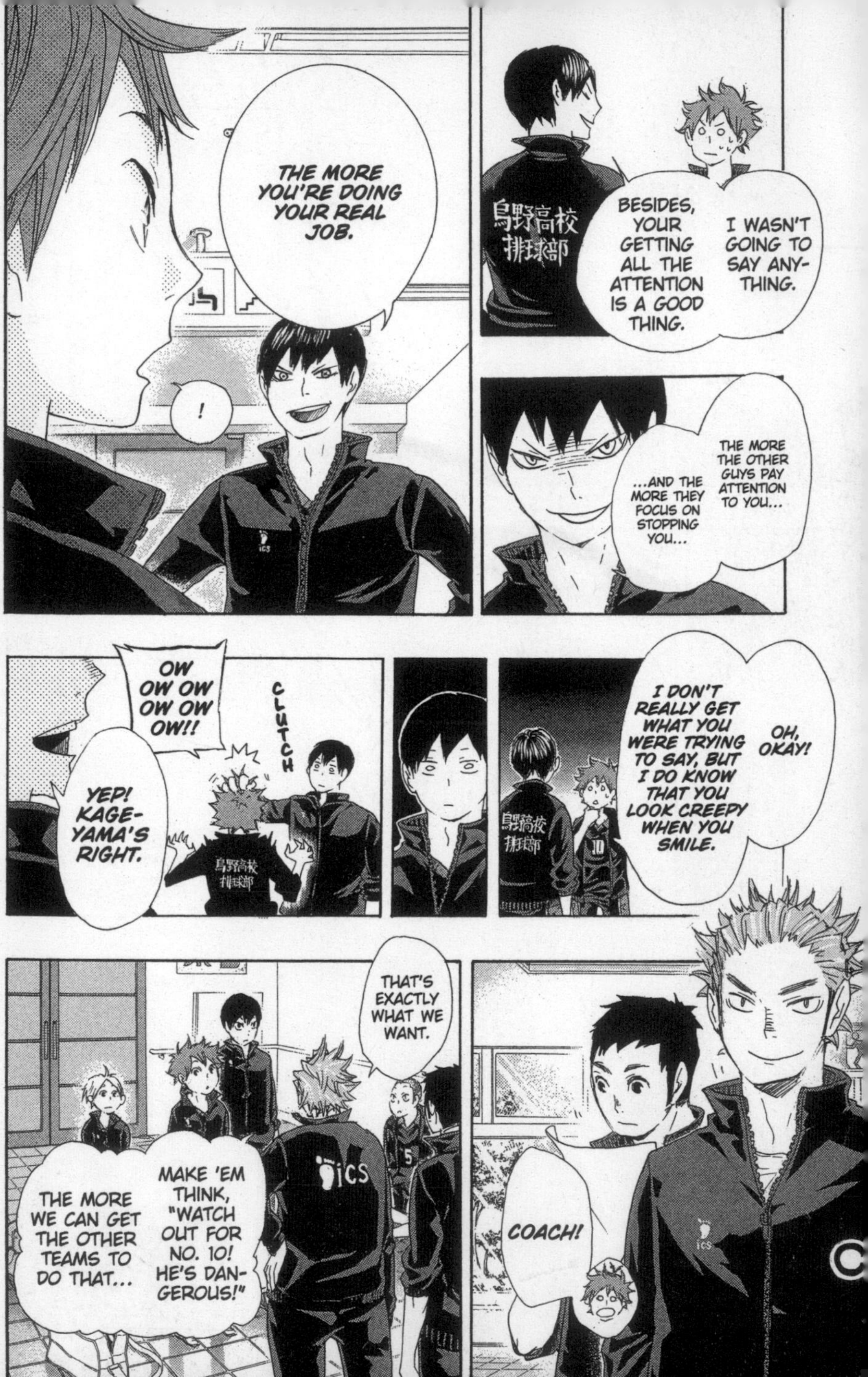
I WASN'T GOING TO SAY ANY-THING.
BESIDES, YOUR GETTING ALL THE ATTENTION IS A GOOD THING.
THE MORE THE OTHER GUYS PAY ATTENTION TO YOU...
...AND THE MORE THEY FOCUS ON STOPPING YOU...
THE MORE YOU'RE DOING YOUR REAL JOB.
!
OH, OKAY!
I DON'T REALLY GET WHAT YOU WERE TRYING TO SAY, BUT I DO KNOW THAT YOU LOOK CREEPY WHEN YOU SMILE.
OW OW OW OW OW!!
CLUTCH
YEP! KAGE-YAMA'S RIGHT.
COACH!
THAT'S EXACTLY WHAT WE WANT.
MAKE 'EM THINK, "WATCH OUT FOR NO. 10! HE'S DAN-GEROUS!"
THE MORE WE CAN GET THE OTHER TEAMS TO DO THAT...

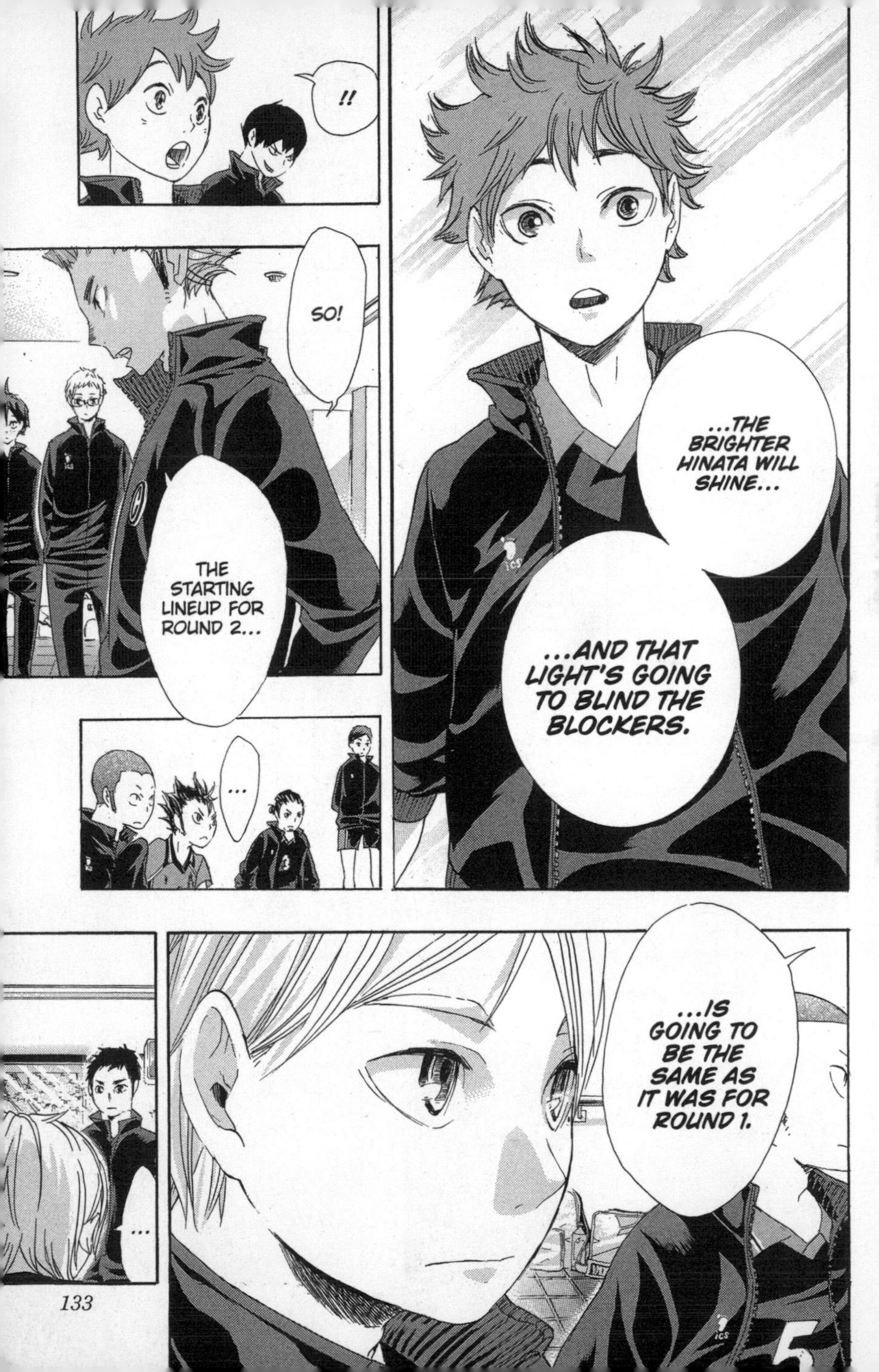
...THE BRIGHTER HINATA WILL SHINE...
...AND THAT LIGHT'S GOING TO BLIND THE BLOCKERS.
!!
SO!
THE STARTING LINEUP FOR ROUND 2...
...
...IS GOING TO BE THE SAME AS IT WAS FOR ROUND 1.
...

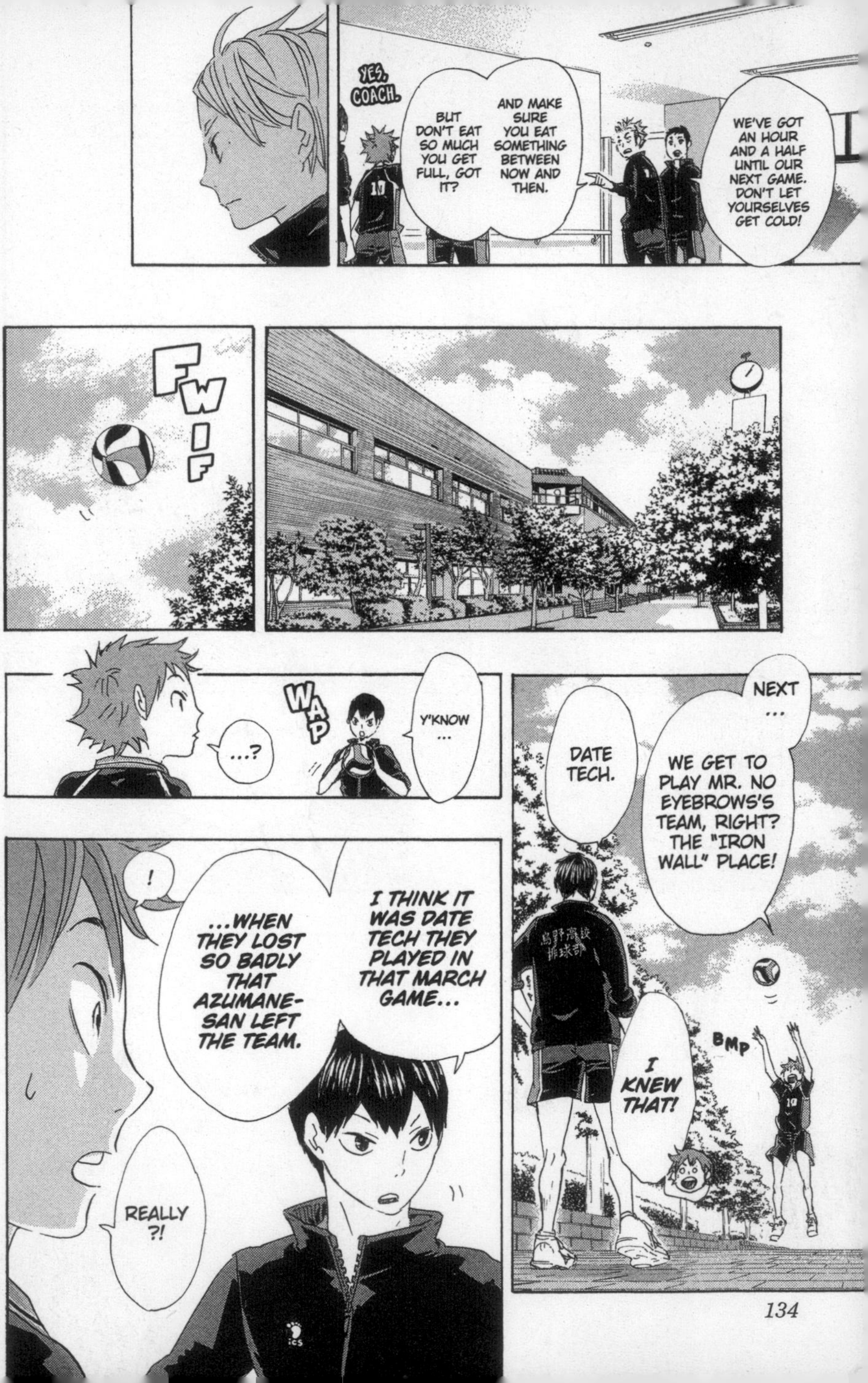
WE'VE GOT AN HOUR AND A HALF UNTIL OUR NEXT GAME. DON'T LET YOURSELVES GET COLD!
AND MAKE SURE YOU EAT SOMETHING BETWEEN NOW AND THEN.
BUT DON'T EAT SO MUCH YOU GET FULL, GOT IT?
YES, COACH.
FWIF
NEXT...
WE GET TO PLAY MR. NO EYEBROWS'S TEAM, RIGHT? THE "IRON WALL" PLACE!
DATE TECH.
I KNEW THAT!
BMP
Y'KNOW...
WAP
...?
I THINK IT WAS DATE TECH THEY PLAYED IN THAT MARCH GAME...
...WHEN THEY LOST SO BADLY THAT AZUMANE-SAN LEFT THE TEAM.
!
REALLY?!

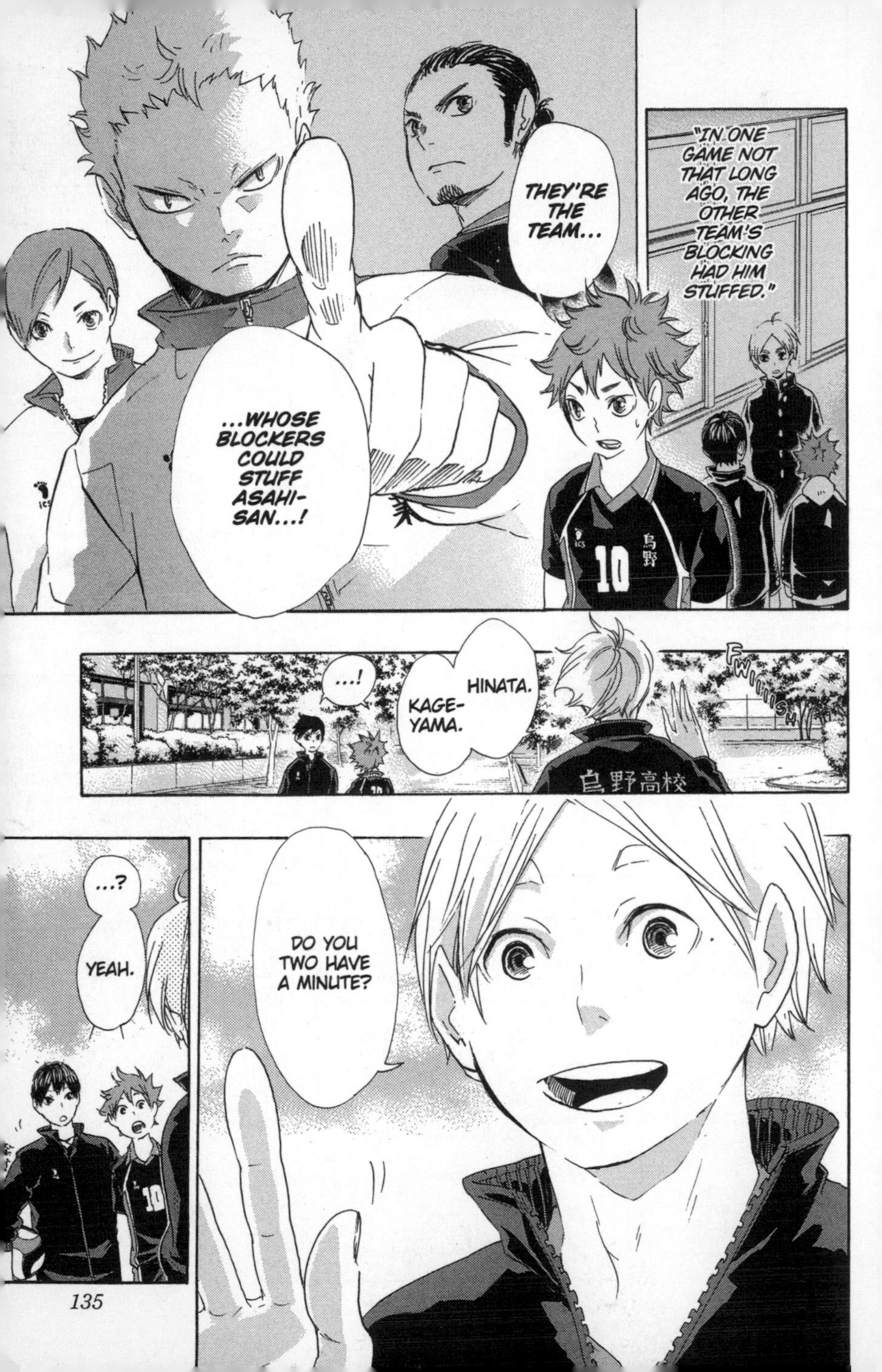
"IN ONE GAME NOT THAT LONG AGO, THE OTHER TEAM'S BLOCKING HAD HIM STUFFED."
THEY'RE THE TEAM...
...WHOSE BLOCKERS COULD STUFF ASAHI-SAN...!
FWIIIISH
HINATA. KAGE-YAMA.
...!
烏野高校
DO YOU TWO HAVE A MINUTE?
...?
YEAH.

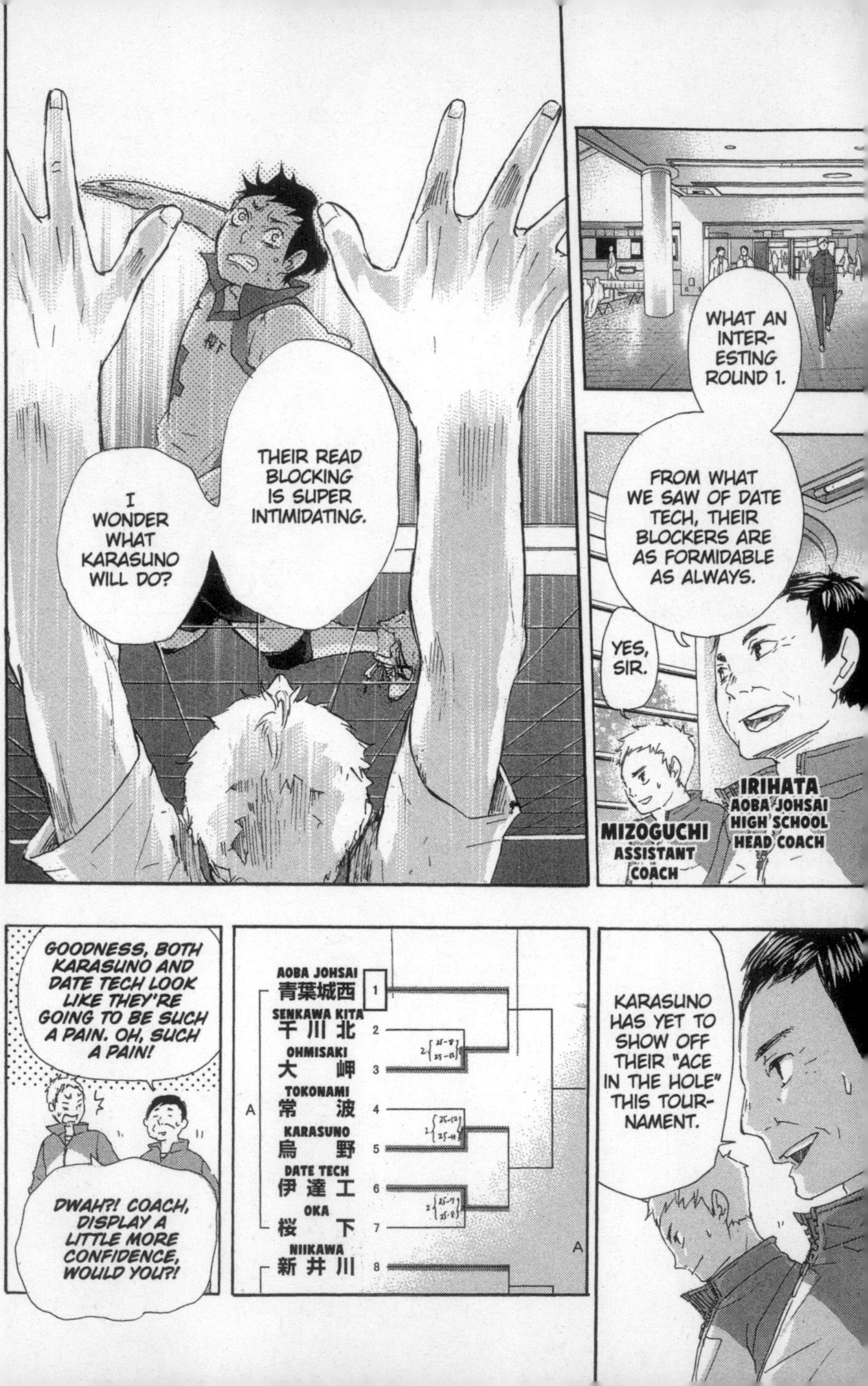

WHAT AN INTERESTING ROUND 1.
FROM WHAT WE SAW OF DATE TECH, THEIR BLOCKERS ARE AS FORMIDABLE AS ALWAYS.
YES, SIR.
IRIHATA AOBA JOHSAI HIGH SCHOOL HEAD COACH
MIZOGUCHI ASSISTANT COACH
THEIR READ BLOCKING IS SUPER INTIMIDATING.
I WONDER WHAT KARASUNO WILL DO?
KARASUNO HAS YET TO SHOW OFF THEIR "ACE IN THE HOLE" THIS TOURNAMENT.
AOBA JOHSAI 青葉城西 1
SENKAWA KITA 千川北 2
OHMISAKI 大岬 3
TOKONAMI 常波 4
KARASUNO 烏野 5
DATE TECH 伊達工 6
OKA 桜下 7
NIIKAWA 新井川 8
A
A
GOODNESS, BOTH KARASUNO AND DATE TECH LOOK LIKE THEY'RE GOING TO BE SUCH A PAIN. OH, SUCH A PAIN!
DWAH?! COACH, DISPLAY A LITTLE MORE CONFIDENCE, WOULD YOU?!

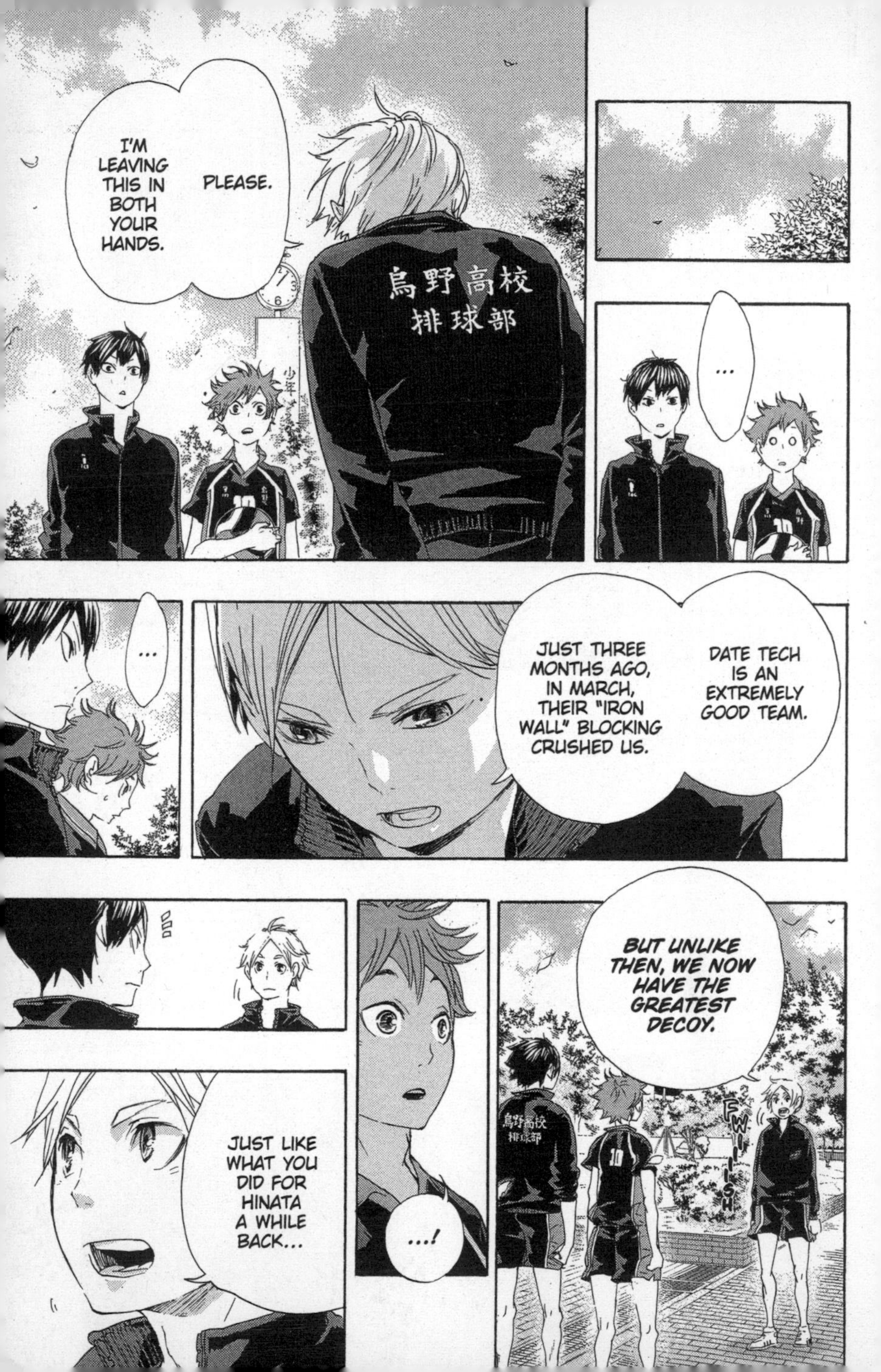
...
PLEASE.
I'M LEAVING THIS IN BOTH YOUR HANDS.
烏野高校
排球部
DATE TECH IS AN EXTREMELY GOOD TEAM.
JUST THREE MONTHS AGO, IN MARCH, THEIR "IRON WALL" BLOCKING CRUSHED US.
...
BUT UNLIKE THEN, WE NOW HAVE THE GREATEST DECOY.
FWIIISH
...!
JUST LIKE WHAT YOU DID FOR HINATA A WHILE BACK...

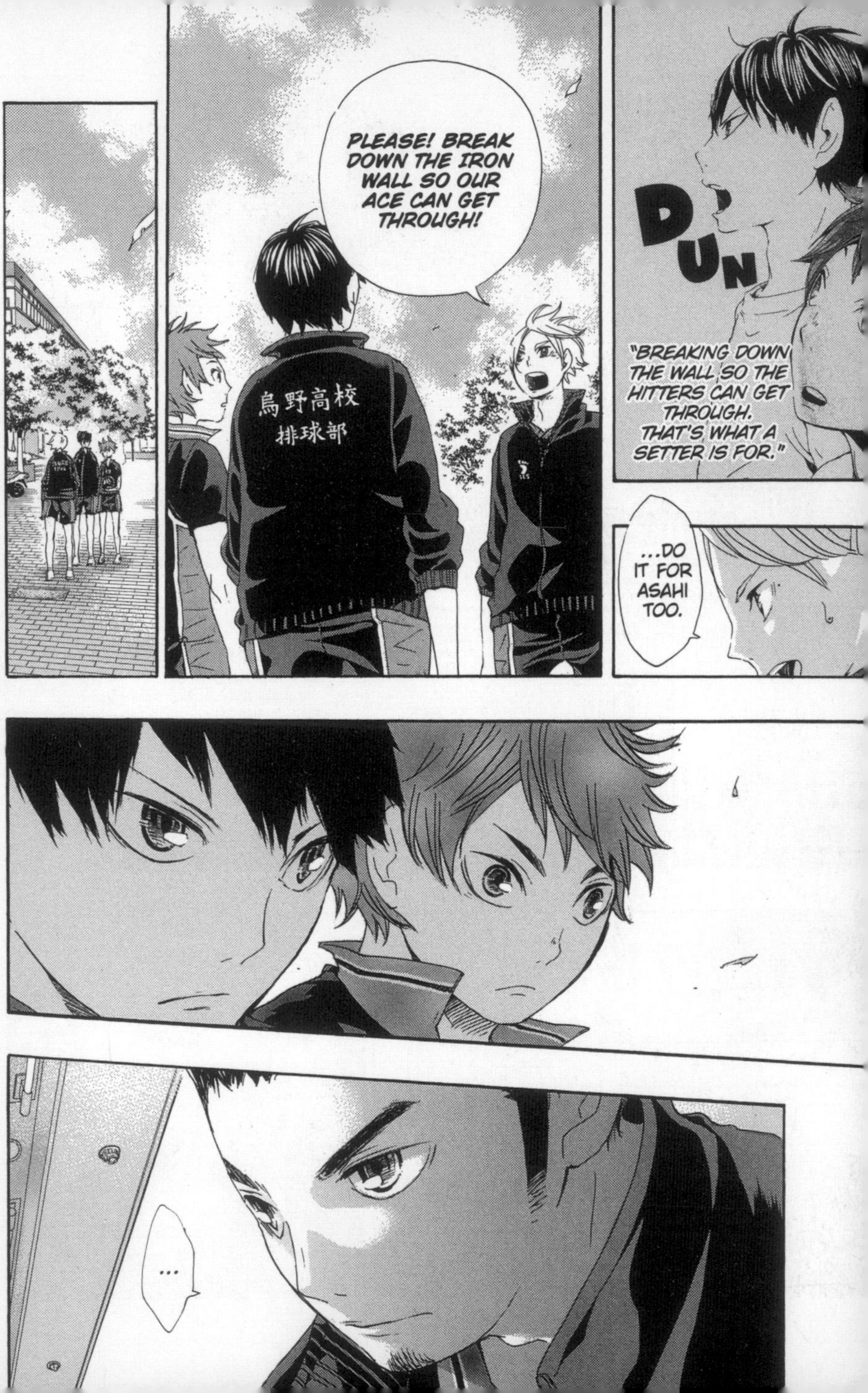
DUN
"BREAKING DOWN THE WALL SO THE HITTERS CAN GET THROUGH. THAT'S WHAT A SETTER IS FOR."
...DO IT FOR ASAHI TOO.
PLEASE! BREAK DOWN THE IRON WALL SO OUR ACE CAN GET THROUGH!
烏野高校
排球部
...

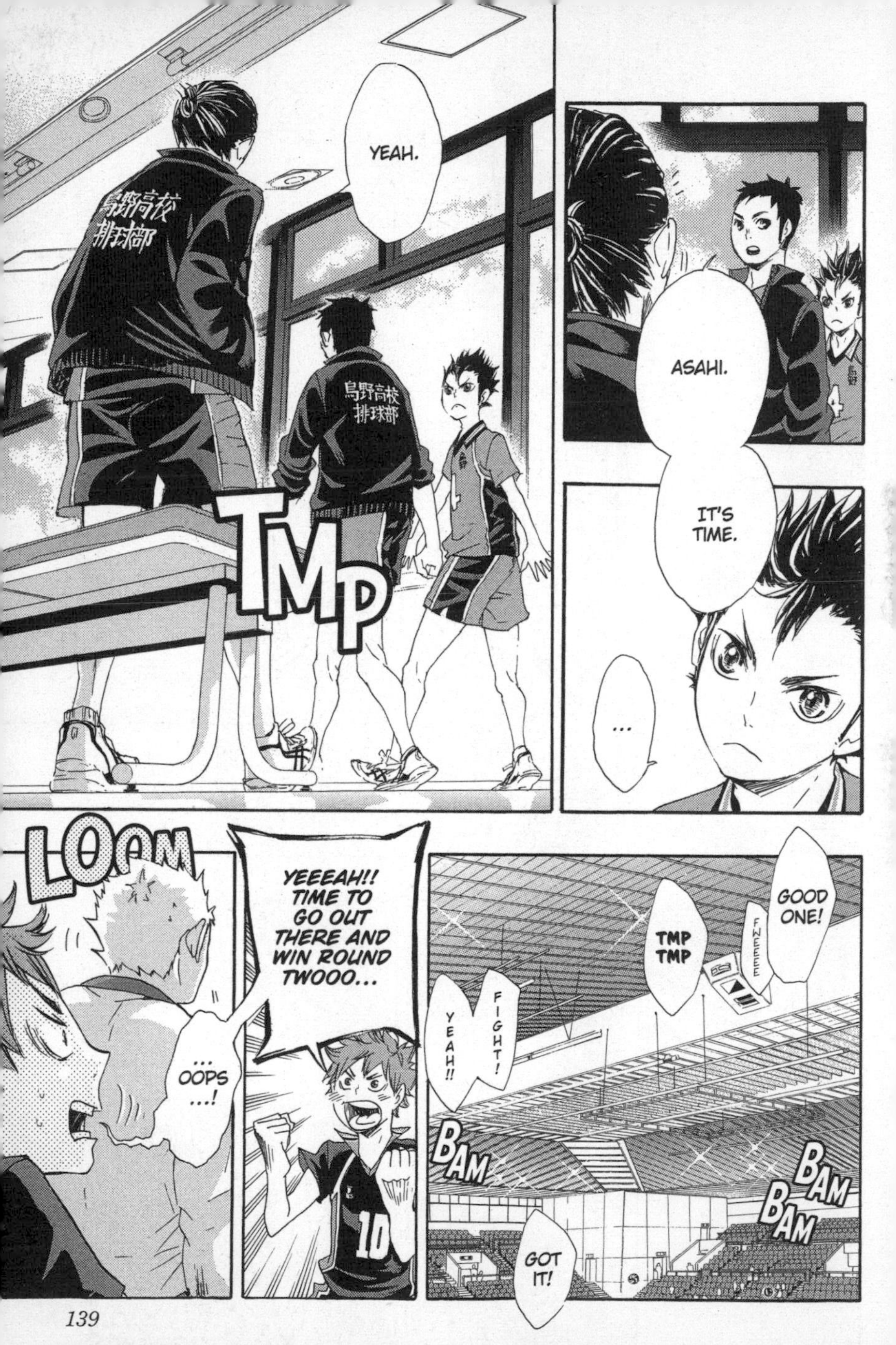
ASAHI.
IT'S TIME.
...
YEAH.
烏野高校排球部
TMP
GOOD ONE!
FWEEEE
TMP TMP
FIGHT!
YEAH!!
BAM
BAM BAM
GOT IT!
YEEEAH!! TIME TO GO OUT THERE AND WIN ROUND TWOOO...
LOOM
... OOPS ...!

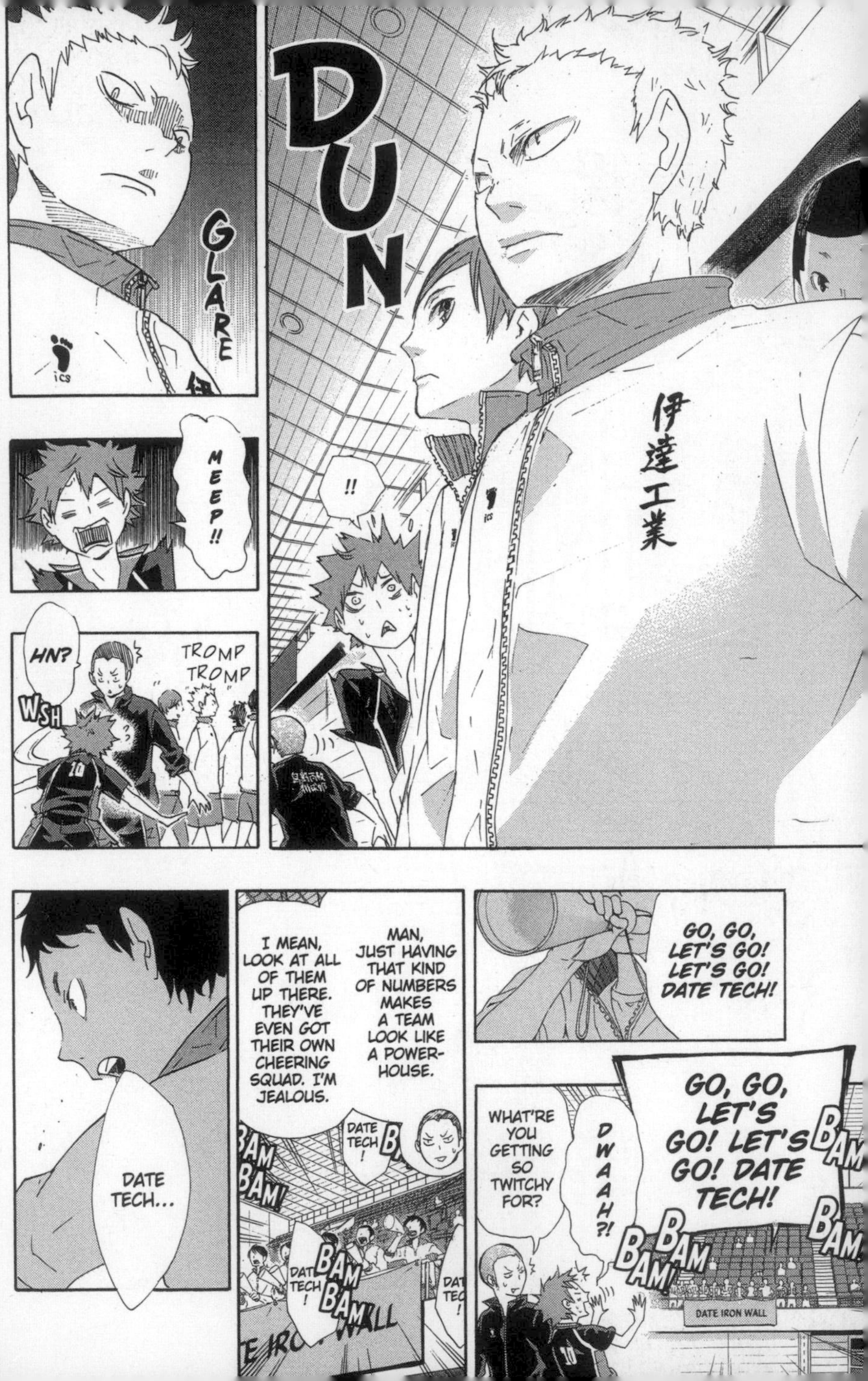
DUN
!!
伊達工業
GLARE
MEEP!!
HN?
TROMP TROMP
WSH
GO, GO, LET'S GO! LET'S GO! DATE TECH!
GO, GO, LET'S GO! LET'S GO! DATE TECH!
BAM
BAM
BAM BAM
DWAAAH?!
WHAT'RE YOU GETTING SO TWITCHY FOR?
DATE IRON WALL
MAN, JUST HAVING THAT KIND OF NUMBERS MAKES A TEAM LOOK LIKE A POWER-HOUSE.
I MEAN, LOOK AT ALL OF THEM UP THERE. THEY'VE EVEN GOT THEIR OWN CHEERING SQUAD. I'M JEALOUS.
DATE TECH!
BAM BAM!
DATE TECH!
BAM BAM
DATE TECH...

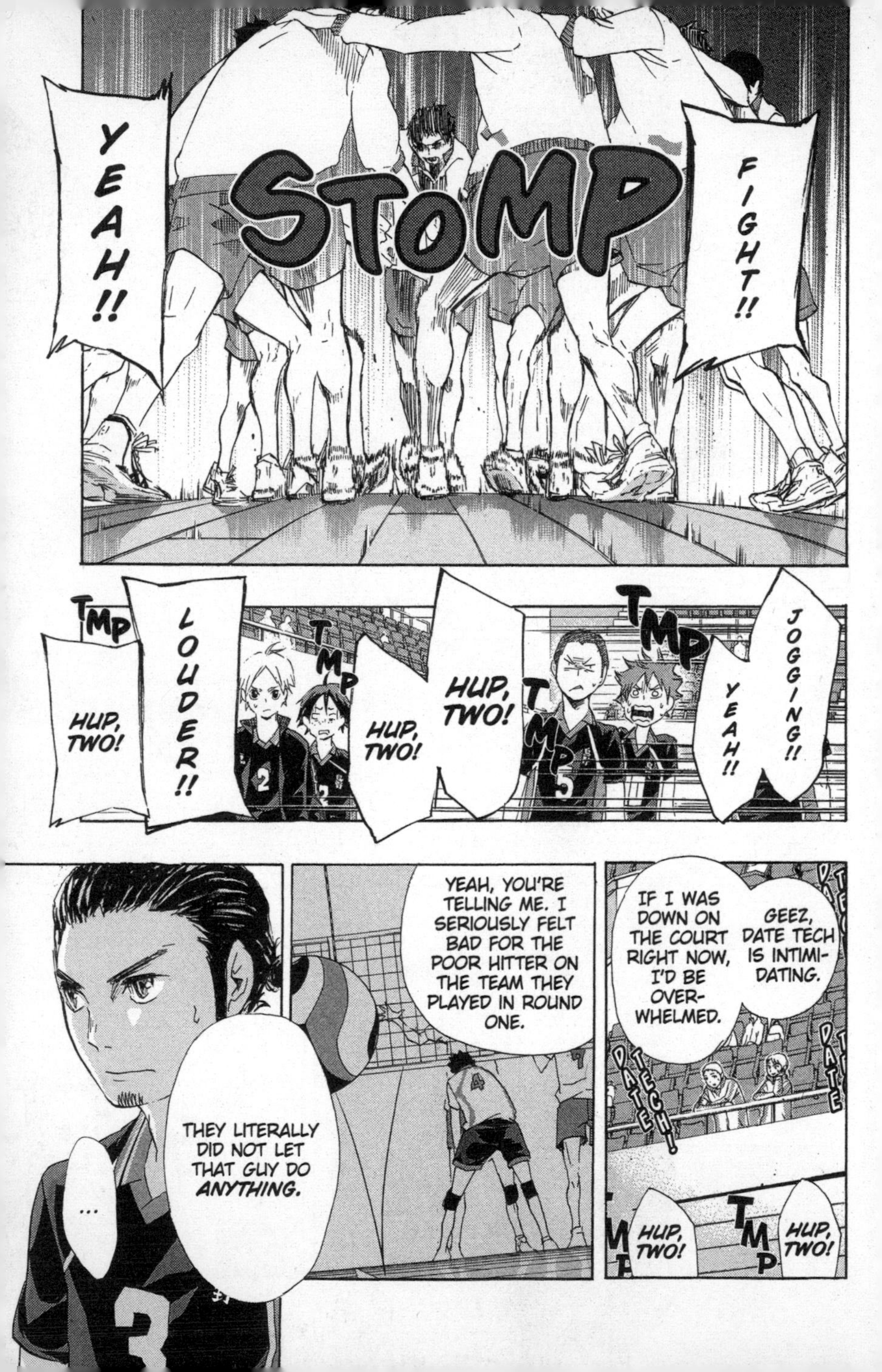
FIGHT!!
STOMP
YEAH!!
JOGGING!!
YEAH!!
TMP
TMP
HUP, TWO!
HUP, TWO!
TMP
LOUDER!!
TMP
HUP, TWO!
GEEZ, DATE TECH IS INTIMIDATING.
IF I WAS DOWN ON THE COURT RIGHT NOW, I'D BE OVERWHELMED.
DATE TECH!
HUP, TWO!
TMP
HUP, TWO!
YEAH, YOU'RE TELLING ME. I SERIOUSLY FELT BAD FOR THE POOR HITTER ON THE TEAM THEY PLAYED IN ROUND ONE.
THEY LITERALLY DID NOT LET THAT GUY DO *ANYTHING.*
...

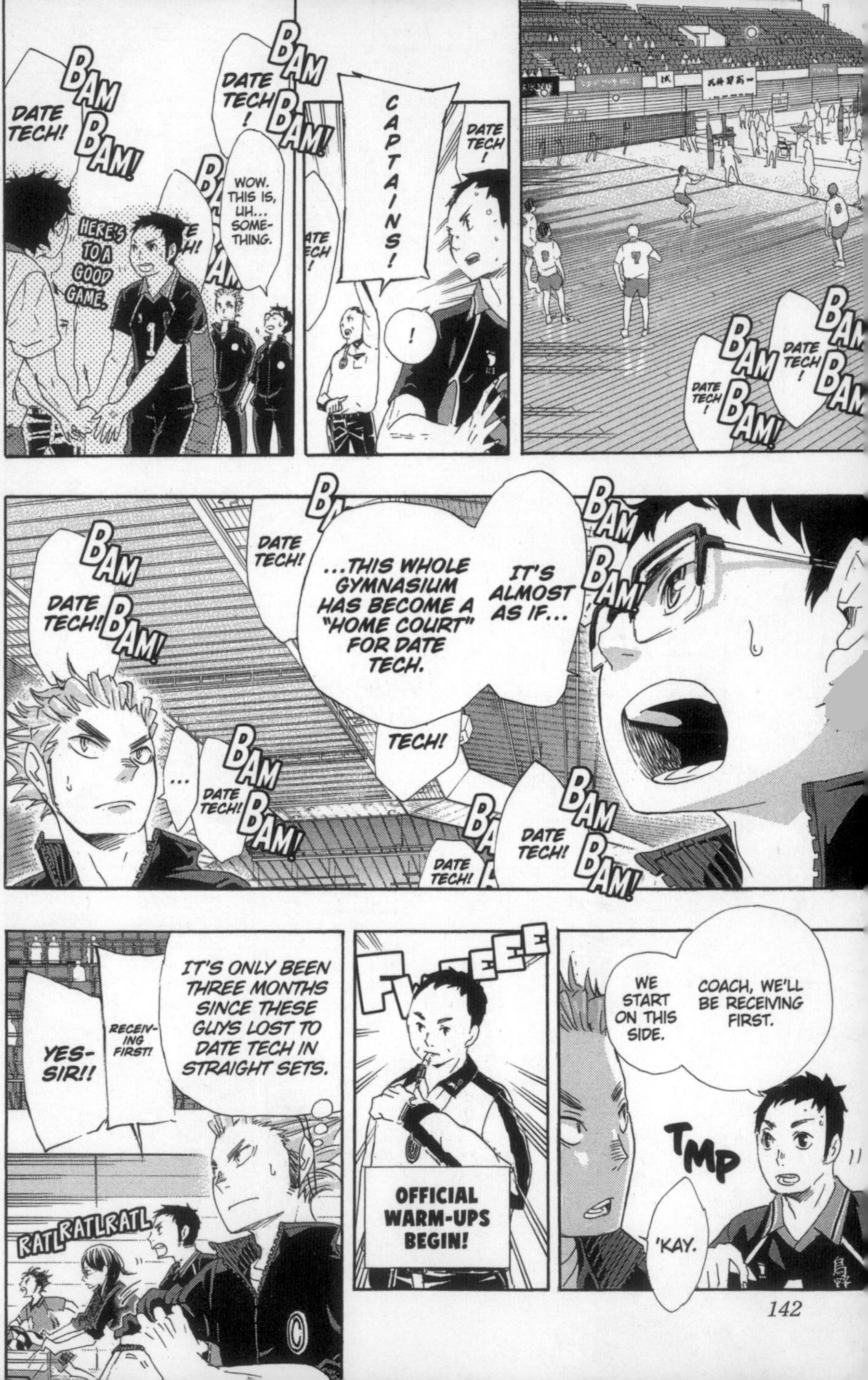
BAM BAM BAM!
DATE TECH!
DATE TECH!
DATE TECH!
CAPTAINS!
!
BAM BAM!
DATE TECH!
WOW. THIS IS, UH... SOMETHING.
DATE TECH!
BAM BAM!
HERE'S TO A GOOD GAME.
IT'S ALMOST AS IF...
...THIS WHOLE GYMNASIUM HAS BECOME A "HOME COURT" FOR DATE TECH.
BAM BAM!
BAM BAM!
DATE TECH!
TECH!
DATE TECH!
DATE TECH!
BAM BAM!
DATE TECH!
BAM BAM!
...
DATE TECH!
COACH, WE'LL BE RECEIVING FIRST.
WE START ON THIS SIDE.
TMP
'KAY.
FWEEEE
OFFICIAL WARM-UPS BEGIN!
IT'S ONLY BEEN THREE MONTHS SINCE THESE GUYS LOST TO DATE TECH IN STRAIGHT SETS.
RECEIVING FIRST!
YES-SIR!!
RATLRATLRATL

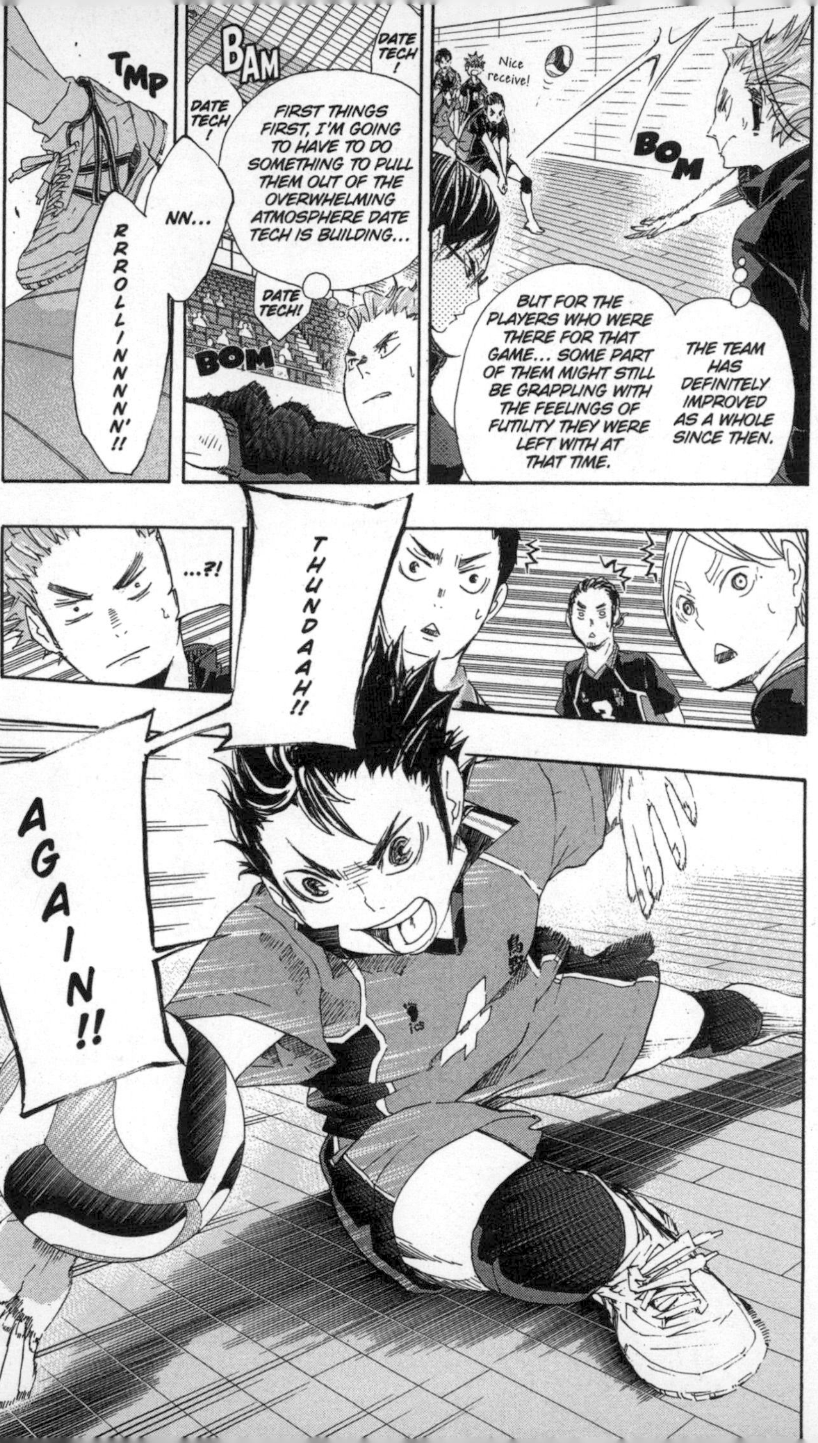
Nice receive!
BOM
THE TEAM HAS DEFINITELY IMPROVED AS A WHOLE SINCE THEN.
BUT FOR THE PLAYERS WHO WERE THERE FOR THAT GAME... SOME PART OF THEM MIGHT STILL BE GRAPPLING WITH THE FEELINGS OF FUTILITY THEY WERE LEFT WITH AT THAT TIME.
DATE TECH!
BAM
DATE TECH!
FIRST THINGS FIRST, I'M GOING TO HAVE TO DO SOMETHING TO PULL THEM OUT OF THE OVERWHELMING ATMOSPHERE DATE TECH IS BUILDING...
DATE TECH!
BOM
TMP
NN...
RRROLLINNNNN'!!
THUNDAAAH!!
...?!
AGAIN!!

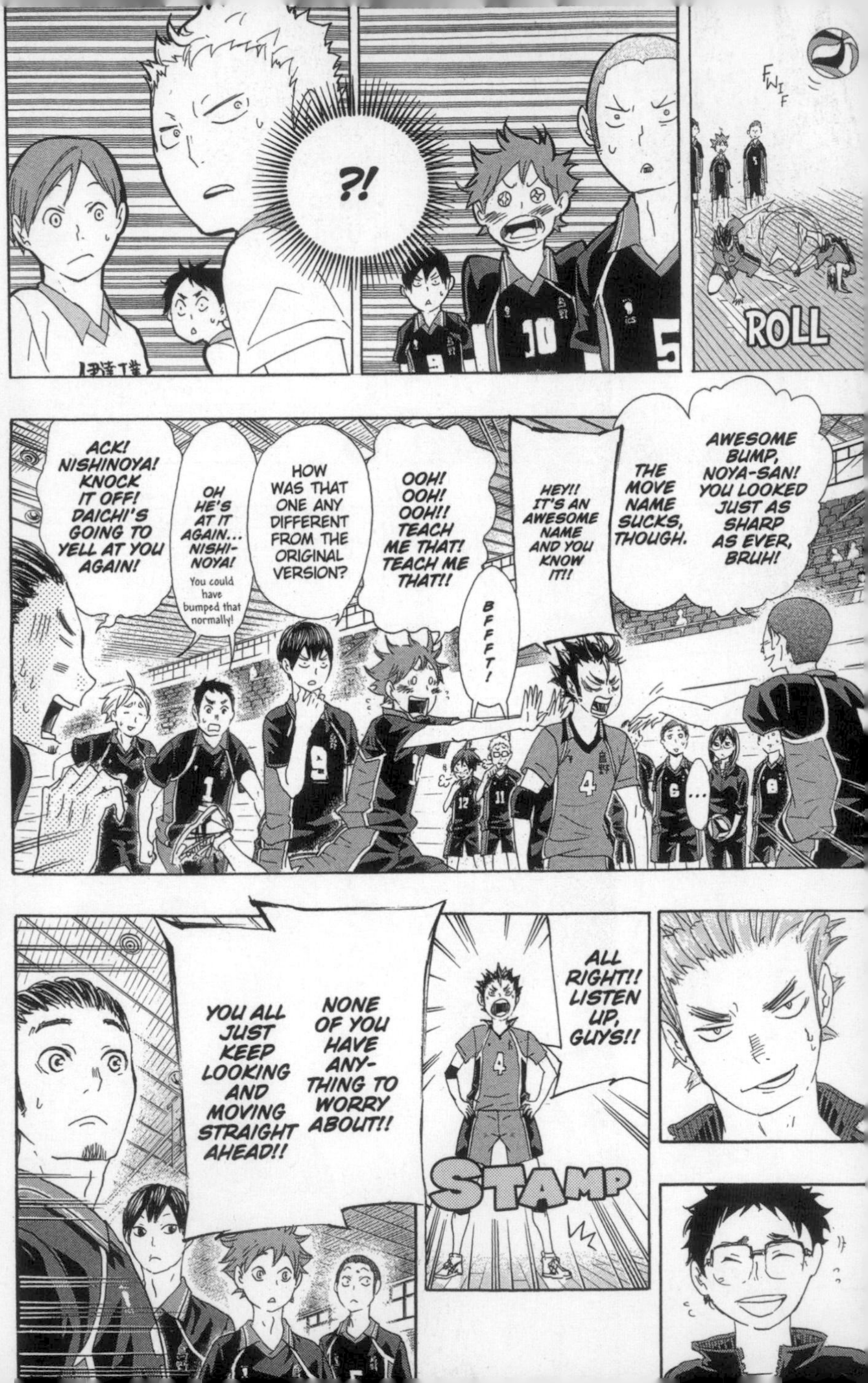

FWIF
ROLL
?!
AWESOME BUMP, NOYA-SAN! YOU LOOKED JUST AS SHARP AS EVER, BRUH!
THE MOVE NAME SUCKS, THOUGH.
HEY!! IT'S AN AWESOME NAME AND YOU KNOW IT!!
BFFFT!
OOH! OOH! OOH!! TEACH ME THAT! TEACH ME THAT!!
HOW WAS THAT ONE ANY DIFFERENT FROM THE ORIGINAL VERSION?
OH HE'S AT IT AGAIN... NISHI-NOYA!
You could have bumped that normally!
ACK! NISHINOYA! KNOCK IT OFF! DAICHI'S GOING TO YELL AT YOU AGAIN!
...
ALL RIGHT!! LISTEN UP, GUYS!!
STAMP
NONE OF YOU HAVE ANY-THING TO WORRY ABOUT!!
YOU ALL JUST KEEP LOOKING AND MOVING STRAIGHT AHEAD!!

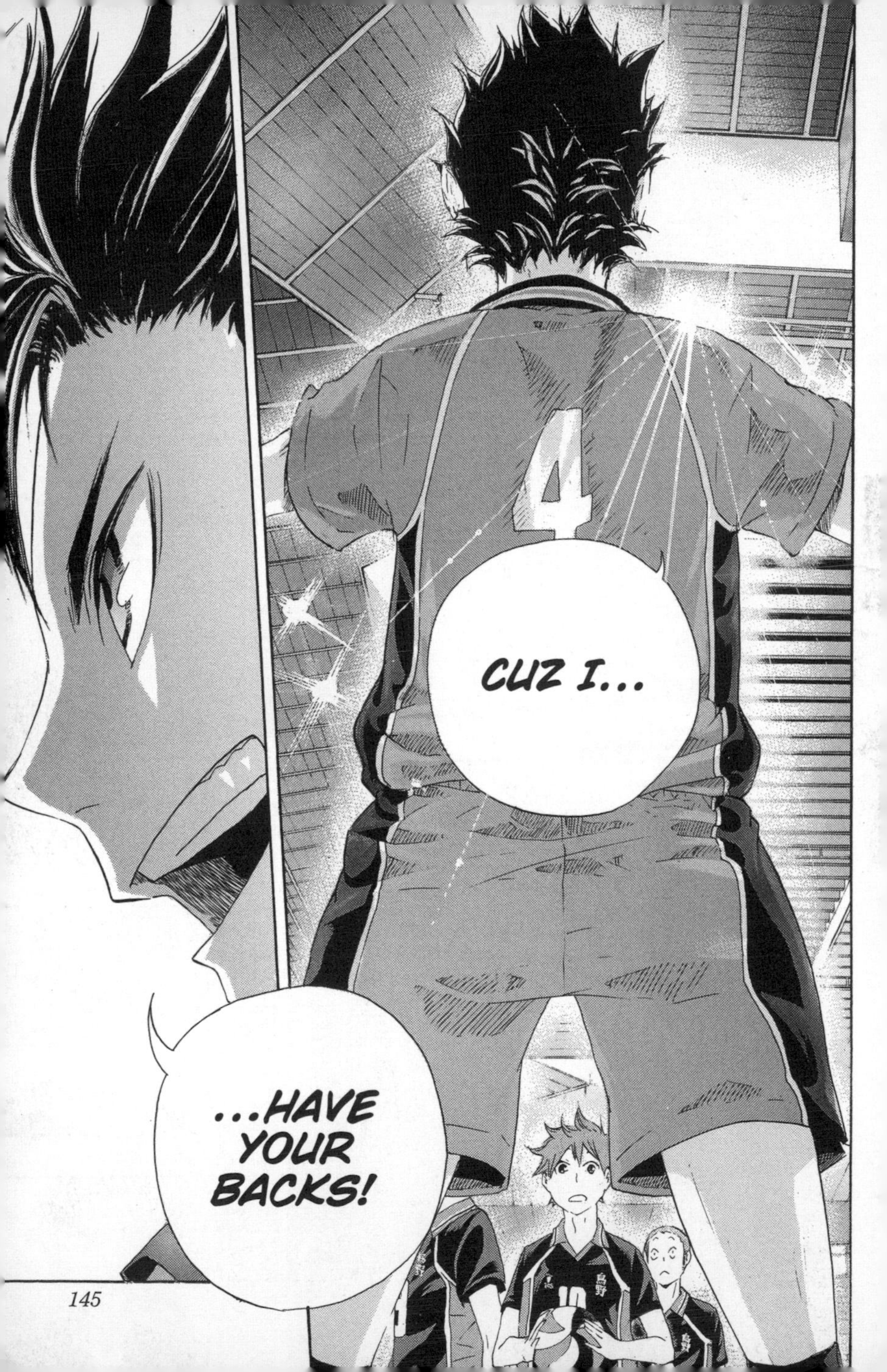
CUZ I...
...HAVE YOUR BACKS!

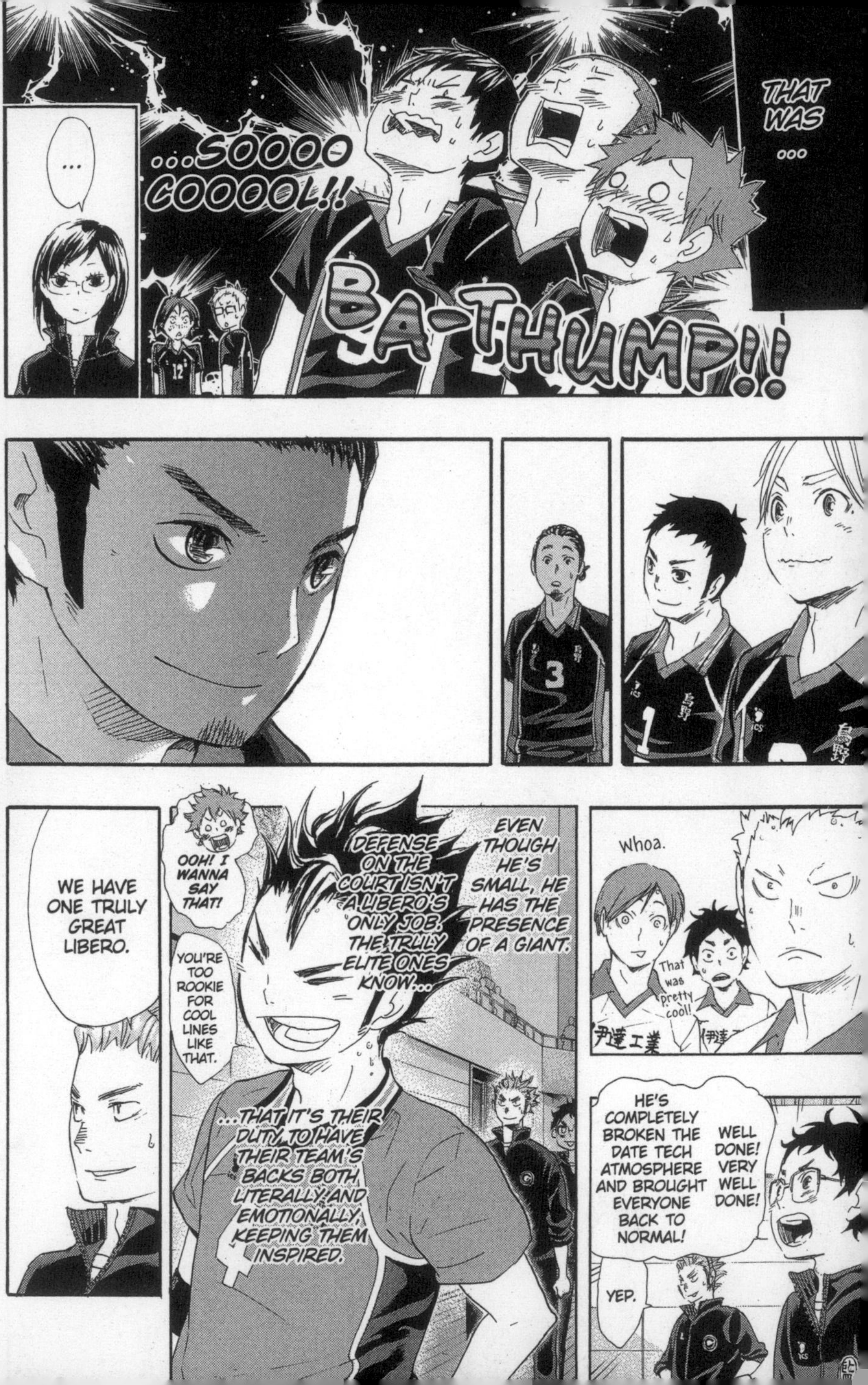
THAT WAS ...
...SOOOO COOOOL!!
BA-THUMP!!
...
Whoa.
That was pretty cool!
HE'S COMPLETELY BROKEN THE DATE TECH ATMOSPHERE AND BROUGHT EVERYONE BACK TO NORMAL!
WELL DONE! VERY WELL DONE!
YEP.
EVEN THOUGH HE'S SMALL, HE HAS THE PRESENCE OF A GIANT.
DEFENSE ON THE COURT ISN'T A LIBERO'S ONLY JOB. THE TRULY ELITE ONES KNOW...
OOH! I WANNA SAY THAT!
YOU'RE TOO ROOKIE FOR COOL LINES LIKE THAT.
...THAT IT'S THEIR DUTY TO HAVE THEIR TEAM'S BACKS BOTH LITERALLY AND EMOTIONALLY, KEEPING THEM INSPIRED.
WE HAVE ONE TRULY GREAT LIBERO.

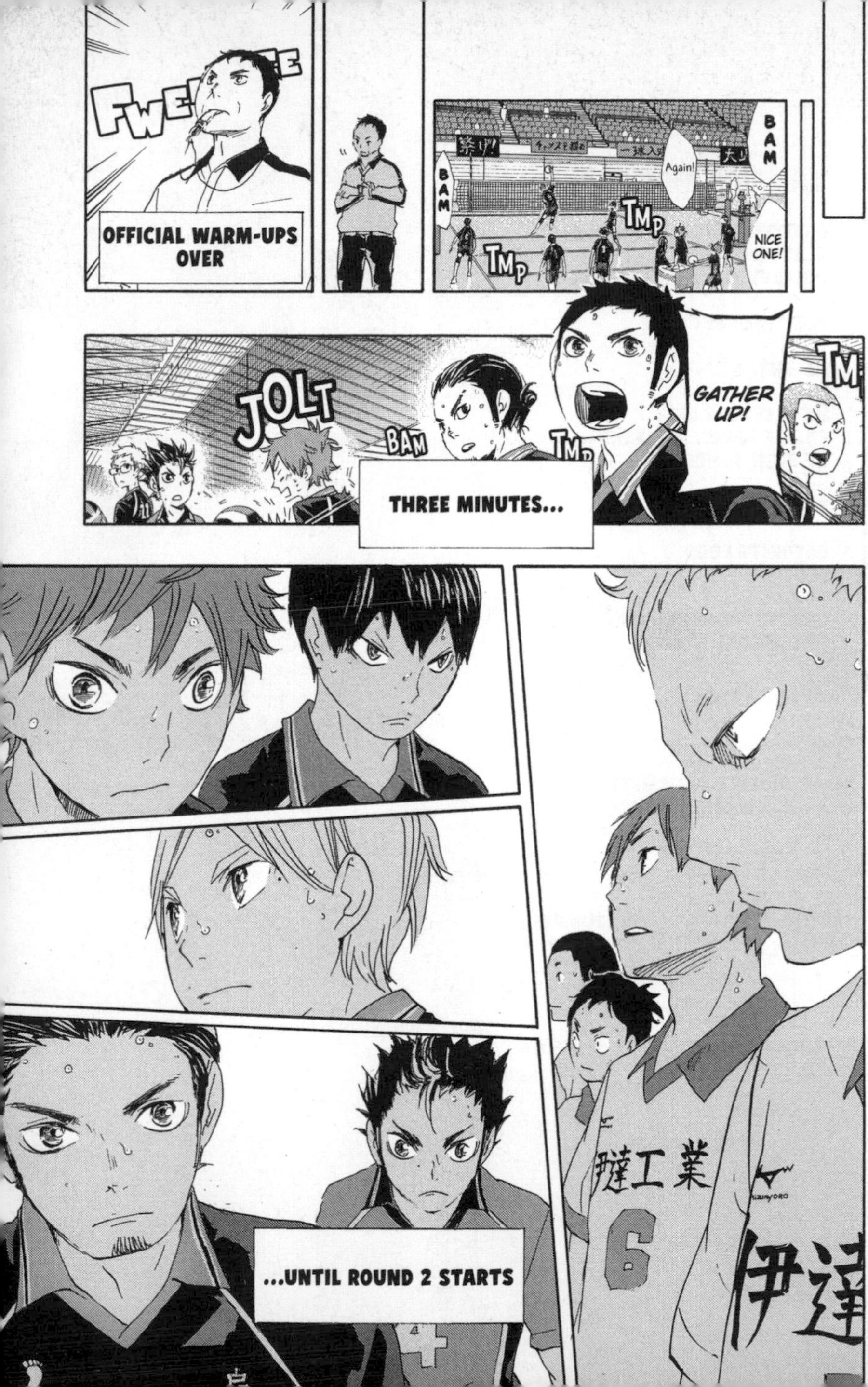

OFFICIAL WARM-UPS OVER
BAM
Again!
NICE ONE!
TMP
BAM
TMP
TM
GATHER UP!
TMP
BAM
JOLT
THREE MINUTES...
...UNTIL ROUND 2 STARTS

KANAME MONIWA

DATE TECHNICAL HIGH SCHOOL
CLASS 3-C
VOLLEYBALL CLUB CAPTAIN

POSITION: SETTER

HEIGHT: 5'9"

WEIGHT: 149 LBS.
(AS OF APRIL, 3RD YEAR
OF HIGH SCHOOL)

BIRTHDAY: SEPTEMBER 6

FAVORITE FOOD:
FOOD

CURRENT WORRY:
THE SECOND YEARS.

ABILITY PARAMETERS
(5-POINT SCALE)

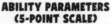

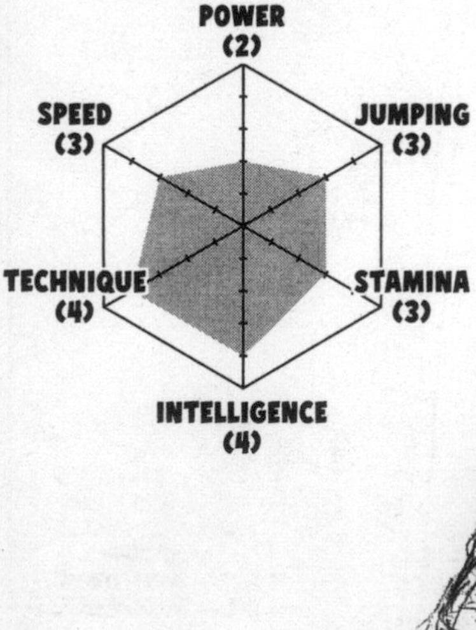
POWER
(2)
JUMPING
(3)
STAMINA
(3)
INTELLIGENCE
(4)
TECHNIQUE
(4)
SPEED
(3)

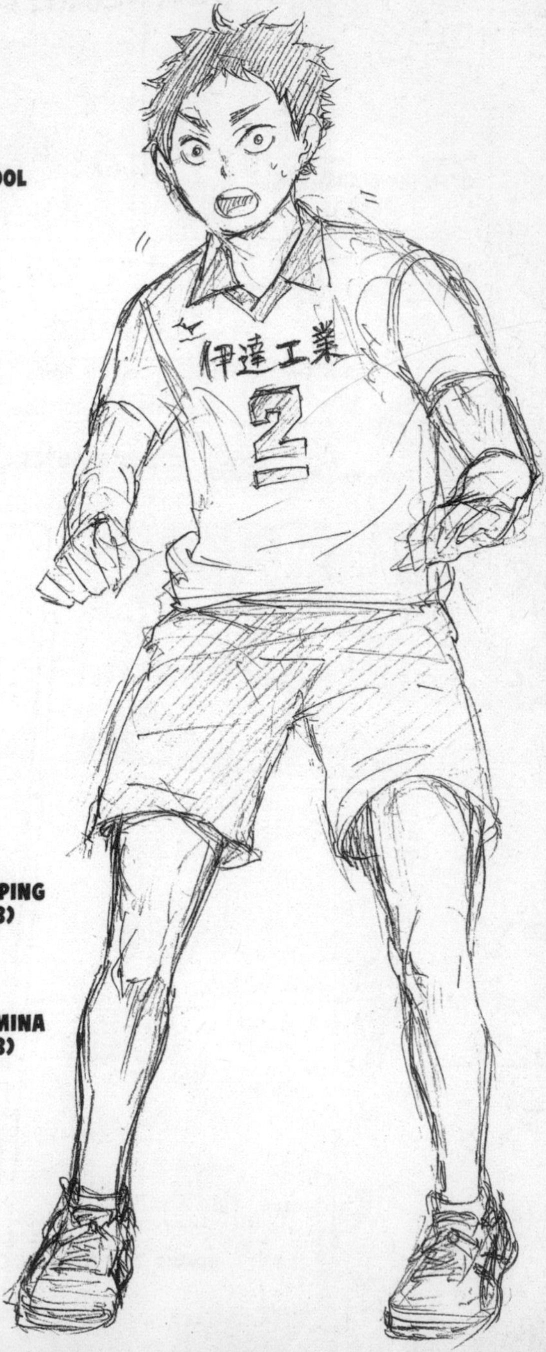
伊達工業
2

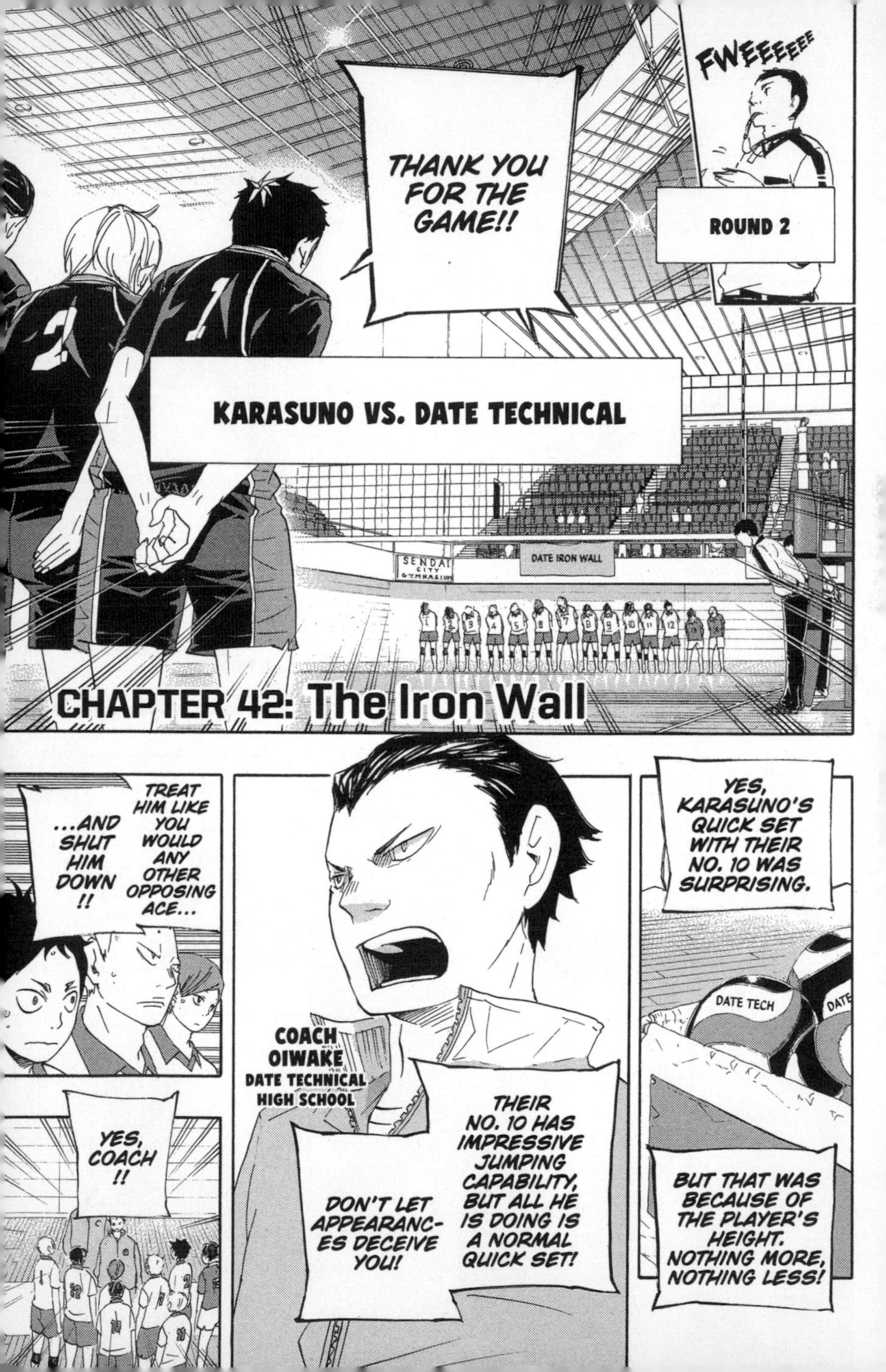

FWEEEEEE
ROUND 2
THANK YOU FOR THE GAME!!
KARASUNO VS. DATE TECHNICAL
SENDAI CITY GYMNASIUM
DATE IRON WALL
CHAPTER 42: The Iron Wall
YES, KARASUNO'S QUICK SET WITH THEIR NO. 10 WAS SURPRISING.
DATE TECH
BUT THAT WAS BECAUSE OF THE PLAYER'S HEIGHT. NOTHING MORE, NOTHING LESS!
COACH OIWAKE
DATE TECHNICAL HIGH SCHOOL
THEIR NO. 10 HAS IMPRESSIVE JUMPING CAPABILITY, BUT ALL HE IS DOING IS A NORMAL QUICK SET!
DON'T LET APPEARANC-ES DECEIVE YOU!
TREAT HIM LIKE YOU WOULD ANY OTHER OPPOSING ACE...
...AND SHUT HIM DOWN!!
YES, COACH!!

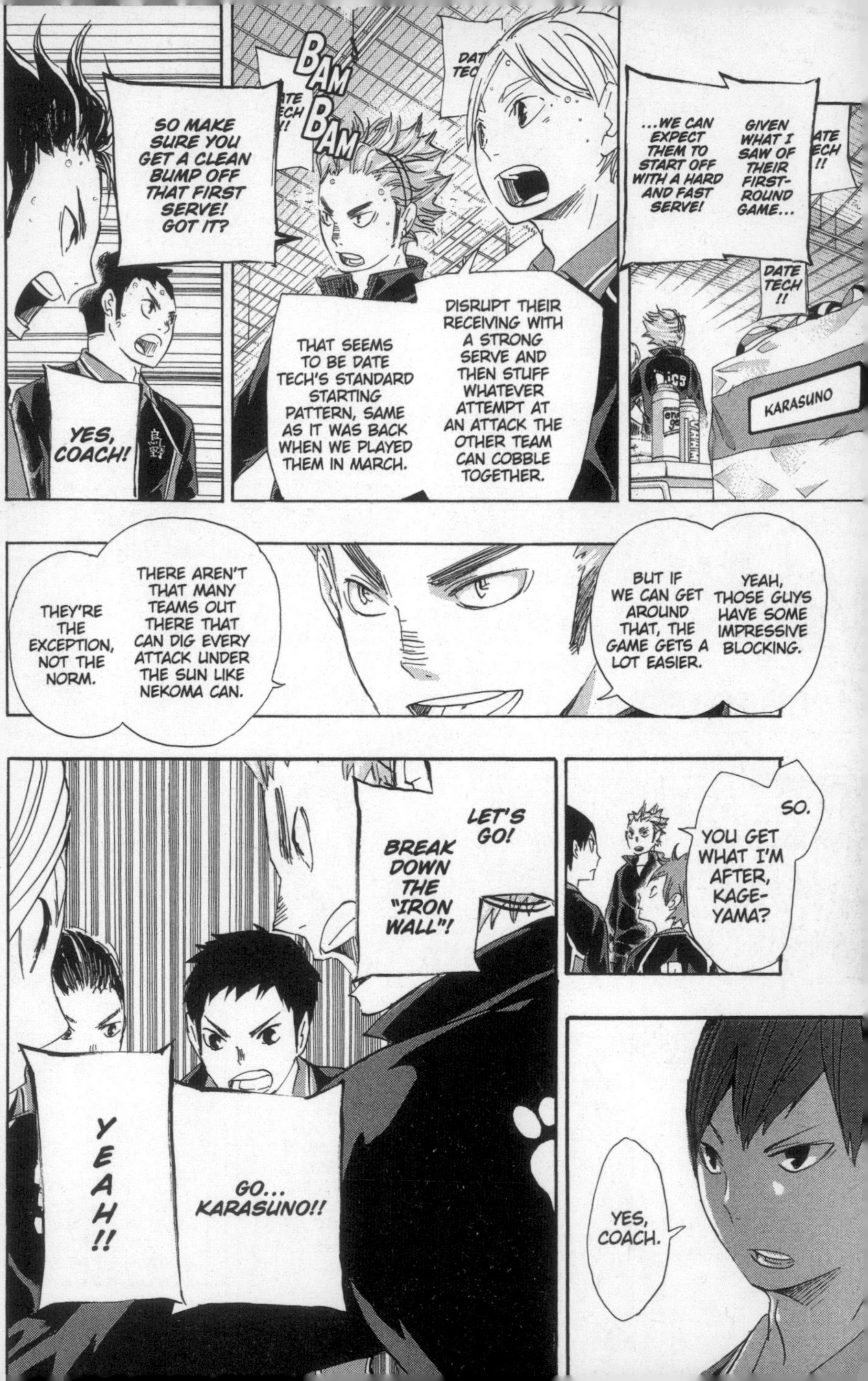
GIVEN WHAT I SAW OF THEIR FIRST-ROUND GAME...
...WE CAN EXPECT THEM TO START OFF WITH A HARD AND FAST SERVE!
DATE TECH !!
KARASUNO
BAM BAM
DISRUPT THEIR RECEIVING WITH A STRONG SERVE AND THEN STUFF WHATEVER ATTEMPT AT AN ATTACK THE OTHER TEAM CAN COBBLE TOGETHER.
THAT SEEMS TO BE DATE TECH'S STANDARD STARTING PATTERN, SAME AS IT WAS BACK WHEN WE PLAYED THEM IN MARCH.
SO MAKE SURE YOU GET A CLEAN BUMP OFF THAT FIRST SERVE! GOT IT?
YES, COACH!
YEAH, THOSE GUYS HAVE SOME IMPRESSIVE BLOCKING.
BUT IF WE CAN GET AROUND THAT, THE GAME GETS A LOT EASIER.
THERE AREN'T THAT MANY TEAMS OUT THERE THAT CAN DIG EVERY ATTACK UNDER THE SUN LIKE NEKOMA CAN.
THEY'RE THE EXCEPTION, NOT THE NORM.
SO.
YOU GET WHAT I'M AFTER, KAGE-YAMA?
YES, COACH.
LET'S GO!
BREAK DOWN THE "IRON WALL"!
GO... KARASUNO!!
YEAH!!

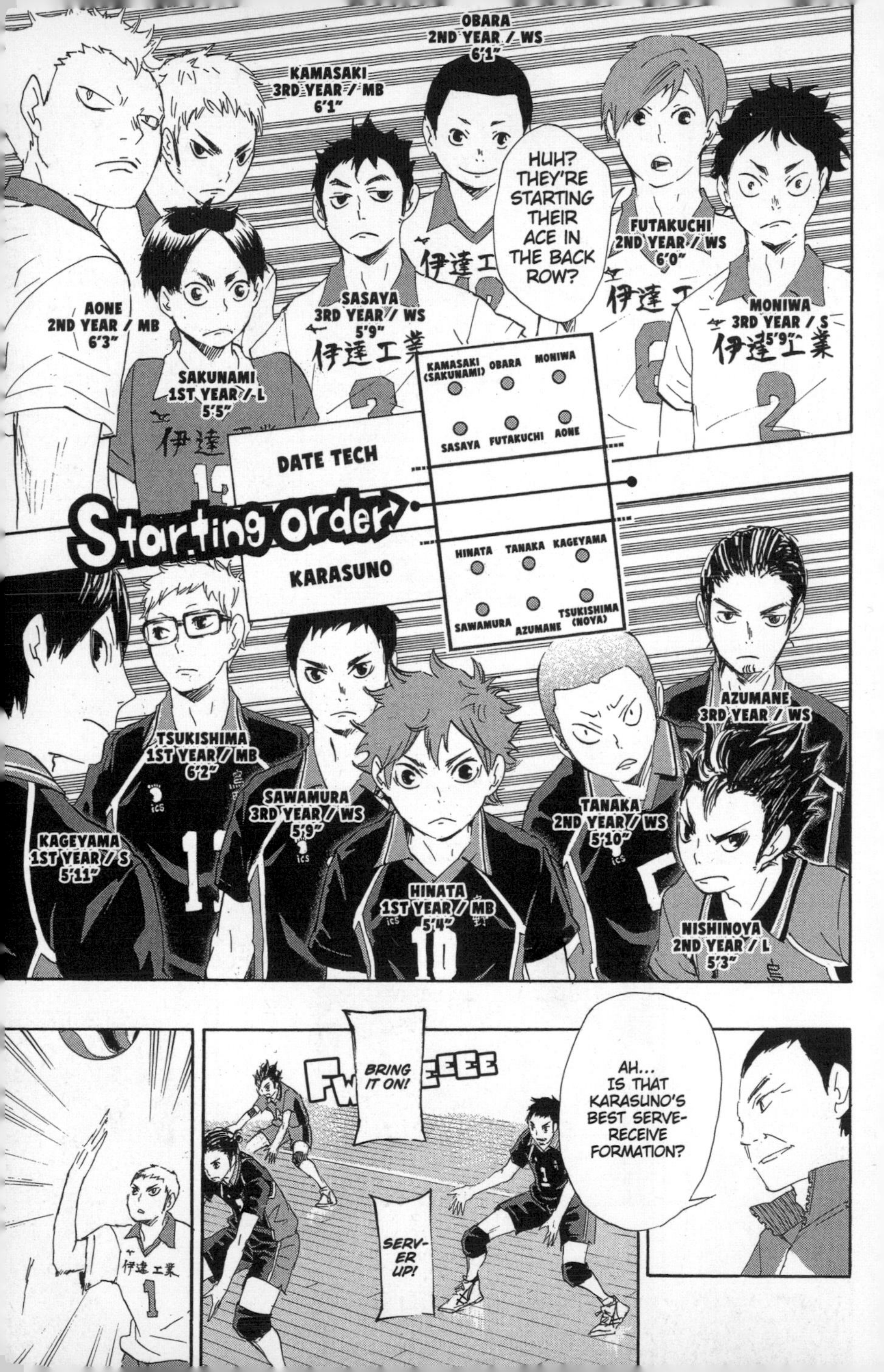

OBARA
2ND YEAR / WS
6'1"
KAMASAKI
3RD YEAR / MB
6'1"
MONIWA
3RD YEAR / S
5'9"
FUTAKUCHI
2ND YEAR / WS
6'0"
HUH? THEY'RE STARTING THEIR ACE IN THE BACK ROW?
SASAYA
3RD YEAR / WS
5'9"
AONE
2ND YEAR / MB
6'3"
SAKUNAMI
1ST YEAR / L
5'5"
Starting order
DATE TECH
KAMASAKI (SAKUNAMI) OBARA MONIWA
SASAYA FUTAKUCHI AONE
KARASUNO
HINATA TANAKA KAGEYAMA
SAWAMURA AZUMANE TSUKISHIMA (NOYA)
AZUMANE
3RD YEAR / WS
NISHINOYA
2ND YEAR / L
5'3"
TANAKA
2ND YEAR / WS
5'10"
HINATA
1ST YEAR / MB
5'4"
SAWAMURA
3RD YEAR / WS
5'9"
TSUKISHIMA
1ST YEAR / MB
6'2"
KAGEYAMA
1ST YEAR / S
5'11"
AH... IS THAT KARASUNO'S BEST SERVE-RECEIVE FORMATION?
BRING IT ON!
FWEEEE
SERVER UP!

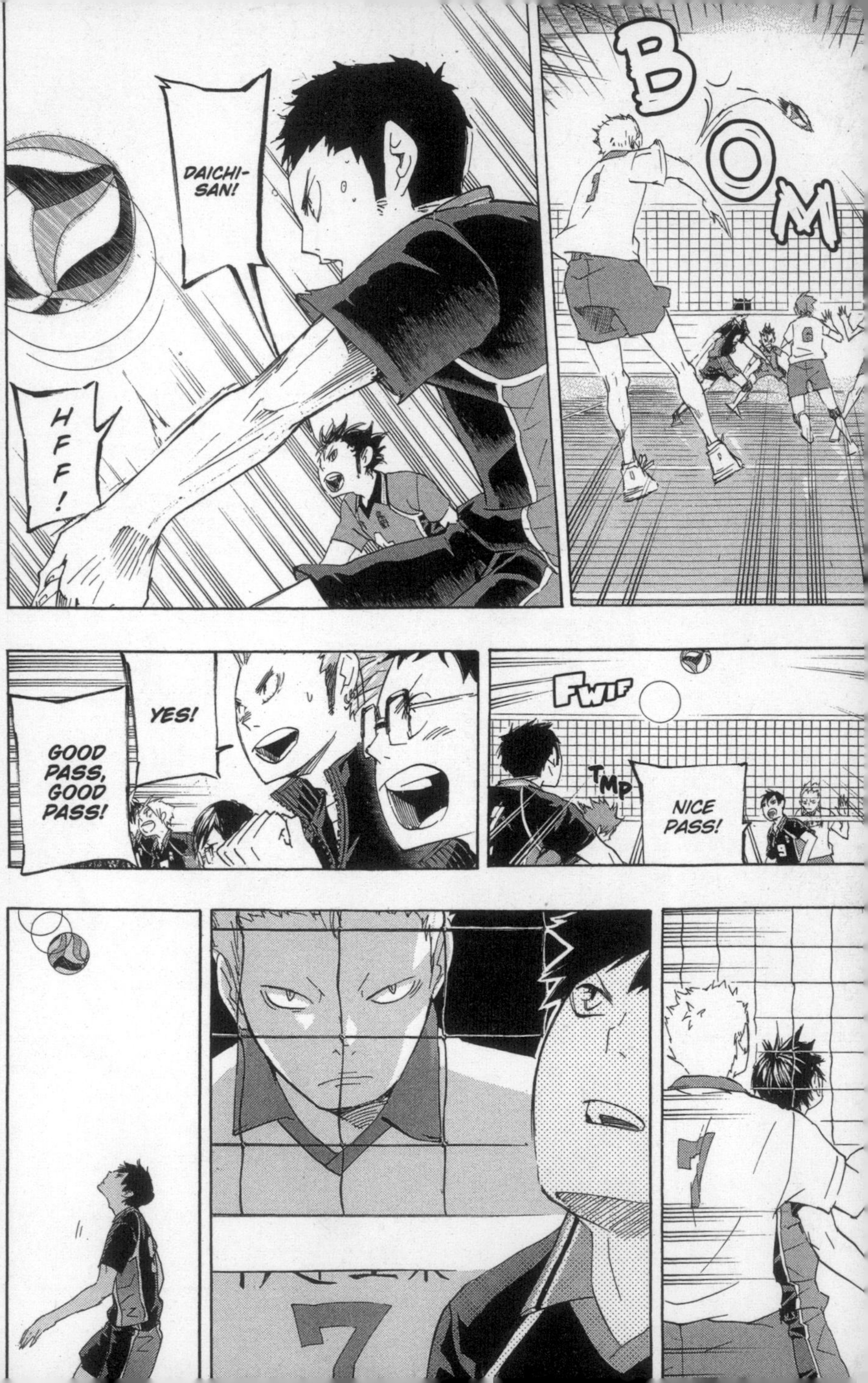
BOM
DAICHI-SAN!
HFF!
FWIF
TMP
NICE PASS!
YES!
GOOD PASS, GOOD PASS!

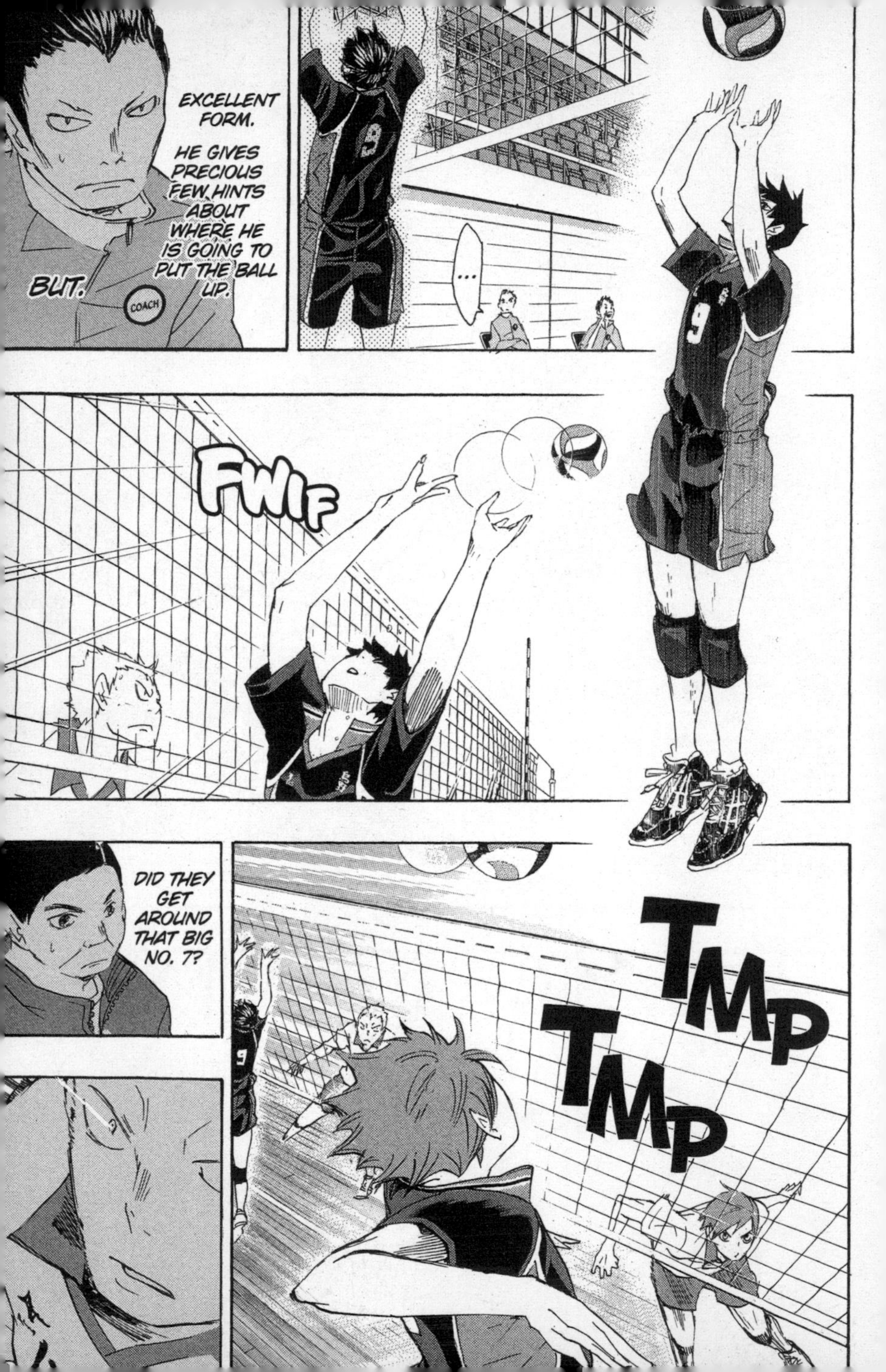
...
EXCELLENT FORM.
HE GIVES PRECIOUS FEW HINTS ABOUT WHERE HE IS GOING TO PUT THE BALL UP.
BUT.
COACH
FWIF
TMP TMP
DID THEY GET AROUND THAT BIG NO. 7?

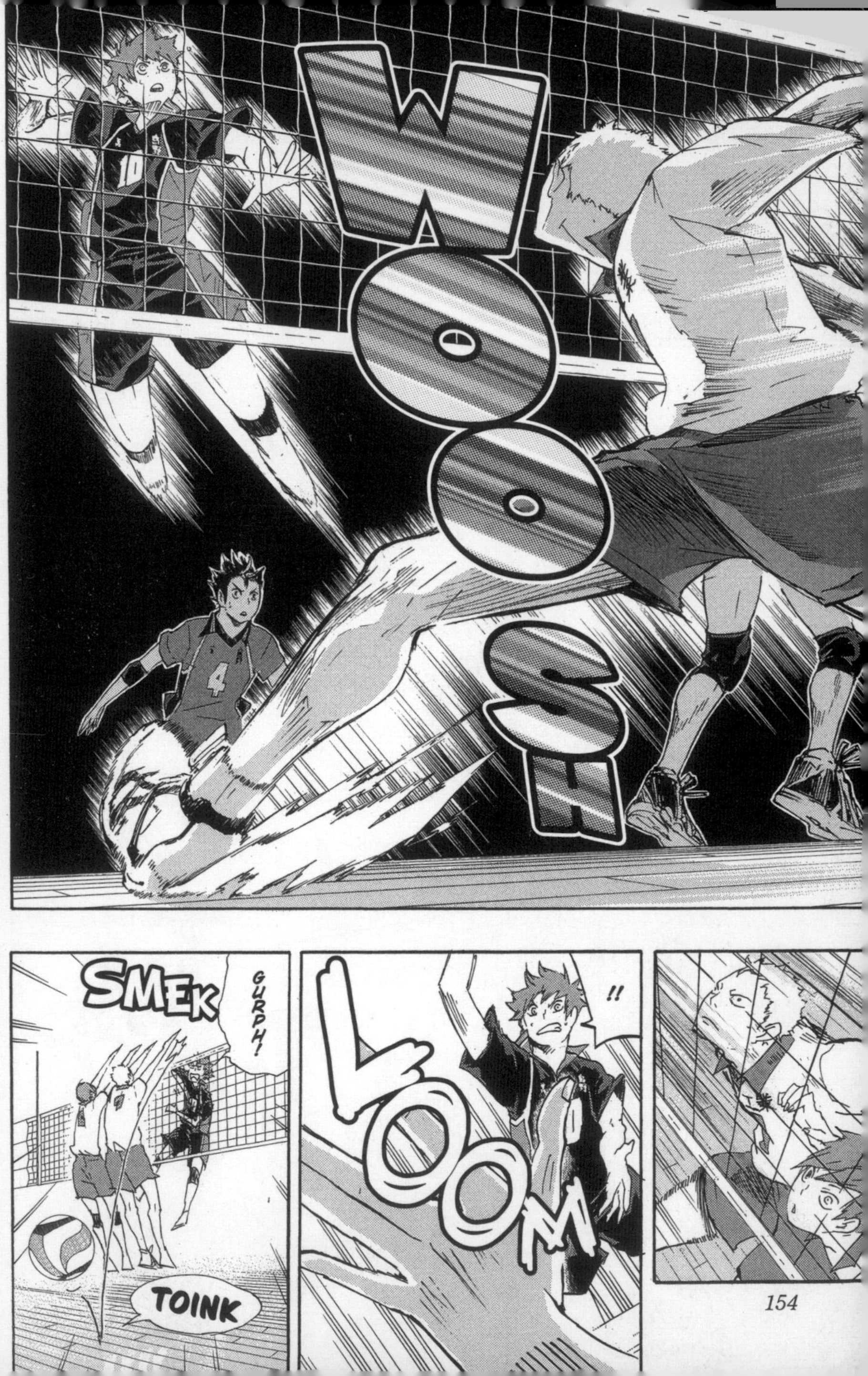
WOOOSH
!!
LOOOM
GURPH!
SMEK
TOINK

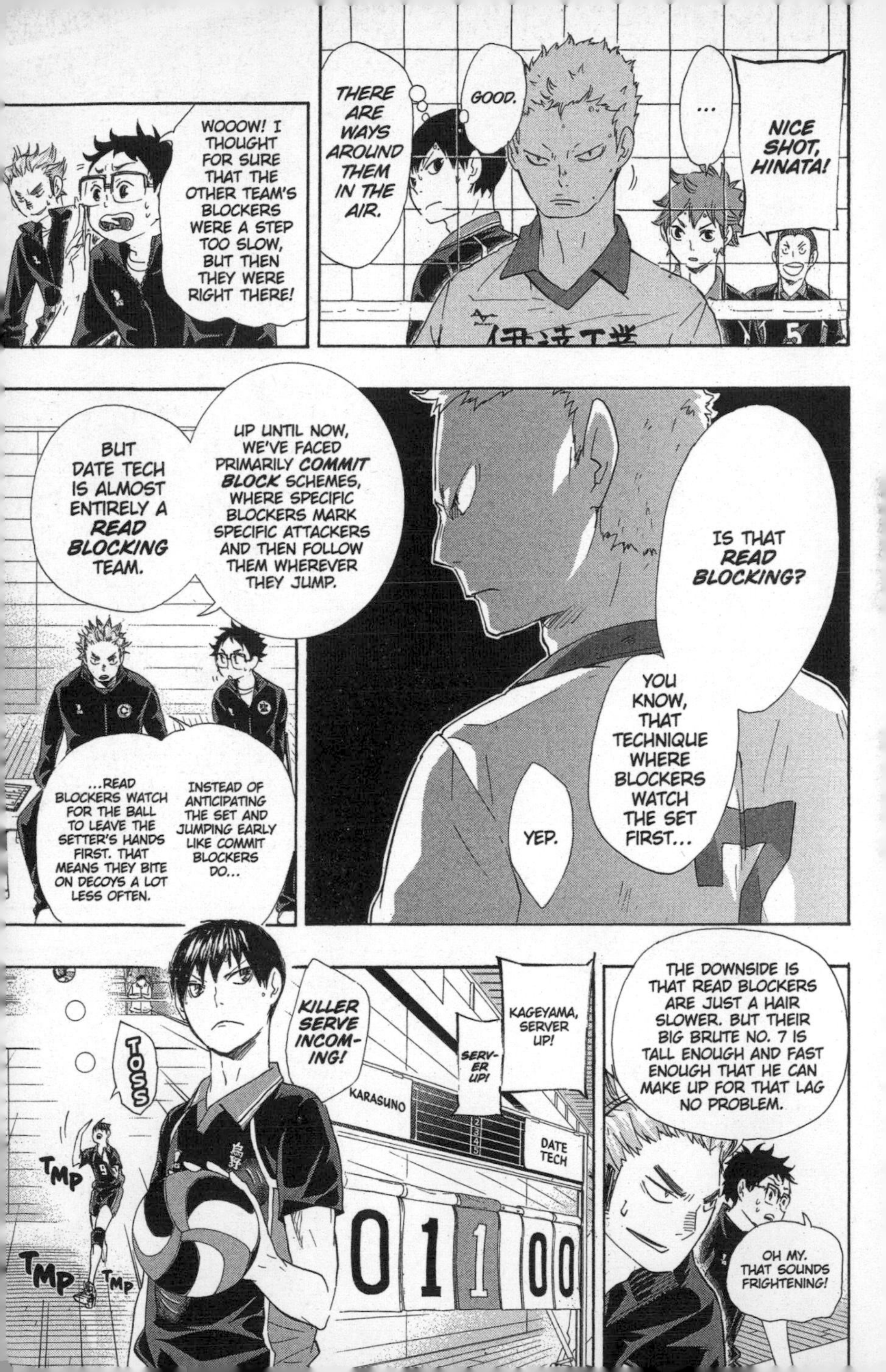
NICE SHOT, HINATA!
...
GOOD.
THERE ARE WAYS AROUND THEM IN THE AIR.
WOOOW! I THOUGHT FOR SURE THAT THE OTHER TEAM'S BLOCKERS WERE A STEP TOO SLOW, BUT THEN THEY WERE RIGHT THERE!
IS THAT READ BLOCKING?
YOU KNOW, THAT TECHNIQUE WHERE BLOCKERS WATCH THE SET FIRST...
YEP.
UP UNTIL NOW, WE'VE FACED PRIMARILY COMMIT BLOCK SCHEMES, WHERE SPECIFIC BLOCKERS MARK SPECIFIC ATTACKERS AND THEN FOLLOW THEM WHEREVER THEY JUMP.
BUT DATE TECH IS ALMOST ENTIRELY A READ BLOCKING TEAM.
INSTEAD OF ANTICIPATING THE SET AND JUMPING EARLY LIKE COMMIT BLOCKERS DO...
...READ BLOCKERS WATCH FOR THE BALL TO LEAVE THE SETTER'S HANDS FIRST. THAT MEANS THEY BITE ON DECOYS A LOT LESS OFTEN.
THE DOWNSIDE IS THAT READ BLOCKERS ARE JUST A HAIR SLOWER. BUT THEIR BIG BRUTE NO. 7 IS TALL ENOUGH AND FAST ENOUGH THAT HE CAN MAKE UP FOR THAT LAG NO PROBLEM.
OH MY. THAT SOUNDS FRIGHTENING!
KAGEYAMA, SERVER UP!
SERV-ER UP!
KILLER SERVE INCOM-ING!
KARASUNO
DATE TECH
TOSS
TMP
TMP
TMP

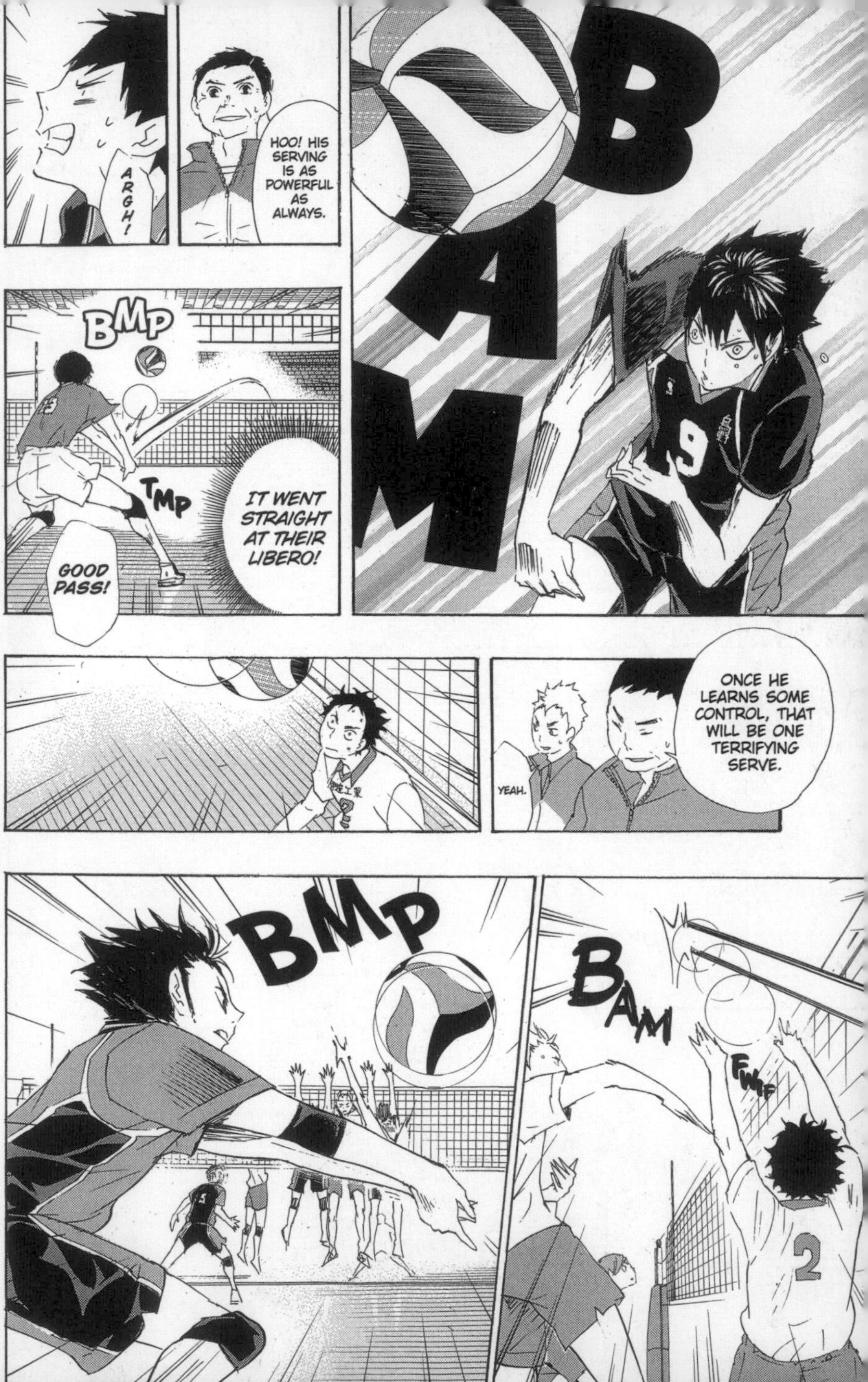
BAM
HOO! HIS SERVING IS AS POWERFUL AS ALWAYS.
ARGH!
BMP
IT WENT STRAIGHT AT THEIR LIBERO!
TMP
GOOD PASS!
ONCE HE LEARNS SOME CONTROL, THAT WILL BE ONE TERRIFYING SERVE.
YEAH.
BAM
FWIP
BMP

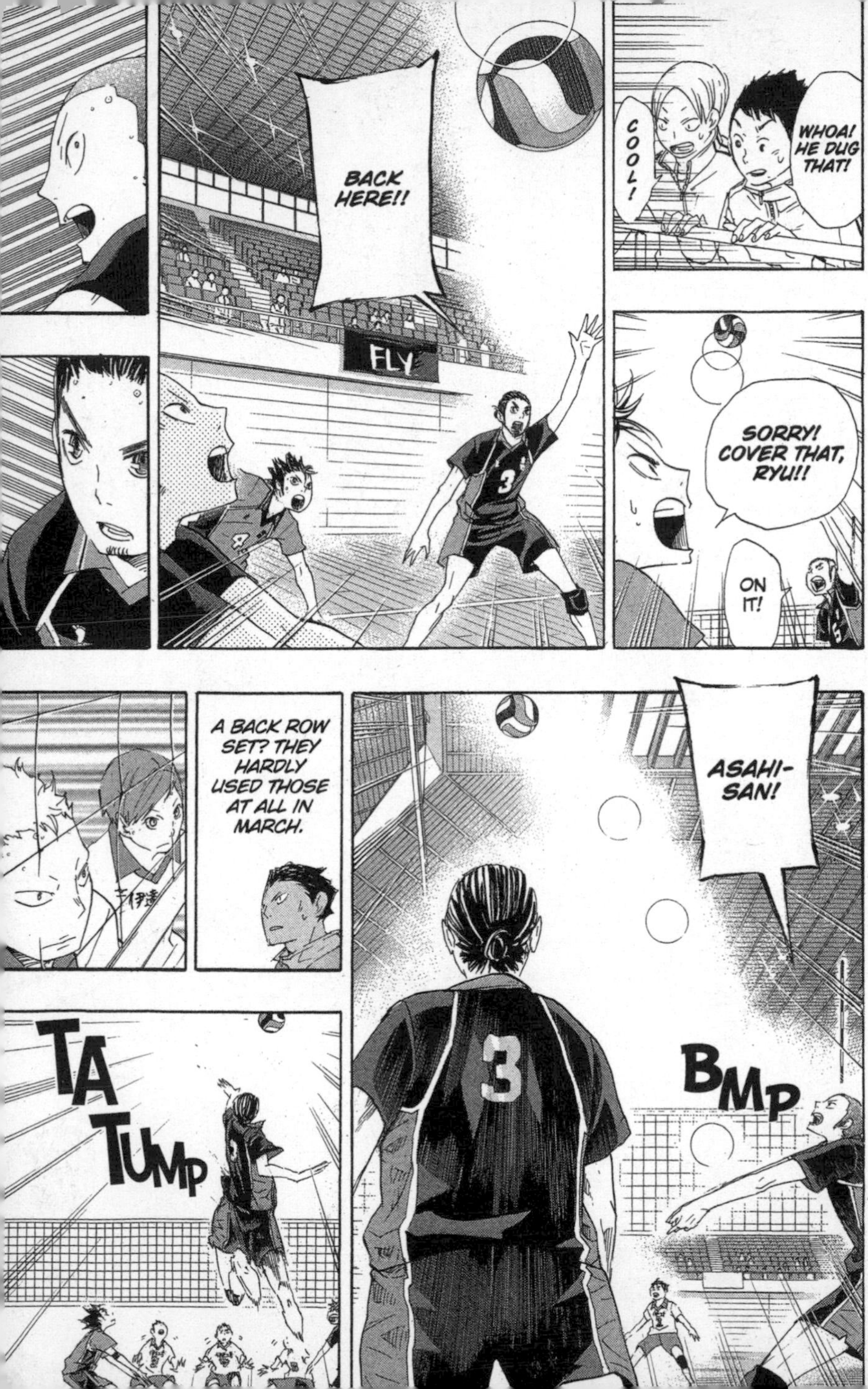
WHOA! HE DUG THAT!
COOL!
SORRY! COVER THAT, RYU!!
ON IT!
BACK HERE!!
FLY
ASAHI-SAN!
BMP
A BACK ROW SET? THEY HARDLY USED THOSE AT ALL IN MARCH.
TA TUMP

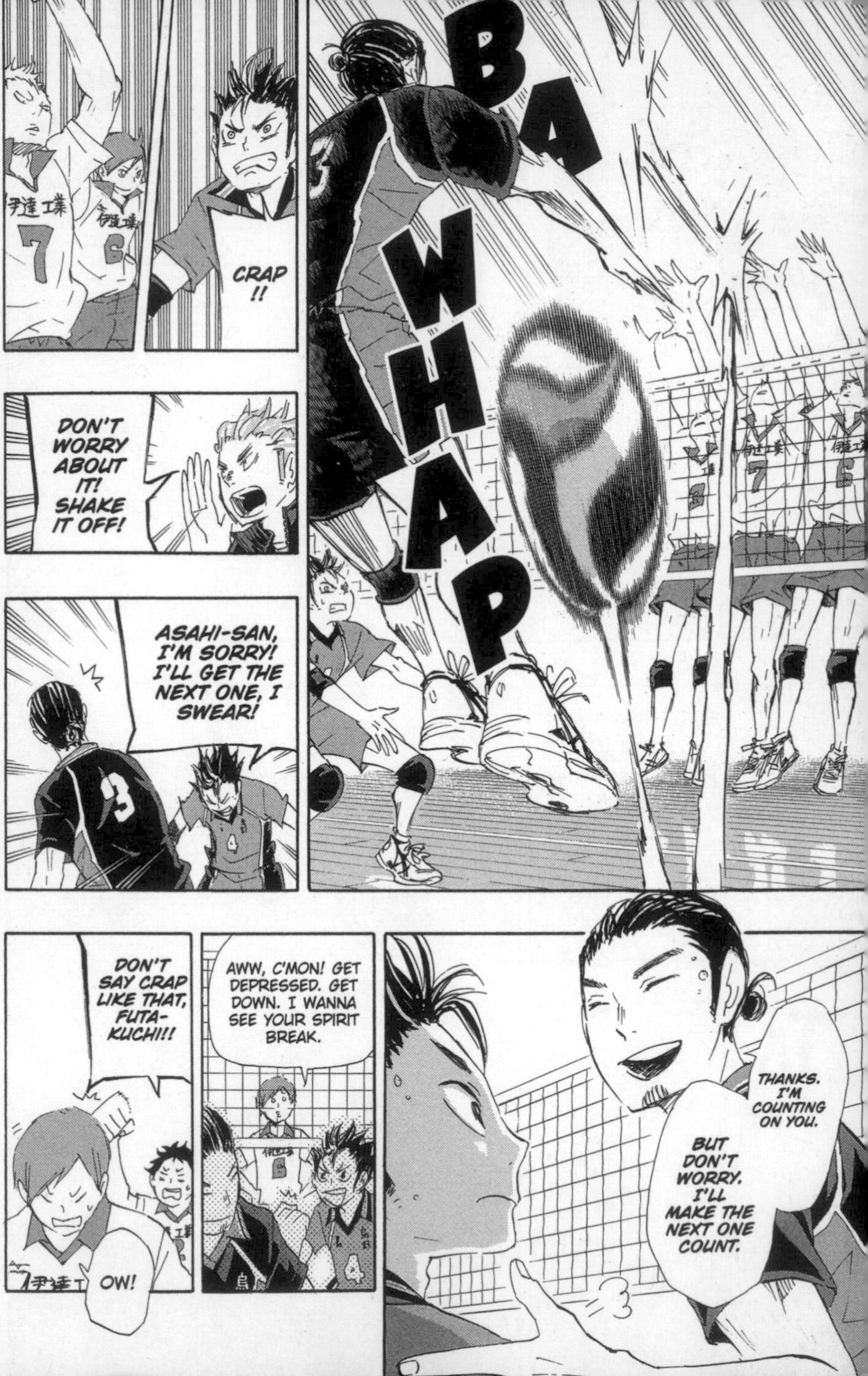
BA WHAP
CRAP !!
DON'T WORRY ABOUT IT! SHAKE IT OFF!
ASAHI-SAN, I'M SORRY! I'LL GET THE NEXT ONE, I SWEAR!
THANKS. I'M COUNTING ON YOU.
BUT DON'T WORRY. I'LL MAKE THE NEXT ONE COUNT.
AWW, C'MON! GET DEPRESSED. GET DOWN. I WANNA SEE YOUR SPIRIT BREAK.
DON'T SAY CRAP LIKE THAT, FUTA-KUCHI!!
OW!

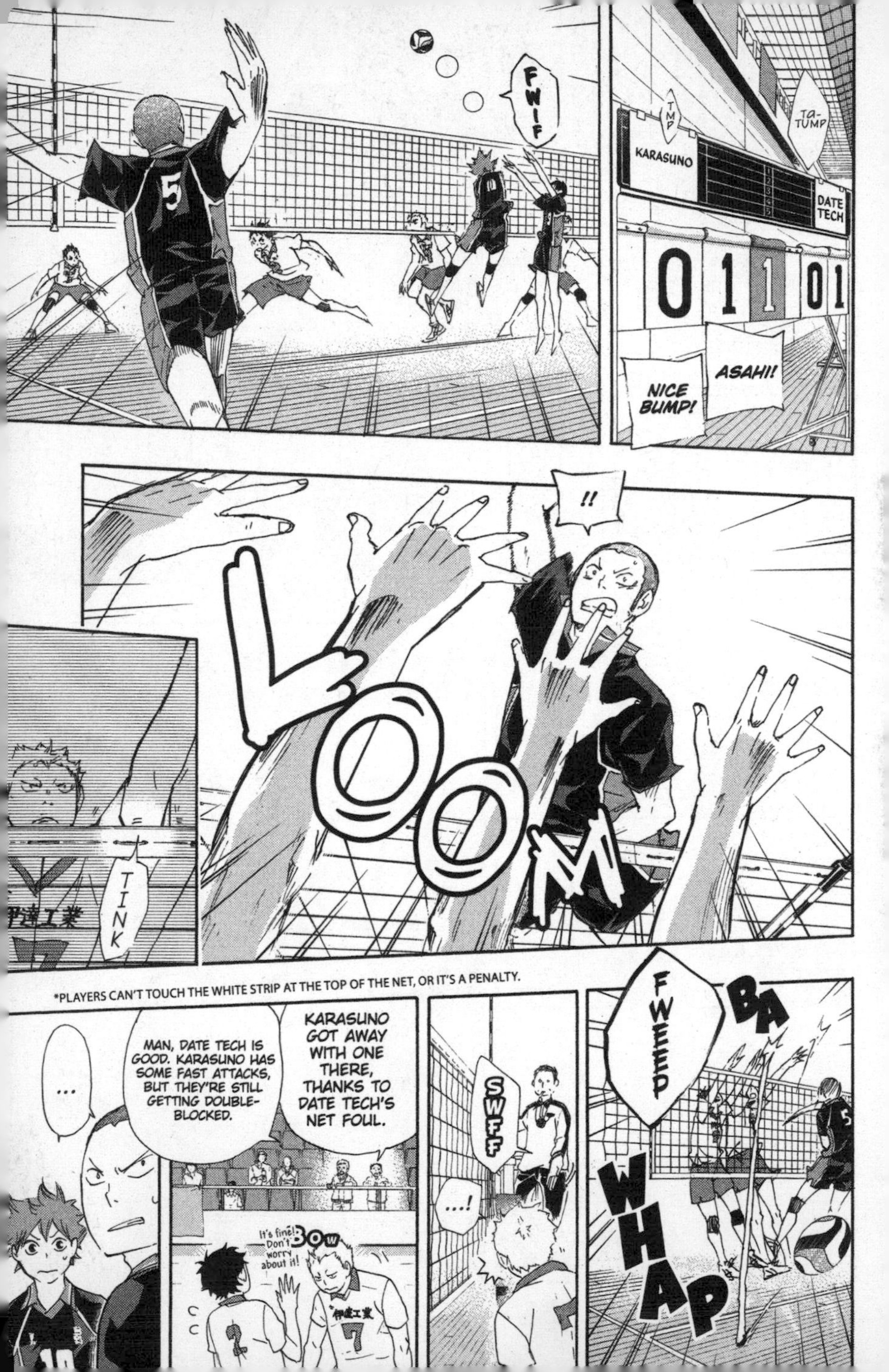
Ta-TUMP
TMP
KARASUNO
DATE TECH
ASAHI!
NICE BUMP!
FWIF
!!
LOOOM
TINK
BA
FWEEP
WHHAP
SWFF
...!
KARASUNO GOT AWAY WITH ONE THERE, THANKS TO DATE TECH'S NET FOUL.
It's fine! Don't worry about it!
BOW
MAN, DATE TECH IS GOOD. KARASUNO HAS SOME FAST ATTACKS, BUT THEY'RE STILL GETTING DOUBLE-BLOCKED.
...
*PLAYERS CAN'T TOUCH THE WHITE STRIP AT THE TOP OF THE NET, OR IT'S A PENALTY.

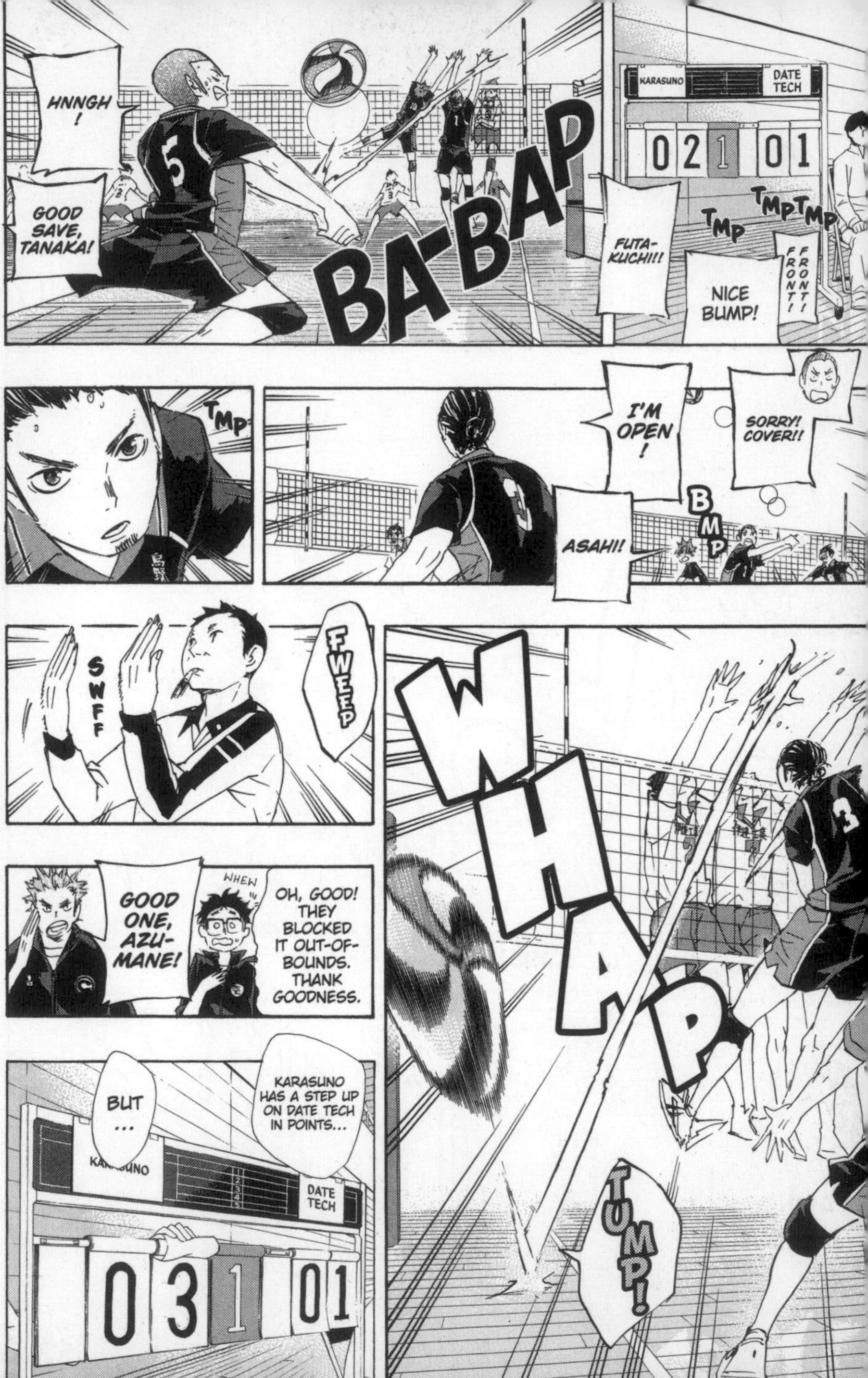
DATE TECH
KARASUNO
02 1 01
FRONT!
FRONT!
TMPTMP
TMP
NICE BUMP!
FUTA-KUCHI!!!
BA-BAP
HNNGH!
GOOD SAVE, TANAKA!
SORRY! COVER!!
I'M OPEN!
BMP
ASAHI!
TMP
WHAP
TUMP!
FWEEP
SWFF
OH, GOOD! THEY BLOCKED IT OUT-OF-BOUNDS. THANK GOODNESS.
WHEW
GOOD ONE, AZUMANE!
KARASUNO HAS A STEP UP ON DATE TECH IN POINTS...
BUT ...
KARASUNO
DATE TECH
03 1 01

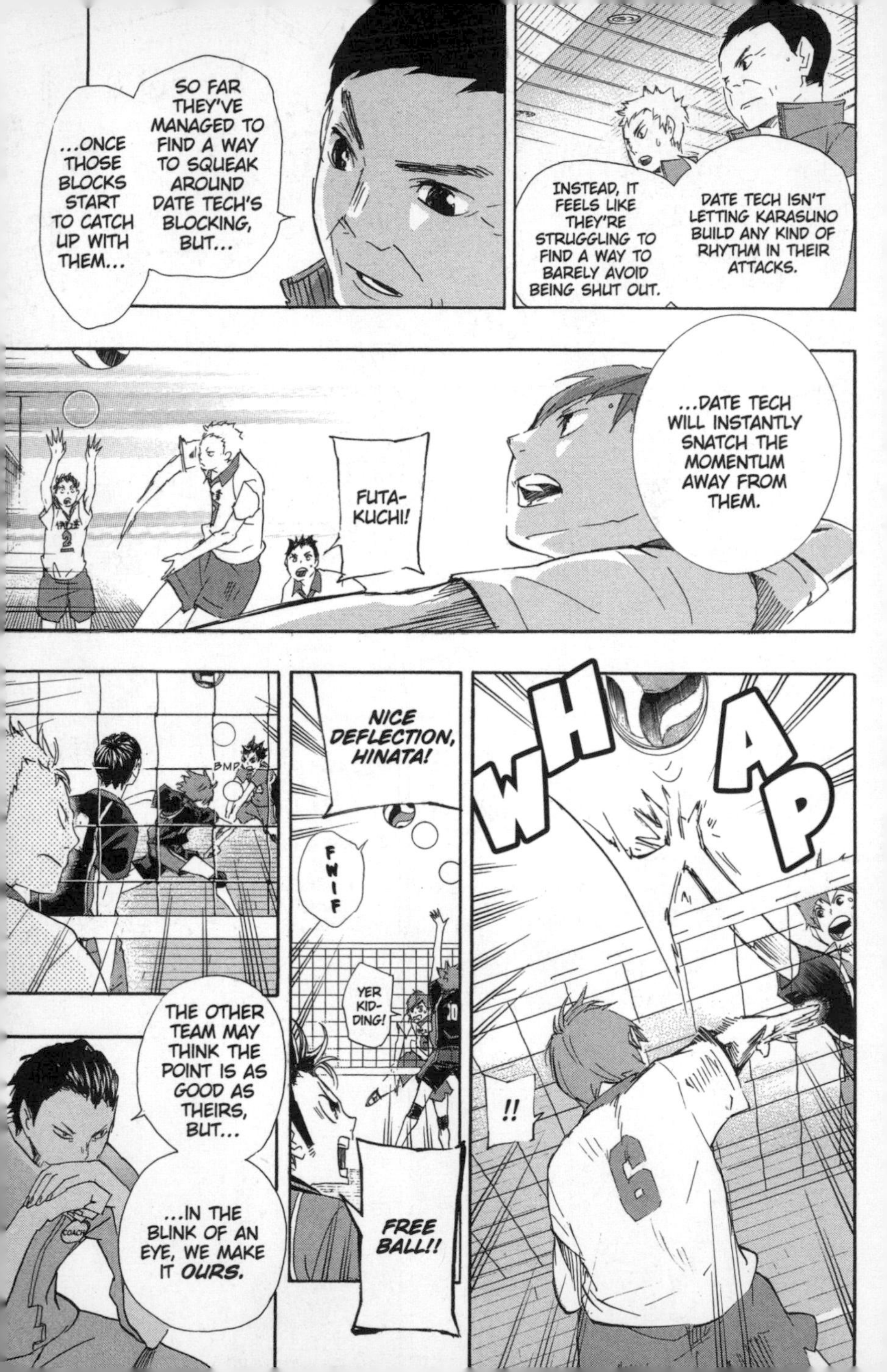
DATE TECH ISN'T LETTING KARASUNO BUILD ANY KIND OF RHYTHM IN THEIR ATTACKS.
INSTEAD, IT FEELS LIKE THEY'RE STRUGGLING TO FIND A WAY TO BARELY AVOID BEING SHUT OUT.
SO FAR THEY'VE MANAGED TO FIND A WAY TO SQUEAK AROUND DATE TECH'S BLOCKING, BUT...
...ONCE THOSE BLOCKS START TO CATCH UP WITH THEM...
...DATE TECH WILL INSTANTLY SNATCH THE MOMENTUM AWAY FROM THEM.
FUTA-KUCHI!
WHAP
!!
NICE DEFLECTION, HINATA!
FWIF
YER KID-DING!
FREE BALL!!
BMP
THE OTHER TEAM MAY THINK THE POINT IS AS GOOD AS THEIRS, BUT...
...IN THE BLINK OF AN EYE, WE MAKE IT *OURS.*
COACH

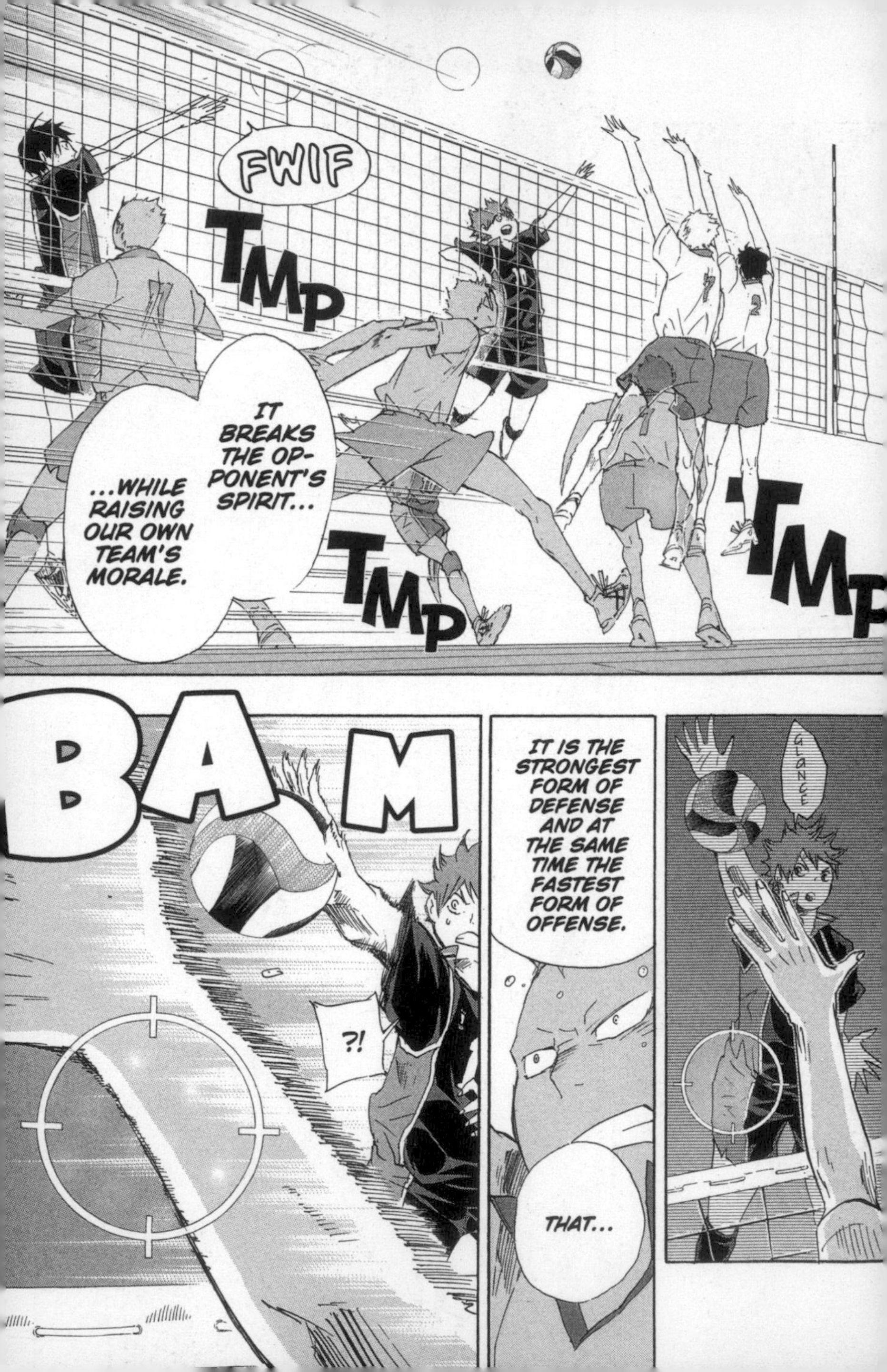
FWIF
TMP
TMP
TMP
IT BREAKS THE OPPONENT'S SPIRIT...
...WHILE RAISING OUR OWN TEAM'S MORALE.
GLANCE
IT IS THE STRONGEST FORM OF DEFENSE AND AT THE SAME TIME THE FASTEST FORM OF OFFENSE.
THAT...
BAM
?!

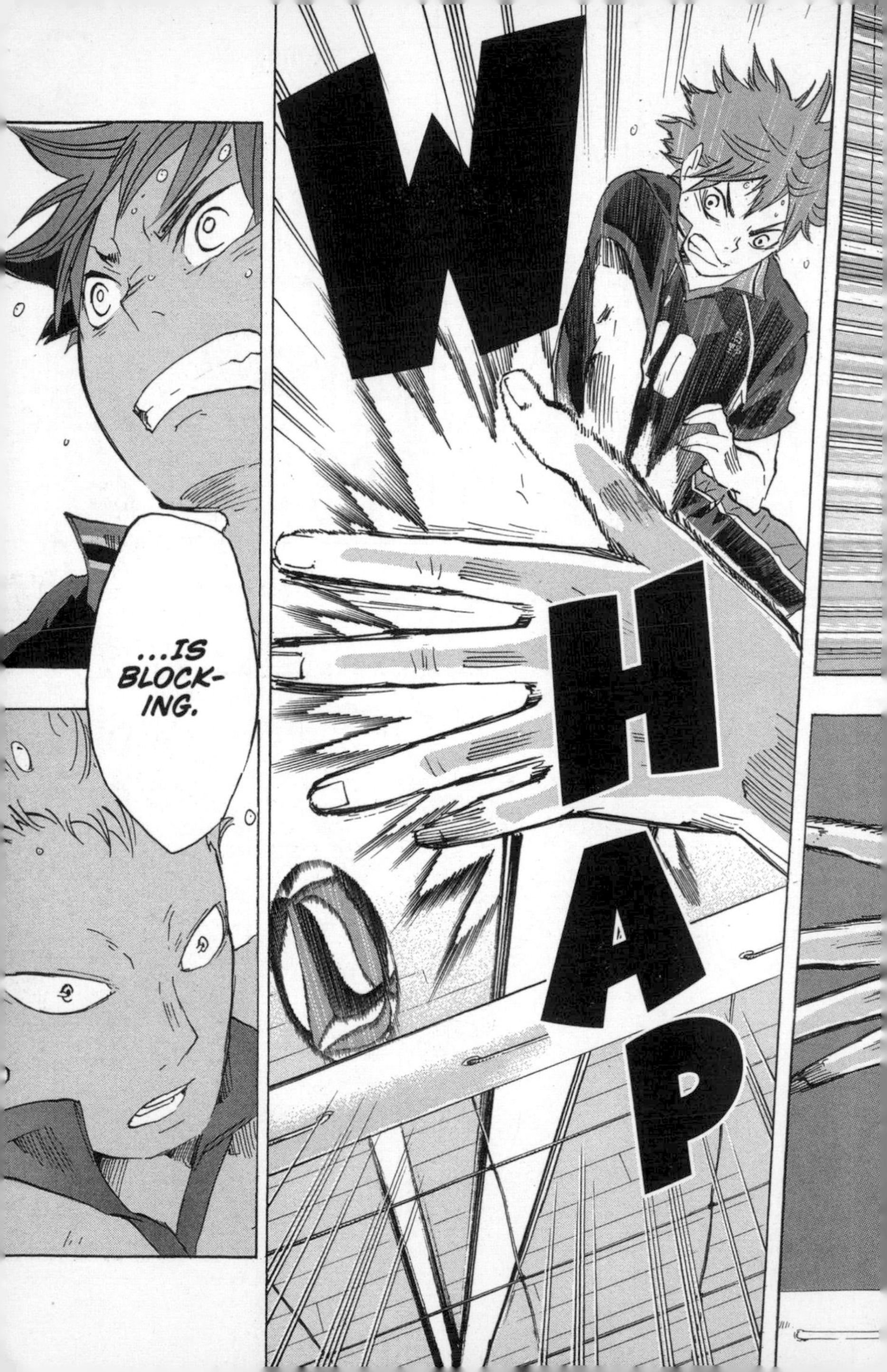
WHAP
...IS BLOCKING.

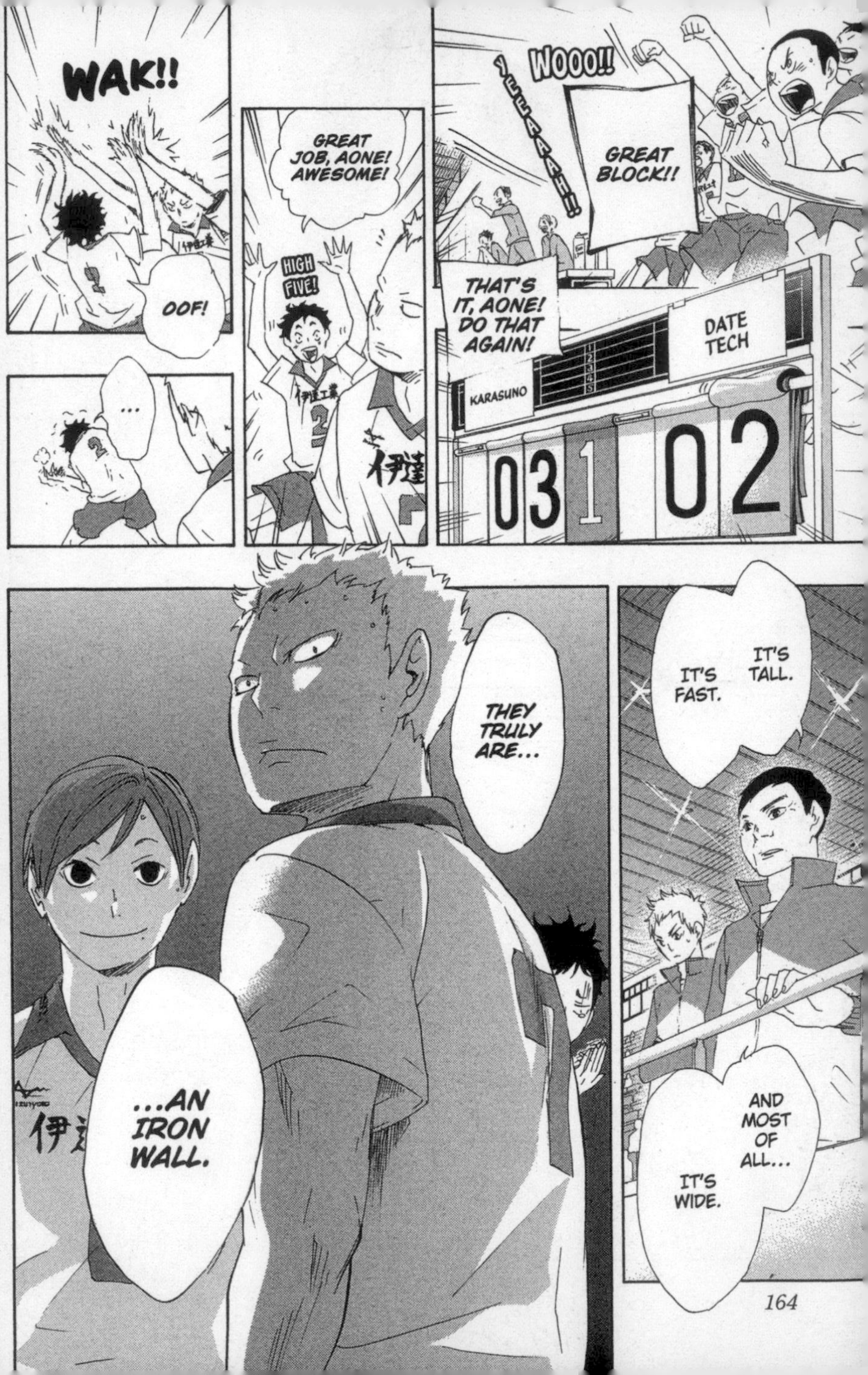
WOOO!!
YEEAAAHH!!
GREAT BLOCK!!
THAT'S IT, AONE! DO THAT AGAIN!
DATE TECH
KARASUNO
03
1
02
GREAT JOB, AONE! AWESOME!
HIGH FIVE!
WAK!!
OOF!
...
IT'S TALL.
IT'S FAST.
AND MOST OF ALL...
IT'S WIDE.
THEY TRULY ARE...
...AN IRON WALL.

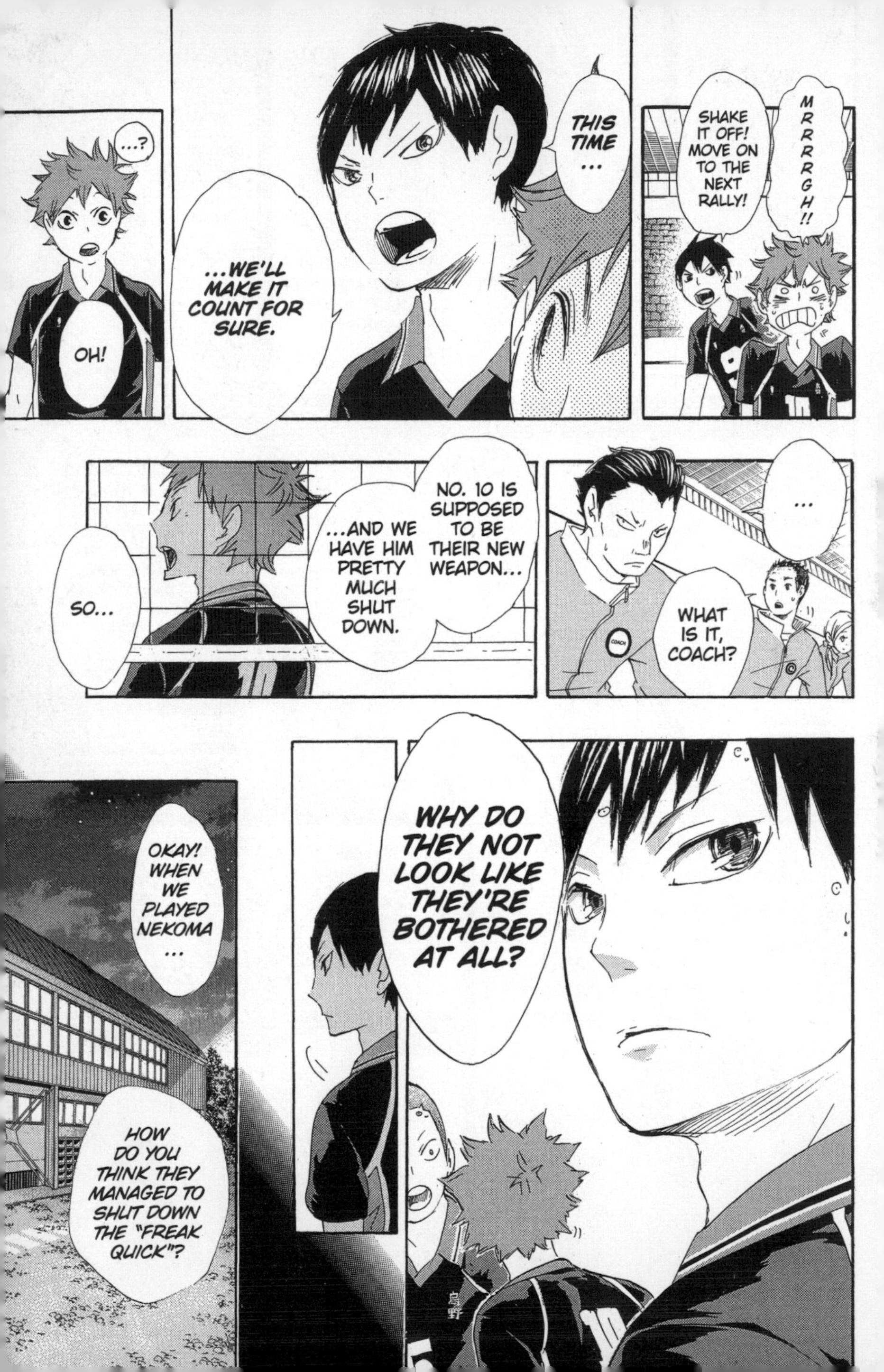
MRRRRGH!!
SHAKE IT OFF! MOVE ON TO THE NEXT RALLY!
THIS TIME...
...WE'LL MAKE IT COUNT FOR SURE.
...?
OH!
...
WHAT IS IT, COACH?
NO. 10 IS SUPPOSED TO BE THEIR NEW WEAPON...
...AND WE HAVE HIM PRETTY MUCH SHUT DOWN.
SO...
WHY DO THEY NOT LOOK LIKE THEY'RE BOTHERED AT ALL?
OKAY! WHEN WE PLAYED NEKOMA...
HOW DO YOU THINK THEY MANAGED TO SHUT DOWN THE "FREAK QUICK"?

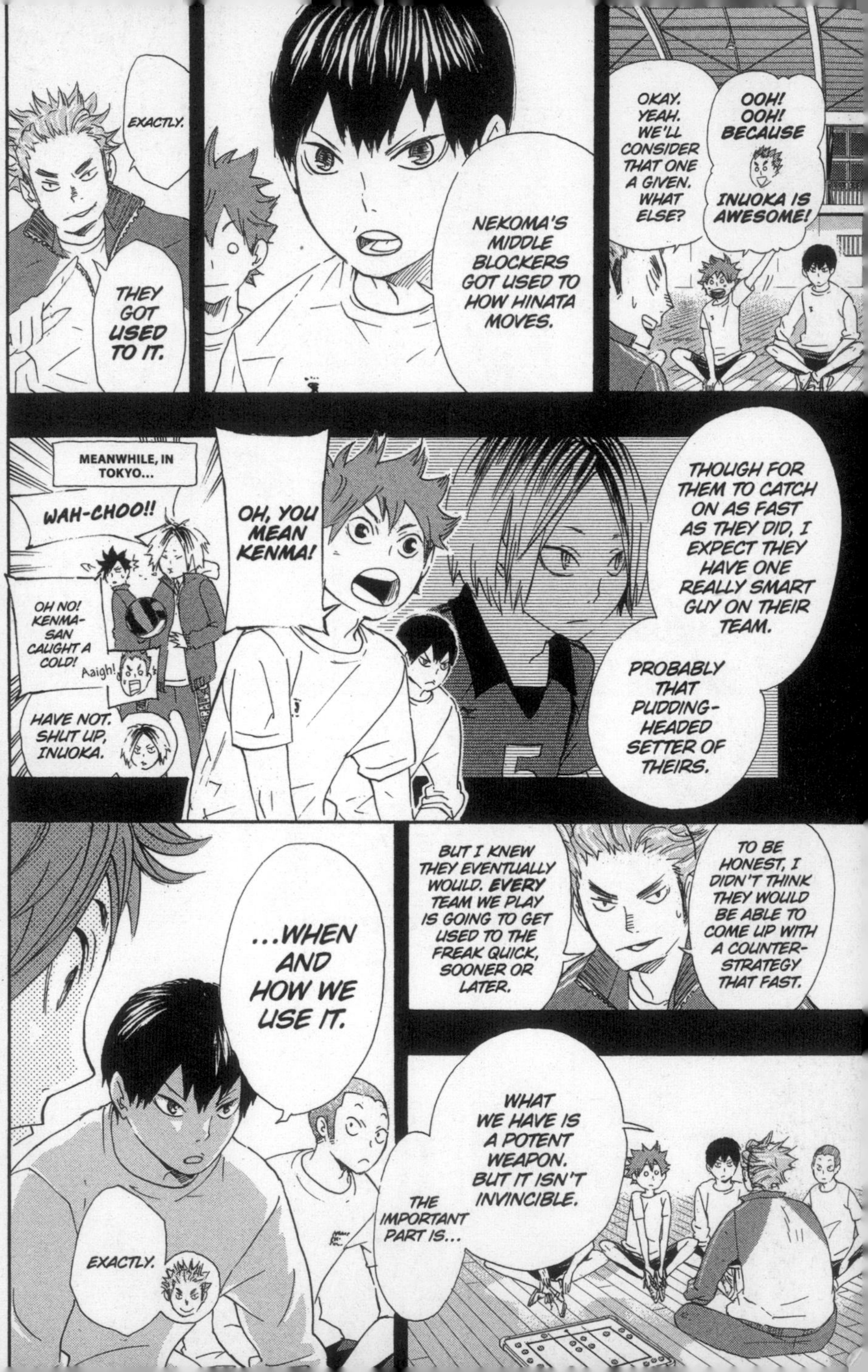
OOH! OOH! BECAUSE INUOKA IS AWESOME!
OKAY. YEAH. WE'LL CONSIDER THAT ONE A GIVEN. WHAT ELSE?
NEKOMA'S MIDDLE BLOCKERS GOT USED TO HOW HINATA MOVES.
EXACTLY.
THEY GOT USED TO IT.
THOUGH FOR THEM TO CATCH ON AS FAST AS THEY DID, I EXPECT THEY HAVE ONE REALLY SMART GUY ON THEIR TEAM.
PROBABLY THAT PUDDING-HEADED SETTER OF THEIRS.
OH, YOU MEAN KENMA!
MEANWHILE, IN TOKYO...
WAH-CHOO!!
OH NO! KENMA-SAN CAUGHT A COLD!
Aaigh!
HAVE NOT. SHUT UP, INUOKA.
TO BE HONEST, I DIDN'T THINK THEY WOULD BE ABLE TO COME UP WITH A COUNTER-STRATEGY THAT FAST.
BUT I KNEW THEY EVENTUALLY WOULD. EVERY TEAM WE PLAY IS GOING TO GET USED TO THE FREAK QUICK, SOONER OR LATER.
WHAT WE HAVE IS A POTENT WEAPON. BUT IT ISN'T INVINCIBLE.
THE IMPORTANT PART IS...
...WHEN AND HOW WE USE IT.
EXACTLY.

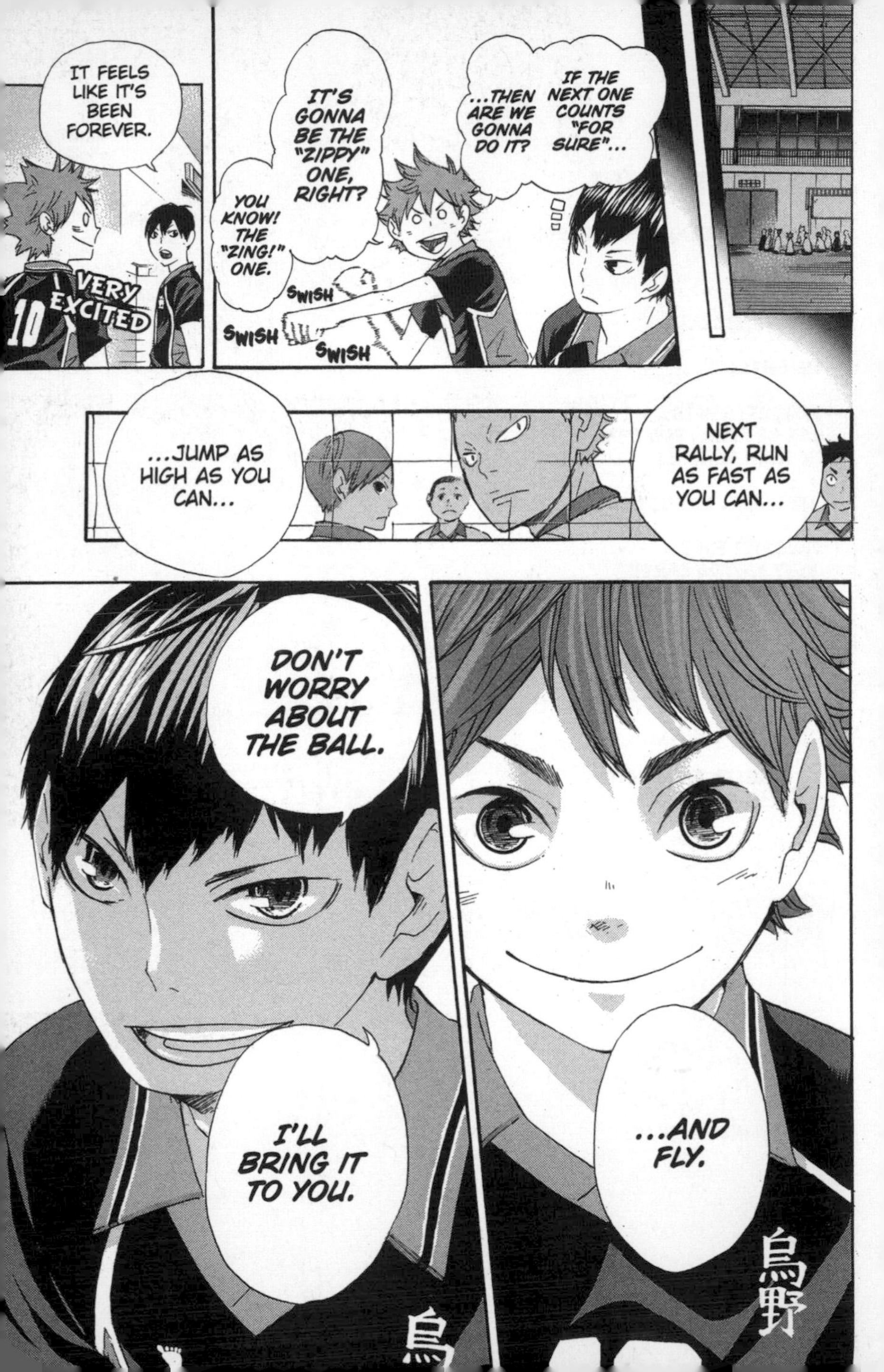
IF THE NEXT ONE COUNTS "FOR SURE"...
...THEN ARE WE GONNA DO IT?
IT'S GONNA BE THE "ZIPPY" ONE, RIGHT?
YOU KNOW! THE "ZING!" ONE.
SWISH
SWISH
SWISH
IT FEELS LIKE IT'S BEEN FOREVER.
VERY EXCITED
NEXT RALLY, RUN AS FAST AS YOU CAN...
...JUMP AS HIGH AS YOU CAN...
...AND FLY.
烏野
DON'T WORRY ABOUT THE BALL.
I'LL BRING IT TO YOU.
烏

TAKANOBU AONE

DATE TECHNICAL HIGH SCHOOL
CLASS 2-A

POSITION:
MIDDLE BLOCKER

HEIGHT: 6'3"

WEIGHT: 194 LBS.
(AS OF APRIL, 2ND YEAR OF HIGH SCHOOL)

BIRTHDAY: AUGUST 13

FAVORITE FOOD:
KURI KINTON **CANDIED CHESTNUT DUMPLINGS**

CURRENT WORRY:
WHEN HE SITS DOWN ON THE TRAIN, NO ONE EVER SITS NEAR HIM.

ABILITY PARAMETERS
(5-POINT SCALE)

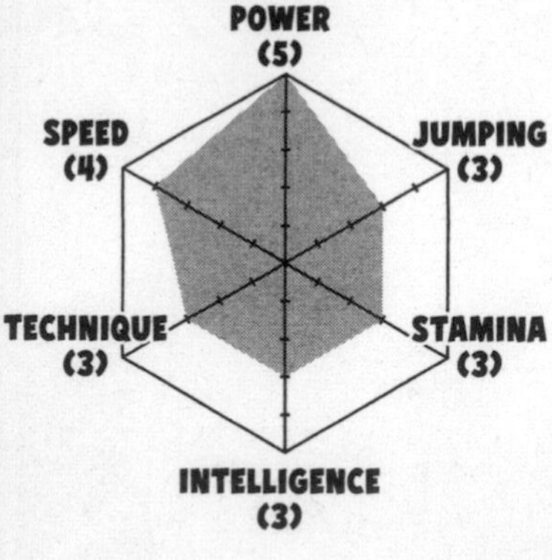
POWER (5)
JUMPING (3)
STAMINA (3)
INTELLIGENCE (3)
TECHNIQUE (3)
SPEED (4)

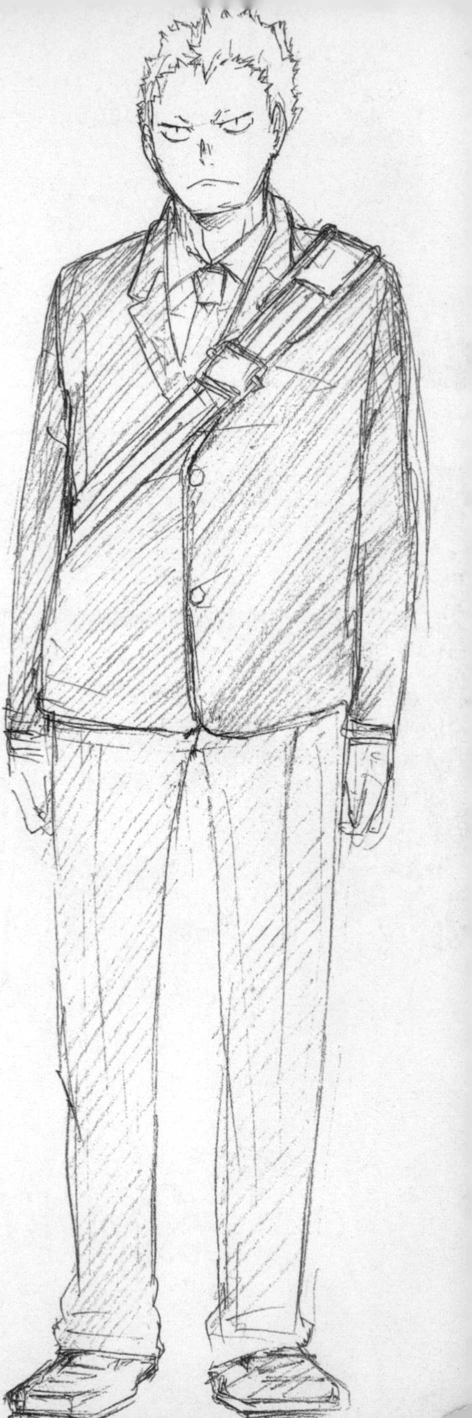

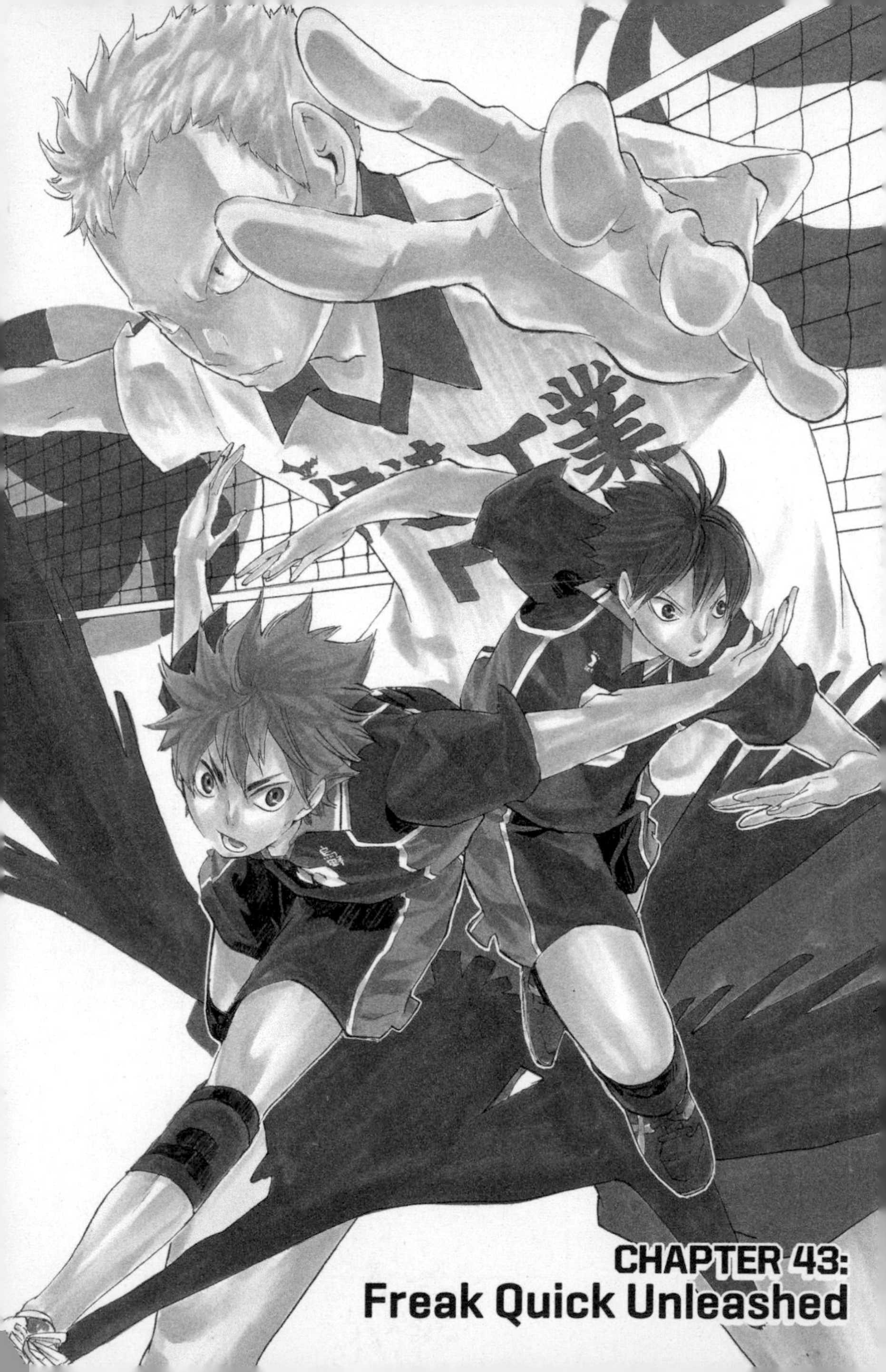

CHAPTER 43:
Freak Quick Unleashed

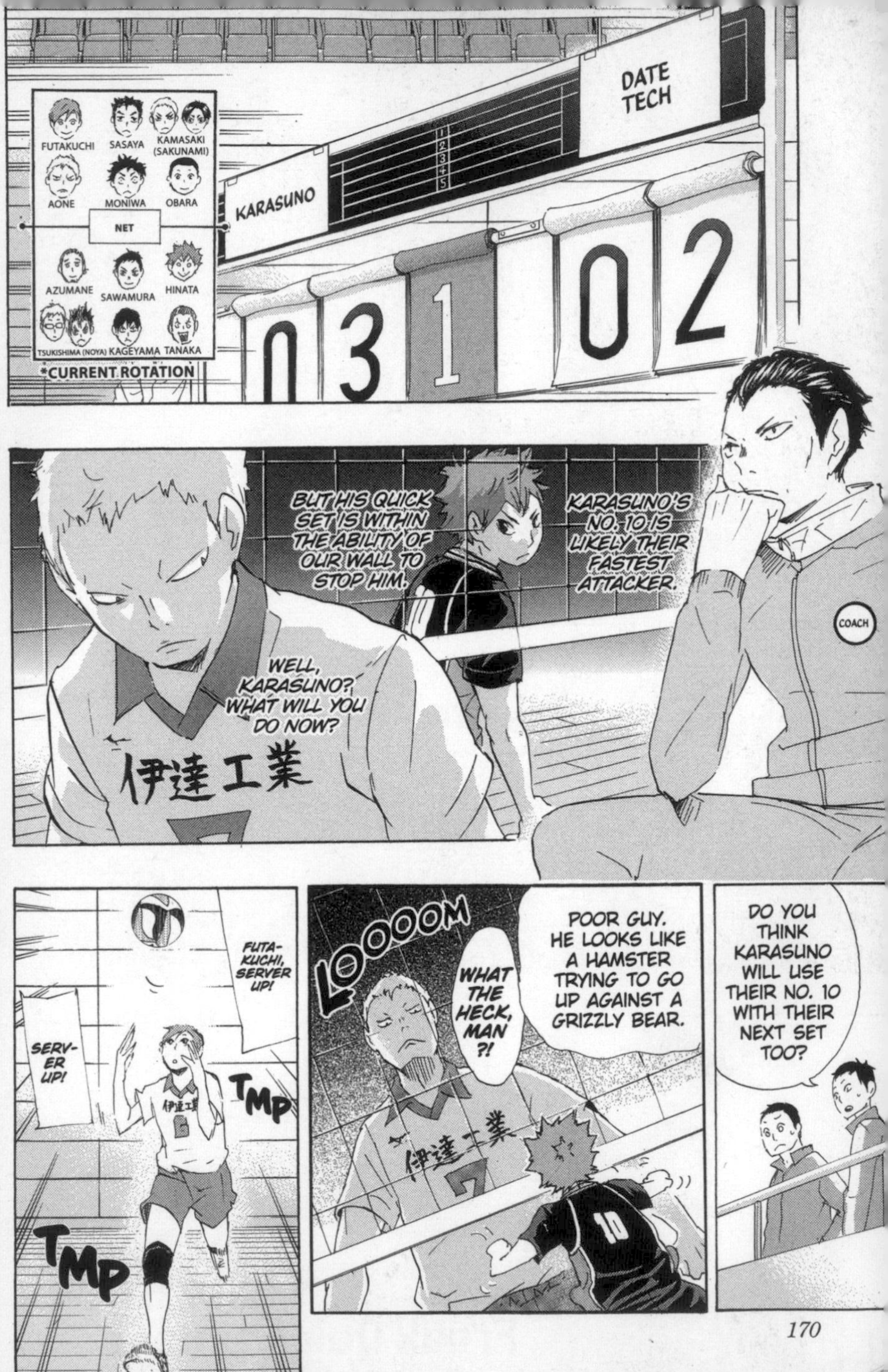

DATE TECH
FUTAKUCHI
SASAYA
KAMASAKI (SAKUNAMI)
AONE
MONIWA
OBARA
NET
AZUMANE
SAWAMURA
HINATA
TSUKISHIMA (NOYA)
KAGEYAMA
TANAKA
*CURRENT ROTATION
KARASUNO
1
2
3
4
5
0 3 1 0 2
KARASUNO'S NO. 10 IS LIKELY THEIR FASTEST ATTACKER.
COACH
BUT HIS QUICK SET IS WITHIN THE ABILITY OF OUR WALL TO STOP HIM.
WELL, KARASUNO? WHAT WILL YOU DO NOW?
DO YOU THINK KARASUNO WILL USE THEIR NO. 10 WITH THEIR NEXT SET TOO?
POOR GUY. HE LOOKS LIKE A HAMSTER TRYING TO GO UP AGAINST A GRIZZLY BEAR.
WHAT THE HECK, MAN?!
LOOOOM
FUTA-KUCHI, SERVER UP!
SERV-ER UP!
TMP
TMP

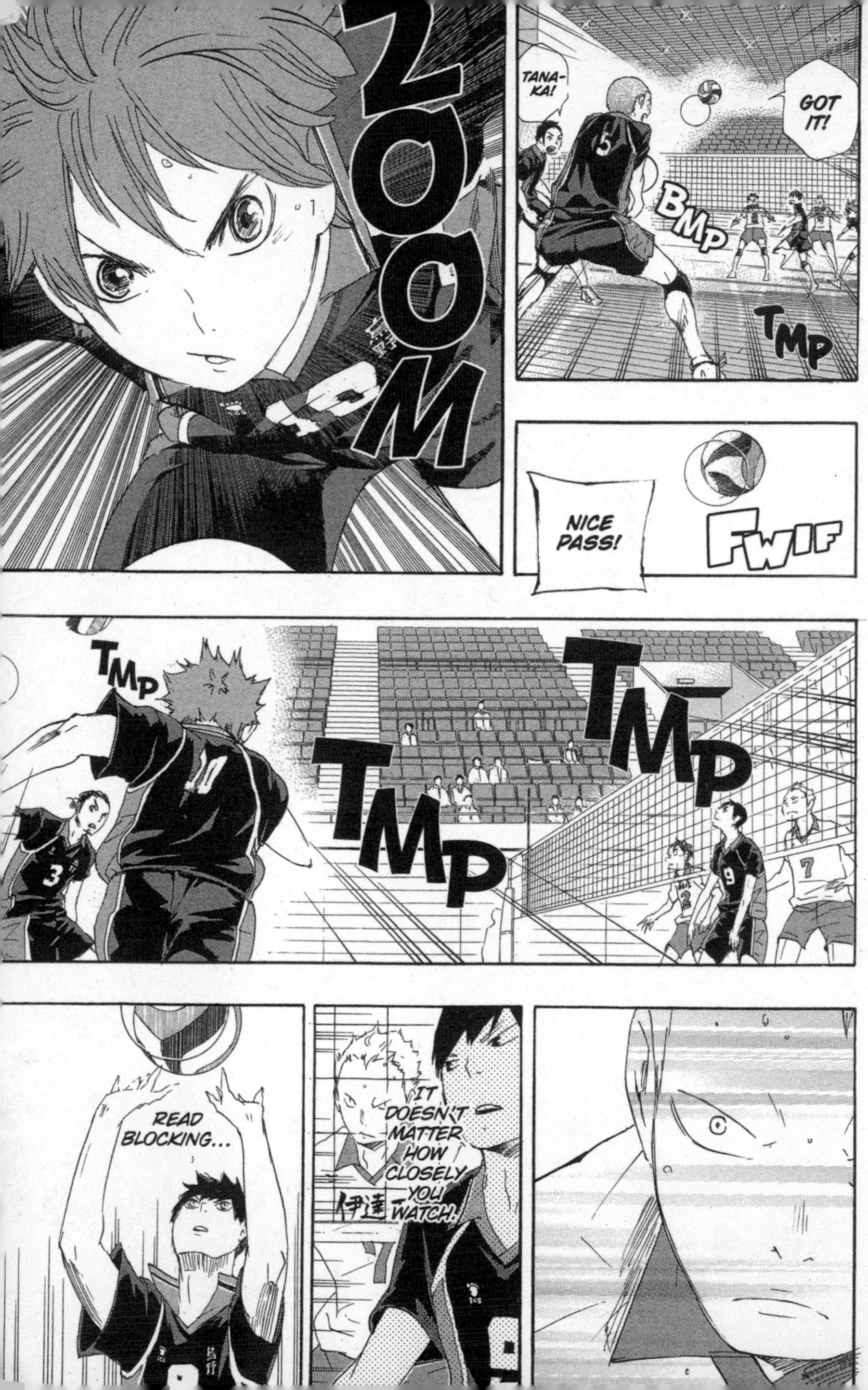
GOT IT!
TANAKA!
BMP
TMP
FWIF
NICE PASS!
ZOOM
TMP
TMP
TMP
IT DOESN'T MATTER HOW CLOSELY YOU WATCH.
READ BLOCKING...

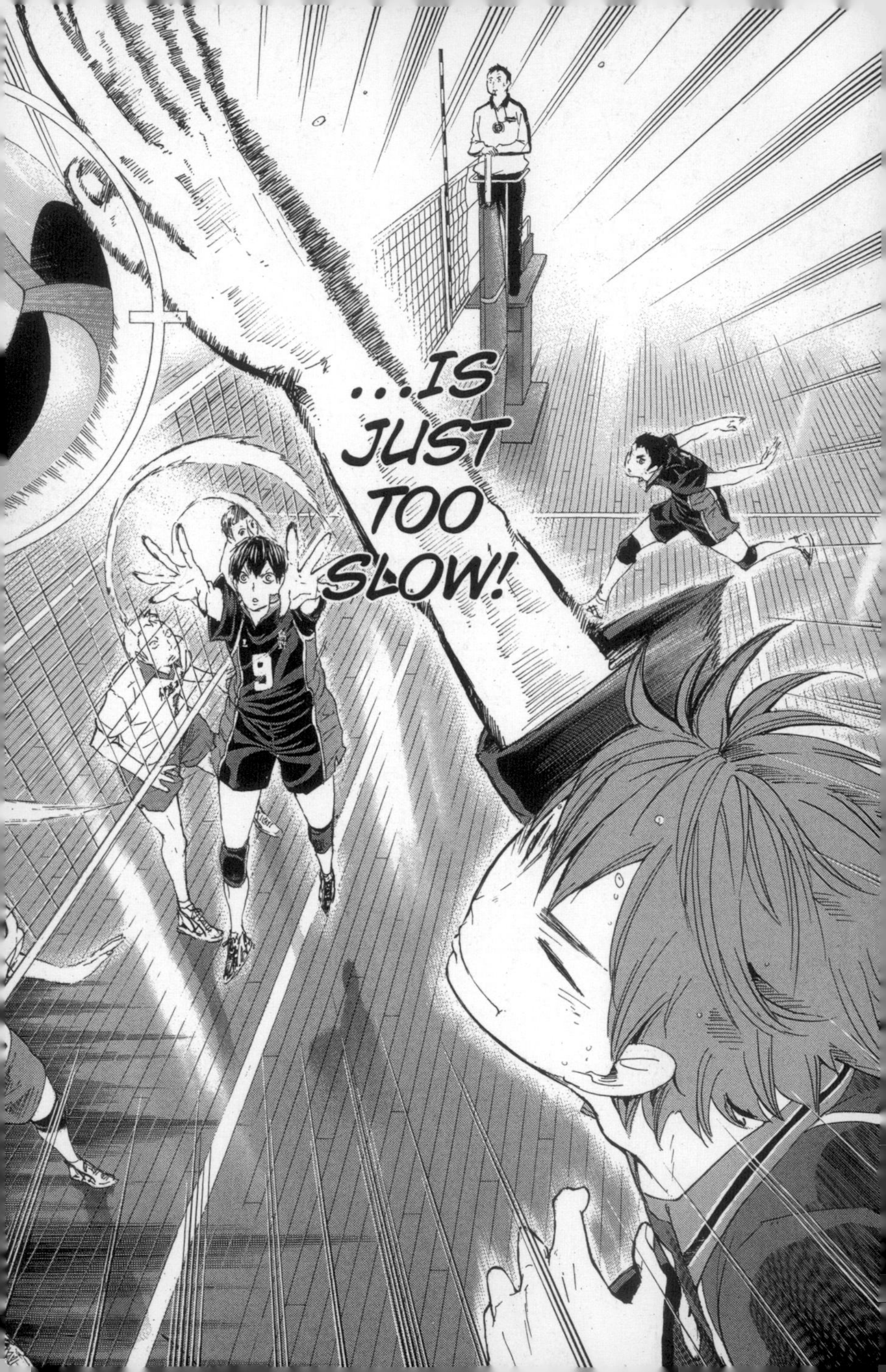
...IS JUST TOO SLOW!

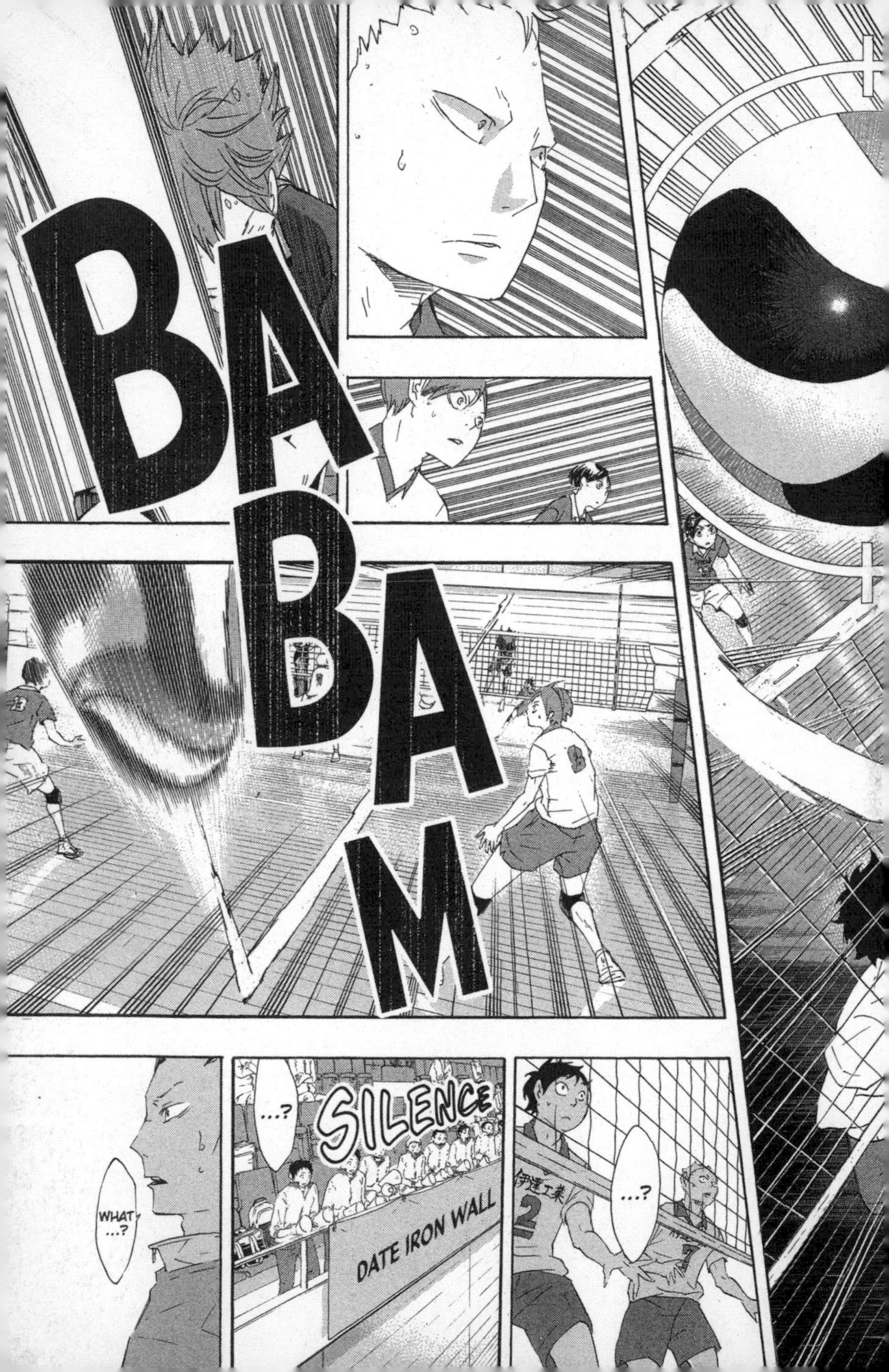
BABABAM
...?
...?
SILENCE
DATE IRON WALL
WHAT ...?

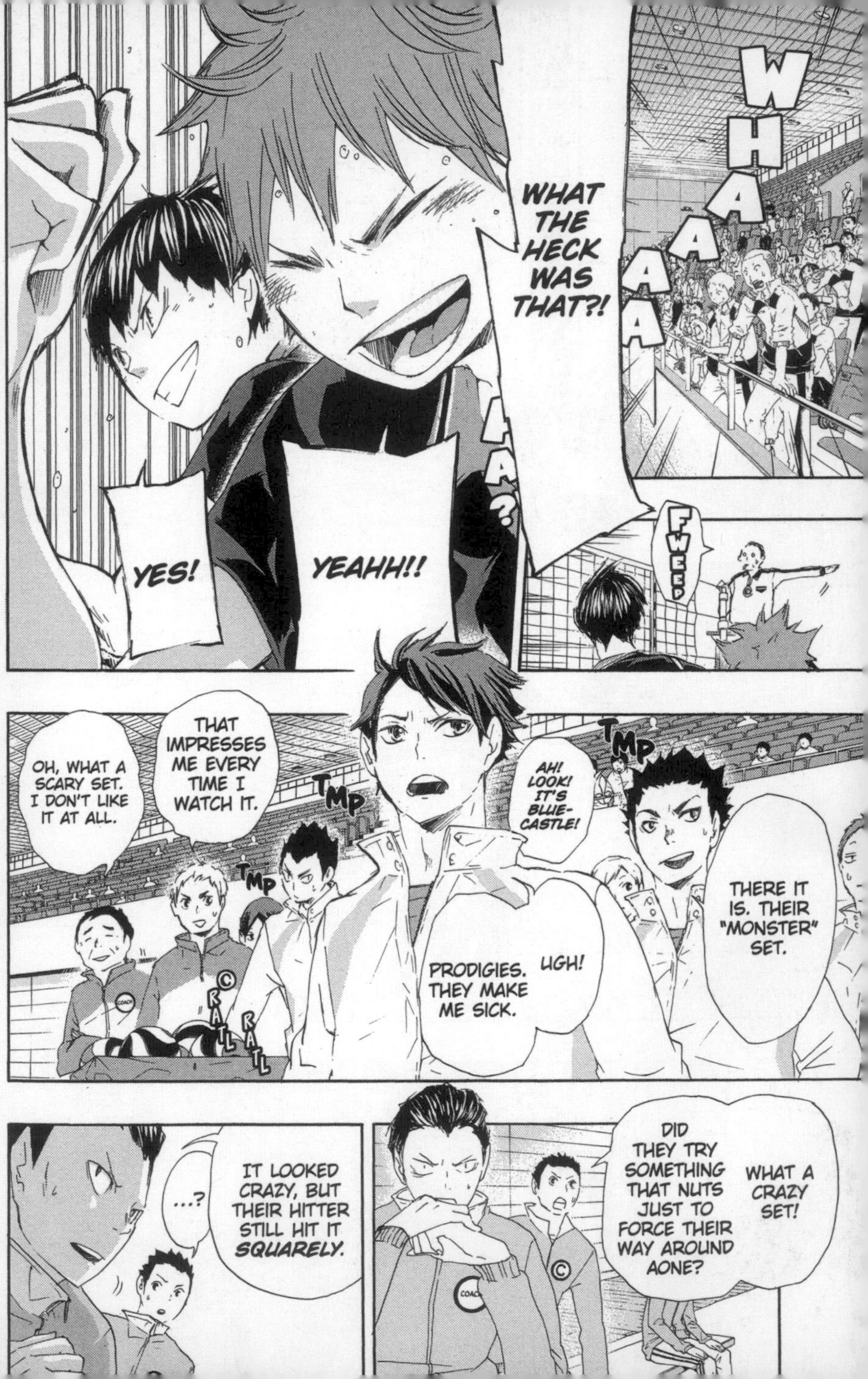
WHAAAAA
WHAT THE HECK WAS THAT?!
FWEEP
AA?
YEAHH!!
YES!
THERE IT IS. THEIR "MONSTER" SET.
AH! LOOK! IT'S BLUE-CASTLE!
TMP
UGH!
PRODIGIES. THEY MAKE ME SICK.
TMP
TMP
THAT IMPRESSES ME EVERY TIME I WATCH IT.
OH, WHAT A SCARY SET. I DON'T LIKE IT AT ALL.
RATTL RATTL
WHAT A CRAZY SET!
DID THEY TRY SOMETHING THAT NUTS JUST TO FORCE THEIR WAY AROUND AONE?
IT LOOKED CRAZY, BUT THEIR HITTER STILL HIT IT SQUARELY.
...?

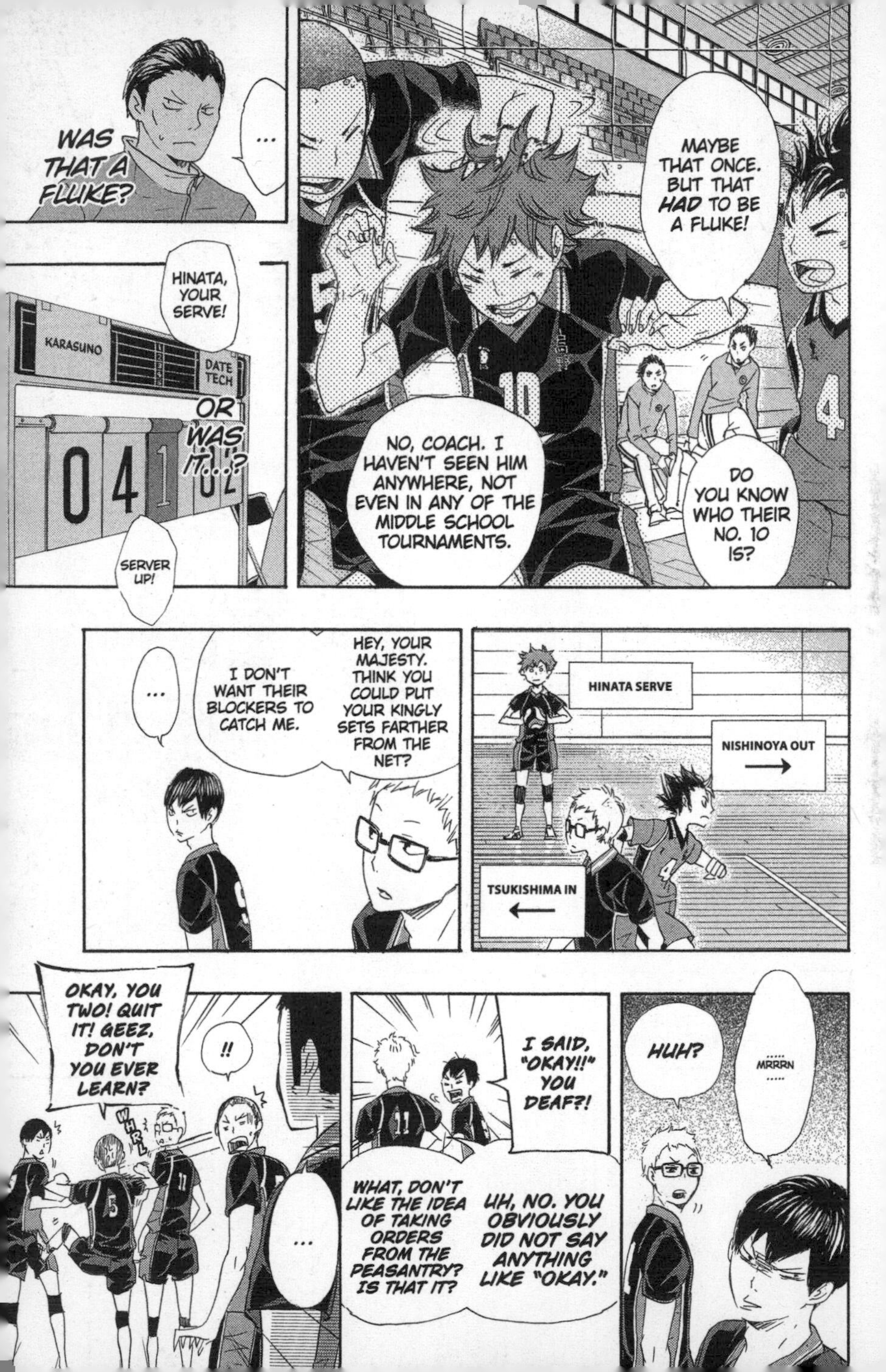
MAYBE THAT ONCE. BUT THAT *HAD* TO BE A FLUKE!
DO YOU KNOW WHO THEIR NO. 10 IS?
NO, COACH. I HAVEN'T SEEN HIM ANYWHERE, NOT EVEN IN ANY OF THE MIDDLE SCHOOL TOURNAMENTS.
...
WAS THAT A FLUKE?
HINATA, YOUR SERVE!
KARASUNO
DATE TECH
OR WAS IT...?
SERVER UP!
HINATA SERVE
NISHINOYA OUT
TSUKISHIMA IN
HEY, YOUR MAJESTY. THINK YOU COULD PUT YOUR KINGLY SETS FARTHER FROM THE NET?
I DON'T WANT THEIR BLOCKERS TO CATCH ME.
...
......MRRRN......
HUH?
I SAID, "OKAY!!" YOU DEAF?!
UH, NO. YOU OBVIOUSLY DID NOT SAY ANYTHING LIKE "OKAY."
WHAT, DON'T LIKE THE IDEA OF TAKING ORDERS FROM THE PEASANTRY? IS THAT IT?
!!
OKAY, YOU TWO! QUIT IT! GEEZ, DON'T YOU EVER LEARN?
WHRL
...

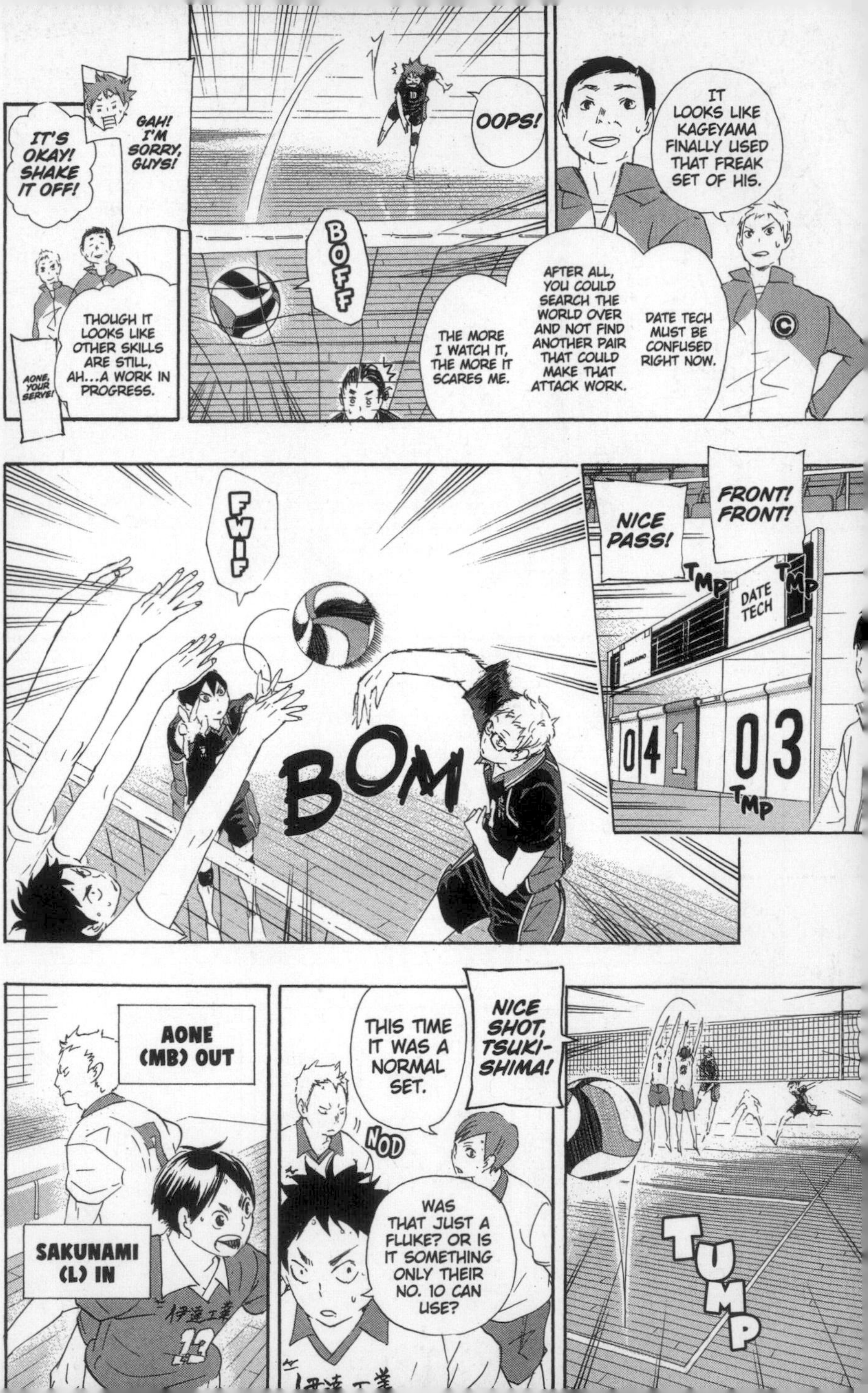
IT LOOKS LIKE KAGEYAMA FINALLY USED THAT FREAK SET OF HIS.
DATE TECH MUST BE CONFUSED RIGHT NOW.
AFTER ALL, YOU COULD SEARCH THE WORLD OVER AND NOT FIND ANOTHER PAIR THAT COULD MAKE THAT ATTACK WORK.
THE MORE I WATCH IT, THE MORE IT SCARES ME.
OOPS!
BOFF
GAH! I'M SORRY, GUYS!
IT'S OKAY! SHAKE IT OFF!
THOUGH IT LOOKS LIKE OTHER SKILLS ARE STILL, AH...A WORK IN PROGRESS.
AONE, YOUR SERVE!
FRONT! FRONT!
NICE PASS!
TMP
TMP
DATE TECH
041
03
TMP
FWIF
BOM
TUMP
NICE SHOT, TSUKISHIMA!
THIS TIME IT WAS A NORMAL SET.
NOD
WAS THAT JUST A FLUKE? OR IS IT SOMETHING ONLY THEIR NO. 10 CAN USE?
AONE (MB) OUT
SAKUNAMI (L) IN

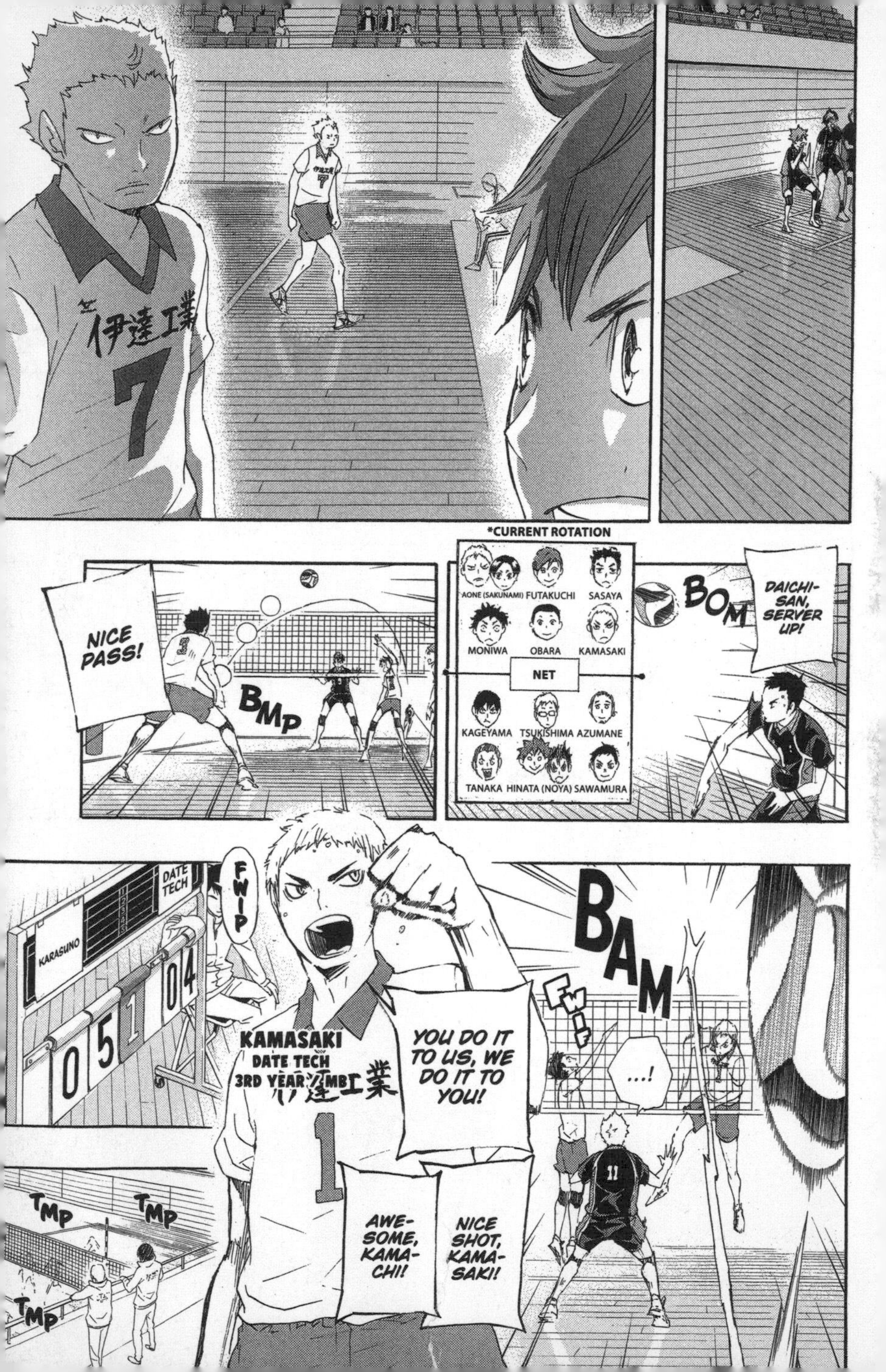
DAICHI-SAN, SERVER UP!
BOM
*CURRENT ROTATION
AONE (SAKUNAMI) FUTAKUCHI SASAYA
MONIWA OBARA KAMASAKI
NET
KAGEYAMA TSUKISHIMA AZUMANE
TANAKA HINATA (NOYA) SAWAMURA
NICE PASS!
BMP
BAM
FWIF
...!
YOU DO IT TO US, WE DO IT TO YOU!
KAMASAKI
DATE TECH
3RD YEAR MB
FWIP
DATE TECH
KARASUNO
NICE SHOT, KAMASAKI!
AWE-SOME, KAMA-CHI!
TMP
TMP
TMP

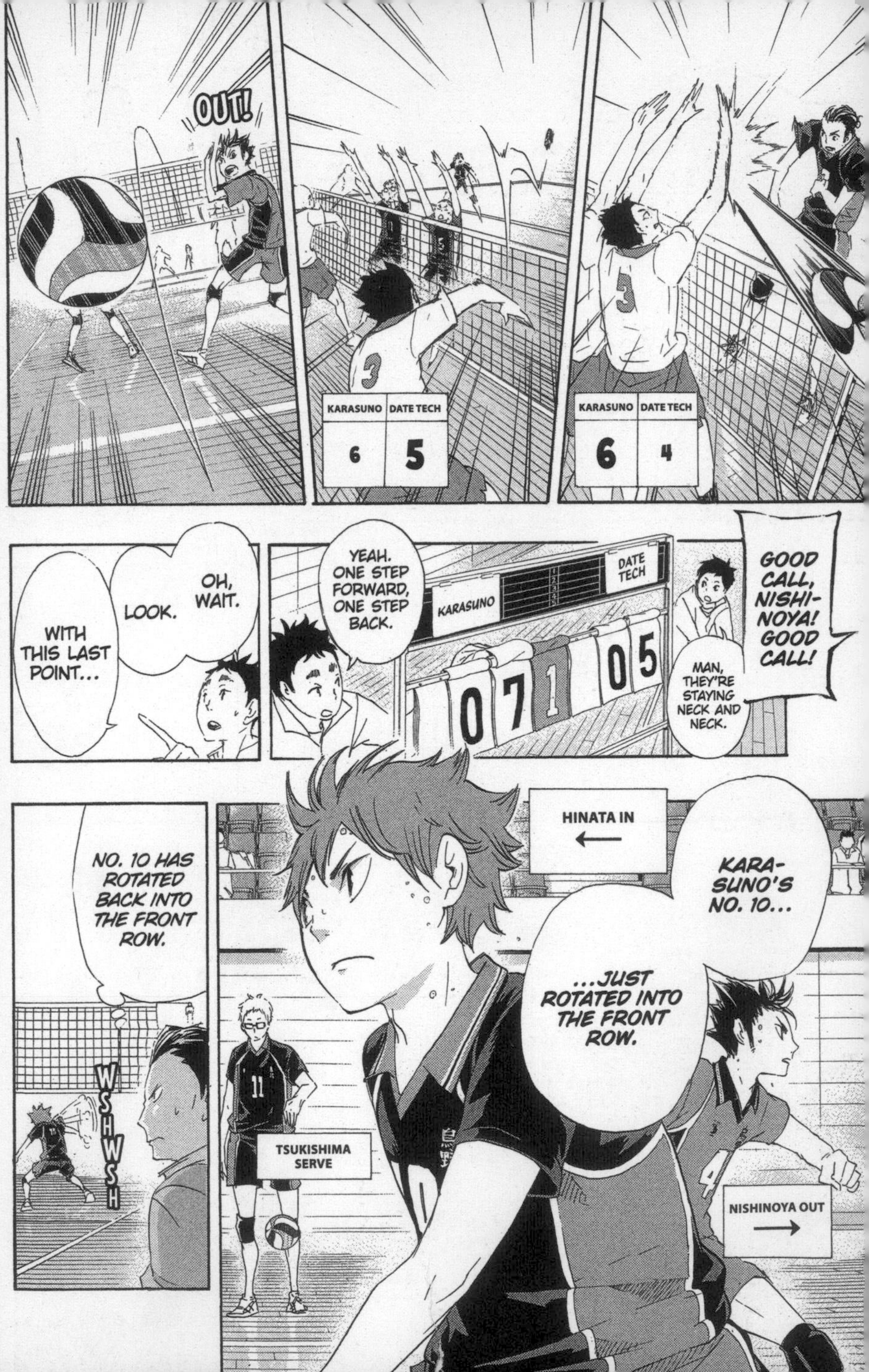
KARASUNO
DATE TECH
6
4
KARASUNO
DATE TECH
6
5
OUT!
GOOD CALL, NISHINOYA! GOOD CALL!
MAN, THEY'RE STAYING NECK AND NECK.
DATE TECH
KARASUNO
07
1
05
YEAH. ONE STEP FORWARD, ONE STEP BACK.
OH, WAIT.
LOOK.
WITH THIS LAST POINT...
HINATA IN
KARA-SUNO'S NO. 10...
...JUST ROTATED INTO THE FRONT ROW.
NISHINOYA OUT
TSUKISHIMA SERVE
NO. 10 HAS ROTATED BACK INTO THE FRONT ROW.
WSHWSH

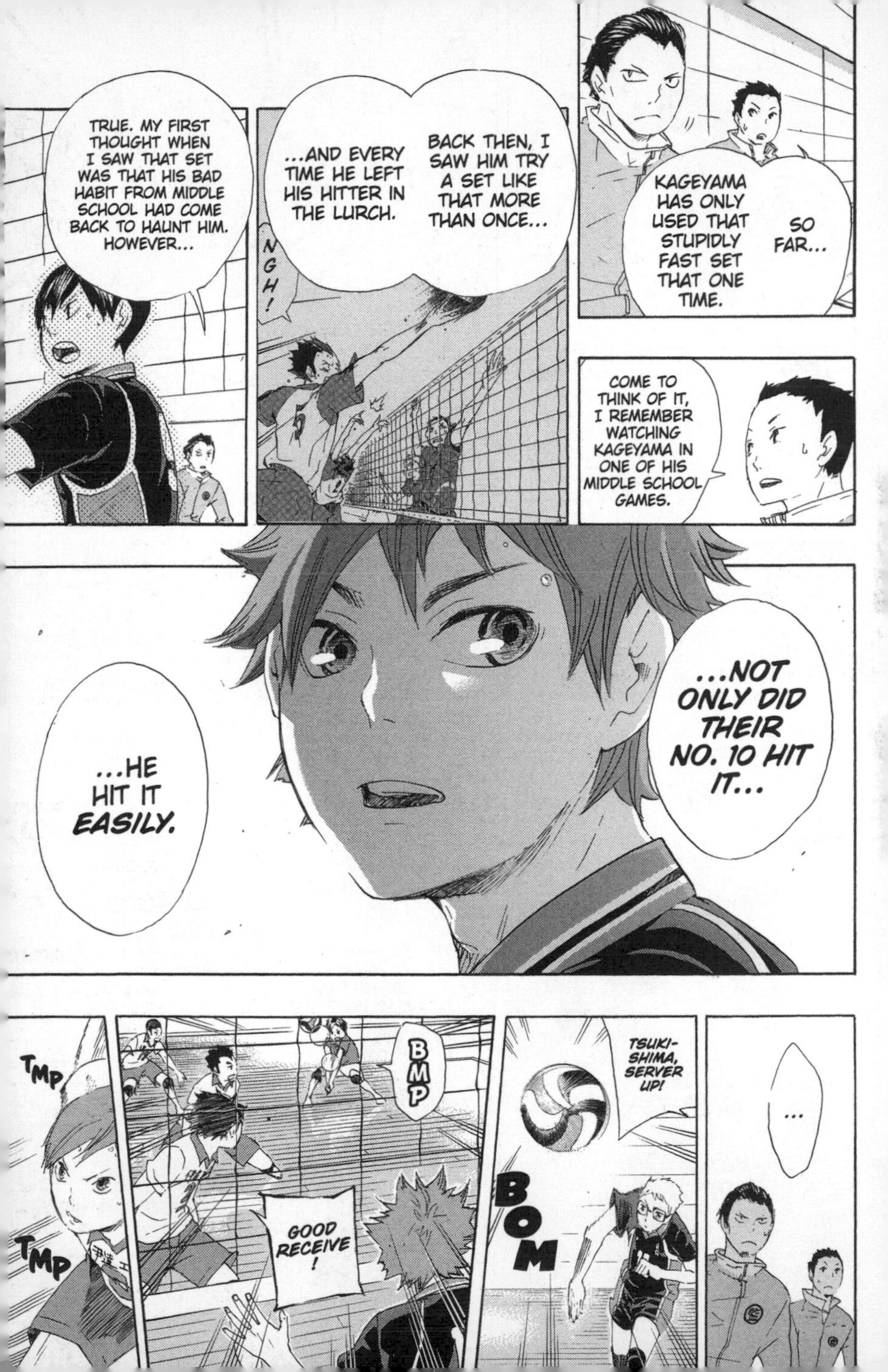
SO FAR...
KAGEYAMA HAS ONLY USED THAT STUPIDLY FAST SET THAT ONE TIME.
COME TO THINK OF IT, I REMEMBER WATCHING KAGEYAMA IN ONE OF HIS MIDDLE SCHOOL GAMES.
BACK THEN, I SAW HIM TRY A SET LIKE THAT MORE THAN ONCE...
...AND EVERY TIME HE LEFT HIS HITTER IN THE LURCH.
NGH!
TRUE. MY FIRST THOUGHT WHEN I SAW THAT SET WAS THAT HIS BAD HABIT FROM MIDDLE SCHOOL HAD COME BACK TO HAUNT HIM. HOWEVER...
...NOT ONLY DID THEIR NO. 10 HIT IT...
...HE HIT IT EASILY.
...
TSUKISHIMA, SERVER UP!
BOM
BMP
GOOD RECEIVE!
TMP
TMP

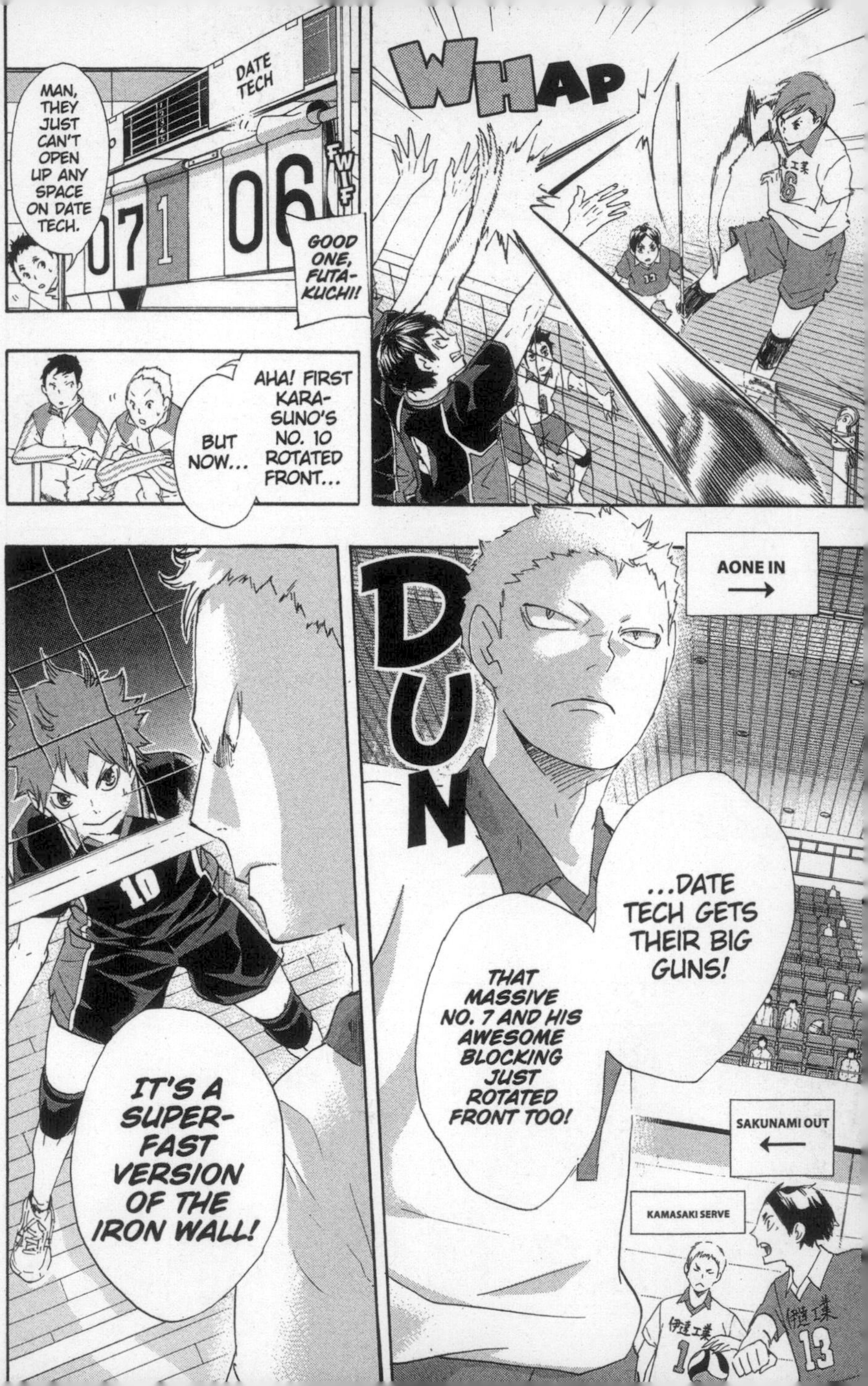
WHAP
DATE TECH
07 1 06
FWIF
GOOD ONE, FUTAKUCHI!
MAN, THEY JUST CAN'T OPEN UP ANY SPACE ON DATE TECH.
AHA! FIRST KARASUNO'S NO. 10 ROTATED FRONT...
BUT NOW...
AONE IN →
DUN
...DATE TECH GETS THEIR BIG GUNS!
THAT MASSIVE NO. 7 AND HIS AWESOME BLOCKING JUST ROTATED FRONT TOO!
SAKUNAMI OUT ←
KAMASAKI SERVE
IT'S A SUPER-FAST VERSION OF THE IRON WALL!

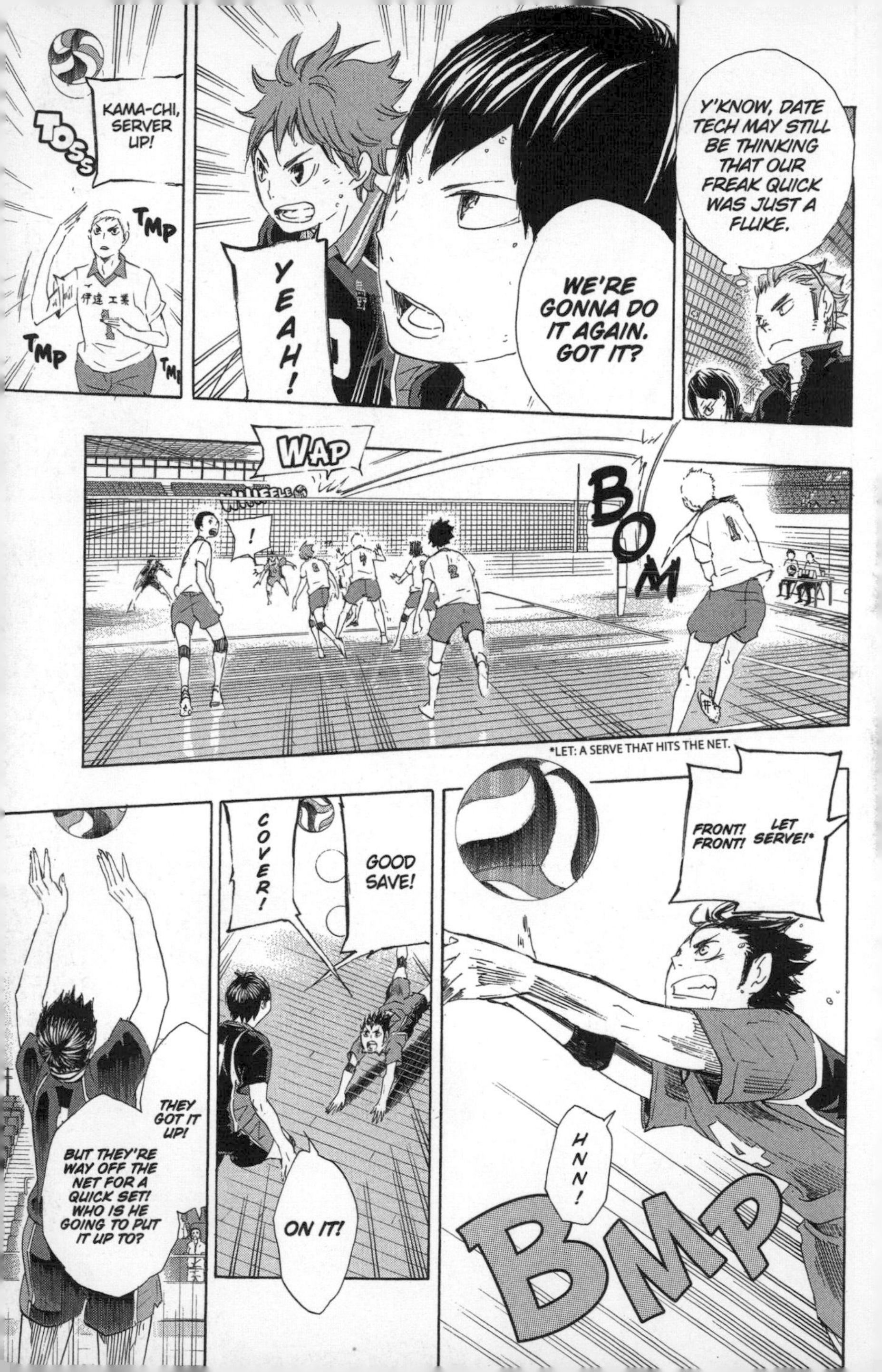
Y'KNOW, DATE TECH MAY STILL BE THINKING THAT OUR FREAK QUICK WAS JUST A FLUKE.
WE'RE GONNA DO IT AGAIN. GOT IT?
YEAH!
KAMA-CHI, SERVER UP!
TOSS
TMP
TMP
TMP
WAP
BOM
!
LET SERVE!*
FRONT! FRONT!
HNN!
BMP
GOOD SAVE!
COVER!
ON IT!
THEY GOT IT UP!
BUT THEY'RE WAY OFF THE NET FOR A QUICK SET! WHO IS HE GOING TO PUT IT UP TO?

*LET: A SERVE THAT HITS THE NET.

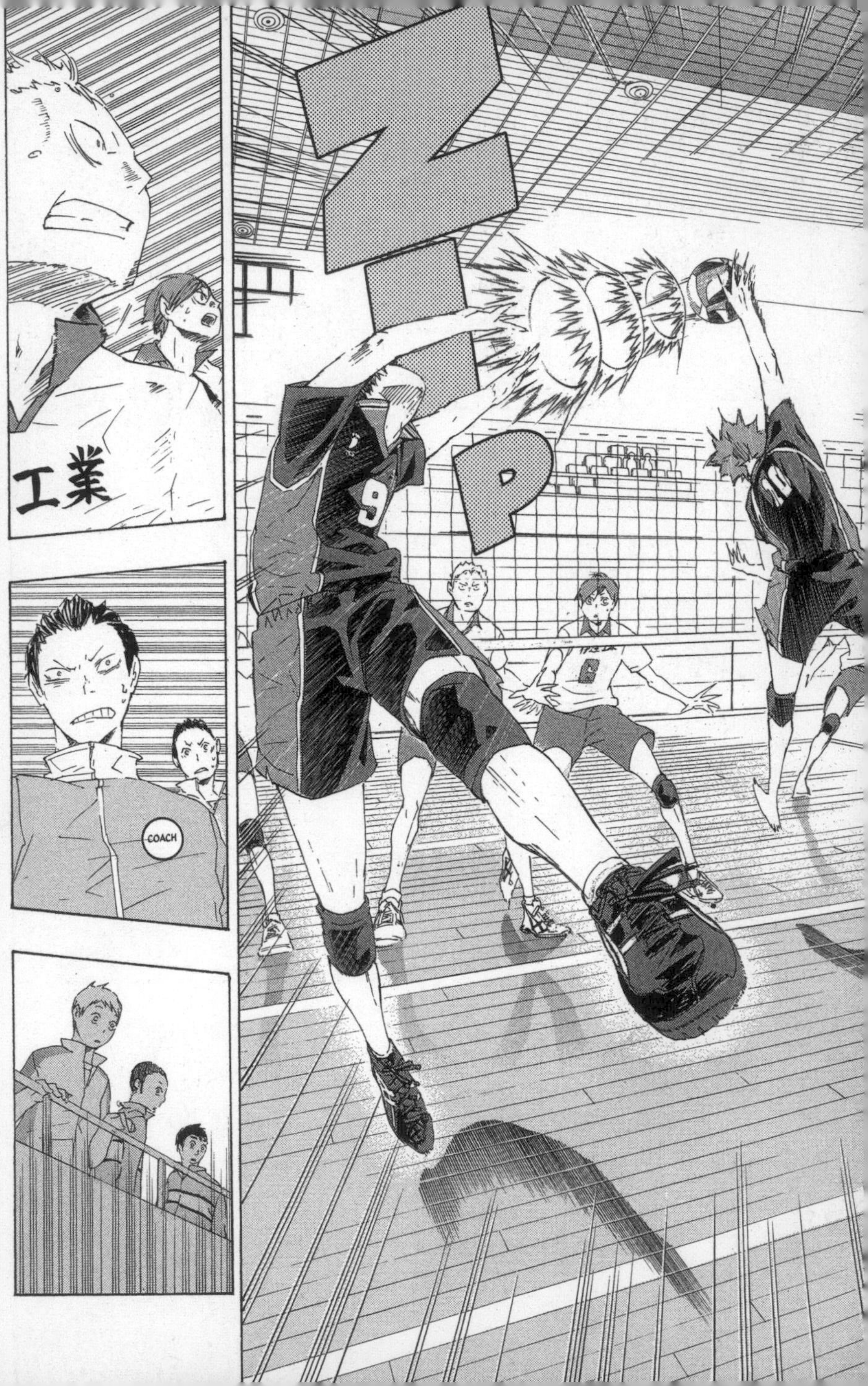
ZIP
工業
COACH

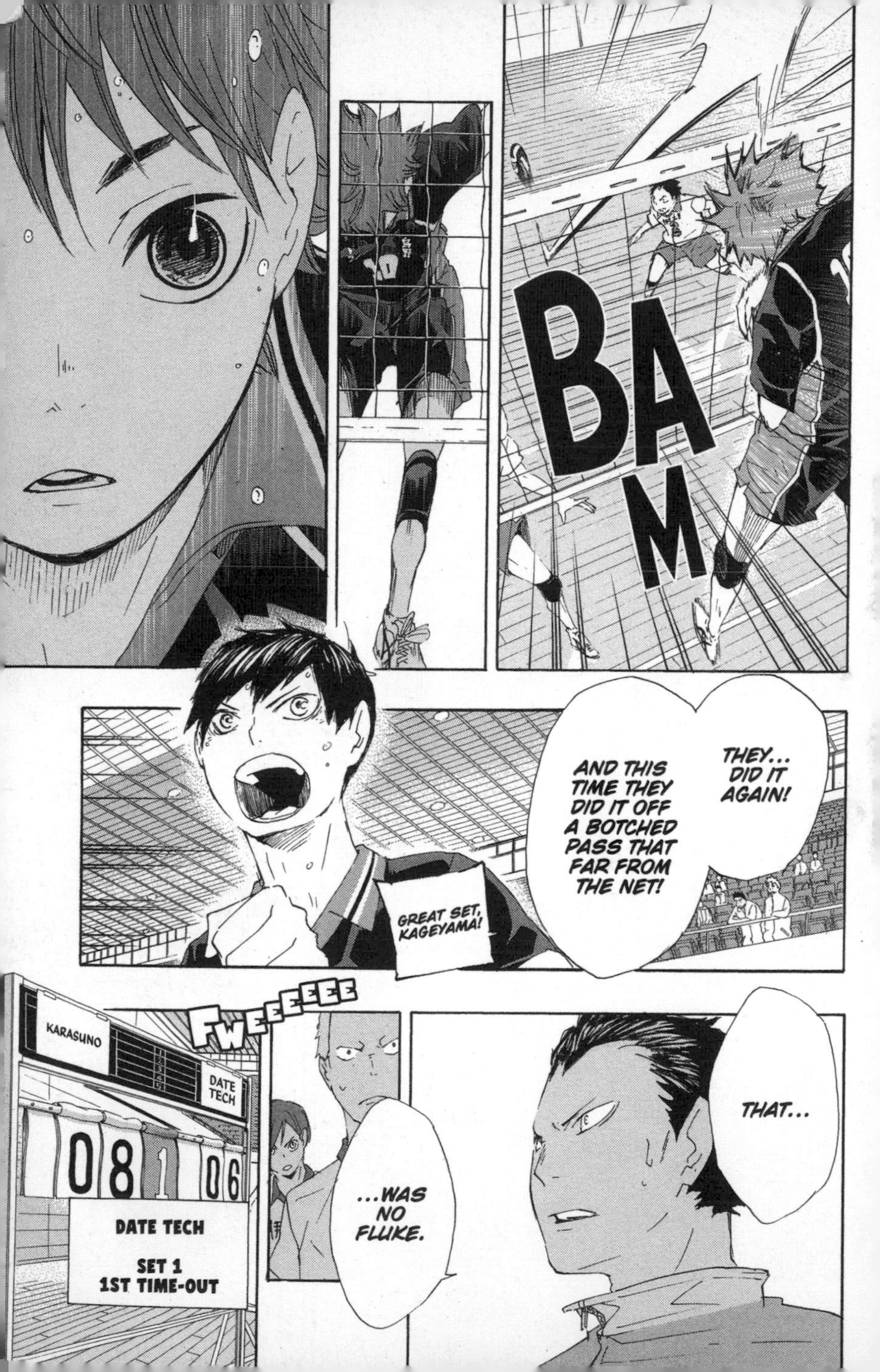
BAM
THEY... DID IT AGAIN!
AND THIS TIME THEY DID IT OFF A BOTCHED PASS THAT FAR FROM THE NET!
GREAT SET, KAGEYAMA!
THAT...
...WAS NO FLUKE.
FWEEEEEE
KARASUNO
DATE TECH
08 1 06
DATE TECH
SET 1
1ST TIME-OUT

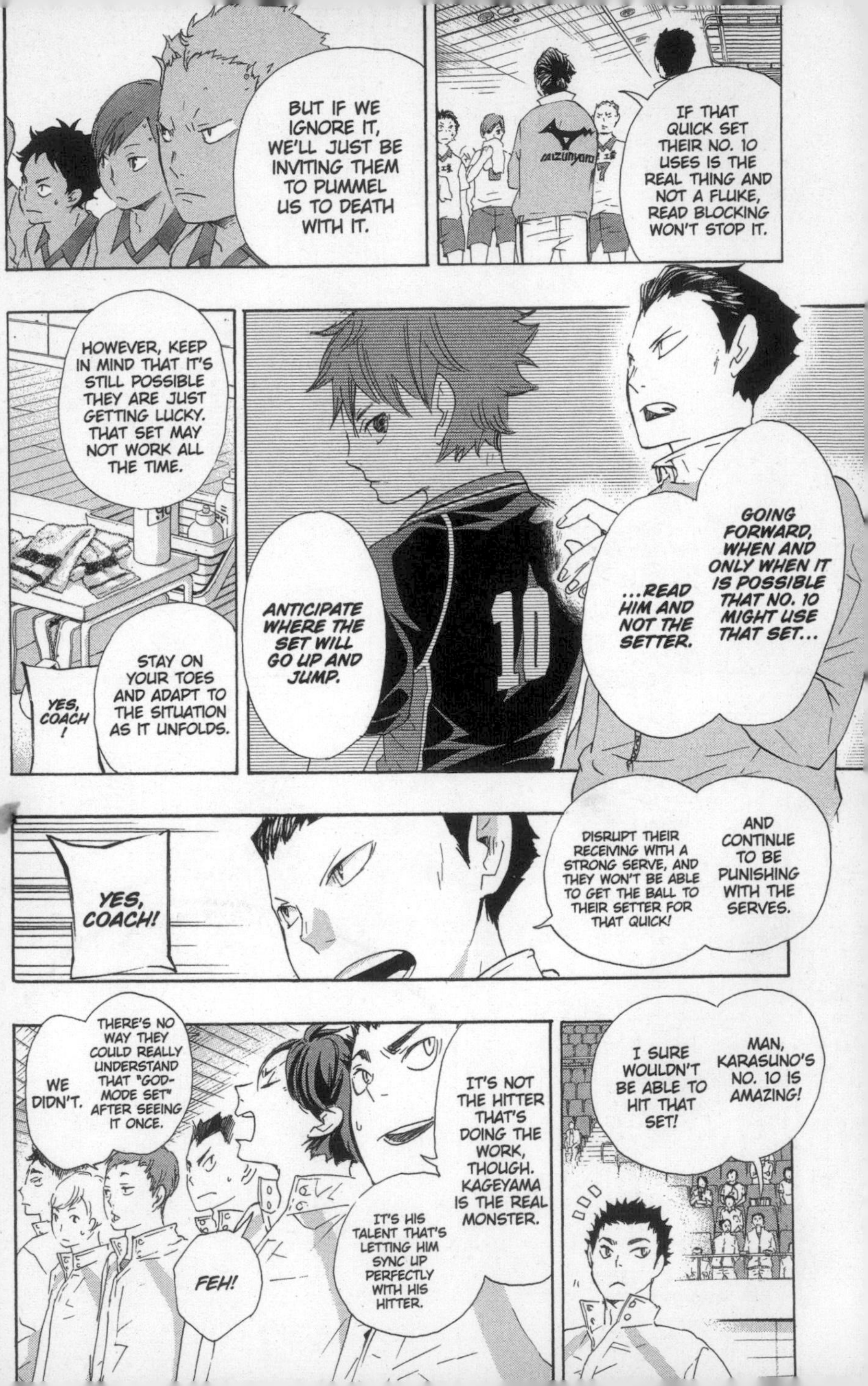
IF THAT QUICK SET THEIR NO. 10 USES IS THE REAL THING AND NOT A FLUKE, READ BLOCKING WON'T STOP IT.
BUT IF WE IGNORE IT, WE'LL JUST BE INVITING THEM TO PUMMEL US TO DEATH WITH IT.
GOING FORWARD, WHEN AND ONLY WHEN IT IS POSSIBLE THAT NO. 10 MIGHT USE THAT SET...
...READ HIM AND NOT THE SETTER.
ANTICIPATE WHERE THE SET WILL GO UP AND JUMP.
HOWEVER, KEEP IN MIND THAT IT'S STILL POSSIBLE THEY ARE JUST GETTING LUCKY. THAT SET MAY NOT WORK ALL THE TIME.
STAY ON YOUR TOES AND ADAPT TO THE SITUATION AS IT UNFOLDS.
YES, COACH!
DISRUPT THEIR RECEIVING WITH A STRONG SERVE, AND THEY WON'T BE ABLE TO GET THE BALL TO THEIR SETTER FOR THAT QUICK!
AND CONTINUE TO BE PUNISHING WITH THE SERVES.
YES, COACH!
MAN, KARASUNO'S NO. 10 IS AMAZING!
I SURE WOULDN'T BE ABLE TO HIT THAT SET!
IT'S NOT THE HITTER THAT'S DOING THE WORK, THOUGH. KAGEYAMA IS THE REAL MONSTER.
IT'S HIS TALENT THAT'S LETTING HIM SYNC UP PERFECTLY WITH HIS HITTER.
THERE'S NO WAY THEY COULD REALLY UNDERSTAND THAT "GOD-MODE SET" AFTER SEEING IT ONCE.
WE DIDN'T.
FEH!

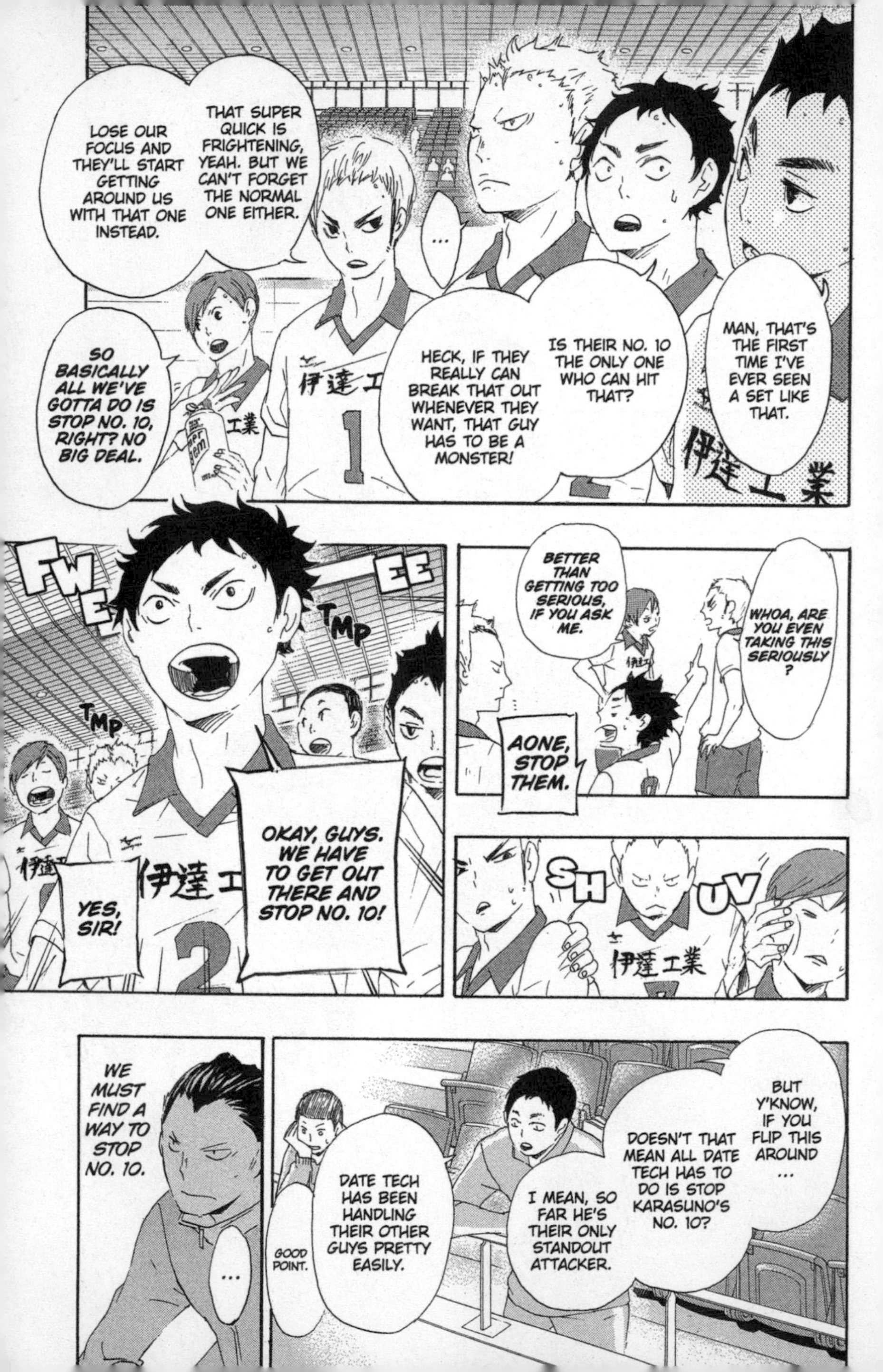
MAN, THAT'S THE FIRST TIME I'VE EVER SEEN A SET LIKE THAT.
IS THEIR NO. 10 THE ONLY ONE WHO CAN HIT THAT?
HECK, IF THEY REALLY CAN BREAK THAT OUT WHENEVER THEY WANT, THAT GUY HAS TO BE A MONSTER!
...
THAT SUPER QUICK IS FRIGHTENING, YEAH. BUT WE CAN'T FORGET THE NORMAL ONE EITHER.
LOSE OUR FOCUS AND THEY'LL START GETTING AROUND US WITH THAT ONE INSTEAD.
SO BASICALLY ALL WE'VE GOTTA DO IS STOP NO. 10, RIGHT? NO BIG DEAL.
WHOA, ARE YOU EVEN TAKING THIS SERIOUSLY?
BETTER THAN GETTING TOO SERIOUS, IF YOU ASK ME.
AONE, STOP THEM.
SH UV
FWEE
TMP
TMP
OKAY, GUYS. WE HAVE TO GET OUT THERE AND STOP NO. 10!
YES, SIR!
BUT Y'KNOW, IF YOU FLIP THIS AROUND...
DOESN'T THAT MEAN ALL DATE TECH HAS TO DO IS STOP KARASUNO'S NO. 10?
I MEAN, SO FAR HE'S THEIR ONLY STANDOUT ATTACKER.
DATE TECH HAS BEEN HANDLING THEIR OTHER GUYS PRETTY EASILY.
GOOD POINT.
WE MUST FIND A WAY TO STOP NO. 10.
...

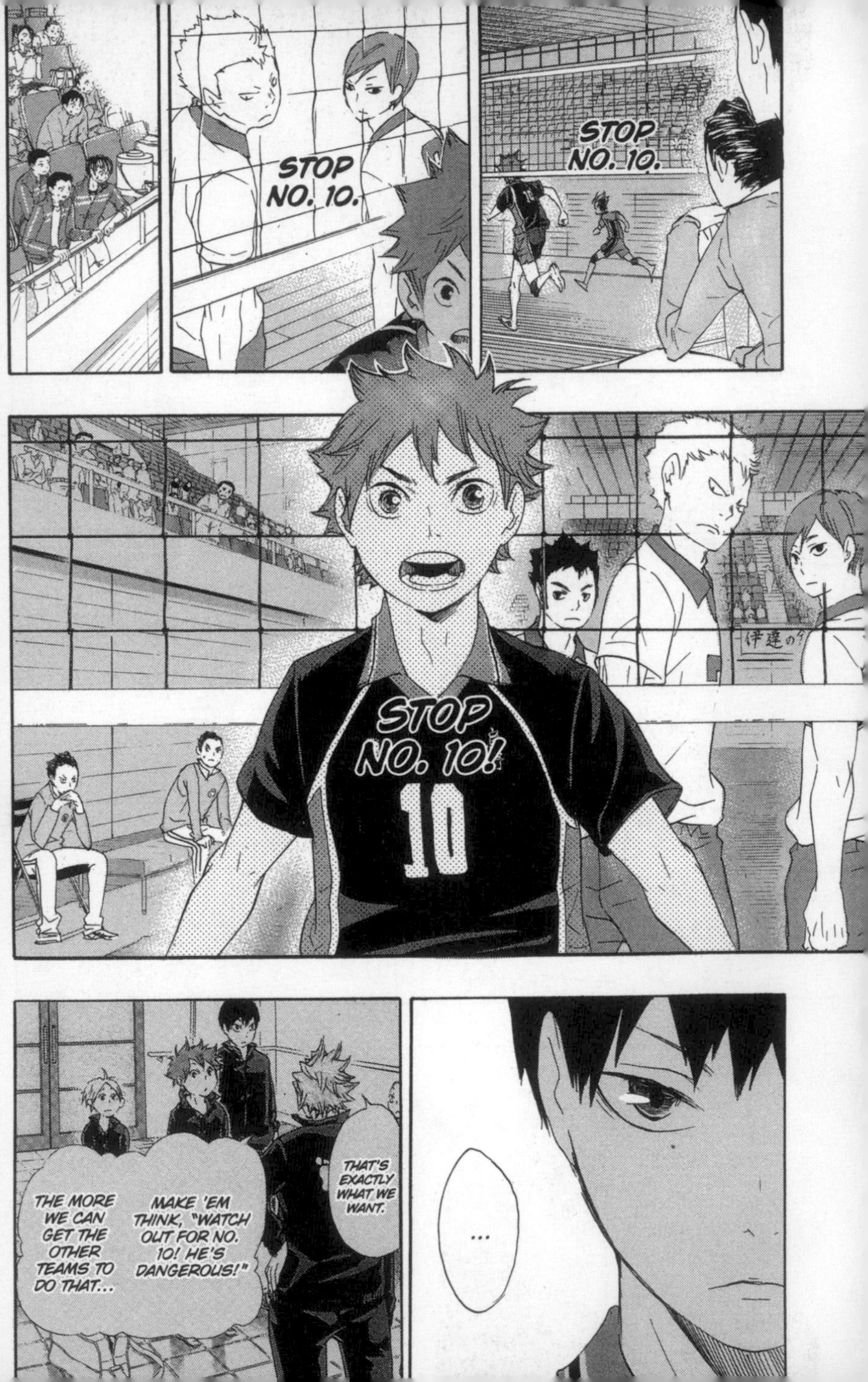
STOP NO. 10.
STOP NO. 10.
STOP NO. 10!
...
THAT'S EXACTLY WHAT WE WANT.
MAKE 'EM THINK, "WATCH OUT FOR NO. 10! HE'S DANGEROUS!"
THE MORE WE CAN GET THE OTHER TEAMS TO DO THAT...

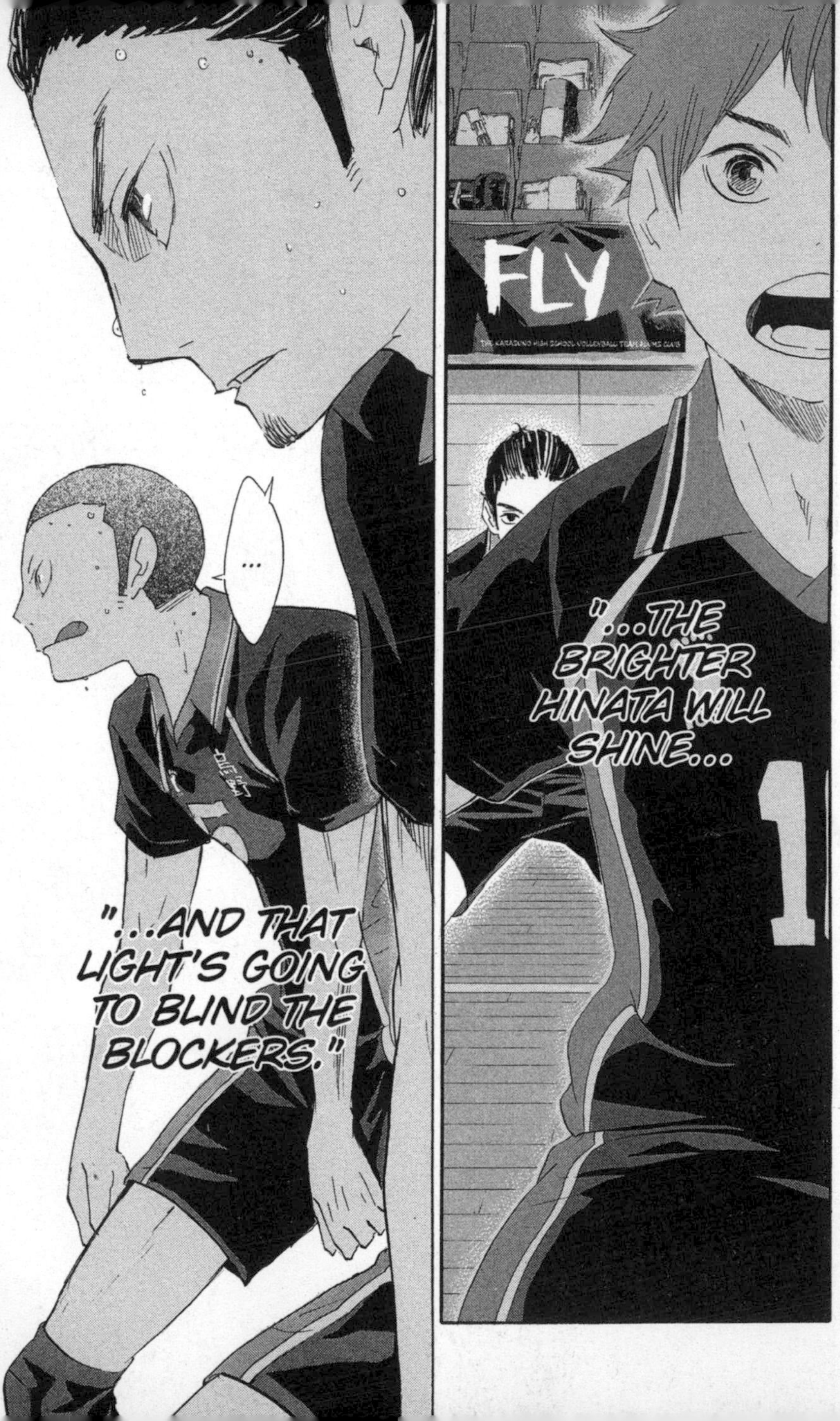
FLY
"...THE BRIGHTER HINATA WILL SHINE...
...
"...AND THAT LIGHT'S GOING TO BLIND THE BLOCKERS."

KENJI FUTAKUCHI

DATE TECHNICAL HIGH SCHOOL
CLASS 2-A

POSITION:
WING SPIKER

HEIGHT: 6'0"

WEIGHT: 158 LBS.
(AS OF APRIL, 2ND YEAR
OF HIGH SCHOOL)

BIRTHDAY: NOVEMBER 10

FAVORITE FOOD:
SOUR GUMMIES

CURRENT WORRY:
HE HAS TO GO GET HIS
WISDOM TEETH REMOVED.

ABILITY PARAMETERS
(5-POINT SCALE)

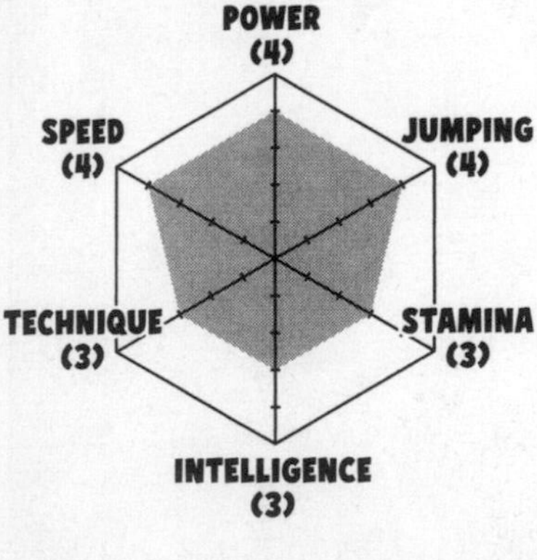
POWER (4)
JUMPING (4)
STAMINA (3)
INTELLIGENCE (3)
TECHNIQUE (3)
SPEED (4)

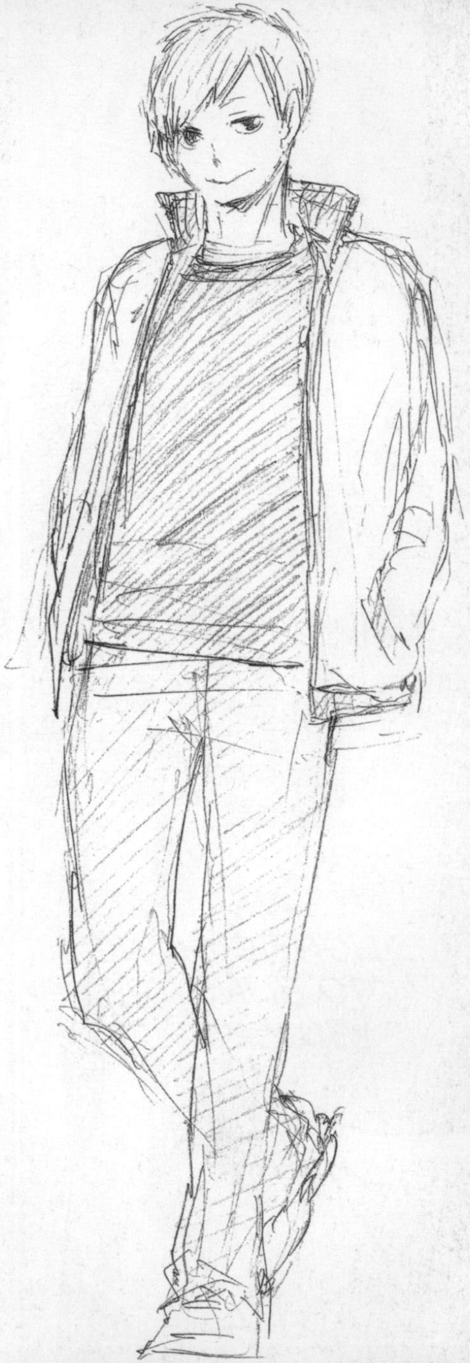

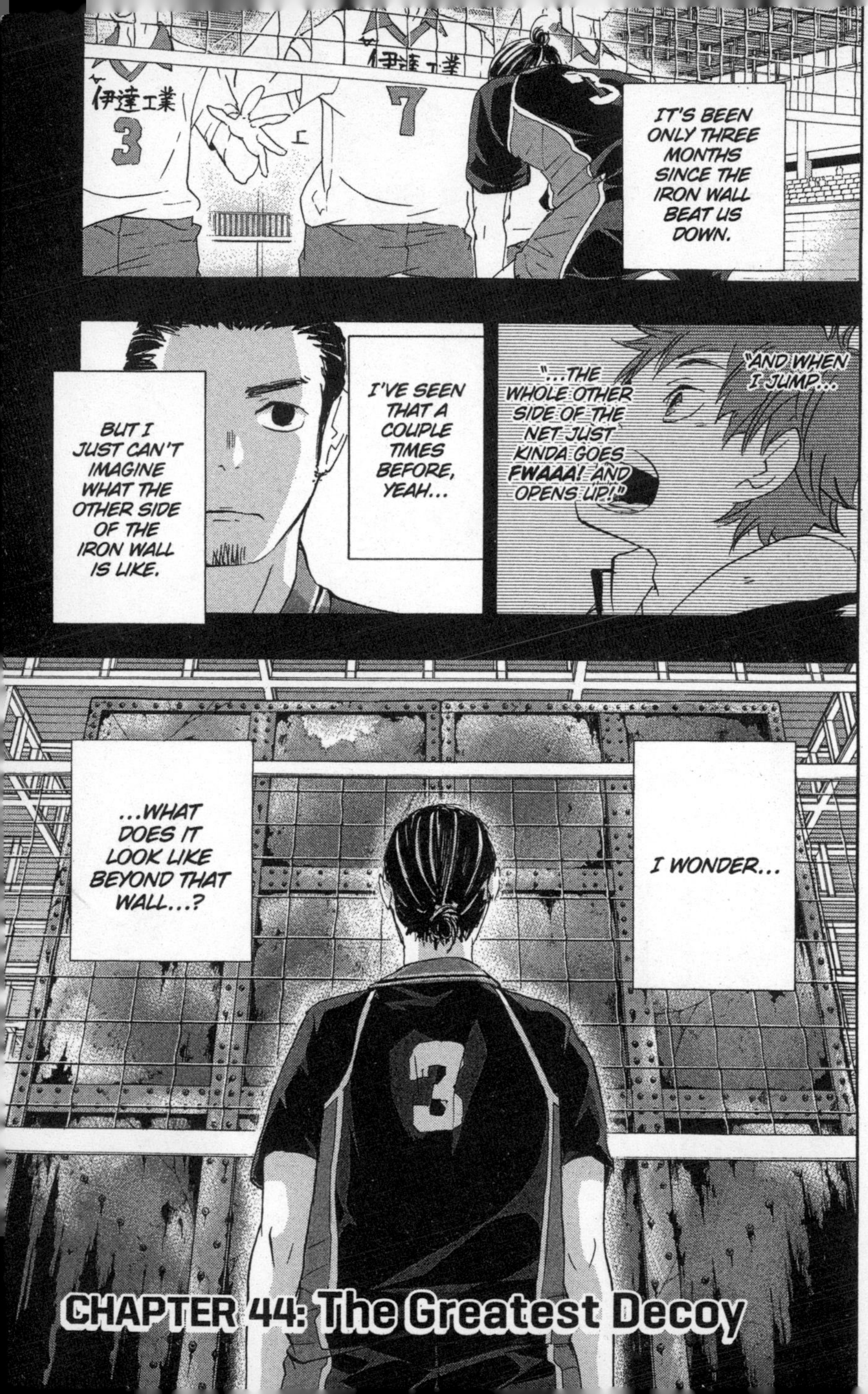
伊達工業
伊達工業
IT'S BEEN ONLY THREE MONTHS SINCE THE IRON WALL BEAT US DOWN.
"AND WHEN I JUMP...
"...THE WHOLE OTHER SIDE OF THE NET JUST KINDA GOES FWAAA! AND OPENS UP!"
I'VE SEEN THAT A COUPLE TIMES BEFORE, YEAH...
BUT I JUST CAN'T IMAGINE WHAT THE OTHER SIDE OF THE IRON WALL IS LIKE.
I WONDER...
...WHAT DOES IT LOOK LIKE BEYOND THAT WALL...?
CHAPTER 44: The Greatest Decoy

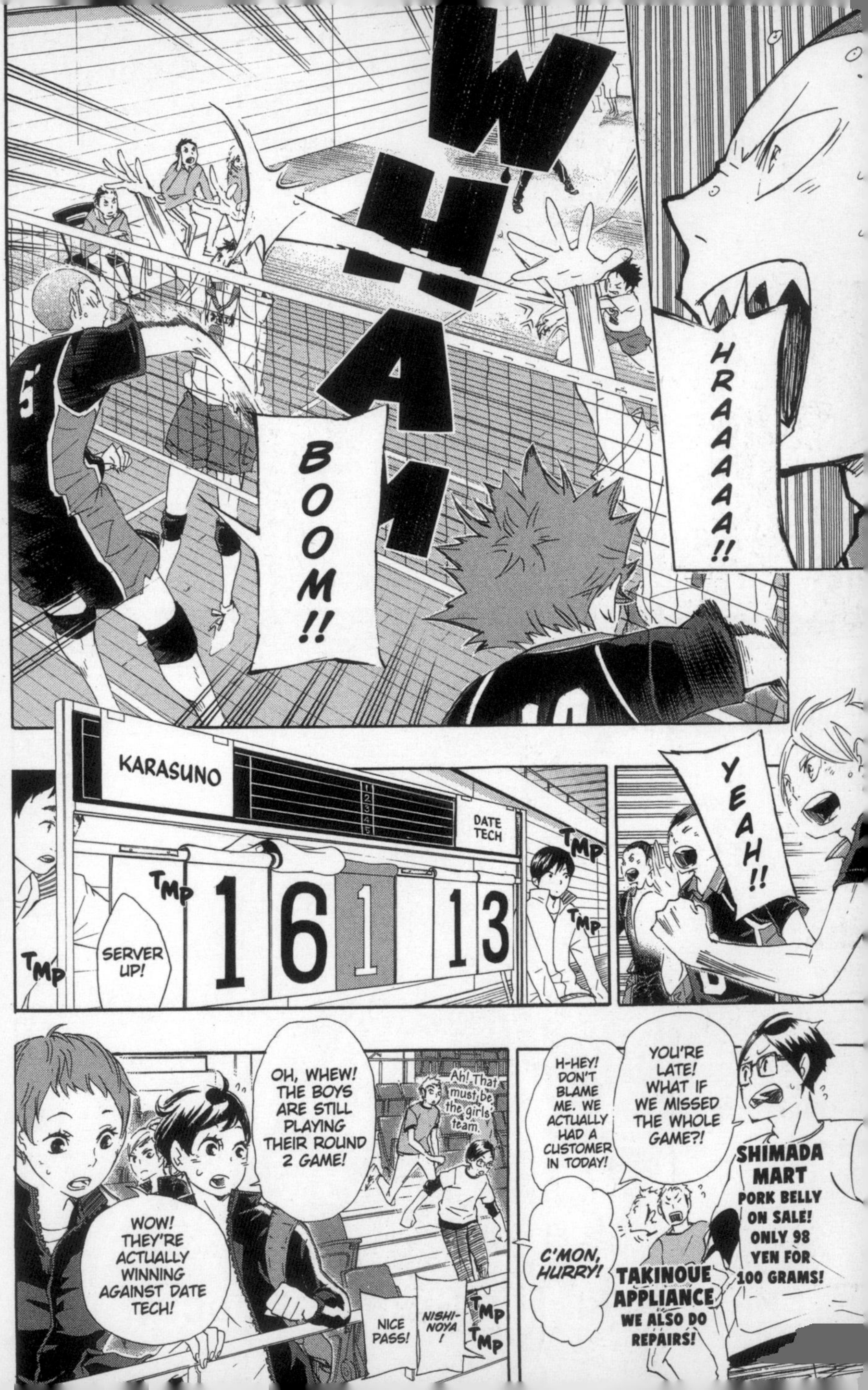
HRAAAAAA!!
WHAM
BOOM!!
YEAH!!
TMP
KARASUNO
DATE TECH
16
1
13
TMP
TMP
SERVER UP!
TMP
YOU'RE LATE! WHAT IF WE MISSED THE WHOLE GAME?!
H-HEY! DON'T BLAME ME. WE ACTUALLY HAD A CUSTOMER IN TODAY!
SHIMADA MART PORK BELLY ON SALE! ONLY 98 YEN FOR 100 GRAMS!
C'MON, HURRY!
TAKINOUE APPLIANCE WE ALSO DO REPAIRS!
OH, WHEW! THE BOYS ARE STILL PLAYING THEIR ROUND 2 GAME!
Ah! That must be the girls' team.
WOW! THEY'RE ACTUALLY WINNING AGAINST DATE TECH!
TMP
TMP
NISHI-NOYA!
NICE PASS!

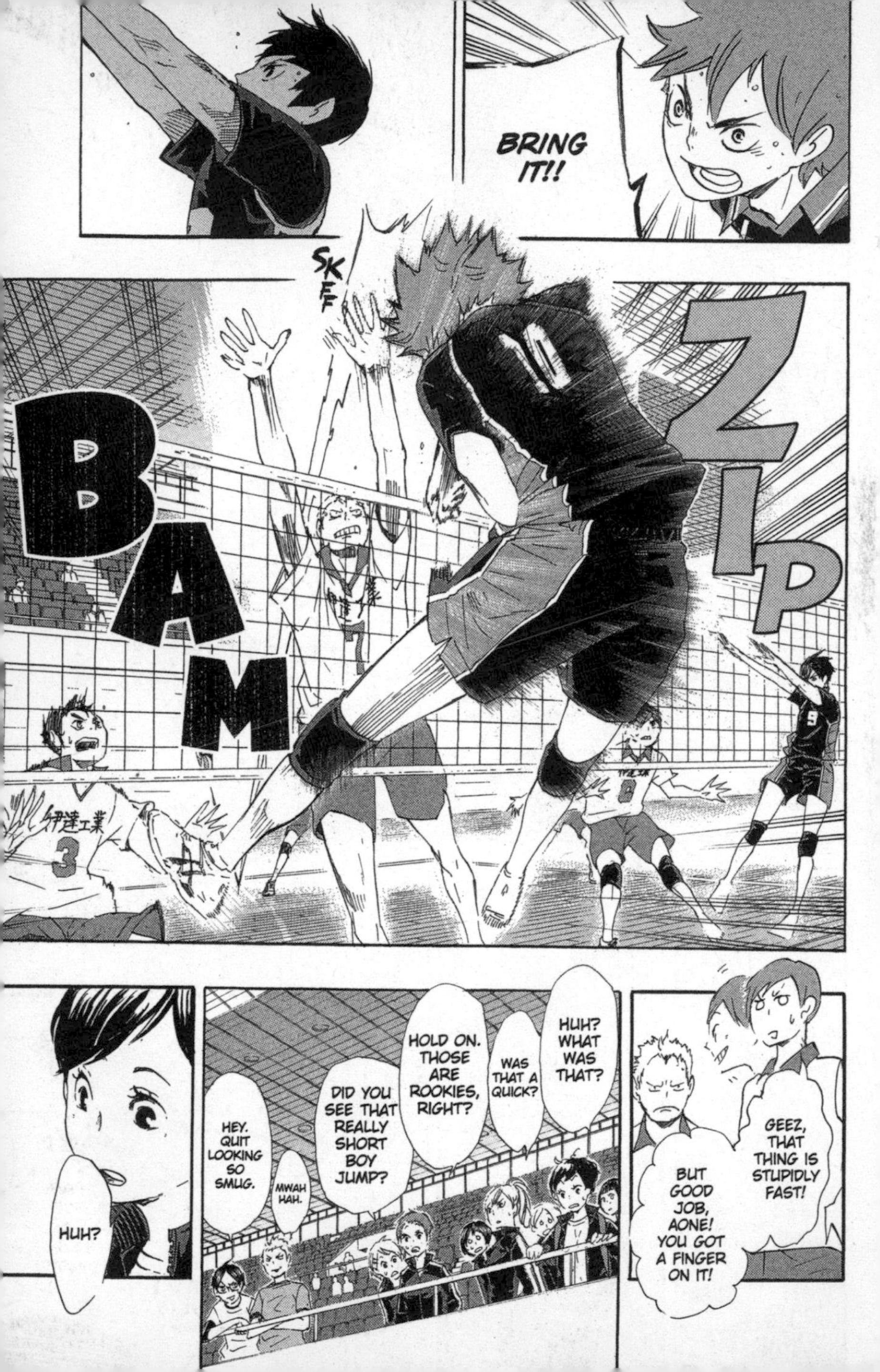
BRING IT!!
ZIP
SKFF
BAM
GEEZ, THAT THING IS STUPIDLY FAST!
BUT GOOD JOB, AONE! YOU GOT A FINGER ON IT!
HUH? WHAT WAS THAT?
WAS THAT A QUICK?
HOLD ON. THOSE ARE ROOKIES, RIGHT?
DID YOU SEE THAT REALLY SHORT BOY JUMP?
MWAH HAH.
HEY. QUIT LOOKING SO SMUG.
HUH?

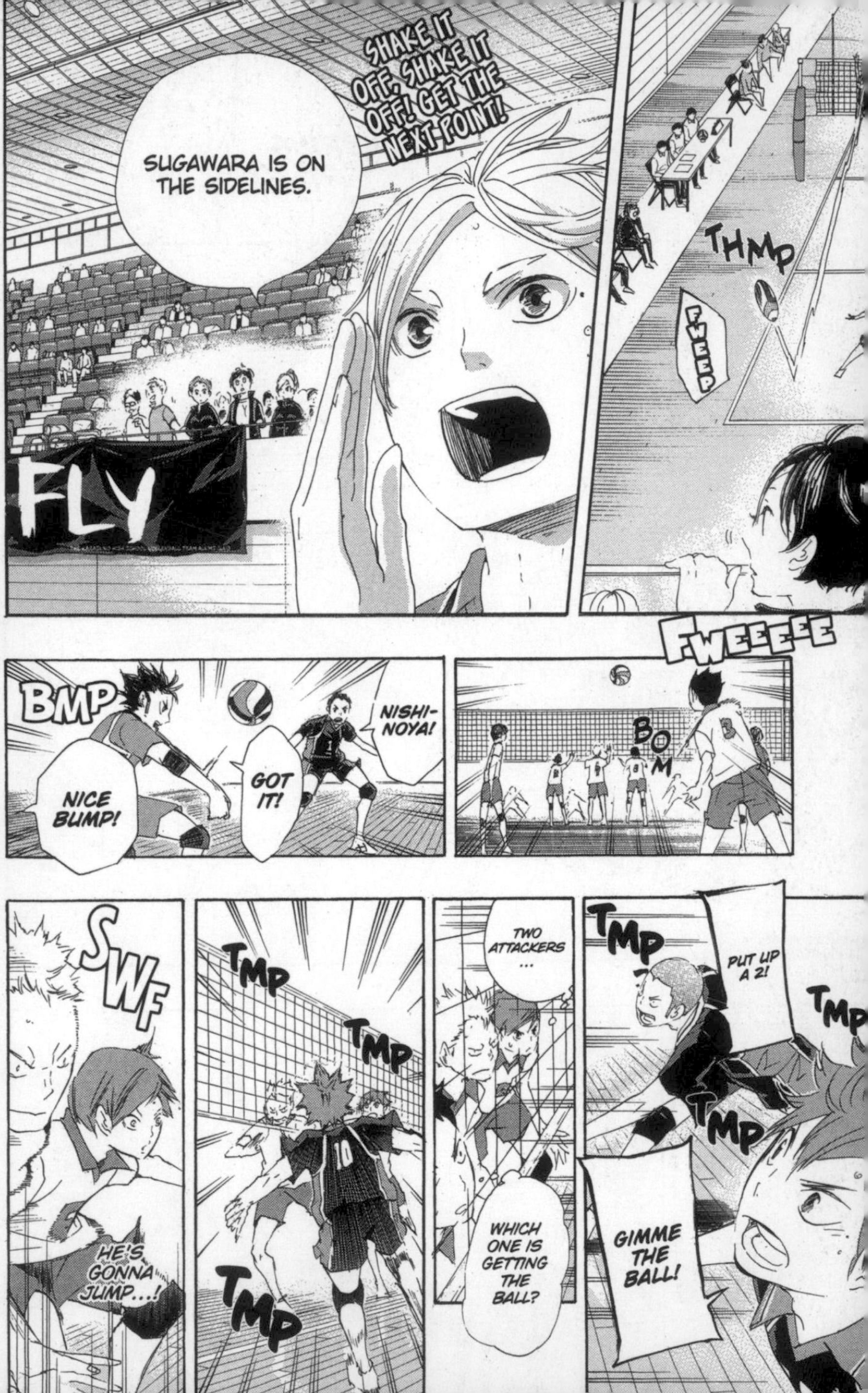
THMP
FWEEP
SHAKE IT OFF, SHAKE IT OFF! GET THE NEXT POINT!
SUGAWARA IS ON THE SIDELINES.
FLY
FWEEEE
BOM
NISHI-NOYA!
GOT IT!
BMP
NICE BUMP!
TMP
PUT UP A 2!
TMP
TMP
GIMME THE BALL!
TWO ATTACKERS ...
WHICH ONE IS GETTING THE BALL?
TMP
TMP
TMP
SWF
HE'S GONNA JUMP...!

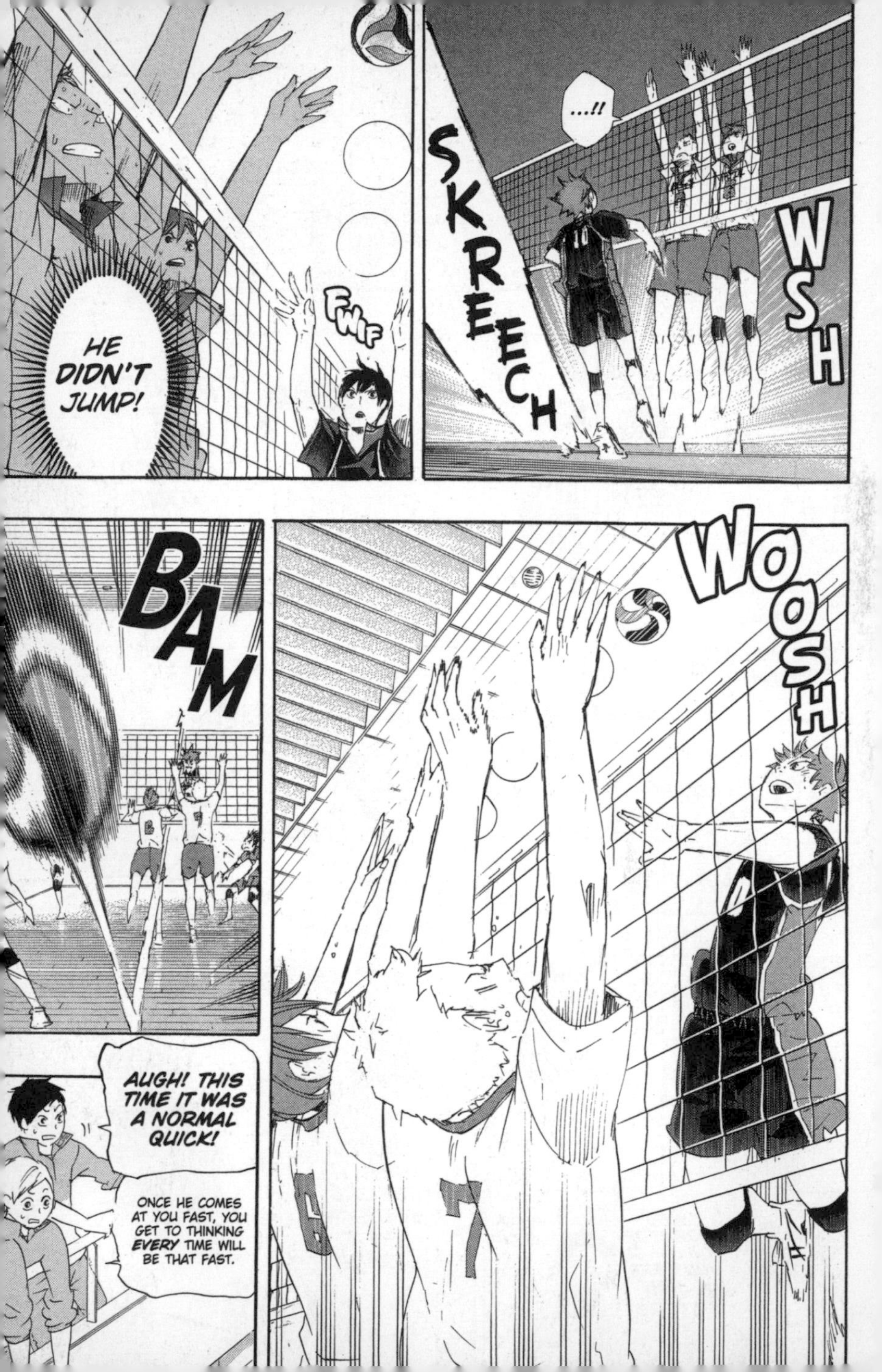
...!!
SKREECH
WSH
HE DIDN'T JUMP!
FWIF
WOOSH
BAM
AUGH! THIS TIME IT WAS A NORMAL QUICK!
ONCE HE COMES AT YOU FAST, YOU GET TO THINKING EVERY TIME WILL BE THAT FAST.

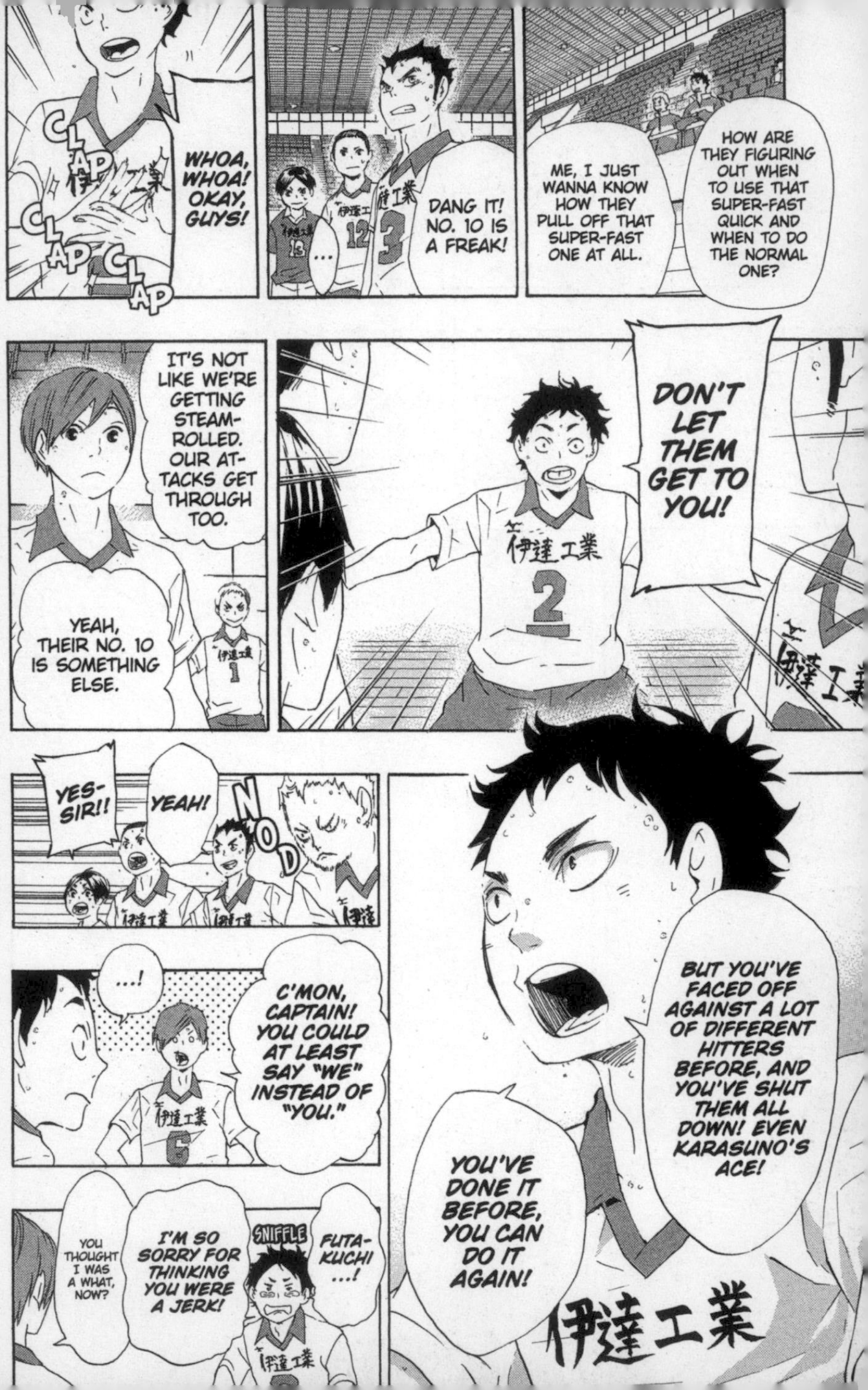
HOW ARE THEY FIGURING OUT WHEN TO USE THAT SUPER-FAST QUICK AND WHEN TO DO THE NORMAL ONE?
ME, I JUST WANNA KNOW HOW THEY PULL OFF THAT SUPER-FAST ONE AT ALL.
DANG IT! NO. 10 IS A FREAK!
...
WHOA, WHOA! OKAY, GUYS!
CLAP
CLAP
CLAP
CLAP
DON'T LET THEM GET TO YOU!
IT'S NOT LIKE WE'RE GETTING STEAM-ROLLED. OUR AT-TACKS GET THROUGH TOO.
YEAH, THEIR NO. 10 IS SOMETHING ELSE.
BUT YOU'VE FACED OFF AGAINST A LOT OF DIFFERENT HITTERS BEFORE, AND YOU'VE SHUT THEM ALL DOWN! EVEN KARASUNO'S ACE!
YOU'VE DONE IT BEFORE, YOU CAN DO IT AGAIN!
伊達工業
NOD
YEAH!
YES-SIR!!
C'MON, CAPTAIN! YOU COULD AT LEAST SAY "WE" INSTEAD OF "YOU."
...!
FUTA-KUCHI ...!
SNIFFLE
I'M SO SORRY FOR THINKING YOU WERE A JERK!
YOU THOUGHT I WAS A WHAT, NOW?

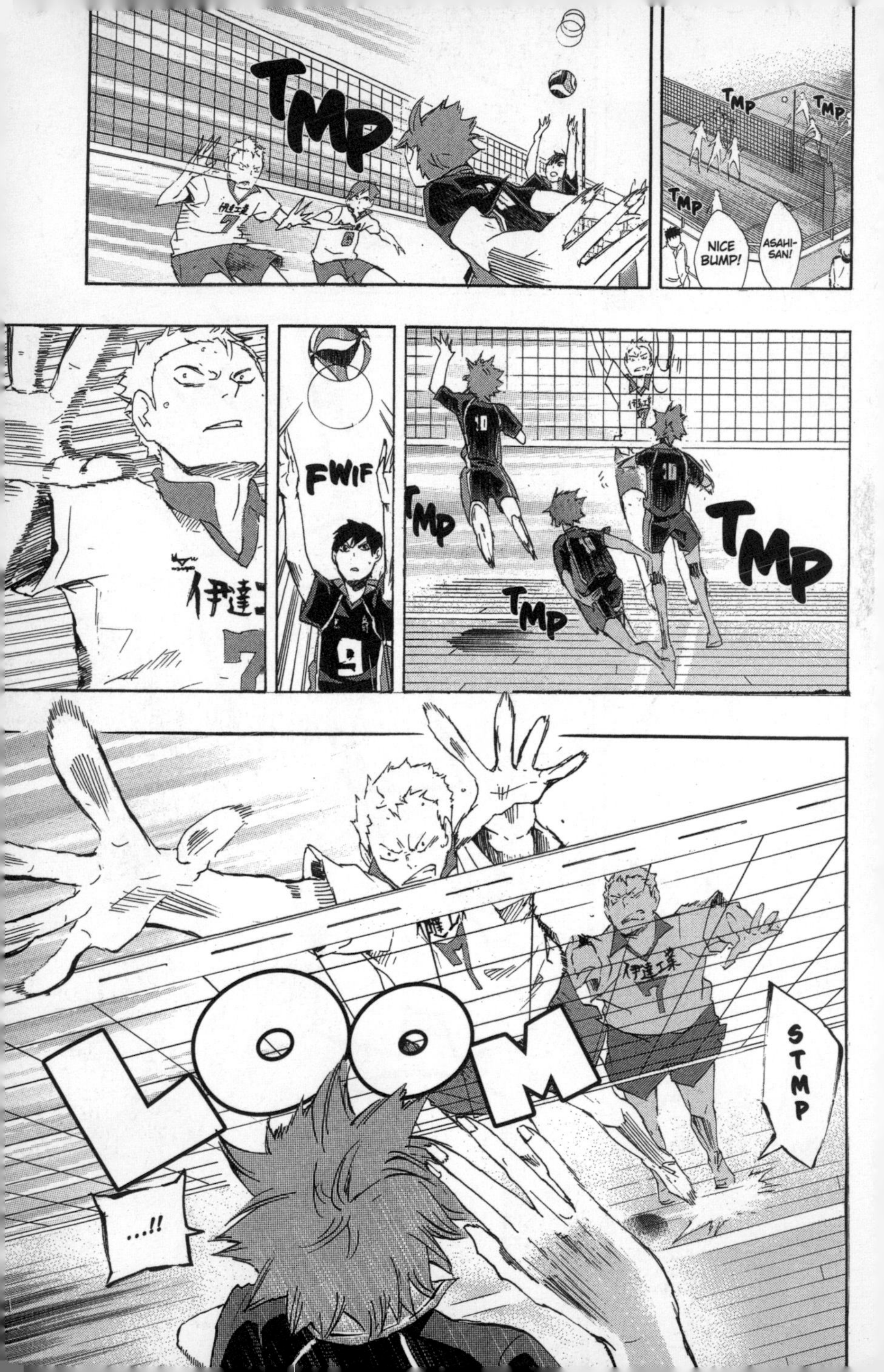
TMP
TMP
TMP
ASAHI-SAN!
NICE BUMP!
TMP
TMP
TMP
TMP
FWIF
STMP
LOOM
...!!

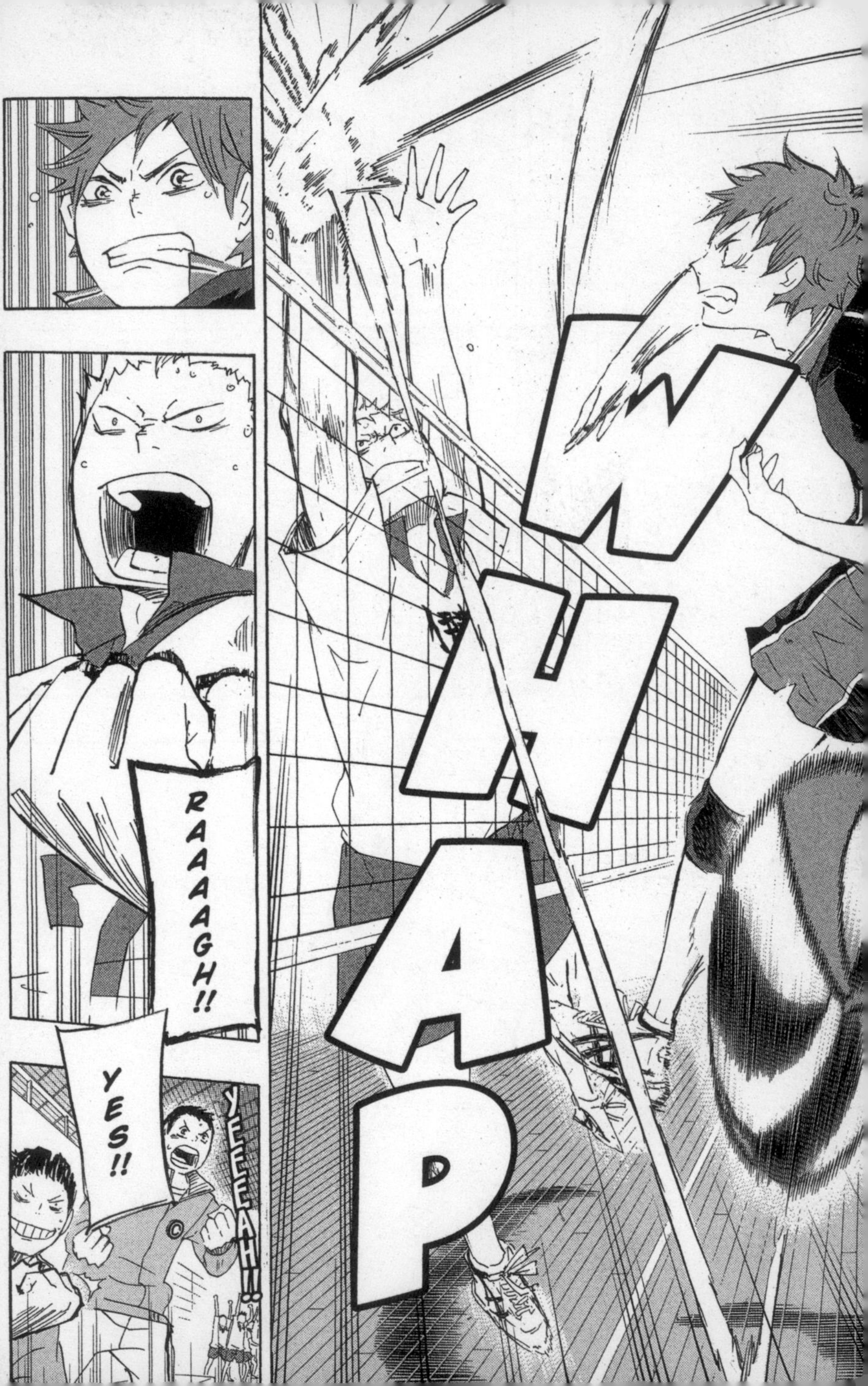
WHAP
RAAAAAGH!!
YEEEEAH!!
YES!!

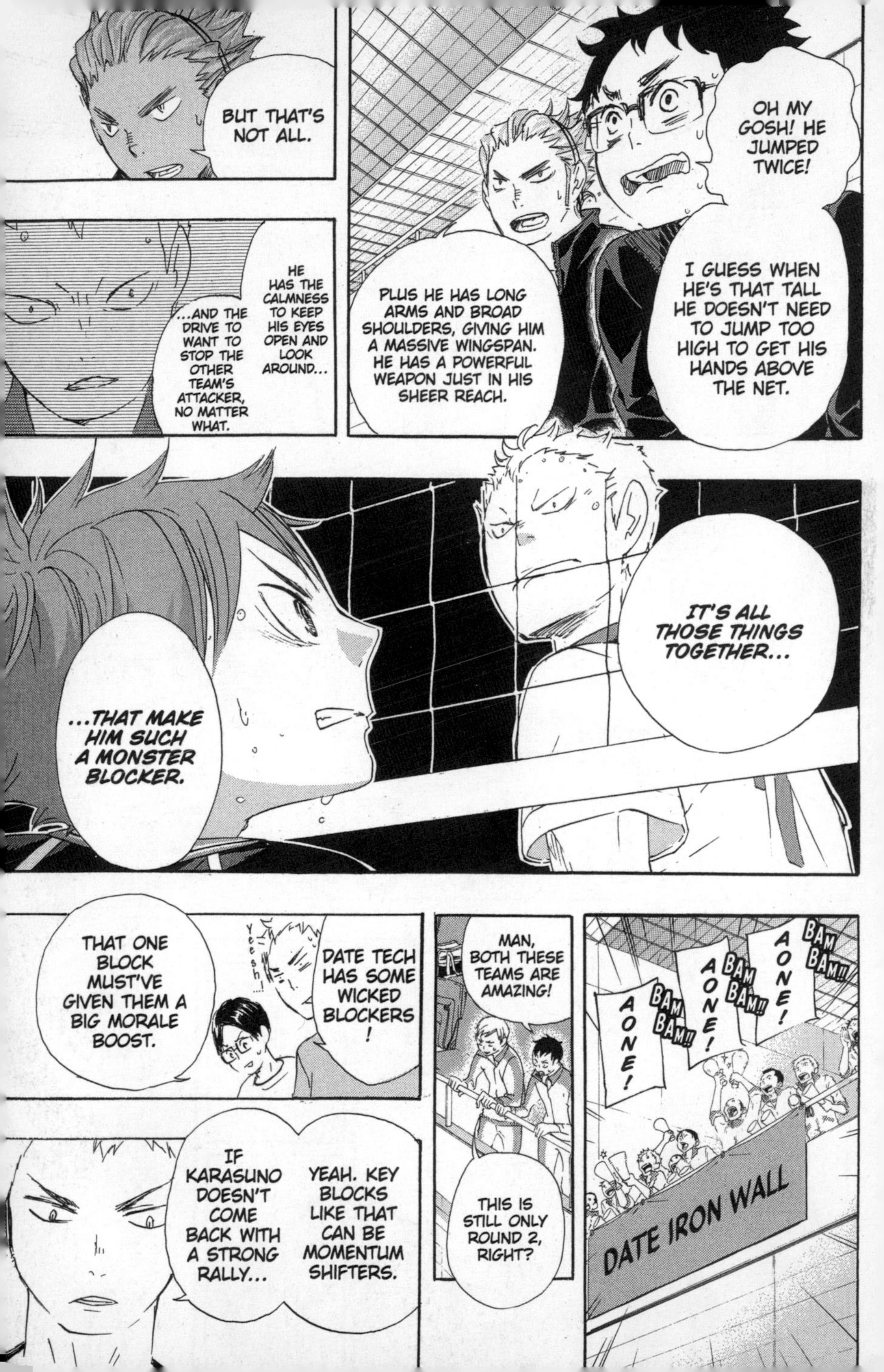
OH MY GOSH! HE JUMPED TWICE!
I GUESS WHEN HE'S THAT TALL HE DOESN'T NEED TO JUMP TOO HIGH TO GET HIS HANDS ABOVE THE NET.
PLUS HE HAS LONG ARMS AND BROAD SHOULDERS, GIVING HIM A MASSIVE WINGSPAN. HE HAS A POWERFUL WEAPON JUST IN HIS SHEER REACH.
BUT THAT'S NOT ALL.
HE HAS THE CALMNESS TO KEEP HIS EYES OPEN AND LOOK AROUND...
...AND THE DRIVE TO WANT TO STOP THE OTHER TEAM'S ATTACKER, NO MATTER WHAT.
IT'S ALL THOSE THINGS TOGETHER...
...THAT MAKE HIM SUCH A MONSTER BLOCKER.
BAM BAM!!
AONE!
BAM BAM!!
AONE!
BAM BAM!!
AONE!
DATE IRON WALL
MAN, BOTH THESE TEAMS ARE AMAZING!
THIS IS STILL ONLY ROUND 2, RIGHT?
DATE TECH HAS SOME WICKED BLOCKERS!
Yeesh!...
THAT ONE BLOCK MUST'VE GIVEN THEM A BIG MORALE BOOST.
YEAH. KEY BLOCKS LIKE THAT CAN BE MOMENTUM SHIFTERS.
IF KARASUNO DOESN'T COME BACK WITH A STRONG RALLY...

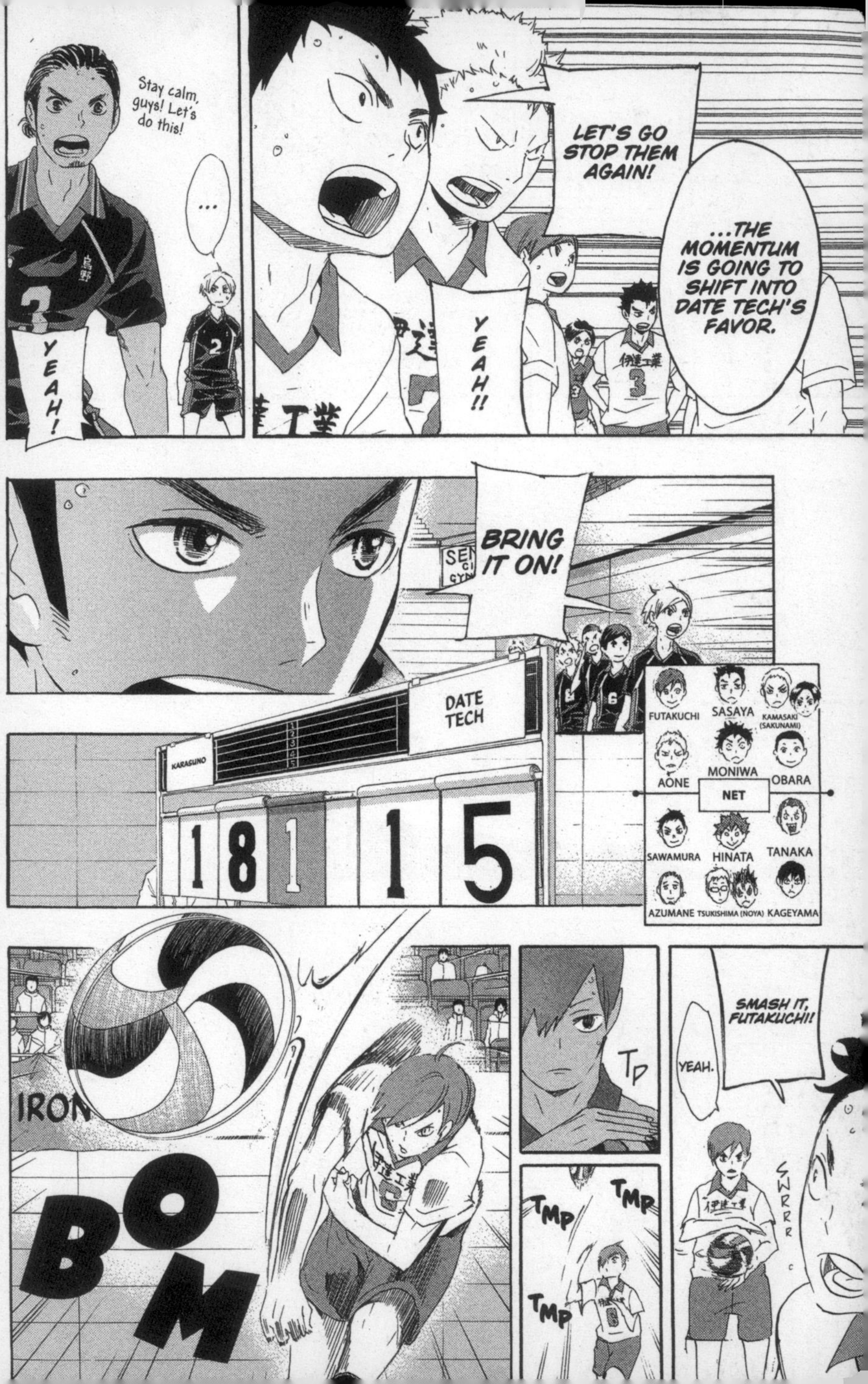
LET'S GO STOP THEM AGAIN!
YEAH!!
...THE MOMENTUM IS GOING TO SHIFT INTO DATE TECH'S FAVOR.
Stay calm, guys! Let's do this!
...
YEAH!
BRING IT ON!
SEN
DATE TECH
KARASUNO
18
1
15
FUTAKUCHI
SASAYA
KAMASAKI (SAKUNAMI)
AONE
MONIWA
OBARA
NET
SAWAMURA
HINATA
TANAKA
AZUMANE
TSUKISHIMA (NOYA)
KAGEYAMA
SMASH IT, FUTAKUCHI!
YEAH.
SWRRR
TP
TMP
TMP
TMP
IRON
BOOM

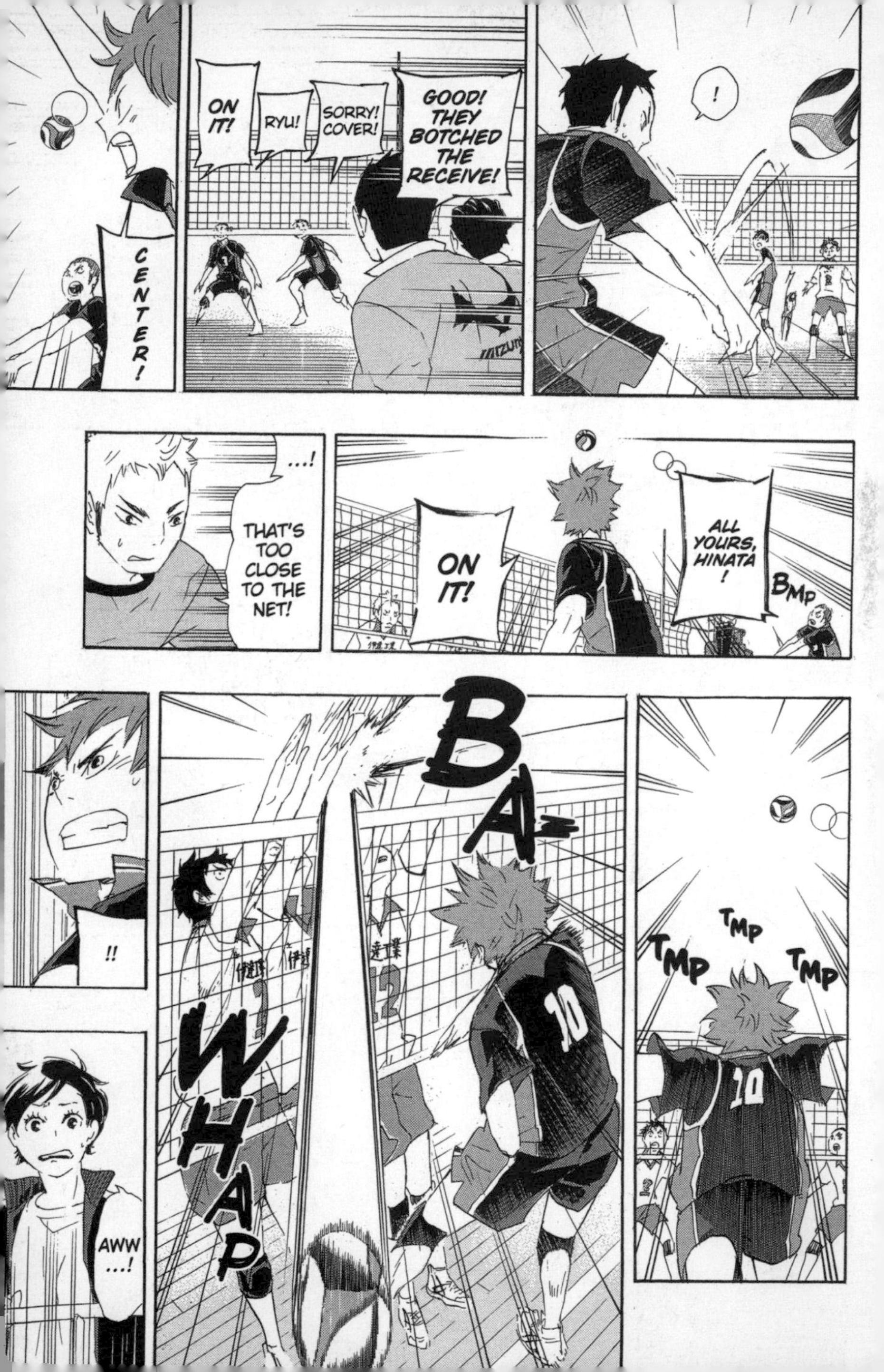
!
GOOD! THEY BOTCHED THE RECEIVE!
SORRY! COVER!
RYU!
ON IT!
CENTER!
ALL YOURS, HINATA!
BMP
ON IT!
...!
THAT'S TOO CLOSE TO THE NET!
TMP
TMP
TMP
BA-
WHAP
!!
AWW ...!

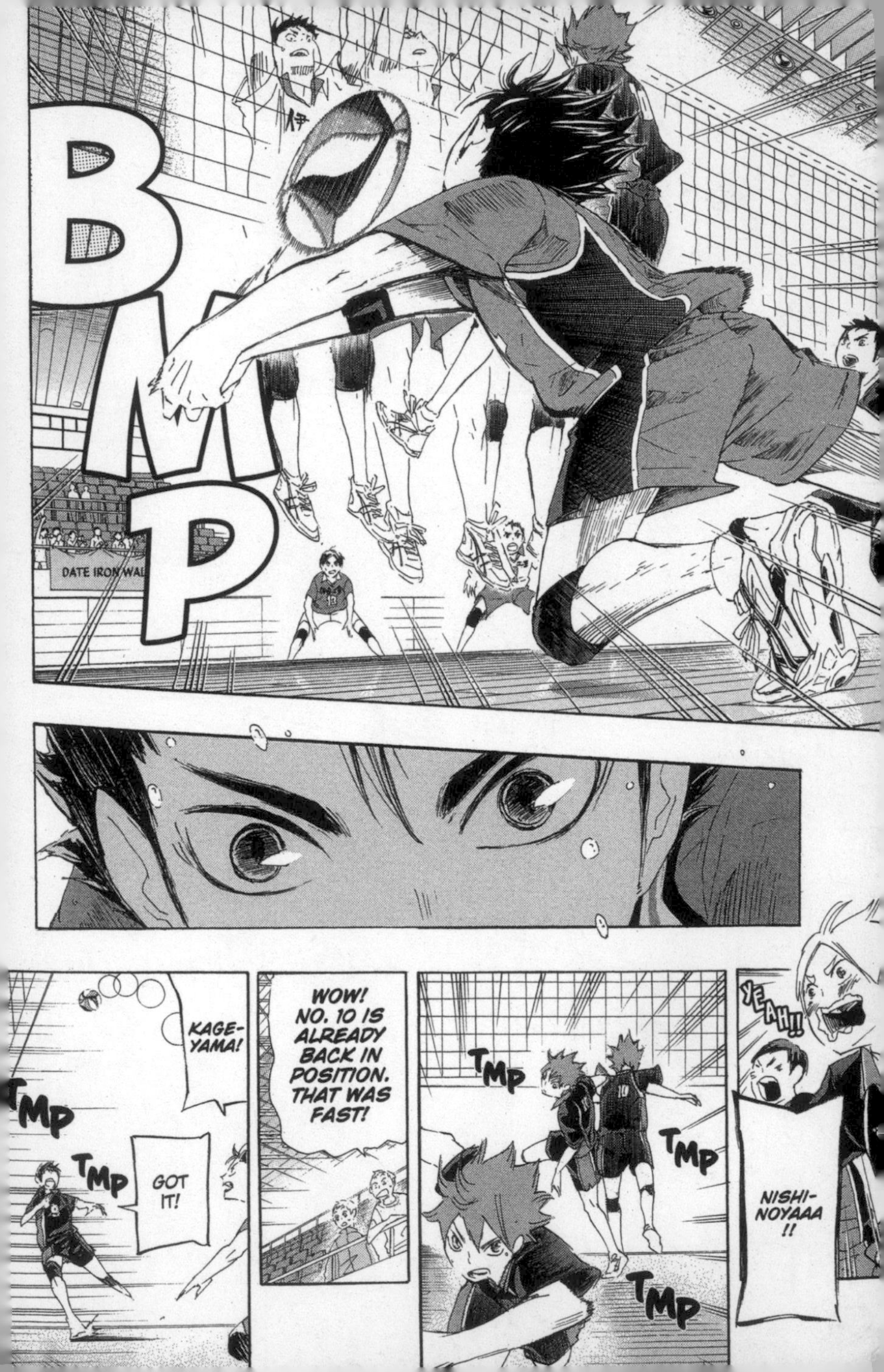
BMP
DATE IRON WALL
YEAH!!
NISHI-NOYAAA !!
TMP
TMP
TMP
WOW! NO. 10 IS ALREADY BACK IN POSITION. THAT WAS FAST!
KAGE-YAMA!
GOT IT!
TMP
TMP

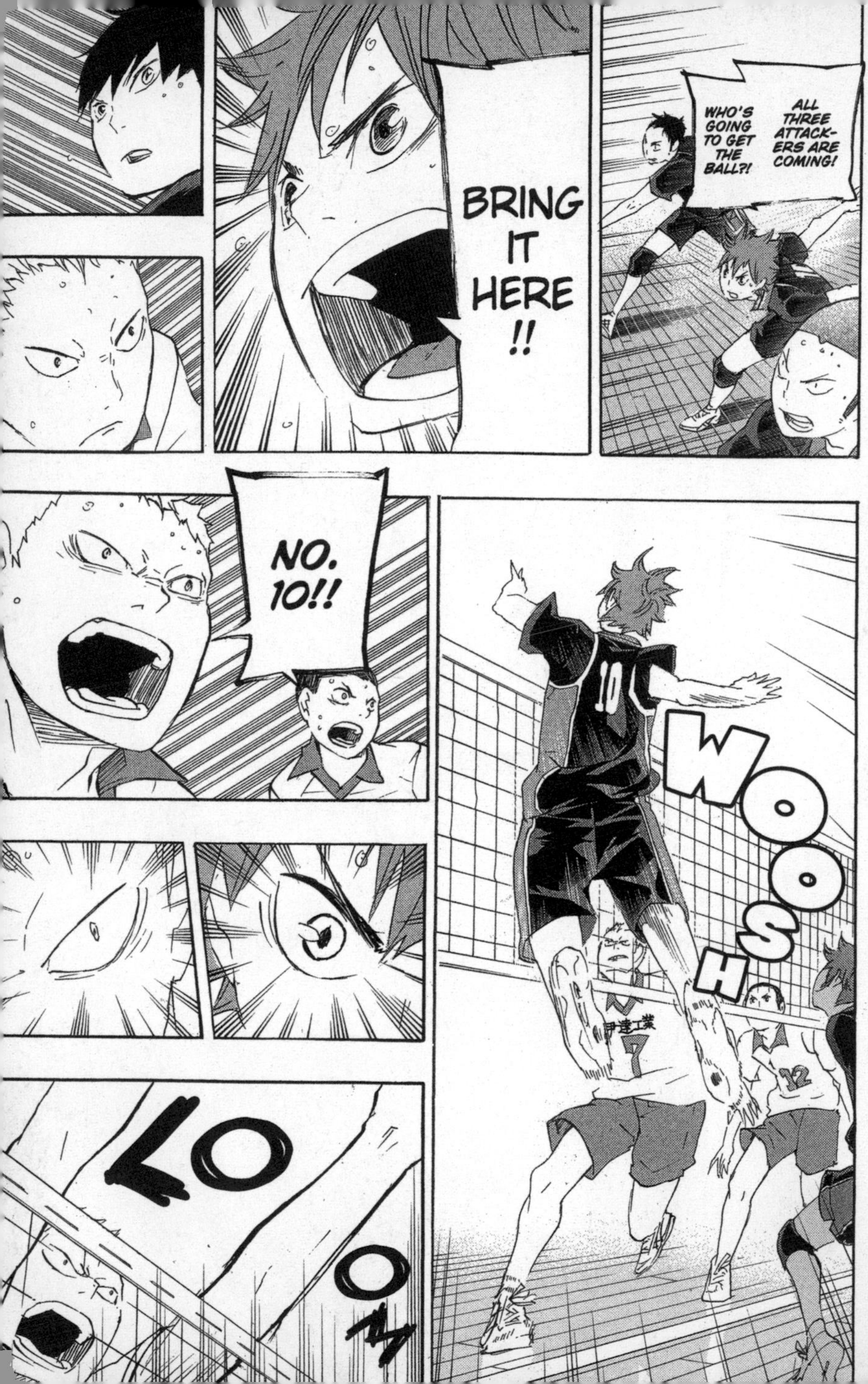
ALL THREE ATTACKERS ARE COMING!
WHO'S GOING TO GET THE BALL?!
BRING IT HERE!!
WOOOSH
NO. 10!!
BOOM

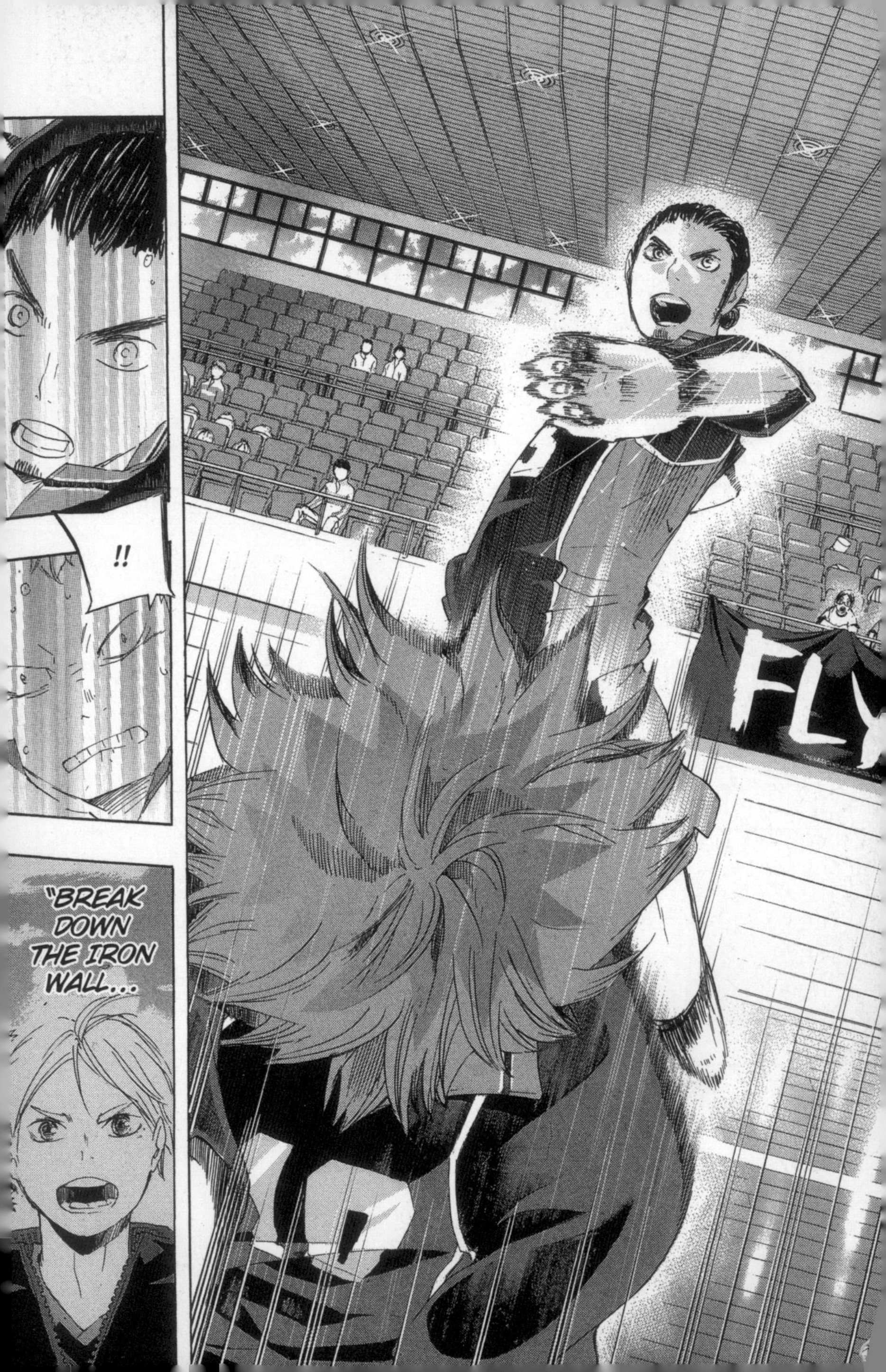
FLY
!!
"BREAK DOWN THE IRON WALL...

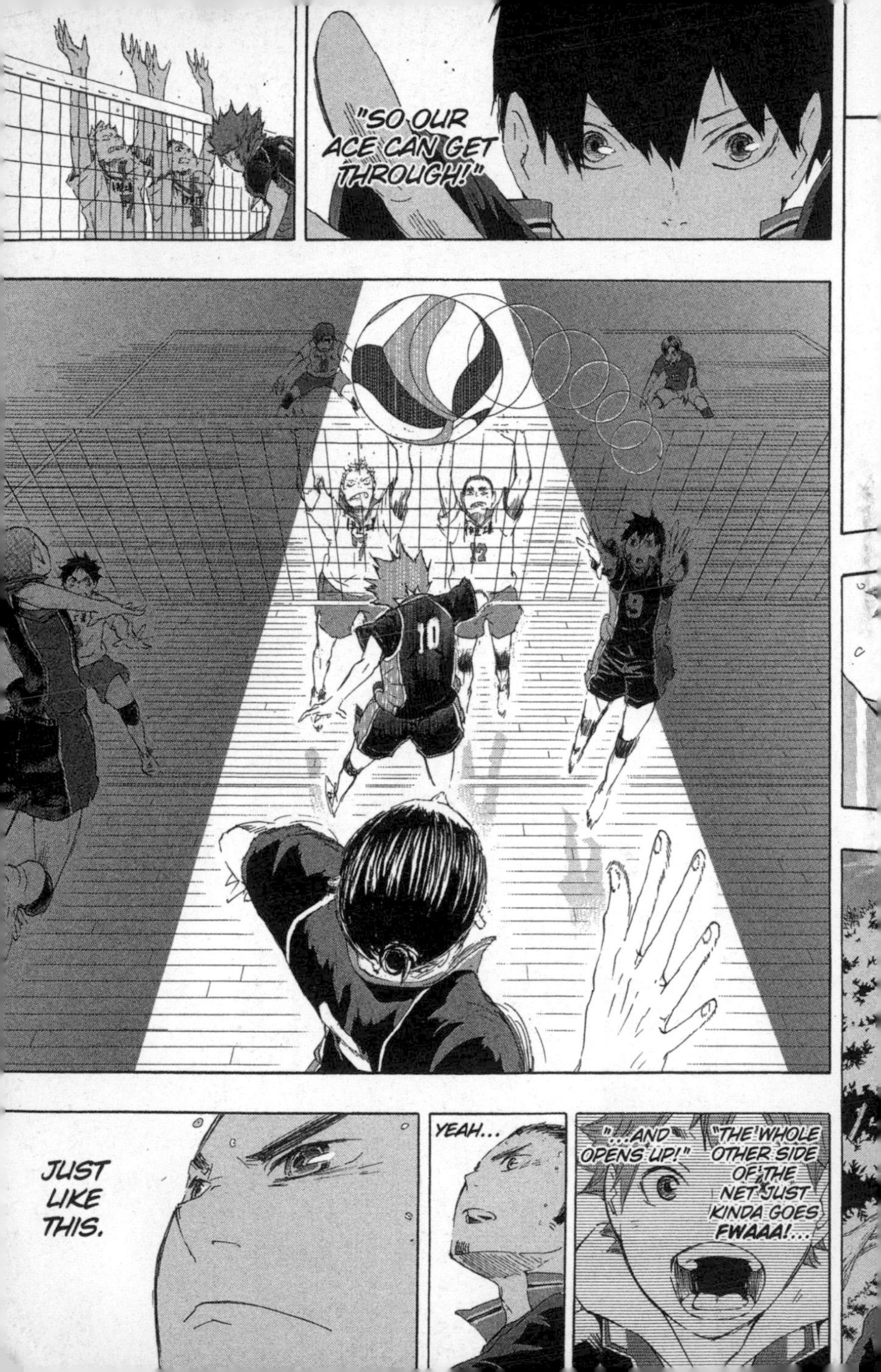
"SO OUR ACE CAN GET THROUGH!"
"THE WHOLE OTHER SIDE OF THE NET JUST KINDA GOES FWAAA!...
"...AND OPENS UP!"
YEAH...
JUST LIKE THIS.

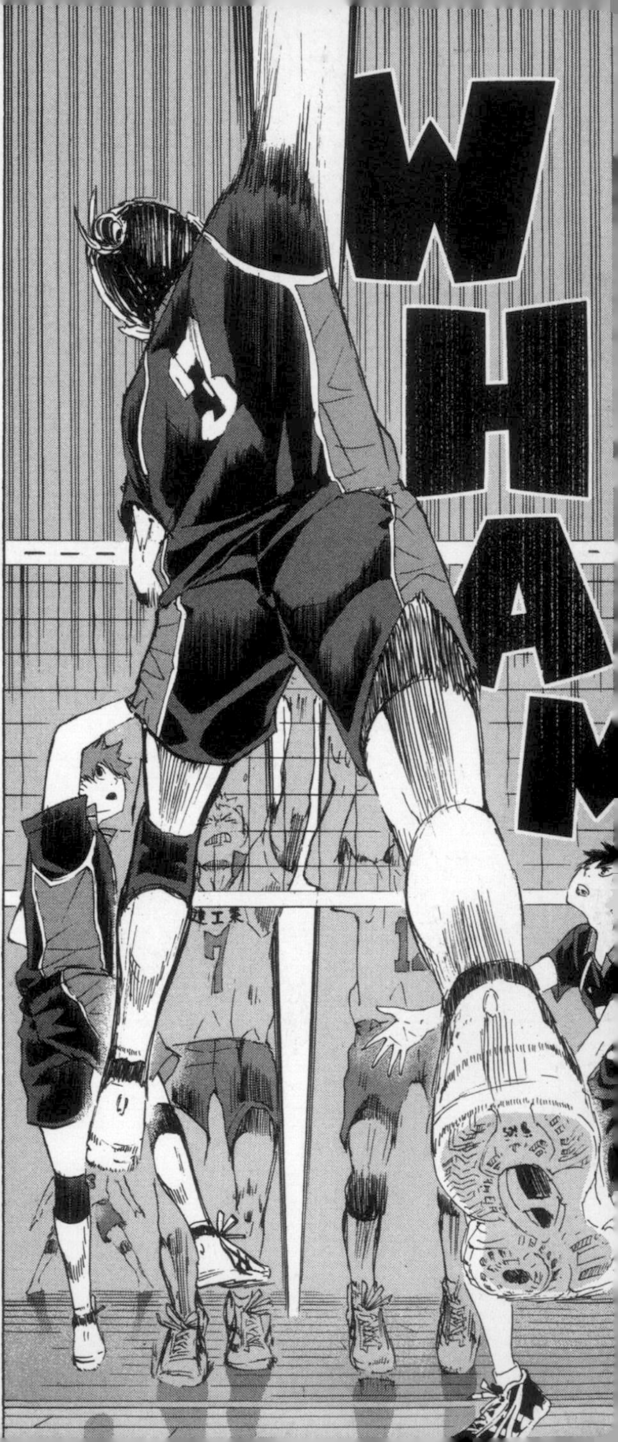
WHAM

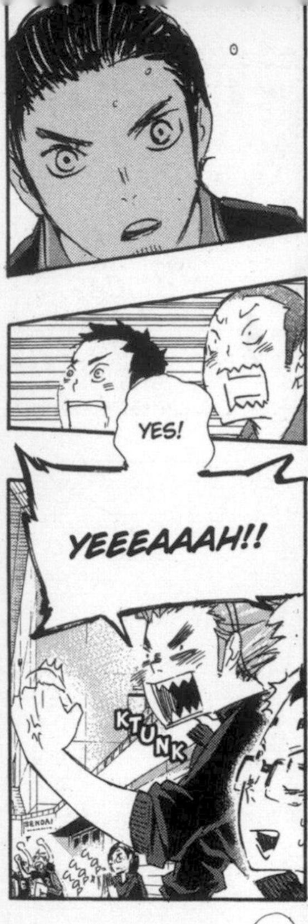
YES!
YEEEAAAH!!
KTUNK
A PIPE*!
THEY USED THE SAME PLAY NEKOMA USED ON THEM!

*PIPE: A SET WHERE A FRONT ROW ATTACKER FAKES THE QUICK AND THE REAL ATTACK COMES FROM THE BACK.

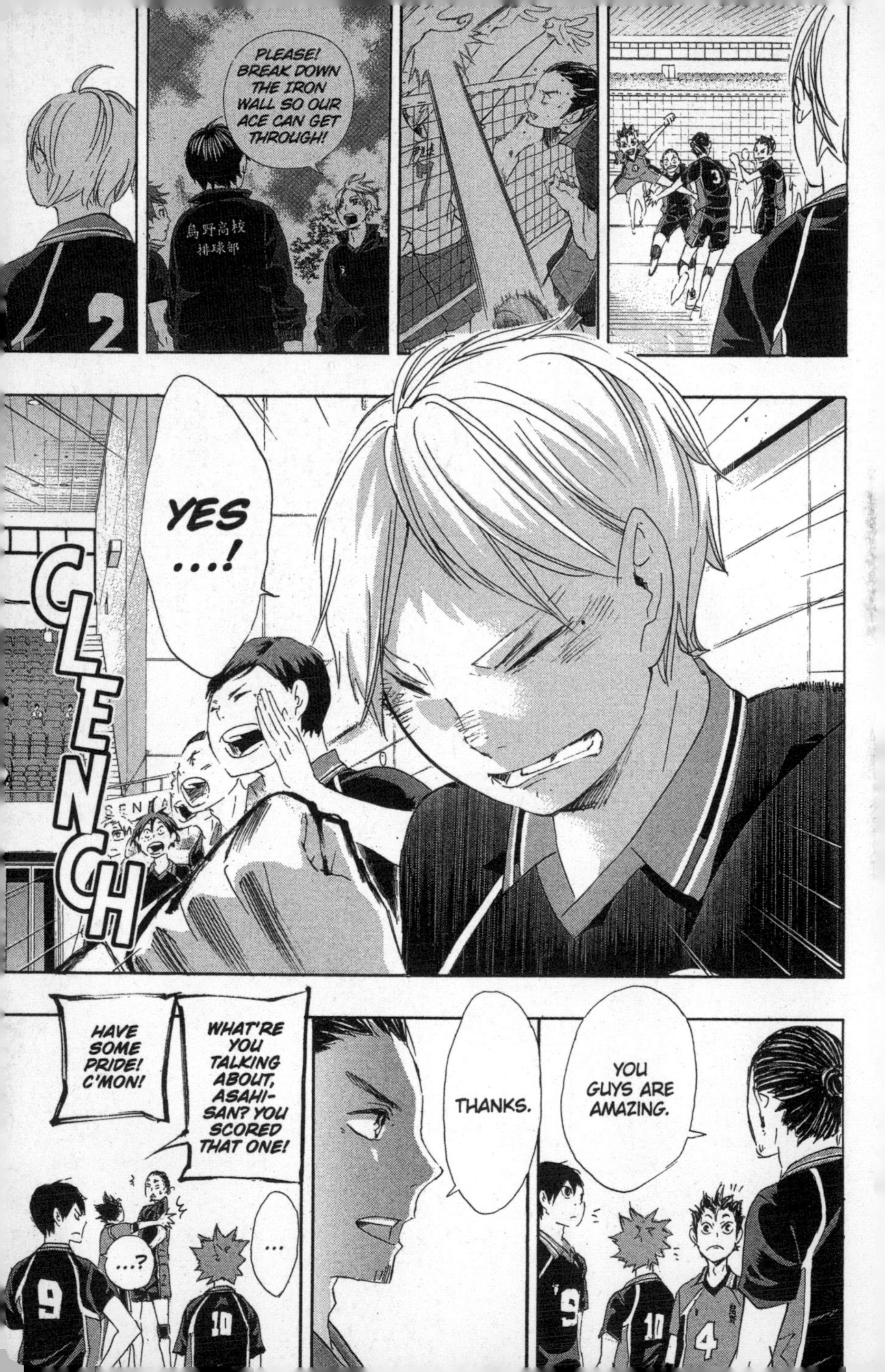
PLEASE! BREAK DOWN THE IRON WALL SO OUR ACE CAN GET THROUGH!
烏野高校
排球部
YES ...!
CLENCH
YOU GUYS ARE AMAZING.
THANKS.
...
WHAT'RE YOU TALKING ABOUT, ASAHI-SAN? YOU SCORED THAT ONE!
HAVE SOME PRIDE! C'MON!
...?

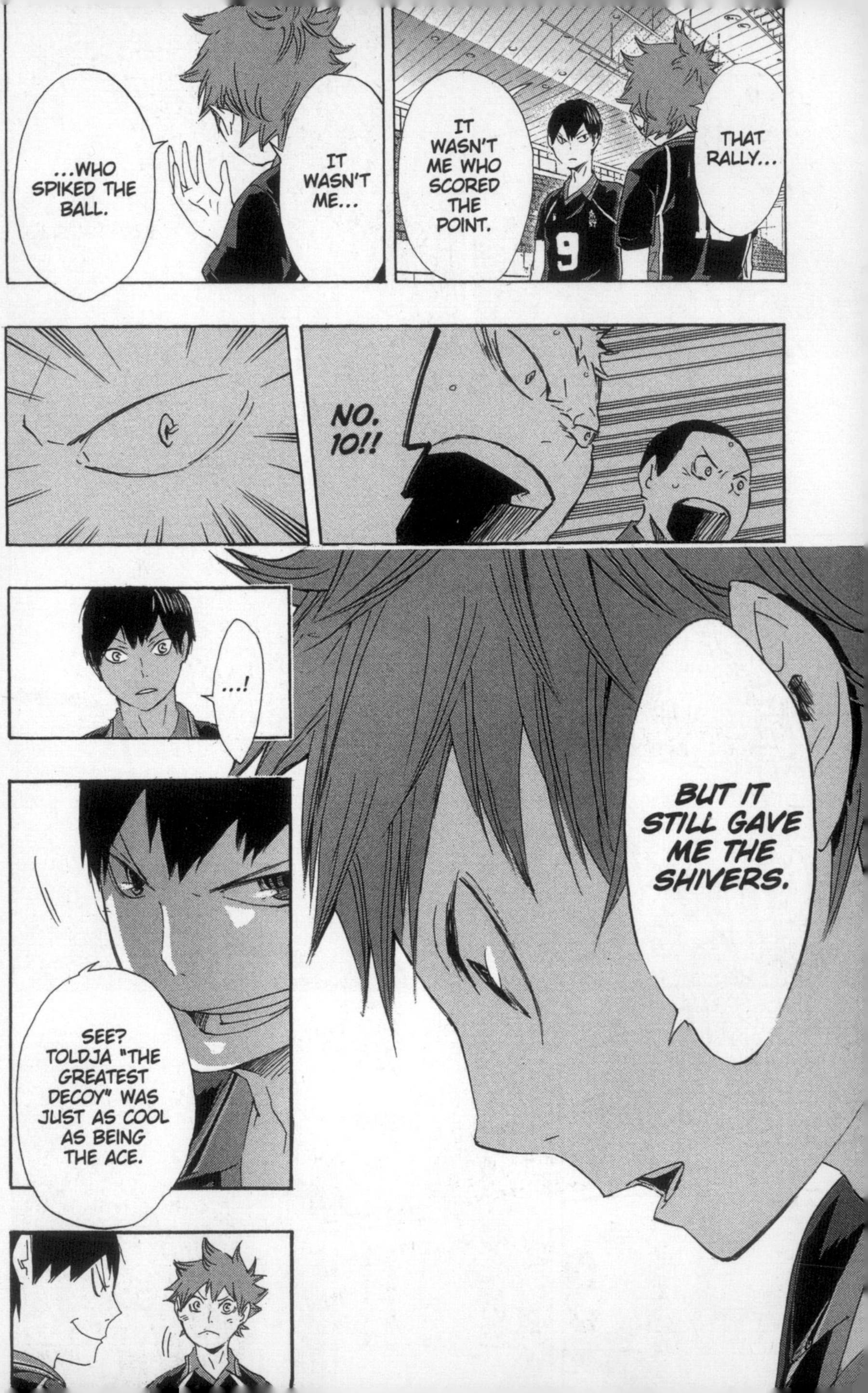
THAT RALLY...
IT WASN'T ME WHO SCORED THE POINT.
IT WASN'T ME...
...WHO SPIKED THE BALL.
NO. 10!!
BUT IT STILL GAVE ME THE SHIVERS.
...!
SEE? TOLDJA "THE GREATEST DECOY" WAS JUST AS COOL AS BEING THE ACE.

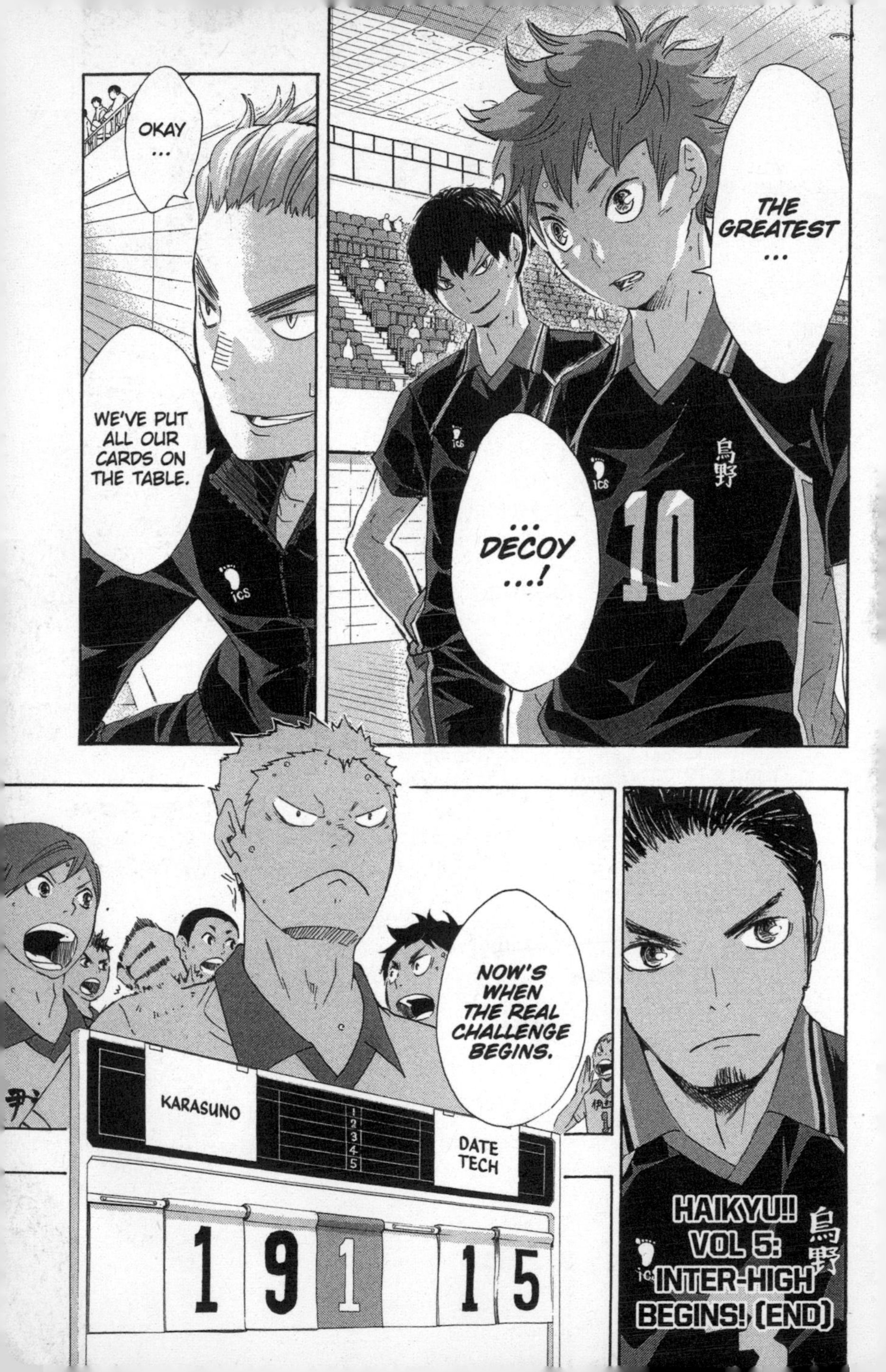
THE GREATEST ...
... DECOY ...!
OKAY ...
WE'VE PUT ALL OUR CARDS ON THE TABLE.
HAIKYU!! VOL 5: INTER-HIGH BEGINS! (END)
NOW'S WHEN THE REAL CHALLENGE BEGINS.
KARASUNO
DATE TECH
19 1 15

EDITOR'S NOTES

The English edition of Haikyu!! maintains the honorifics used in the original Japanese version. For those of you who are new to these terms, here's a brief explanation to help with your reading experience!

When saying someone's name in Japanese, a suffix is often attached to indicate how familiar the speaker is with the person. Some are more polite and respectful, while others are endearing.

1 ***-kun*** is often used for young men or boys, usually someone you are familiar with.

2 ***-chan*** is used for young children and can be used as a term of endearment.

3 ***-san*** is used for someone you respect or are not close to, or to be polite.

4 ***Senpai*** is used for someone who is older than you or in a higher position or grade in school.

5 ***Kohai*** is used for someone who is younger than you or in a lower position or grade in school.

6 ***Sensei*** means teacher.

7 ***Bluecastle*** is a nickname for Aoba Johsai. It is a combination of *Ao* (blue) and *Joh* (castle).

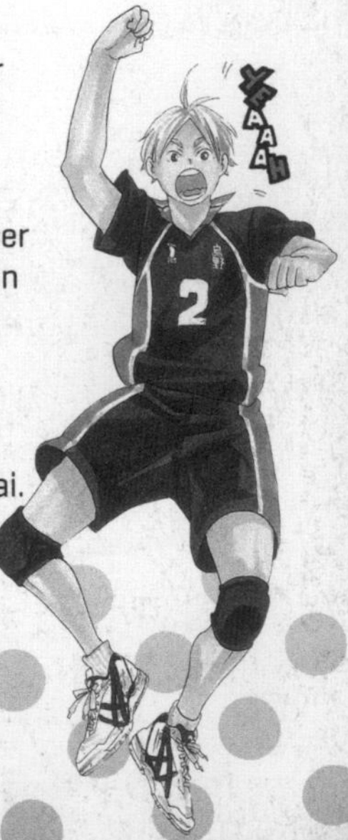
YEAAAH

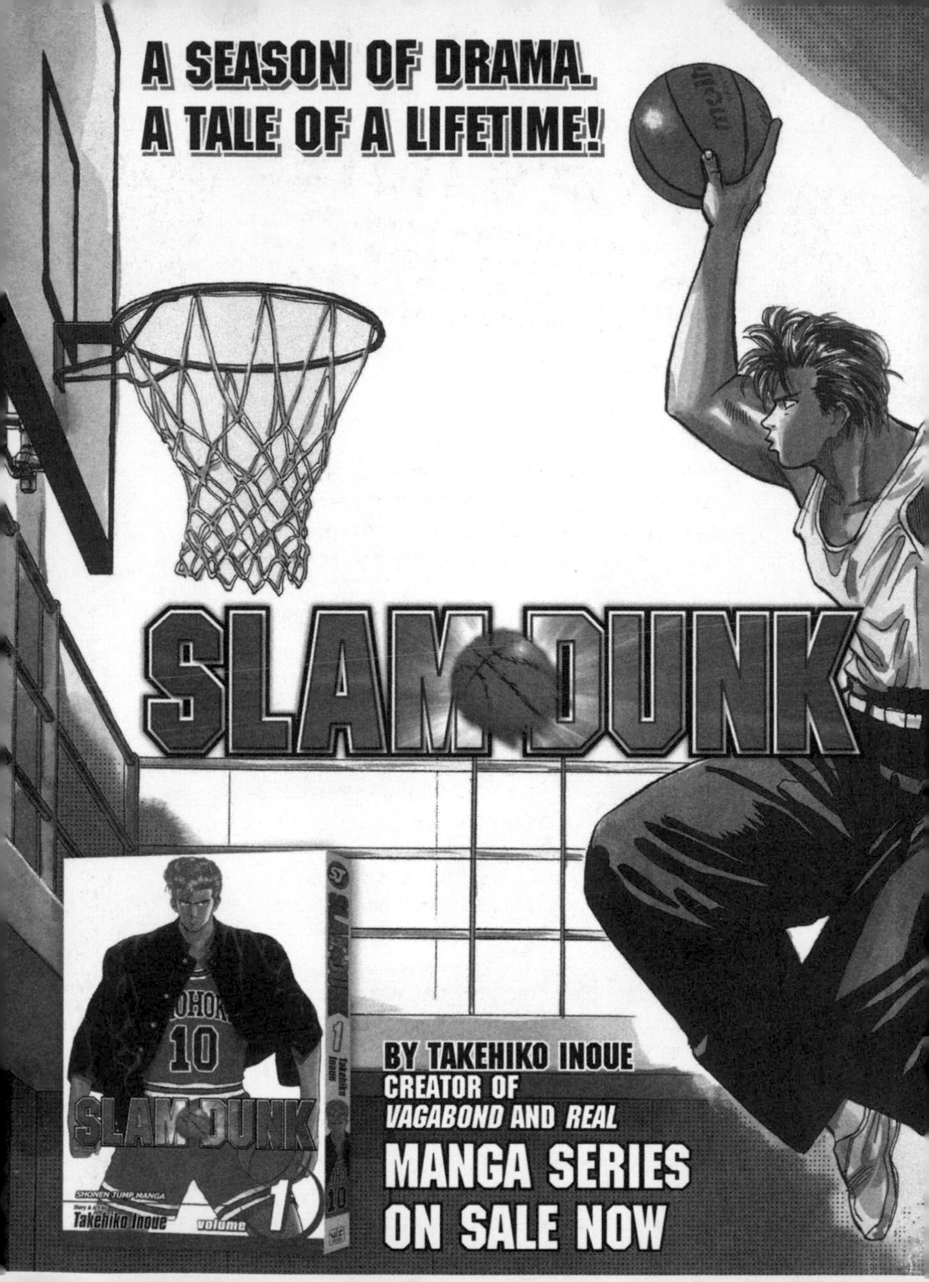
A SEASON OF DRAMA.
A TALE OF A LIFETIME!
SLAM DUNK
BY TAKEHIKO INOUE
CREATOR OF
VAGABOND AND REAL
MANGA SERIES
ON SALE NOW
SLAM DUNK
SHONEN JUMP MANGA
Takehiko Inoue
volume 1

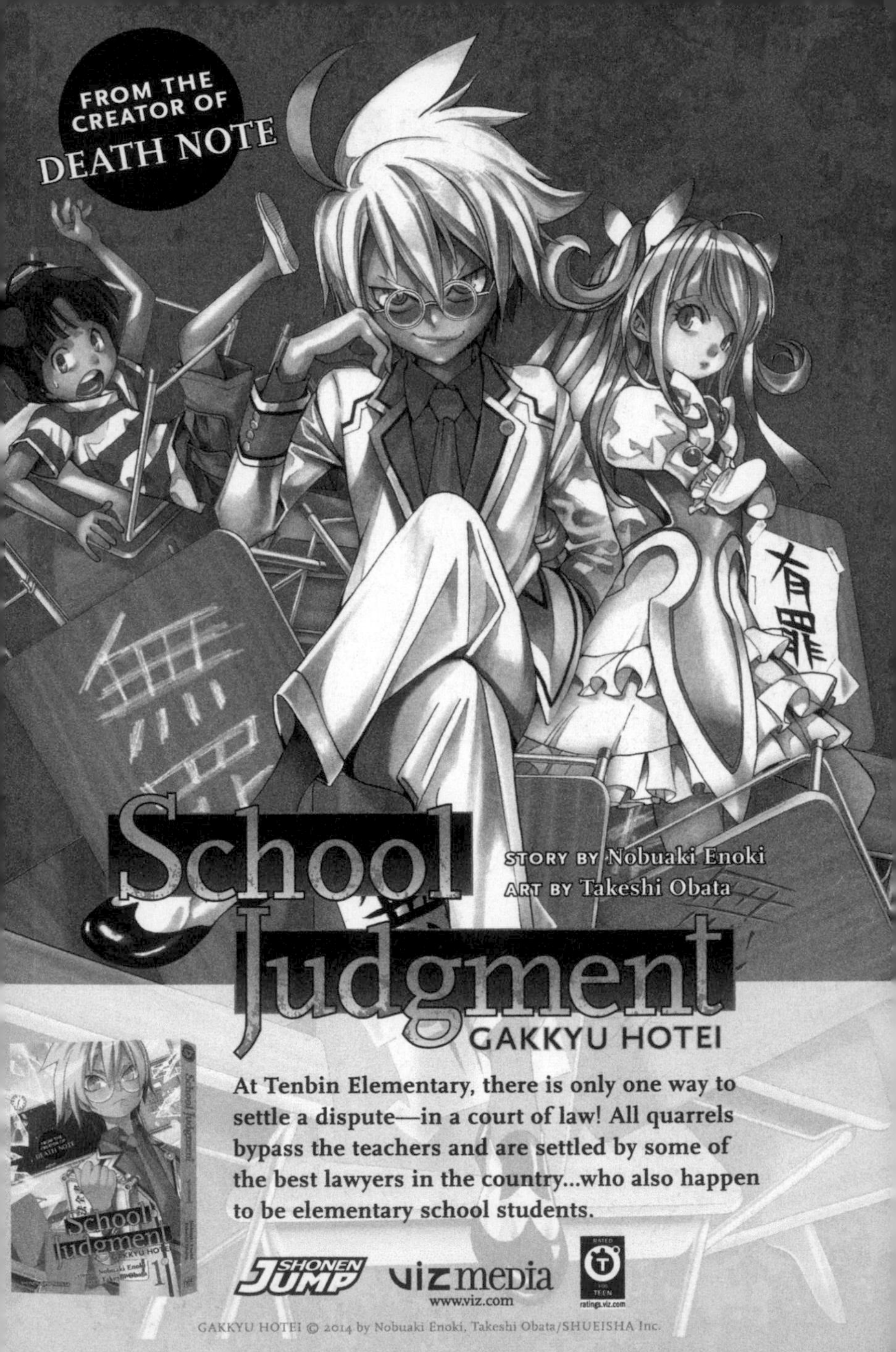
FROM THE CREATOR OF DEATH NOTE
有罪
School Judgment
GAKKYU HOTEI
STORY BY Nobuaki Enoki
ART BY Takeshi Obata
At Tenbin Elementary, there is only one way to settle a dispute—in a court of law! All quarrels bypass the teachers and are settled by some of the best lawyers in the country...who also happen to be elementary school students.
SHONEN JUMP
VIZ media
www.viz.com
RATED T FOR TEEN
ratings.viz.com

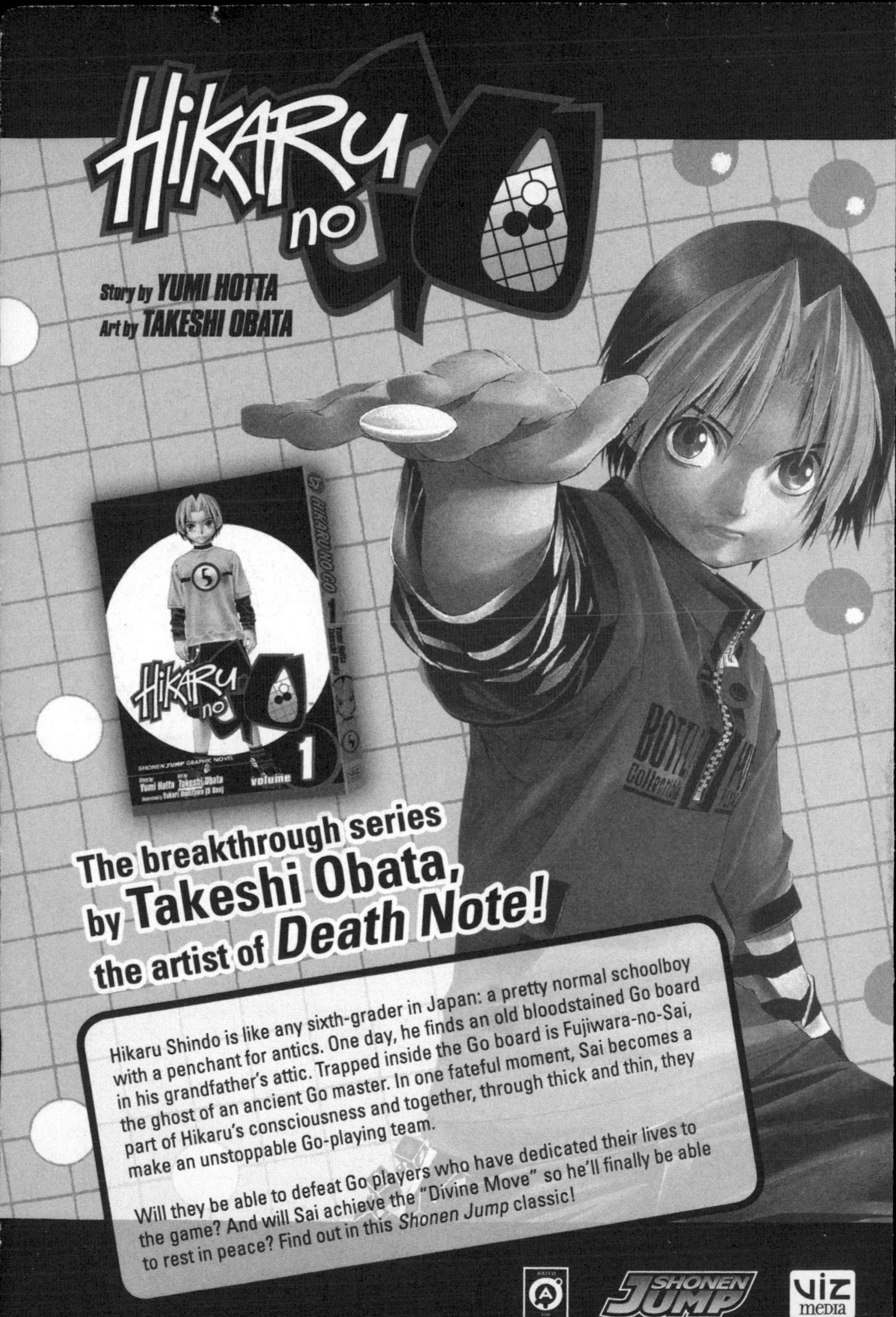

HIKARU no GO
Story by YUMI HOTTA
Art by TAKESHI OBATA
HIKARU NO GO
HIKARU no GO
SHONEN JUMP GRAPHIC NOVEL
volume 1
The breakthrough series by Takeshi Obata, the artist of Death Note!
Hikaru Shindo is like any sixth-grader in Japan: a pretty normal schoolboy with a penchant for antics. One day, he finds an old bloodstained Go board in his grandfather's attic. Trapped inside the Go board is Fujiwara-no-Sai, the ghost of an ancient Go master. In one fateful moment, Sai becomes a part of Hikaru's consciousness and together, through thick and thin, they make an unstoppable Go-playing team.
Will they be able to defeat Go players who have dedicated their lives to the game? And will Sai achieve the "Divine Move" so he'll finally be able to rest in peace? Find out in this *Shonen Jump* classic!
RATED A FOR ALL AGES
ratings.viz.com
SHONEN JUMP
www.shonenjump.com
viz media
www.viz.com

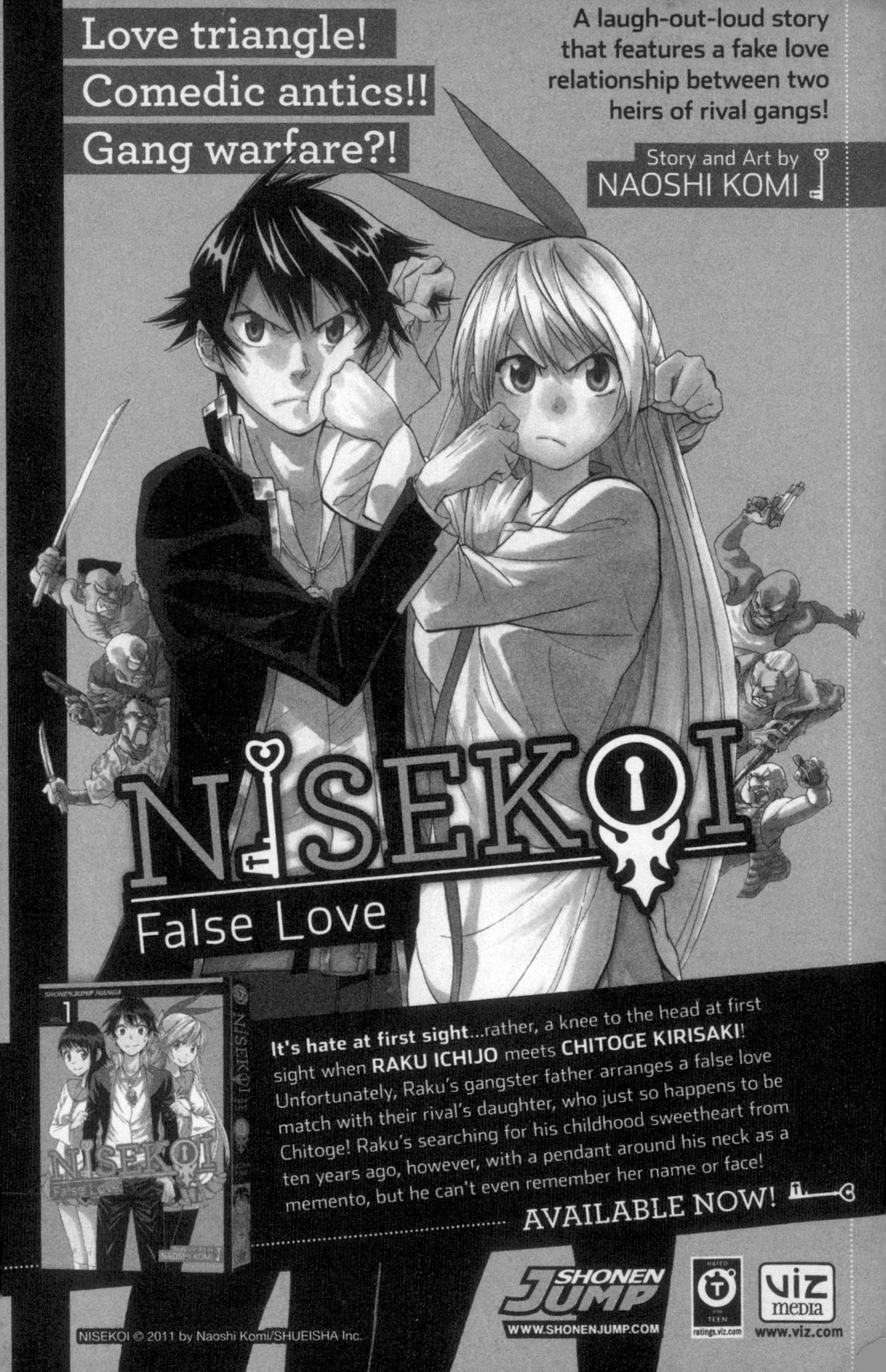
Love triangle!
Comedic antics!!
Gang warfare?!
A laugh-out-loud story that features a fake love relationship between two heirs of rival gangs!
Story and Art by NAOSHI KOMI
NISEKOI
False Love
It's hate at first sight...rather, a knee to the head at first sight when RAKU ICHIJO meets CHITOGE KIRISAKI! Unfortunately, Raku's gangster father arranges a false love match with their rival's daughter, who just so happens to be Chitoge! Raku's searching for his childhood sweetheart from ten years ago, however, with a pendant around his neck as a memento, but he can't even remember her name or face!
AVAILABLE NOW!
SHONEN JUMP
WWW.SHONENJUMP.COM
RATED T TEEN
ratings.viz.com
viz media
www.viz.com
NISEKOI © 2011 by Naoshi Komi/SHUEISHA Inc.

Food Wars!
SHOKUGEKI NO SOMA

Saucy, action-packed food battles!

Story by **Yuto Tsukuda**
Art by **Shun Saeki**
Contributor **Yuki Morisaki**

Soma Yukihira's old man runs a small family restaurant in the less savory end of town. Aiming to one day surpass his father's culinary prowess, Soma hones his skills day in and day out until one day, out of the blue, his father decides to enroll Soma in a classy culinary school! Can Soma really cut it in a school that prides itself on a 10 percent graduation rate? And can he convince the beautiful, domineering heiress of the school that he belongs there at all?!

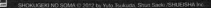

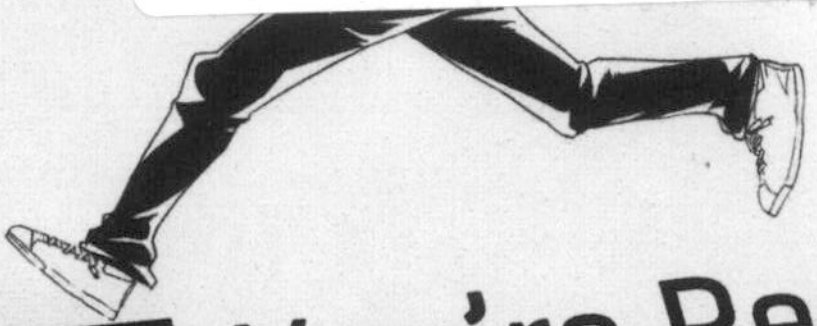

You're Reading the WRONG WAY!

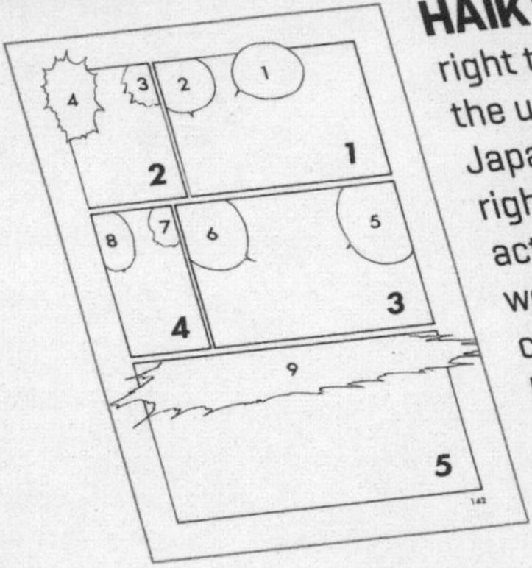

HAIKYU!! reads from right to left, starting in the upper-right corner. Japanese is read from right to left, meaning that action, sound effects and word-balloon order are completely reversed from English order.

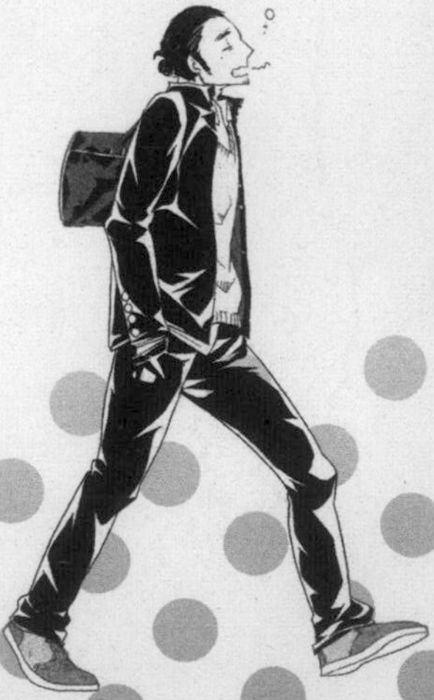